LEADERS OF THE WORLD

BIOGRAPHICAL SERIES

General Editor: ROBERT MAXWELL, M.C.

Morarji Desai

THE STORY OF MY LIFE

Volume 2

LEADERS OF THE WORLD

BIOGRAPHICAL SERIES

General Editor: ROBERT MAXWELL, M.C.

MORARJI DESAI

Prime Minister of India

LEONID ILYICH BREZHNEV

President of the Presidium of the Supreme Soviet of the USSR, General Secretary of the Communist Party of the Soviet Union

Volumes in preparation

JIMMY CARTER

President of the United States of America

HUA GUO-FENG

Premier and Chairman of the Central Committee of the Chinese Communist Party

KURT WALDHEIM

Secretary-General of the United Nations

The author.

Morarji Desai

THE STORY OF MY LIFE

Volume 2

PERGAMON PRESS

OXFORD · NEW YORK · TORONTO · SYDNEY · PARIS · FRANKFURT

U.K.	Pergamon Press Ltd., Headington Hill Hall, Oxford OX3 0BW, England
U.S.A.	Pergamon Press Inc., Maxwell House, Fairview Park, Elmsford, New York 10523, U.S.A.
CANADA	Pergamon of Canada, Suite 104, 150 Consumers Road, Willowdale, Ontario M2J 1P9, Canada
AUSTRALIA	Pergamon Press (Aust.) Pty. Ltd., P.O. Box 544, Potts Point, N.S.W. 2011, Australia
FRANCE	Pergamon Press SARL, 24 rue des Ecoles, 75240 Paris, Cedex 05, France
FEDERAL REPUBLIC OF GERMANY	Pergamon Press GmbH, 6242 Kronberg-Taunus, Pferdstrasse 1, Federal Republic of Germany

First edition 1979

British Library Cataloguing in Publication Data

Desai, Morarji
The story of my life.-(Leaders of the world: biographical series).
1. Desai, Morarji 2. Prime ministers - India - Biography
I. Title II. Series
954.04'092'4 DS481.D385 78-40613

ISBN 0-08-023566-2

Published throughout the World excluding India by Pergamon Press by arrangement with S. Chand & Company Ltd, New Delhi—110055

Printed in India at Rajendra Ravindra Printers (Pvt) Ltd, New Delhi—110055

Contents

Plates

1

Chief Minister of Bombay State

THE INDIAN National Congress was making preparations like other Indian parties, during the last six months of 1951, for the general elections which were to be held, according to the new Constitution, in 1952. I was a member of the Congress Parliamentary Board at the time. The four Pradesh Congress Committees of Bombay State were considering the problem of selecting candidates for the elections. Shri Balasaheb Kher, the then Chief Minister, had declared his decision not to contest. I tried to persuade him to do so, telling him that I had no desire to be the Chief Minister of Bombay. But he refused to change his decision as he felt that several people in the State did not like the attitude of impartiality which he brought to bear on his work. He therefore insisted that I take over the Chief Ministership.

Shri S. K. Patil was President of the Bombay Pradesh Congress Committee at the time. Shri Bhausaheb Hiray was President in Maharashtra, Shri Kanjibhai Desai in Gujarat and Shri Nijalingappa in Karnatak. We were very careful in the selection of candidates and the Central Parliamentary Board therefore accepted the recommendations of these four Pradesh Congress Committees with very few alterations.

The opposition parties had offered a strong challenge and had created a feeling in the country that the Congress was very unpopular and would not get the support of the people. They predicted that the Congress would not get a majority in several States. There was similar propaganda in the press too. From December 1951 onwards I toured all the districts of Bombay State and did some propaganda for the elections. Though I toured in Gujarat for about three weeks, I could not visit my own constituency, Bulsar, more than twice, spending a total of six or seven days there. Shri Bhailalbhai Patel and others had started a Peasants' Party in Gujarat and Saurashtra to fight the elections. This party was converted later on into the Gujarat unit of the Swatantra Party. The Peasants' Party contested most of the seats in almost every district in 1952.

A dacoit named Bhupat had created a great deal of terror in Saurashtra. The Peasants' Party exploited the popular anxiety concerning the ravages of this dacoit to build up a feeling among the people against the Congress. Shri Samldas Gandhi was then the leader of the opposition to the Congress in Saurashtra. I therefore spent some extra time touring Saurashtra. I explained the programmes and policies of the Indian National Congress and demonstrated their superiority over those of the other parties. This created a very favourable atmosphere for the Congress in Saurashtra and, that year, the voters' response to our campaign was very favourable. Most of my colleagues also worked hard in the elections and we scored very well in the elections. The Peasants' Party was defeated and all their tall talk of defeating the Congress came to nothing.

Earlier, in November or December 1951, I had some personal misgivings regarding the elections. As Balasaheb did not contest them it was almost certain that I would have to take the responsibility of forming a Government in Bombay State if the Congress won the majority. This was also generally the feeling of my colleagues then. At that time I feared it might be difficult for me to pursue truth as Chief Minister. Howsoever careful I might be about speaking the truth it could not be said with certainty that the people with whom I would have to work in running the Government would do the same. However careful I might be, I would have to do my work trusting my colleagues. It was possible that not all that they would tell me would be wholly truthful and since I would be acting on their advice I might sometimes do something which would not be in accordance with truth.

The possibility of a reorganisation of Bombay State was at that time in the air. The Karnatak Division of Bombay State, particularly wanted to merge with Mysore State. There was also a possibility of Maharashtra and Gujarat becoming separate States as a result. I, on my part, believed firmly that the strength of the Indian nation lay in maintaining Bombay State as it was. The composite Bombay State had contributed very greatly in creating an atmosphere of unity in the country. Many people, however, wanted a reorganisation of the States on a linguistic basis. They honestly believed that the administration of the states would become simpler and more efficient if they were linguistically homogeneous as the contact between the people and the government in such states would be very close and effective. Moreover, as the administration would be conducted in the people's language, they would be able to take more interest in it. The Congress also had become strong in the struggle for freedom after the Pradesh Congress Committees were organised on a linguistic basis at the suggestion of Mahatma Gandhi. Work in the Pradesh Committees of the Indian National Congress was carried on in the language of the state or pradesh and, as a result, the people's interest in it considerably increased. This was the background for the demand for linguistic provinces in the country.

One found, however, on studying the circumstances which obtained in India for the last three centuries that the proper integration of India could not be effected without creating a burning sense of patriotism among the people for the whole country. I, therefore, felt that a linguistic reorganisation of the states at that stage would make the task of the unification of India, its political integration, more difficult. If the Bombay State was maintained as it was, I believed it would be possible to counter the propaganda for linguistic states. I therefore saw the possibility of a very strong controversy with my close colleagues on this question. Many of them wanted linguistic states both in Maharashtra and Gujarat.

In the circumstances, I was doubtful about how effective I could be if I had to head the State Ministry. I also felt that the responsibility of running a government hindered my search for truth. These things worried me. After a good deal of consideration of all the circumstances, I came to the conclusion that I could attain my ideal of serving the people only if I could pursue the realisation of truth successfully. I had decided to serve the people through the Indian National Congress, and could not, therefore, refuse to take the responsibility of running the State if my colleagues in the Congress wanted me to do so. For a long time I played with the idea that I could save myself from the responsibility of Government if I failed in the elections. This thought came to me several times during November and December 1951. I did not then realise that this kind of thought was contrary to the principle that I had followed in my life of not running away from responsibilities that came to me.

Ever since I resolved to serve the people for the rest of my life, I had decided that I should not create any institution or organisation myself, and that while I should not make any effort to attain any position, I should do whatever work came to me naturally and to fulfil whatever responsibility fell to my lot. Just as I would not take any steps to get any position, I should not try to escape any responsibility that came to me naturally.

When I lost in the general elections of 1952 I came to the conclusion, after considering the whole position, that that defeat was a great lesson for me and that I should not have thought of running away from my responsibility. I thought that God had sent me this defeat to make me understand my mistake.

The constituency in which I was a candidate was for me a completely safe one. This was proved in the general elections of 1957. In 1957 I stood for Parliament, but another Congress worker from Bulsar took my place as candidate for the Bombay Legislative Assembly. I was defeated in 1952 by 19 votes but this Congressman, who was my colleague and had worked for my election in 1952, defeated the same opponent by 19,000 votes in 1957.

Through the defeat in 1952 God taught me that I should not have attempted to run away from the responsibility of running the Government which had come to me naturally. There was no doubt also left in my mind that if one acted honestly in whatever situation one was placed and one performed one's duties conscientiously, God or truth could be realised, whatever the situation and whatever the nature of responsibilities.

It is commonly believed that a politician is seldom able to pursue the path of truth but one must have faith that it is possible to pursue truth even though one is an active politician. The example of King Janaka is before us to prove the truth of this. If a person keeps God constantly before him and surrenders himself to Him and goes on living his life with a sense of duty, without any sense of self-interest, and if he fulfils his responsibility in that spirit, he can pursue truth successfully even while running a Government. This is how I understood things after my defeat in 1952.

On the first counting of the votes in 1952, I was supposed to have been defeated by 219 votes, but when a recount was ordered and some boxes were recounted, 200 more votes came to my share and the difference between me and the winner fell to only 19. Though a few more boxes had to be still recounted, my rival opposed further recounting. Perhaps he feared that if there was a recount of the ballots in the balance of the boxes, his majority would be eroded and I would be declared elected. He therefore opposed further recounting. I was advised over the telephone at Bombay that I should not insist on a full recount as it was being said that I was taking advantage of my position as Home Minister in getting the recounting done. Considering this I felt it would be best if I accepted my defeat. I therefore instructed my representative at Bulsar accordingly even though my colleagues there felt that if the remaining boxes had been recounted I would have won by more votes than 19 instead of getting defeated by that number. I however felt that no good would be achieved by winning in this manner and therefore accepted my defeat cheerfully and stopped further recounting.

When I received information about my defeat it was clear in

my mind that I must resign from the Government and should not think of getting re-elected to the Assembly. However, before I could send in my resignation to Shri Kher the latter sent me a message that I should not make any statement or take any step without first having a talk with him. When I met him he told me immediately that I must not resign and that I must stand for re-election as I had to undertake the responsibility of the Chief Ministership of Bombay State. I then told him that I was not able to appreciate the suggestion very much. If I could not win in the general election it only showed God's wish that I should not continue in Government. I should therefore get out from this kind of politics. That did not mean that I would not be able to serve the Congress outside the Legislative Assembly. It was possible that I might be able to serve the Congress organisation better outside the Legislature. Balasaheb's reply was that if the Government was run well the organisation also would be stronger and that I should be able to serve the Congress better in that manner. Under the then circumstances, I would be able to render better service to the people through the Government. He insisted that I give up the idea of getting out of the Government because I had been defeated in the election. He also argued that in many democratic countries those who were defeated once in elections did not give up parliamentary work but contested elections again and won after one or two or even three defeats. There was nothing improper, he said, in that procedure. I replied that I did agree that that was the general practice in democratic countries. I however did not consider it proper for me to adopt it in view of the ideal of life which I had kept before me. Shri Kher again argued that it would be difficult to find another person acceptable to the people in Bombay State as Chief Minister if I did not accept the responsibility. I asked him what would happen if I left the world. Then another arrangement would *have* to be made and it was possible that that arrangement might even be better. I still therefore considered that it was my duty to get out of the Government. Shri Balasaheb replied that if I was not alive the question would not arise. I was however, still available and he did not think there was then another man in the party who could do this work as well as I could. If, however, I could suggest to him a more suitable person he would certainly consider it. I could not honestly recommend any other person who would be able to undertake this responsibility equally well and I therefore told Balasaheb that I could accept his suggestion and act on it only if all the Presidents of the four Pradesh Congress Committees unanimously and voluntarily agreed with it. It was even more necessary that Jawaharlalji and the Central Parliamentary Board should agree with him in this matter. I also laid down the condition that he must not persuade other people to agree with him and that they must do it voluntarily themselves. If all agreed in this matter I would consider it my duty to accept his suggestion. He promised to abide by my conditions.

We received a letter from Jawaharlalji the very next morning in which he had expressed sorrow and astonishment at my defeat. He also pressed that I should get re-elected and that I should not leave the Government. He also said definitely that he was not prepared to consider any alternative. The Presidents of all the four Pradesh Congress Committees of the Bombay State also pressed the same proposal. The Working Committee of the Congress, which met soon after, also pressed me similarly. I sent word through Shri Gulzari Lal Nanda and other friends to Shri Jawaharlalji that if other ministers who were defeated in this election were not to contest the election again and if I alone was to recontest it would not be very fair and that it would create jealousies. Shri Jawaharlalji immediately sent word that I must not think on those lines and that whatever might be decided in the matter of other people he had no doubt that I must contest an election again. The Working Committee passed a resolution directing that the other ministers who had been defeated in the general elections should not contest elections in the near future. However, the members of the Committee had all insisted that I must stand for election again and accept the Chief Minister's position in Bombay State. I therefore ultimately accepted this suggestion.

During the 1952 elections somebody in a village had asked me what I had to say about the boast of my opponent that he would be defeating me. I had replied that I did not know whether he would defeat me but it was possible that he would lose his deposit. I remembered this incident when I was defeated and some people also reminded me about it. I realised that I had spoken with arrogance and that was also perhaps one of the reasons for my defeat. I fully realised then that one should not have any arrogance of this kind and this realisation benefited me immensely.

When I was analysing the causes of my defeat, I also remembered the saying of ancient rishis: *Satyam api Priyam Bruyat, Na Bruyat Satyam Apriyam* ; i.e. one should tell the truth in a pleasant manner and should not tell the truth which is likely to generate unpleasantness. I used to believe before this that it would not always be possible to speak the truth in a pleasant manner when the truth itself may not be pleasant to some people. I therefore believed one should not hesitate to speak the truth even if somebody took it ill. When, however, I considered deeply the incidents in connection with the elections of 1952 it was brought home to me very clearly that the rishis were far wiser than myself and that I knew very little in comparison with them. I also realised that my earlier attitude was wrong. I argued to myself that truth could not be unpleasant for anybody because truth meant what existed; and what was a fact could not be unpleasant to anybody. The question then arose: why was the truth unpleasant for some people? I felt on further consideration that there were two possibilities for this happening. It might so happen that the 'truth' which I was telling somebody might have been taken by me from somebody else and on his assurance I might say something which might not actually be the truth. If therefore what I said on somebody else's information might not be the truth, it might be disliked by the person to whom it was told. Secondly, if I disliked a person, the truth that I would be telling him would be told in an unpleasant manner because my dislike would influence the language I used and the manner in which I said it, and would be conveyed to the person concerned through the words that I used whether I wished it or not. Coming to this conclusion I realised that I must not harbour any dislike for anybody. This view was confirmed for me when I realised through experience that a person never took the truth I told him amiss if there was friendly feeling between us. This realisation brought about a very healthy change in me and I became very careful to see that I did not speak in an unpleasant manner.

I had discussed this moral problem with Shri Kishorelalbhai Mashruwala also in Bombay and with one or two other friends who were spiritually very advanced. All of them supported Balasaheb's stand and suggestion and told me that considering all the circumstances in the State it was my duty to act upon Balasaheb's advice. Balasaheb had also consulted legal experts to find out whether the suggestion that he was making was legally and morally proper. He would not have made the suggestion of re-election to the Assembly if he was not convinced that it was morally and legally proper and justifiable.

As a whole, we did very well in the 1952 general elections in Bombay State and had a very comfortable majority. My tour and propaganda throughout the State had contributed to this success. This was the view of many. When somebody talked to Jawaharlalji in Delhi about my defeat, he replied, 'He is the victorious leader of a victorious party.'

Considering therefore all the sides of the problem and the

pressing view of Jawaharlalji and all the Presidents of the Bombay Pradesh Congress Committees and Balasaheb Kher I agreed to be the Chief Minister of Bombay State.

After this decision was taken Balasaheb encountered difficulty in the constitution of the Bombay Congress Legislature Party to my getting elected as leader. The constitution laid down that only a member of the Legislative Assembly could be so elected. Even a member of the Bombay Legislative Council could not be elected as leader. The election of the leader of the party was to take place in a few days and had to be done within about six weeks. There was no possibility of my getting elected to the Legislative Assembly during this period. It was therefore necessary to amend the constitution as, without the necessary amendment, I could not have been elected leader of the Congress Legislature Party. Balasaheb therefore called a meeting of the Congress Legislature Party for making the necessary amendment in the constitution.

Those who were not in favour of my becoming Chief Minister wrote to Jawaharlalji that it was very improper that the party's constitution should be amended in this manner. Jawaharlalji wrote to us saying that since the outgoing party was going to be replaced by the newly elected party, the former should not amend the constitution in a hurry. Jawaharlalji did not know of the difficulty that was facing us in the election of the leader. This is perhaps why he wrote in this manner. I immediately replied and explained to him the whole position. I also wrote to him that because of the difficulties and misunderstandings that would have arisen I was not willing to stand for re-election to the Legislative Assembly. I therefore even requested him, with all the force that I could command, to relieve me from the responsibility. If I had to be elected leader of the Congress Legislature Party in Bombay it would not be possible without amending the constitution of the party. If therefore his consent was not received before the date which was fixed for the meeting of the party, the meeting would be cancelled and the proposal to amend the constitution would be given up. I would also then refuse to be the leader of the Legislature Party. Jawaharlalji immediately replied that he had not realised all these difficulties and he therefore asked us to hold the meeting of the party and make the necessary amendment to the constitution.

So, after the constitution had been duly amended I first got elected to the Bombay Legislative Council from a local board constituency, i.e. local self-government constituency of Ahmedabad of which the seat was vacant. As I felt, however, that I should be elected as the leader only as a member of the Legislative

Assembly, when two or three months later there was a vacancy in the Legislative Assembly from a labour constituency at Ahmedabad I contested and was elected with a very large majority.

After I was elected to the Bombay Legislative Council the Congress Legislature Party elected me its leader unanimously. Before the election, however, I explained my position so that the members might take their decision after full consideration. I told them I was very grateful to all of them for deciding to choose me as their leader even though I had been defeated in the elections. I however had to place before them my fundamental beliefs and would request them to elect me as their leader only after they understood them. It was possible that a question might arise on which there would be a difference of opinion between me on the one side and the members of the party on the other. If members of the party felt that their view was in the interest of the people, while I believed that my view alone was proper and correct, that it was in the best interests of the people and that great harm would be done to the State if the members' view was accepted, I would press for my view to be accepted by the party. If the party felt that I must act on their view I would give up the leadership and the party would have to elect another leader. If, however, the party wanted me to continue as the leader of the party they would have to accept my decision even when it was opposed to theirs. Only, if the members of the party agreed with this position of mine should they elect me as their leader. If they did not, they should not elect me and it would be better that they choose some other suitable leader.

The members of the party accepted my position unanimously and I was elected leader of the party. *The Times of India* and some other papers criticised this decision very severely and had even said that my attitude was against democratic principles. I have not been able to understand, even now, the propriety of such criticism. I saw that only those who were personally opposed to me expressed such opinions. There is a greater onus on the leader of the party than on the ordinary members in a democracy, especially in a difficult situation. If, in a difficult situation, the leader was led by the party instead of leading it, he would put democracy and the country in great danger. It was very clear to me that the leader, who did not accept the view of the party and remained firm on his own view, should resign from the leadership, if the party did not accept his view. Where was the question of violating any principles of democracy in this behaviour or in this attitude?

There are times when even amongst the ministers there arises a difference of opinion on some important problem. But in such matters the decision is taken by a majority and even there it is the leader's view which is accorded the utmost attention. If any minister feels that the decision taken is not in accordance with his conscience or that it violates any principle, and if he is firm on his own different opinion, he has to resign his ministership. But, when he accepts a majority decision he must act on it as if it is his own and he must also not express any difference of opinion once the decision is taken and acted upon.

The question of conscience does not arise in every decision or in every matter. There are many questions which are ideological. Some ideas and opinions are personal and others are dependent on the policies of the party to which one belongs. There is no question of the conscience or any conflict of principle in such matters. In the matter of differences of opinion or ideas it would be better and most proper for a person to accept the majority view and to act on it.

The work of the Bombay Ministry was appreciated all over the country because it worked with unity of purpose. If, on any matter, differences of opinion arose, nobody outside knew about them. We in the Ministry observed a rule, during the ten years we were in power (from 1946 to 1956), that every Minister would accept the decision of the Chief Minister in the case of a difference of opinion. This did not mean that the Chief Minister acted arbitrarily. A chief minister cannot carry on for long if he acts arbitrarily, without taking members of his cabinet and his party into confidence and carrying them with him in the decisions he takes. It is the responsibility of the chief minister to win the affection and respect of his colleagues and to create confidence in his impartiality among all his colleagues. He has to be ready to discuss whatever has to be discussed with everyone of his colleagues. There will be rare occasions on which he will differ with his colleagues and in such cases his colleagues will accept his decision cheerfully.

After being elected leader of the Bombay Legislative Congress Party, I encountered some difficulties in the formation of the Ministry. The President of the Maharashtra Pradesh Congress Committee, Bhausaheb Hiray, insisted that I should select men from Maharashtra only with his agreement. Shri M.P. Patil from Karnatak insisted that he would not join the Ministry unless I included at least two ministers from Karnatak.

I discussed the question first with the Presidents of all the Pradesh Congress Committees. It was unanimously decided to have a cabinet of nine ministers: four from Maharashtra, one from

Karnatak, one from Bombay and three from Gujarat. I was included in the Gujarat quota. I had received the concurrence of Shri S.K. Patil on the person to be included in the cabinet from Bombay, but Shri Hiray accepted only two names, his own and Shri Yashwantrao Chavan's of the four ministers I had decided to take from Maharashtra. He insisted that I should choose afresh for the other two places still available for Maharashtra and that only people acceptable to him be appointed. He wanted Shri D.K. Kunte to be one of these two.

I tried to persuade Shri Hiray to see that there could not be two leaders in the cabinet and the ministers should be chosen keeping this principle in view. The leader alone had to select the ministers. If he accepted people chosen by somebody else, he would not get the necessary loyalty from these ministers. The two other persons from Maharashtra whom I had decided to include in the cabinet were Shri Naik Nimbalkar and Shri G.D. Tapase. Shri Nimbalkar was the ex-ruler of the erstwhile Phalton State. He had handed over all the balances of the State to the Bombay Government, when it was merged in Bombay State, retaining for himself only his ancestral home, a bungalow and some land. Dr. Jivaraj Mehta had been taken as a minister from the erstwhile Baroda State of Gujarat and we thought it would be appropriate to take Shri Naik Nimbalkar from the Maharashtra State.

When Balasaheb invited Shri Naik Nimbalkar to join his Cabinet earlier he said: 'I am not a Congressman and if I become one in order to be a Minister, it would not be consistent with my self-respect. Moreover, I have taken to agriculture after the merger of my State in Bombay State and have invested a large sum in it. If I join the Ministry, I will perhaps lose my investment as nobody will be able to look after it.' I persuaded him to agree saying, 'We will not press you to join the Congress. You can join it whenever you think it proper and you are free not to join it if you do not want to do so. You can entrust the agricultural undertaking to your sons and you should join the Ministry, so that the Cabinet can be strengthened and we get a proper representative from the merged Maharashtra State.'

Shri Naik Nimbalkar is a very straight, simple and honest gentleman and was known to be a good administrator of his State. He is also humble by temperament. We felt that if a man of such integrity joined the Ministry, the Cabinet would be strengthened. He ultimately accepted the invitation and joined the earlier Ministry in 1950, and did very good work during the term of his office.

It was with this background that I considered it my duty to

include him in my Cabinet in 1952. I explained this to Shri Hiray and also that I had to include a Harijan, and Shri Tapase was the fittest candidate. He had experience and had worked well in the previous Ministry. Even though I tried hard to persuade Bhausaheb to agree, he did not give up his insistence on the inclusion of two men of his choice. When I told him that I could not agree, he refused to join the Ministry himself, and the discussions ended there.

When Shri M.P. Patil told me that he would not be able to join the Ministry unless at least two ministers from Karnatak were included, I told him that I would not be able to take more than one from there and that if he did not consider this adequate he might not join the Cabinet.

I then consulted Shri Yashwantrao Chavan about Shri Hiray's stand. I asked him whether he was willing to join the Cabinet in view of this position. When he asked for my advice, I said, 'You have to take the decision yourself. You have to decidc whether the advice I give you would be advantageous to you or not. If you agree with Bhausaheb Hiray's position, you must support him. But if you agree with me and feel that you run no political risk in joining my Ministry, you should join it. I cannot say for certain how long the Ministry will last in view of the circumstances in which I am forming it, and if I resign on account of some difficulties arising in the future, you will be in a very awkward position, particularly because Shri Bhausaheb Hiray will be very much displeased at your joining my Ministry and your political future will therefore be in danger. If, therefore, you consider that there is a risk in your joining my Cabinet and decide not to join it, I assure you I shall not take it amiss.'

Shri Yashwantrao Chavan immediately replied: 'I am not bothered about any risk. I believe it is my duty to join your Cabinet. I must not worry about the future.' I congratulated him on his courageous decision. I then consulted Shri Naik Nimbalkar and Shri Tapase and asked them to tell me without any hesitation whether they would be willing to join my Cabinet despite Shri Hiray's attitude. They too immediately agreed, and three names out of four to be taken from Maharashtra were thus settled.

I then decided to keep the fourth place vacant for a month and try to persuade Shri Bhausaheb Hiray to accept the place during the interval. If he did not agree, I planned to take another person from Maharashtra. I had also made arrangements to take another person from Karnatak if Shri M.P. Patil did not join the Ministry. I informed Jawaharlalji on the phone about the circumstances in which I was forming my Cabinet. He suggested that I would be helped in the process if I went to Delhi and discussed the matter with his colleagues there. Shri N.V. Gadgil who was a Central Minister at the time had asked for permission from Jawaharlalji to go to Bombay to help in the formation of the Bombay Ministry. Jawaharlalji told me that he had not permitted this.

Shri Bhausaheb Hiray had told me on the phone that he was also going to Delhi. When I mentioned this to Jawaharlalji, he asked me whether he should see Shri Hiray who wanted to see him. I told Jawaharlalji: 'You ought to see him and hear him. You should not take any decision merely on the basis of what I tell you without hearing others. It is but proper that you see him.'

I went to Delhi the next day. Shri Hiray travelled on the same plane. I explained all the facts to Jawaharlalji when I met him. He suggested we might discuss the question in a meeting of the Central Parliamentary Board but I told him that I would not be able to change my position and discussion in the Parliamentary Board might only make things more difficult. I therefore offered to act as Jawaharlalji advised me. He appreciated this. I had also told him that Shri Hiray, when he met him, would not make any oral statement, but would give him a written one as he would not be able to argue the matter with him. After Shri Hiray had met Jawaharlalji and given him a written statement, Jawaharlalji asked me what reply he should give him. 'It is proper that you advise him as you think best,' I said. In spite of this, when he persisted, I said, 'It would be a good thing if you would advise him to join my Ministry.' (Jawaharlalji told me later that he had advised Shri Hiray accordingly.)

Jawaharlalji then suggested that it would be good if we discussed several matters that were under consideration with Maulana Saheb. Maulana Azad was a member of the Central Parliamentary Board. Jawaharlalji was its Chairman. He then very tactfully called in some other colleagues also and included them in the discussion. When four or five of us thus met, Jawaharlalji referred to the question of the formation of the Bombay Cabinet also while discussing other matters. He stated that he had agreed with the arrangements which I had decided to make and asked for the views of the other colleagues. I had not included a Muslim in the list of nine persons whom I had selected for the Cabinet, but I had included a Muslim amongst the deputy ministers to be appointed. Maulana Saheb said, 'You ought to take a Muslim. You are very alive to this problem and have always pressed for giving a proper representation to Muslims. I hope therefore that you will accept my suggestion.' 'There is nobody amongst the Muslim MLAs,' I said, 'whom I consider capable enough to be taken in the Cabinet. I have therefore decided to take a Muslim as a deputy minister and not as a minister.'

To this the Maulana countered, 'What if I suggest a suitable Muslim name?' But I was firm. 'My opinion alone must be the deciding factor about the fitness or otherwise of the persons who are going to work with me in Bombay.' I said, 'Therefore if I do not agree with your view, how can I accept it?' Maulana Saheb, however, continued to press his view and asked Jawaharlalji whether he did not agree that a Muslim should be taken in the Ministry. Jawaharlalji replied that if a suitable person was found he should be taken. I then said: 'There is no suitable person.' When Maulana Saheb persisted in his demand in spite of what I said, I told him: 'If you feel that I would be considered correct in my attitude only if I include a Muslim in my Cabinet, it is not proper. You should not press me to act against my judgment in this manner.' The others present supported me and the matter ended there.

After settling this difficulty, I returned to Bombay. Shri Hiray also immediately returned to Bombay. I called him again and asked him to reconsider his decision. I told him that we should elect Shri Kunte Speaker and thus his view would be respected to that extent. Shri Hiray was of the view that Shri Kunte would not accept the Speakership. 'I shall persuade him to do so,' I said, 'I shall also give you the Agricultural Department in addition to the Revenue Department. This will give you added importance in the Cabinet and you should not now refuse to join the Ministry. If you feel dissatisfied with the working of the Ministry after joining it, you can certainly resign from it. But it is in the interest of everybody, that you should join the Cabinet now.' After a little hesitation, Shri Hiray agreed and the crisis was thus resolved.

I then called Shri M.P. Patil and said, 'I cannot take two ministers from Karnatak. If you accept this position and agree to join the Cabinet I will include you. If, however, you refuse the offer, I shall have to think of an alternative. Shri Hiray has already agreed to join.' Shri Patil told me he would give me his reply after consulting the President of the Karnatak Pradesh Congress Committee. I asked him to let me have it by seven the same evening.

We had met at four in the afternoon, and when I reminded Shri Patil at seven he told me that he had not been able to get in touch with the President of the Pradesh Congress Committee. Nevertheless, he agreed to join the Ministry. I was thus able to send the names of the Ministers to the Governor at about 8 p.m. and we were sworn in by the Governor the next morning.

Shri N.V. Gadgil who met me after the formation of the Ministry, told me that as a result of my attitude, my Ministry would not last long and that I would have to change it. 'I am not going to make any changes in the Ministry later on,' I told him, 'If such an occasion arises I shall not continue as Chief Minister. I am, however, confident that this Ministry will be able to work effectively for the full term of five years.'

I then persuaded Shri Kunte to accept the Speakership. As Shri Hiray had promised to include him in the Ministry, Shri Kunte was dissatisfied with my decision. Even though we were on very good terms, I found it somewhat difficult to persuade him, but ultimately he agreed to be the Speaker.

2

Administrative Reforms

When we presented the budget after the formation of the Cabinet, we proposed a large increase in the sales tax from which we were to receive an additional revenue of Rs. 10 to 11 crores. Besides this increase, we also proposed to levy a surcharge on land revenue which would have yielded an additional Rs. 1 crore. Dr. Jivaraj Mehta was the Finance Minister. I left for Delhi soon after the budget was presented in the Assembly as I had to attend a meeting of the Congress Working Committee the next day. A meeting of the Congress Legislature Party was called for a discussion of the budget that very evening at Poona where the Assembly session was meeting. Poona was the Monsoon Headquarters of the Government in those days.

Soon after I reached Delhi I was informed over the phone that strong opposition had been offered to the additional taxes in the Party meeting and that Shri Hiray and Dr. Jivaraj Mehta had not succeeded in satisfying the opposition. As the opposition had not abated, I advised them to adjourn the meeting until my return, and this was done.

After I returned from Delhi, a meeting of the Party was held again. I asked for a frank expression of the views of the members. Many expressed their opposition to the additional taxation with much politeness. They told me that they would not be able to satisfy the people about the propriety of these taxes and that the opposition in the Assembly would be strengthened and, as a result, the Congress Party would be weakened. I explained the financial position of the State and how necessary all the new taxes were. I also pointed out that it was not proper to surrender to the mistaken propaganda of the opposition and that we should not hesitate or feel diffident in explaining the correct position to the people. I warned them at the end of the discussion: 'If we tinker with the budget in this manner, it will be difficult to carry on the government of the State, and the Party also will be weakened. If therefore you do not agree with this budget, the only solution that I can suggest is that you should elect another leader as I will not be able to continue as leader under these conditions. You should therefore think very seriously on the whole matter and give me your considered reply.'

My presentation of the facts had a healthy effect, and the opposition was withdrawn. The MLAs assured me of their full support, without any reservations, for whatever I decided to do in the matter. I then asked them to leave the decision to me. After a good deal of consideration of all factors, I decided to give up the surcharge on land revenue, but did not make any concessions in regard to the sales tax increase which was to yield a very large revenue. The Party accepted my decision.

I then called a special meeting of the Party for three days and had a very free and frank discussion with the members as regards the transaction of the Party's business. I spoke to them for nearly two and a half hours and frankly placed before them my views on the attitude the Party should adopt and how we should work in the Party. I told the MLAs clearly how harmful it would be to the Party if we discussed the problem in the Party in the manner in which the budget had been discussed in my absence. I concluded, saying: 'There are some matters on which I should take action without saying anything to anyone else. I must act without making explanations as such prior explanations would lessen the effectiveness of the action. I have discussed these matters so frankly as I am anxious to see that no awkward situation arises in the Party in future.' All the members appreciated my arguments and told me that they did not consider it necessary to have any further discussion on the matter. The Party meeting therefore ended peacefully and no awkward or difficult situation ever arose in the Party since then until I left Bombay to join the Central Government. All of us worked like a happy family.

When Kaka Saheb Gadgil came to Poona and met me after this incident, he referred to the budget and said that I should not have given up the proposed surcharge on land revenue. 'Shri Bhausaheb Hiray is your friend,' I said, 'he had given his approval to this surcharge in the Cabinet but did not support it very strongly in the Party meeting. This encouraged some of the members to oppose it. I had to take all these factors into consideration and this is why I had to give up the proposed cess on land revenue. You should therefore convey your disapproval to Bhausaheb and not to me.' He must have then talked about it to Shri Hiray, as a result of which the latter who attended an informal meeting of the Cabinet the next day, said to me, 'It was not proper of you to criticise me in your talk with Kaka Saheb Gadgil. If you have no confidence in me, I must resign from the Ministry.' 'I told Kaka Saheb only the facts as he asked me about them,' I replied, 'I did this particularly because he is your friend. I am convinced about the facts. I still believe that what I told him was correct. If you do not approve of what I have said and want to resign from the Ministry, you are free to do so. But I must tell you frankly that this kind of attitude is not proper.' Bhausaheb Hiray appreciated my point and did not talk any further of resigning from the Ministry. In fact, for as long as I remained in Bombay as Chief Minister after that, Shri Hiray never again spoke of resigning.

Shri S. K. Patil, President of the Bombay Pradesh Congress Committee, started an agitation on the matter of sales tax and criticised it very strongly. He did not come to see me about this even though I invited him for a discussion. I reported the matter to Jawaharlalji who disapproved of Shri Patil's attitude. He wrote to Shri Patil about it. We discussed this matter when we met at the Indore AICC meeting a few months later, and Shri Patil agreed to give up his opposition as suggested by Jawaharlalji. Shri Patil had been opposing the sales tax increase as many businessmen were opposed to it and had been complaining to him about it. Shri Patil was worried that, as a result of this opposition from businessmen, the Congress would become unpopular amongst the people. I understood that Shri Patil's opposition was offered with a view to ensure that the Congress did not suffer and my personal relations with him remained cordial.

I have always believed that education and agriculture hold the key to the development of our country and that it is therefore necessary to make strenuous efforts to make people aware of this and to interest them in participating in the developmental activities in these fields. However, as is the rule with me, I never sought to be allotted a particular responsibility which I felt was interesting and important and undertook whatever responsibility was allotted to me to the best of my capacity. Thus, when Balasaheb was Chief Minister, the allotment of the Home and Revenue departments to me was entirely his decision. It was he who thought I could handle these departments best and I think I gave him satisfaction. Balasaheb retained charge of the Education Department right through his Chief Ministership. He too was deeply interested in education and he used regularly to consult me on new policies before they were implemented.

In view of my deep interest in, and the importance I attach to education and agriculture, I should perhaps, when I became Chief Minister, have taken charge of at least the Education Department. However, my colleagues felt that I should retain the Home portfolio, and I felt it would not be right (although I could have managed both departments with ease) to retain too much for myself. I therefore entrusted the Education Department to Shri Dinkerrao Desai.

There was great dissatisfaction with the system of textile control that prevailed in 1951. Dr. Harekrishna Mehtab who was in charge of the relevant Ministry at the centre was advised by us to appoint a Textile Advisory Committee of non-officials and to carry on the work of controlling the textile industry with the advice of that committee. Dr. Mehtab accepted our suggestion but insisted that I should be the Chairman of the Committee. I told him that I had not much free time as I had very heavy work to do in my Ministry and it was difficult for me to undertake any extra responsibility. Kaka Saheb Gadgil and Balasaheb also pressed me to undertake this responsibility and I had therefore to accept it. The members of the Advisory Committee were appointed with my approval which made it easier for me to look after the work of this Committee. I was able to work effectively and many of the complaints which were previously heard against the controls were removed to a large extent.

Before I give some further information about the work of the Ministry I should like to mention an incident. The Chief Minister of Madras was also defeated in the elections of 1952 and the Congress was not able to get a majority in those elections in that State. The question of the formation of a Ministry in Madras therefore had arisen. Before this could be settled, there was the problem of the appointment of the Governor of Madras State and the Prime Minister was considering whom he should appoint. Jawaharlalji had requested Balasaheb Kher to accept the Governorship before I had been elected leader of the Congress Legislature Party in Bombay. He had selected him as he felt it necessary to select a person who would be able to win the confidence of all people in the State. Balasaheb did not stand for election in 1952. Balasaheb did not find the offer acceptable but Jawaharlalji asked him to reconsider his decision. Balasaheb talked to me about it and told me that he did not want to take up a Governorship as he did not like such duties and requested me to persuade Jawaharlalji to give up his suggestion. I told him that if Jawaharlalji consulted me I would certainly try to persuade him not to press the proposal. I received a telephone call from Jawaharlalji the next day and he asked me to persuade Balasaheb to accept. Balasaheb would have had to go to Madras immediately, i.e. before a new Ministry could be formed and the new Assembly began to function. I told Jawaharlalji that if Balasaheb left Bombay and resigned the Chief

Ministership of the State at the moment and went to Madras as Governor, it would be difficult to make the necessary arrangements to fill the vacancy created by Balasaheb's going. 'You are there,' Jawaharlalji said, 'you are, in any case, going to be the leader of the new Party. It is therefore not difficult for you to take up the responsibility right now.' 'I have not yet been elected to either house in Bombay State,' I replied, 'and have been defeated in the elections. Several people from the opposition will therefore raise objections to my taking up the Chief Ministership now and would ask you how you have appointed a defeated person as Chief Minister of Bombay. It would perhaps be difficult for you to give a satisfactory explanation. If, however, you are not worried by such questions and criticism and are confident that you will be able to satisfy such critics, I can certainly persuade Balasaheb Kher to accept the Governorship.' When I put these arguments before him, Jawaharlalji immediately said, 'You are right. I am dropping the idea of appointing Balasaheb Kher as Governor.' He asked me to suggest somebody else for the Governorship of Madras. I suggested Shri Sriprakashji, which he liked and Sriprakashji was appointed as Governor of Madras State immediately.

The selection of a leader of the Congress Legislature Party in Madras State who could form a Ministry there, was quite a problem in 1952. Sriprakashji felt that if Rajaji could be persuaded to accept the leadership it would be best as it would give strength to the weakened Congress Party in Madras and informed Jawaharlalji accordingly. Jawaharlalji said that if it was possible to make such an arrangement he would be happy, but Rajaji should be elected to the Legislative Assembly or to the Legislative Council so that he might be elected leader of the Party. When Sriprakashji mentioned this to Rajaji, the latter refused to stand for election to either house and said that he would accept the leadership only if he was nominated to the upper house, i.e. the Legislative Council. Neither Jawaharlalji nor others like me liked the idea of making a nominated member Chief Minister of a State. But before we could say anything to Sriprakashji, the latter utilised his powers and nominated Rajaji to the upper house. Rajaji was then elected the leader of the Congress Legislature Party in Madras and formed his Ministry. Sriprakashji took this step on his own responsibility as Rajaji could not be persuaded to stand for election to either house. I have not yet understood why Rajaji made this a condition for accepting leadership. But it was no use asking him for reasons in this matter after he had already been nominated and elected the leader.

Shri Yashwantrao Chavan was one of the Ministers in the Ministry I formed in 1952. I had entrusted the Civil Supplies Department to him. This Department was responsible for supply and distribution of food in the State. Shri Rafi Ahmed Kidwai was in charge of this Ministry at the Centre and there was in those days strict food control which had been in operation for quite some time. Ration shops were distributed all over the city of Bombay and a few other cities especially in those areas in the country where foodgrains were scarce. The people were supplied foodgrains from the shops according to the regulations in force. This system had been in force from the time of the war as there was a deficit in the supply of foodgrains in the country. Some 30 to 35 lakh tonnes of foodgrains had to be imported and this is how the deficit was met.

There was great dissatisfaction amongst the people with this control of foodgrains and there was an agitation for its removal. Bapu also had pressed for the removal of these controls when he was alive. The States however could not then remove the controls on account of the deficit supply of foodgrains in the country. Rafisaheb came to the conclusion that it should be removed and made a proposal to this effect in the Central Cabinet. His proposal however was not accepted by the Cabinet. He used to meet me whenever he came to Bombay and also used to consult me about such matters. We had not been close to each other in 1950–51 and, as I have said earlier, I had refused to support him for the election to the Parliamentary Board. Our relations therefore were not quite friendly. But Rafisaheb was a very liberal-hearted person.

A few months after the incident of the 1951 election, there was some dispute between him and Shri Govind Vallabh Pant. When news of the dispute reached Jawaharlalji, he asked Rafisaheb about it. Rafisaheb told Jawaharlalji that he could inquire into the whole matter and added, 'Morarji Desai is not my friend. If you entrust the inquiry to him I shall accept his decision even if he finds fault with me as I have full faith in his objectivity and impartiality.' I then realised that Shri Rafisaheb had good regard for me. When the Central Cabinet did not accept his proposal to abandon controls on foodgrains he came to Bombay and asked me to find out a way to remove the controls. 'There is one way to do it,' I told him, 'If you can make arrangements to supply foodgrains to Bombay city for a few months as it is a deficit area in the matter of foodgrains, I shall certainly support you in your proposal to remove controls and you would be able to implement it easily.' Rafisaheb made arrangements for supply of the required stock of foodgrains to Bombay city after a few days and we took steps to remove controls on foodgrains in actual practice, i.e. the controls were removed in fact, though not formally. When the Central Cabinet saw that the controls had been actually removed without ill effects, they also accepted the position and the people were greatly relieved at the disappearance of controls on foodgrains.

After the war the Government of Bombay had made it compulsory for peasants to raise foodgrains on a fixed proportion of their land. It was however seen that these orders were not effectively implemented and that there was a great increase in corruption amongst the lower subordinates in charge of enforcements. The people raised whatever crops they wanted to raise and got wrong entries made in the village records in collusion with the village officials. It was thus difficult to enforce the orders which had been issued for compulsory raising of crops and we were convinced that we could not succeed in enforcing them. We therefore withdrew this regulation also.

We had taken steps for introducing prohibition in Bombay State and it was fully introduced in 1950. This benefited us greatly in the elections of 1952. One or two communist members were elected to the Legislative Assembly from Bombay city before 1952. These members however opposed the policy of prohibition in the elections of 1952 and they lost in the elections since the people of Bombay were very happy with the policy of prohibition. Prohibition had given great relief to the women-folk of the State and they therefore supported the Congress with great enthusiasm. As I have said earlier I got confirmation of this from the talk I had with one or two European managers of mills. When I asked them about the effects of prohibition on their labour, they described to me the improvement that had taken place in the living standards of the labour as a result. Shri Jayaprakash Narayan and his colleagues had instigated a strike in the textile mills in Bombay city in 1951. Most of the textile labour had been forced by the leaders to join the strike. Textile labour had demanded four months' bonus from the mill-owners but the Labour Tribunal had awarded only two months' bonus to them. Labour was not satisfied with this award and demanded three months' bonus from the mill-owners. As the mill-owners did not accept this demand, this strike was called. There was also some scarcity of cotton at that time and there was a possibility of a situation arising in which several mills would not be able to work fully for want of cotton. I invited the representatives of the mill-owners for talks and asked them whether they were prepared to give three months' bonus. They expressed their inability to do so and requested me to help them to bring an end to the strike. 'If you are patient,' I told them, 'and do not submit to the strike I am quite sure that labour will return to work soon, as the demand is not a reasonable one.'

When the strike had lasted about six weeks the representatives of the workers saw Jawaharlalji and requested him to intervene in their favour. The INTUC was the recognised labour union under the law in force at that time. The INTUC had not joined the strike at the time, but many of its members had been forced to stay away from work by threats and violence on the part of some labour leaders. Jawaharlalji came to Bombay and discussed the strike with me. He asked me how we were justified in recognising the INTUC when the other labour unions had been able to get all the workers to join the strike. He therefore asked me to consider the demands of those people and hear them. I explained to him the position in law and the circumstances under which the strike had been launched. 'If you consider all the facts of the situation carefully,' I explained to him, 'you will find that the demand and the attitude of those who have gone on strike are not proper. Would you like the law to be made by a strike or by the legislature?' When I asked him this question, Jawaharlalji was surprised and asked me, why I was asking the question. I explained to him that we recognised the union which has the largest membership according to our law. If, however, another union acquired a large membership after this recognition we would accept that union as a recognised union and withdraw the recognition of the other union. This law was quite just and fair. It was true that all the labourers in the textile field had joined the strike but if the labour union which had called the strike could prove to have the largest number of labourers, their work would be much easier. They should convince the proper authorities about their larger membership and if they succeed in doing so I would certainly recognise them. But these people were not able to show any larger membership which shows that they have forced the majority of labourers to join the strike by violent actions. Under such circumstances, how could I increase the amount of bonus which has been awarded by the Tribunal? If I was forced by the strike to accept their demand there would be no purpose in appointing the Labour Tribunal.

Jawaharlalji accepted my arguments and, at the end of our discussion, issued a statement to that effect. As he did not support the strikers and as their power of resistance had dwindled, they returned to work unconditionally at the end of a two months' strike. This caused loss to all the mill labourers. In trying to get bonus for one more month they lost wages for two months. This was the outcome of their ill-advised strike. The result was that there was no strike in this sector in the State for ten years after this one.

Balasaheb engaged himself in constructive work, especially that relating to the development of tribals after he retired from the Chief Ministership of Bombay in 1952. Soon after, however, Jawaharlalji offered him the post of High Commissioner at London. Balasaheb discussed this proposal with me and I pressed him to accept it. I was sure that his going to London as High Commissioner would raise the reputation of the country in England and would also strengthen the relations between the two countries. Balasaheb accepted Jawaharlalji's suggestion and he was formally appointed to that post in June of that year. He left for London in the second week of July and took charge of his office by about the middle of July.

He wrote to me from Paris on his way to London and corresponded with me regularly while he was in London. In our correspondence we used to discuss the problems he was facing in London and the problems which I was facing in Bombay. Our relations were very close and there was a deep understanding between us. We also felt the separation after having worked together continuously for ten years.

Balasaheb was very keen to have officers in whom he had confidence when he went to London. He asked for the services of Shri P. V. R. Rao and Shri S. J. Barve and wrote requesting me to make arrangements for sending them there. Shri Rao was in Bombay but Shri Barve had been deputed to the Centre at that time. Shri P. V. R. Rao at first declined to go to London. When I informed Balasaheb about this he told me that if he was not willing I should not bother to ask him again, but he asked me to make arrangements for sending Barve to London. Jawaharlalji was not prepared to spare Barve as his services were required in Faridabad where he had been posted. I therefore persuaded Shri Rao to accept the post in London and he accepted my suggestions saying that he would be going there for three months in the first instance and would continue to work there if the work suited him.

I suggested to Balasaheb in my letter to him in this connection that in such matters he ought to write to Jawaharlalji direct so that no misunderstanding might arise in the matter of such appointments. I suggested that he could send me copies of letters he sent to Jawaharlalji in such matters so that I could expedite the action to be taken on such matters. Balasaheb accepted my suggestion.

Balasaheb was an extremely sensitive person and one never

knew when he would take offence about some matter. When I received two or three letters from him in very formal language, I inquired from him whether I had given him any cause for offence. He then explained to me what was worrying him. I wrote to him and requested him not to misunderstand whatever I might have written and told him also that even if he cut off his relations with me I would not do so and would not allow him to do so. He then admitted that there was a misunderstanding, and assured me that in future there would be no repetition.

Somebody had written to Balasaheb that there had been some changes in the educational policy, which had been laid down by him when he was Chief Minister. This he resented and he mentioned it in a letter. I wrote to him: 'The policy is not changed but we did remove some of the weaknesses so that we could implement it more effectively and we are pursuing that policy with vigour.'

My own attitude in such matters is somewhat different. If a person relinquishes a responsibility and somebody else takes it up, one should not have any attachment to whatever one may have done at the time when he was in charge and should not bother whether his policy is changed or maintained after he has given over charge to someone else. The person who succeeds to the job has as much right to carry out his policy as his predecessor had. I therefore consider it proper that I should adopt a policy and enforce it as I consider proper as long as I am in charge. The moment I give up charge and somebody else takes on the responsibility, it is improper for me to insist that my successor should not depart from my policy. I conveyed these views to Shri Balasaheb Kher in a very discreet manner so that he would not misunderstand me. Balasaheb accepted the correctness of my attitude.

Somebody had complained to him also that there was some laxity in the implementation of prohibition in the Bombay State. When he wrote to me about this I replied that there was no reason for him to fear any slackness in the implementation of the prohibition policy after his departure. I pointed out to him that if there was any slackness in the policy it was at his end after he had gone to London to take charge of his new office. I had heard that he used to serve liquor in London in the course of his duties and wrote to him accordingly. I however told him that I had no dispute in the matter if he had to make compromises in this connection in the circumstances in which he had to work in London. But when one makes such compromises in the matter of accepted principles, one has to be very careful and one has to see that unnecessary compromises are not made. I had such discussions with him on several matters in our correspondence. This correspondence was very useful both to me and him and also brought us closer together.

When I informed Balasaheb in London about the betrothal of my son Kantu he was very happy especially because the proposed marriage was an inter-caste and inter-state one. The betrothal was with a Maharashtrian girl. Balasaheb knew the family of the girl and we were very happy about the new relationship. My daughter-in-law Padma had come to stay with us for a few days soon after the betrothal and I used to teach her Gujarati. When I informed Balasaheb about this he was surprised that I could find time to do this. I believe that a person can find time for doing whatever he wants to do. It is only when he does not want to do something particular that he finds excuses like want of time. The experience that I have had in my life in this connection has confirmed this belief of mine.

Hillary and Tensing were successful in climbing Mount Everest in 1953. In the same year we removed controls over the distribution of cloth on the basis of a decision of the Textile Advisory Committee.

An event of far-reaching importance took place in Kashmir in that year (1953). Sheikh Abdullah, the first Prime Minister of Jammu and Kashmir had pressed Jawaharlalji in 1948 to accept the merger of Kashmir with India as the leader and the President of the National Conference of Kashmir. He firmly believed at that time that Kashmir could not survive as an independent state as was demonstrated by the Pakistani invasion when it was independent. As a result of this experience, Sheikhsaheb played an important part in the merger of Kashmir with India. He held elections for a Constituent Assembly of Jammu and Kashmir and in 1951–52 had declared that Kashmir had been permanently merged with India and that the merger was unalterable.

At the end of 1952 and the beginning of 1953, Sheikhsaheb's thinking appeared to change and he started talking about getting independence for Kashmir. This created a difference of opinion between him and his colleagues. Jawaharlalji tried to dissuade Sheikhsaheb from persisting in making such demands but he failed. The Sheikh even began to criticise the Indian military forces that had been posted in Kashmir at his own request. This encouraged Pakistan in its unreasonable attitude. The position therefore became very serious so far as Jammu and Kashmir State was concerned. These circumstances forced the Government of India to remove Sheikhsaheb from office and also to imprison him.

Shri Ghulam Mohammad Bakshi succeeded him in the post of Prime Minister. Shri Bakshi successfully tackled the situation created by Sheikhsaheb and established peaceful conditions in Kashmir. Sheikhsaheb's volte-face helped Pakistan to reopen the controversy on an international plane. Sheikhsaheb now insisted that a plebiscite be taken in Kashmir and did some very aggressive propaganda amongst the people to that effect. Maulana Abul Kalam Azad also tried to dissuade him, but to no effect. Sheikhsaheb did not even behave courteously with him.

Looking at the history of Kashmir and its merger with India and the manner in which it merged with India and taking into consideration all the facts relating to this State, any person will be convinced how dangerous this talk of taking a plebiscite in Kashmir or of making Kashmir independent and separate from India is and how harmful it is to the people of the Jammu and Kashmir State.

Mr. John Foster Dulles was the Secretary of State in USA in 1953. He came to Delhi to meet Jawaharlalji and discuss relations between the two countries. There was some difference of opinion between America and India at the time and Mr. Dulles had come to discuss this. When he saw Jawaharlalji and talked to him for some time, he found that Jawaharlalji had actually gone to sleep and was not taking any interest in what he was saying. Mr. Dulles felt insulted at this behaviour of Jawaharlalji and ended his talks with him and left him. A short time after this he made an agreement with Pakistan, promising the supply of military equipment and help to Pakistan. Jawaharlalji protested against this but the agreement could not be changed by this protest or opposition after it had already been made. I got this information when I went to Washington for the first time in 1958. When I met Mr. Dulles there I indirectly gathered from him the information I have mentioned above. I felt that if Jawaharlalji had talked with Mr. Dulles without prejudices when he came to India, the position would have been different and the harmful results that followed that visit would not have taken place.

Dr. Homi Bhabha declared in 1953 that India would be able to produce atomic energy in about three years' time. This illustrated how much progress we had made in the field of atomic energy in our country. Dr. Bhabha played the most important role in the production of atomic energy in this country. It would be no exaggeration if I said that if Dr. Bhabha had not been there this task would not have been accomplished for several more years. Dr. Bhabha was a great artist and was a very great patriot besides being one of the most well-known scientists. He worked very hard to make faster progress in the scientific field in our country and did achieve some marvellous progress by his labour. Dr. Bhabha met with tragic death in an aeroplane accident in the beginning of 1966. This country suffered an irreparable loss as a result. I knew him very well and was aware of what great dreams he had for the progress of India. We have been able to produce electricity through atomic energy at Tarapore mainly because of the efforts he made. We are also soon going to produce electricity through atomic energy in two or three other places. Smt. Vijaya Laxmi Pandit became the President of the General Assembly of the United Nations in the year 1953. The credit for her election to this high post went as much to Shrimati Pandit's personality as to the importance which India had in world affairs. She carried out her duties with great credit and contributed to the enhancement of the international reputation of the country.

Shri Jawaharlalji pressed me to stay with him twice or thrice when I went to Delhi for meetings of the Working Committee in 1951–52. I generally used to put up at 4, Ferozeshah Road with Kanjibhai Desai whenever I went to Delhi. I had been doing this ever since 1930 when I went to Surat and also when I went to Delhi after 1950. Shri Jawaharlalji once even said that he would get my kit from Kanjibhai's place so that I could stay with him. I told him, 'My relations with Kanjibhai are such that I cannot put up anywhere else. This is why I am unable to accept your invitation and I hope you will excuse me for my inability to do so.'

I have observed as a rule in my life that I should not change my place of residence except for unavoidable reasons. This was why I had to decline Jawaharlalji's invitations to stay with him. The other reason which also prompted me to decline this offer was that if I stayed there it would be very difficult for many people who used to see me in Delhi to come and see me there on account of the security arrangements in the Prime Minister's house. Jawaharlalji wanted me to stay with him because he thought, and I agreed with him, that if I stayed there we could meet at any time and whenever it was convenient to him and discuss matters. This would have been a very useful arrangement, but, for the reasons given, we could not avail of it.

3

The Medium of Instruction

We took some new steps in the field of education in Bombay State in 1953–54. One of them, which we took after very careful consideration, was to hand over the administration of primary schools fully to the School Boards as we had learnt from experience that the dual system of administration by School Boards and Government resulted in inefficiency.

I had some discussion with Shri Balasaheb on this dual administration before he decided to introduce it. I had accepted his decision even though I differed from his view as he was then Chief Minister and also Education Minister. Experience convinced us that the dual system had to be ended and that the administration of the schools should be made the concern of the School Boards exclusively. We took this decision in 1953 and I informed Shri Balasaheb in London as I knew that he generally did not like any policy initiated by him changed. When I wrote to him he appreciated the steps taken. He realised that no decision can remain unchanged for all time and that changes as and when necessary have to be effected if progress is to be made. Every Government has the right to change its policy and system from time to time, as circumstances require.

The question of medium of instruction had assumed great importance at that time. Instructions had already been issued to ensure that English was not given greater importance than the regional language of the State. The English language question has become a very controversial one in this country. Some people are of the view that not giving adequate importance to English arises from an opposition to the English language. This is, however, not a correct view. The question is whether the languages of the country should develop fully or not. The culture and literature of India are in Indian languages and not in English. Except for the small Anglo-Indian population, every Indian has an Indian language for a mother tongue. Most educational experts the world over are of the view that education must be imparted in the mother tongue if it is to be fully absorbed by a child. If education is imparted in a tongue other than the mother tongue the child has to spend more energy in mastering the other language and finds it difficult to understand the subject concerned fully. A child's intellectual capacity develops most fully only if education is given in his mother tongue. This arrangement alone enables a child to master a subject.

Our people have sufficient intelligence—certainly not less than any other people, perhaps a little more. Nevertheless we have not been able to produce an adequate number of experts in any field. The main reason for this deficiency is that education is imparted in a foreign language. The country will produce experts in sufficient numbers only when education is imparted in the regional languages. The number of experts then will be even larger than that in any other country. If we are not able to produce the required number of experts, the development and progress of the country will not be as quick as we want it to be. I have, therefore, no doubt that education must be imparted in the mother tongue and that necessary steps for this purpose should be taken. I am not opposed to the English language but I only insist that greater importance should not be given to English than to Indian languages and that English should not have a priority over them. As a matter of fact the Indian language should have greater importance in India.

A large majority of our people had accepted Hindi as the national language even before the advent of freedom. There are sixteen main languages in our country. As it is not possible for every citizen to learn all the sixteen languages it is necessary to have one common language for purpose of inter-communication. It is as clear as daylight that English cannot be this common language. In spite of the British rule in this country for 200 years during which they gave greater importance to the English language and suppressed Indian languages, not more than 1 to 2 per cent of our people are today able to read or write English. If this is the position after a full encouragement to English over 200 years, how can English serve as a common language in India now? Nobody claims that Hindi as a language has greater importance than other Indian languages. It is, however, a fact that a large proportion of Indians understand Hindi and use it too. This being so, it is not difficult to create conditions in which all people will understand the Hindi language. I, therefore, consider it appropriate and useful that Hindi should be the government and national language and should replace English in these fields. English should be taught to students to enable them to acquaint themselves with the literature of the Western world and to follow developments in modern science. I believe that many Indians share this view.

We have not yet got used to thinking in terms of the interests of the whole country in preference to other interests and are still used to giving priority to one's individual interests. This attitude is at the root of the language controversy in this country. I am, however, confident that in spite of this controversy the Hindi language will become the language of the Central Government very soon. Hindi will also become the common language for communication between the different states in the country. There is no danger to any other of the Indian languages because of Hindi becoming the common language. If any harm has been caused to the Indian languages, it has been because greater importance has been given to the English language. Hindi will become richer as a result of its becoming the common language of the country and will help other Indian languages to get richer. Our arrangements should be such as to enable the Indian languages to strengthen and enrich one another. When the mother tongue becomes the universal medium of instruction from the beginning to the end of education, I have no doubt that prejudices against the Hindi language will disappear. The regional languages are bound to be enriched. The interest of the country lies in the development of Indian languages and I have full confidence that everybody will understand this necessity soon.

We had accepted the policy in Bombay State of doing away with English as the medium of education and had decided to replace it by the mother tongue at the primary and the secondary levels and also to teach English from the 8th standard onwards. We also decided at the same time that all students should pass an examination in Hindi.

I believed that both regional languages and Hindi should be the medium of instruction at the university level and had, therefore, thought of making Hindi the alternative medium of instruction in Government colleges. I had a difference of opinion with several close colleagues in Gujarat on this issue. Both Gujarati and Hindi were provided as the medium of instruction when Gujarat University was established. Every subject was to be taught either in Hindi or Gujarati and the students could choose whichever language they wanted. Professors could teach in either of the two languages and the students could write their answer papers in examinations in the language they preferred. I considered these steps essential if Hindi was to take the place of English at the national level. Some of my colleagues in Gujarat were of a different view and firmly held that even at the university level the medium of instruction should be only the regional language. Hindi, they said, should be taught as a compulsory subject but should not replace the regional language as the medium of instruction. The Congress Working Committee had also passed a resolution in favour of regional languages as the medium of instruction.

Controversy on this question continued in the Gujarat University as well as in the GPCC. Some people were of the view that Gujarati should not be the medium of instruction at the Gujarat University and that at the university level it should be either Hindi or English. This was strongly opposed by those who wanted only the Gujarati medium at the university level. They felt that the proposal to use Hindi and English would perpetuate English as the medium of instruction and that even the use of Hindi would injure the interests of the regional language. These friends, therefore, got a resolution passed in the Gujarat University by a large majority which directed that only Gujarati could be the medium of instruction in Gujarat University. The resolution urging Hindi and English as the media was lost.

I did not take any active steps to get my views accepted during the time when this controversy went on as I was afraid that my doing so would create much bitterness amongst ourselves. The difference between my colleagues and myself was not a large one as I also believed in the regional language as the medium of instruction. I wanted Hindi to be accepted as an alternative medium only to facilitate the study of those who came from other states and wanted to study in Gujarat colleges. I did not stress my point of view after Gujarati alone was accepted by the Gujarat University. I was convinced that if in the circumstances through which we were passing, we raised a controversy between Hindi and the regional language, the medium of English would probably be perpetuated and there would be nothing more harmful than this. It was very necessary to see that no injustice was done to the regional language and its development was not hampered. It was, therefore, necessary to see that there was no bitterness between the advocates of Hindi and those of the regional language. While I agreed that the regional language should be the medium of instruction at *all* levels, I also thought it proper and essential that nobody should have any opposition to having educational institutions in the non-Hindi States where Hindi might be made the medium of instruction, and some students might prefer to study in it. It is a matter of deep sorrow that this controversy has not yet come to a happy conclusion.

At about this time complaints were made by some members of the Hyderabad State Legislative Congress Party against the Chief

Minister, Ram Krishna Rao. These were considered by the Central Parliamentary Board of the Congress which decided that this question could be decided satisfactorily if Jawaharlalji or somebody from the Parliamentary Board went to Hyderabad and ascertained the majority view of the Congress party there on the leadership issue. Jawaharlalji went to Hyderabad soon after this decision and found that in the Congress Legislative Party the majority view was in favour of Shri Rao and so he continued as the leader of the party.

I have already referred to the fact that Rajaji became Chief Minister of Madras after the 1952 elections. Shri Kamaraj was then the President of Madras Pradesh Congress Committee. He too had suggested the name of Rajaji as leader of the Madras Congress Legislative Party. The relations between Rajaji and Kamaraj got strained within two years of Rajaji becoming the Chief Minister. Shri Kamaraj complained that Rajaji was not behaving properly towards the President of the Congress Committee whom he had criticised even in public. The relations got so strained that it became clear that Kamaraj would not be able to carry on his work in those conditions any longer. The majority of the Central Parliamentary Board supported Shri Kamaraj and did not approve of Rajaji's behaviour. This question was discussed in the Parliamentary Board and I had some discussion with Kamaraj personally also. We were all convinced that it was not possible to continue Rajaji as Chief Minister of the State any longer and suggested to him that he relinquish office. Shri Rajaji accordingly resigned from Chief Ministership of the State.

When we considered the question of Rajaji's successor in Madras in the Parliamentary Board, we all agreed that it was desirable that Shri Kamaraj should be the next Chief Minister. Shri Kamaraj knew only Tamil. He had little knowledge of English in those days. He also did not show any desire to be the Chief Minister of the State. We were of the view that there would be no difficulty in carrying on the Government administration if a minister did not know English and we could not reconcile ourselves to a position where only an English-knowing person could be considered fit to be a minister. We, therefore, proposed that Kamaraj become the Chief Minister. The late Shri Mallya who was a very close friend of Shri Kamaraj persuaded him to accept the position. Shri C. Subramaniam contested the leadership election in the Congress Legislative Party in Madras. It was generally believed that he had become a candidate at the instance of Rajaji. Shri Kamaraj was elected with a very large majority. He included Shri C. Subramaniam in his Ministry which consisted of only seven or eight ministers. Karmaraj, who continued as Chief Minister until the Kamaraj Plan which came into force in 1963, ran the Government and the State very efficiently and successfully.

Rajaji was deeply shocked and pained when he was requested to resign as he felt he had been put aside for a much less educated person. From that time on, Rajaji opposed Kamaraj on every occasion and continued to do so up to 1969. He soon after left Congress and founded the Swatantra Party. He had become a bitter opponent of the Congress. In the beginning Rajaji used to oppose Shri Kamaraj only and particularly did not oppose Shri Jawaharlalji. He began to oppose Jawaharlalji only when he found that Jawaharlalji was supporting Shri Kamaraj, and that the opposition to Kamaraj would not succeed unless Jawaharlalji was weakened. He then believed that and ultimately came to the conclusion that opposition to Jawaharlalji would not be effective unless the Indian National Congress was weakened and so he carried on a strong campaign against the Congress. He continued this campaign until the beginning of 1970.

As a person who has a deep faith in democracy, I strongly believe that it is essential to decentralise power if democracy is to run smoothly, successfully and effectively. We had in this country a system of gram panchayats from ancient times. These panchayats used to manage the affairs of the village. This system almost disappeared during the British rule. A Central Committee under the Presidentship of the late Shri Balwantrai Mehta considered this problem and recommended the establishment of village panchayats, at the village level and taluka panchayats at the taluka level and district panchayats at the district level. This committee also recommended the transfer of effective powers to these bodies. The Congress Working Committee gave careful consideration to the recommendations of the Balwantrai Mehta Committee and recommended within two months of the Committee's Report that the Panchayat Raj system should be introduced in every state. The Central Government issued instructions to all the State Governments to introduce the system as early as possible. Legislation has since been enacted in almost all the States for the introduction of this system. This has, however, not been fully implemented in several States. The Panchayat Raj system has very effectively been established and developed in Maharashtra and Gujarat and it is hoped that this system will be developed soon in other states also.

In Gujarat the whole of land revenue has been handed over to the panchayats. Several other works and duties and responsibilities have also been transferred by the state to the panchayats, including primary education and all the district roads excepting the national highways. This Panchayat Raj system should be so developed that the district panchayat could carry on the administration in the whole district, the taluka panchayat that of the whole taluka and the village panchayat that of the whole village.

If effective panchayat judicial benches were introduced, and their powers gradually widened, many of civil disputes would be disposed of quickly at much less cost and people would get proper justice easily and cheaply and with greater speed. I have been, therefore, impressing upon the Gujarat State Government that more and more powers should be delegated to the panchayats and I have been convinced that the state government also does have such a policy. Much progress has been made in this field in Maharashtra also. If the Panchayat Raj system is fully and properly developed, the administration of the state and central governments would become more efficient and effective.

4

The Executive and the Judiciary

When we formed the Government in Bombay we had already decided that the executive and the judiciary should be separated. We had started this process of separation even earlier. It was completed in 1953 and one of the directive principles in our constitution was thus implemented by us in Bombay State. The then Chief Justice of Bombay High Court, Shri M. C. Chagla, greatly appreciated this step and even praised it publicly.

Even though my personal relations with Shri Chagla were cordial and friendly, our opinions clashed on some political questions. Shri Chagla was very interested in politics and had been active in politics before he joined the judiciary. This interest led him to criticise the Government on some occasions. Shri Chagla and I discussed this matter several times and also had a lengthy correspondence about it. This correspondence pinpointed our respective viewpoints. At the end of our correspondence Shri Chagla accepted my bonafides.

Shri Chagla was known as a very good judge but he had some predetermined notions in political affairs which led him to criticise the Government on some occasions. I had experience of this in the middle of 1952 when we once met at a dinner party. The discussion we started on some remarks made by him assumed serious proportions. I noted down the main points of our discussion after going home. (The correspondence and the note are given in Appendixes 1 and 2 respectively.)

One of the causes of our strained relations related to the appointment of a Judge of the Bombay High Court. Shri P. M. Lad was a member of the ICS and was serving in the judicial branch. Many ICS officers who were on the judicial side reverted to the executive side after the advent of freedom. Shri Lad continued in the judiciary and did not want to come back to the executive as he was deeply interested in law and justice. We, therefore, appointed him as our adviser for legal affairs. He carried out his duties in an admirable manner and whenever we consulted him on matters of law and the enactment of laws, he gave us his objective, honest and independent advice and was thus very useful to us in arriving at correct decisions. The High Court had given decisions against the Bombay Government in some dozen matters but when we took the matters to the Supreme Court we won in most of the appeals. This was mainly due to the correct advice given by Shri Lad. This prejudiced Shri Chagla against Shri Lad. We had recommended Shri Lad for appointment as a Judge of the Bombay High Court as he was a very capable lawyer but Shri Chagla opposed our proposal strongly.

Dr. Kailas Nath Katju was Home Minister at the Centre at that time. I wrote to him pressing for the appointment of Shri Lad as a Judge of the Bombay High Court. Even though Dr. Katju considered my recommendation reasonable and proper, he tried to persuade me not to go against the Chief Justice. I, therefore, wrote to Dr. Katju making it clear, with details of facts and arguments, how injustice had been done to Shri Lad. I also made it clear that if out of prejudice injustice was allowed to prevail I would not be able to take any part in recommendations for such appointments to the High Court in future as I considered it a matter of my self-respect.

The appointment of Shri Lad as a Judge was, therefore, delayed. Dr. Katju did not have the courage to do it. The controversy continued for several months. Shri Lad ultimately felt that if this controversy continued and if the Chief Justice was so violently opposed to him he would not be able to work properly and usefully in the High Court. He would also be very uncomfortable and unhappy in that position. He, therefore, requested me not to press further for his appointment and suggested a way out of the whole situation. As Shri Lad made this request himself and was firm about it, I gave up my recommendation in his favour and instead recommended to the Central Government that they appoint him Secretary in the Information Department at the Centre. Shri Lad was accordingly appointed to that post and gave satisfaction to the Central Government by his ability and devotion to work. He was kept so busy and was so over-worked that his health was completely shattered. He passed away while still in service.

After he became Secretary at the Centre, Shri Lad had prepared a plan for collecting the writings, speeches and letters of Mahatma Gandhi and publishing them. It was envisaged that the Centre should shoulder the responsibility for seeing this plan through. He requested me to help him in implementing this plan and appointed an Advisory Committee to help him in this work. He had also requested me to accept Chairmanship of this Committee which I agreed to do.

Gandhiji's works were to be collected and edited in the first instance in English, Hindi and Gurarati and the project has been carried on since that time. The collection has been far greater in volume than had been estimated. We found that Mahatma Gandhi had written and spoken much more than any other individual in the past. When we started the collection of material for this work we had estimated that there would be about fifty volumes. We found later on that the number would go beyond eighty. We had hoped to complete this work by the end of the birth centenary celebrations of Mahatma Gandhi in 1969 but we have not been able to do this on account of the magnitude of the task and the inherent difficulties involved in it. It will take at least a few more years to complete this project.

I had decided for myself not to enter into public controversy with Shri Chagla even though he publicly criticised the State Government on several occasions. I took this decision as I was convinced that if we entered into public controversy with the judiciary, its prestige would not be maintained. I have no doubt that there is great respect for the judiciary in the public mind and its independence must be maintained for the strengthening and success of democracy. This was why I did not consider it proper to criticise the judiciary even though we were criticised without any restraint. As far as I remember Shri Chagla publicly acknowledged that we had fully carried out this policy of respecting the independence of the judiciary in Bombay when I left that State at the end of 1956.

Balasaheb Kher returned to India from London in 1954 after having been High Commissioner for two years. The main reason of his returning before completing his term was a very serious deterioration in his wife's health. It was discovered in London that she was suffering from cancer and that the disease was developing rapidly. Smt. Kher passed away as a result of her illness on 18 October 1954.

The Central Government had decided to appoint a Hindi Commission to consider and make recommendations concerning steps to be taken in furtherance of the introduction of Hindi as the state language, as required by the Constitution. Balasaheb was considered for the Chairmanship of this Commission and he was requested to accept it. I too persuaded Balasaheb to accept the appointment. I was aware of his great attachment to Hindi and his desire to give impetus to the process of establishment of Hindi as the national language. I, therefore, considered he would be the most appropriate person for this task. Balasaheb was willing to undertake the responsibility provided Shri S. G. Barve was appointed Secretary of the Commission. Shri Barve was accordingly appointed and Balasaheb became the Chairman.

Bombay was a pioneer amongst the states of the Indian Union in starting labour welfare centres. To carry on the work of labour welfare systematically, we constituted the Labour Welfare Board in the middle of 1953. The Board was required to prepare a programme of formation of labour welfare centres. The Board also gave guidance to the welfare centres when they were set up. We also decided in mid-1953 to start boarding schools in adivasi areas. The Bombay State Financial Corporation was formed in the same year for helping medium and small industries.

About this time I was in correspondence with Jawaharlalji concerning the proposal made by some people that the upper houses i.e. the Legislative Councils which were in vogue in several States be abolished. Jawaharlalji was of the opinion that these Upper Houses were not very effective and that, therefore, it would be proper if some non-official member of the legislature would initiate a proposal for abolishing these instead of the State Government doing so. I was against this institution from the very outset and when this resolution came before the Bombay Legislative Assembly a year or two after this correspondence with Jawaharlalji it was unanimously accepted and sent to the Central Government for necessary action. However, before necessary action could be taken, Bombay State was divided into two States—Maharashtra and Gujarat. While Maharashtra retained the Upper House, Gujarat State started without one.

I had some correspondence with Shri S. K. Patil who was the President of the Bombay Pradesh Congress Committee in 1953 in connection with the relations between the Government and the Committee and we decided to discuss matters of dispute between the Presidents of Pradesh Congress Committees in the State and the ministers of the Government and resolve them satisfactorily. Shri Patil insisted that decisions of the Pradesh Congress Committees should be considered as final, but the other three Pradesh Congress Committees agreed with me that whenever a dispute between Government and the Pradesh Congress Committee arose, the decision of either the All India Congress Committee or the Congress Working Committee should be considered final. Shri Patil did not agree with this. Jawaharlalji, whom I had informed about this matter, supported us. Shri Patil did not join in our discussions. He criticised the Government publicly on some matters but I did not enter into public controversy with him. We could, therefore, maintain our cordial personal relations and there was also no difficulty in the administration of the State.

A state of scarcity arose in several districts of Bombay State in the beginning of 1953, involving some districts of Maharashtra also. Relief works were started, according to the established practice, as soon as scarcity conditions arose. I had had very useful and rich experience of such works, first as a revenue officer during British rule, and then as Revenue Minister from 1937 to 1939, and had set up the machinery and issued instructions for the prompt and efficient tackling of scarcity conditions as soon as they arose. Under the system I had devised relief works were started automatically on the appearance of scarcity conditions and the district officers took action themselves without waiting for instructions from Government. Specific rules and directions were issued for starting works for people wanting work, providing relief to persons incapable of doing work, and for making provisions for fodder for cattle in scarcity areas. Standing instructions had also been issued for supplying water to people wherever there was scarcity of water. Relief work therefore started automatically with the appearance of scarcity conditions in 1953.

Shri Bhausaheb Hiray who was the Minister of Revenue at that time asked me how many crores of rupees I intended to provide for relief works. In those days, there was no provision for central assistance for such works. The State had to make its own arrangements. I told Shri Hiray that we should not be bothered about how much money was to be spent for this purpose but should consider what help had to be given and what minimum expenditure was necessary and we should be prepared to meet that expenditure. If necessary, we should curtail expenditure in other fields. He should not therefore, I advised, be worried about the provision of funds but should make proper arrangements for giving relief to the people wherever necessary. This reply satisfied Shri Hiray and he did not press for earmarking any particular amount. We incurred heavy expenditure for these relief works, but it was generally acknowledged that the arrangements we made gave satisfaction to the people affected. Jawaharlalji himself visited the State to see the scarcity relief work that was going on. Shri Bhausaheb Hiray and I accompanied Jawaharlalji on the tour. Jawaharlalji discussed problems with many people wherever he went. We gave him full information about the arrangements that we had made and he expressed a sense of deep satisfaction with the steps taken by us and publicly gave expression to his appreciation. He also stated clearly that the relief work done in the State was better than that done anywhere else. He also said that he was consequently very much relieved. Bhausaheb Hiray wanted that he alone should accompany Shri Jawaharlalji during the tour and that I should not be with them. But I had to go because Jawaharlalji insisted on my joining him. As I learnt from Smt. Padmaja Naidu, who had accompanied Jawaharlalji, Shri Bhausaheb Hiray was unhappy and dissatisfied during the tour, to some extent. At the end of it, however, Shri Hiray's feelings of unhappiness and dissatisfaction disappeared as I later learnt from him. He was satisfied when he saw that I had conveyed to Shri Jawaharlalji fully the efficient and good work done by Shri Hiray.

Jawaharlalji wrote to me in October 1953 to give some financial help to the Urdu poet Sagar Nizami who was in financial difficulties. I gave the necessary help to the poet as desired by Shri Jawaharlalji. I learnt from the poet later on that he was happy with the help that the State had extended to him.

I was asked at that time to recommend the name of a well-known artist from the State for nomination as a member of the Council of State by the President. I could not suggest the name of an artist but I recommended the names of Dr. P.V. Kane, Dr. V.R. Khanolkar and Smt. Hansa Mehta. Jawaharlalji gave preference to Dr. Kane. When I talked to Dr. Kane about the proposal, he told me that it would not be possible for him to be present in the Council of State meetings regularly or for several days together. He told me that he could accept the nomination only if he was not required to be regular in his attendance. When I conveyed this condition to Jawaharlalji, he accepted it and the President of India nominated him as a member of the Council of State.

I also had some correspondence with Jawaharlalji at the end of 1953 about the system which existed at the time in connection with legislation on subjects which were concurrent between the States and the Centre. Whenever a state had to enact legislation on any concurrent subject, it had to take the previous approval of the Centre, but the Centre did not have any previous consultation with the state when it brought in legislation before the Parliament on a concurrent subject. The Centre had, for instance, at that time introduced a bill in the Council of State for regulating advertisements in the newspapers without consulting us. I drew the attention of Shri Jawaharlalji to this matter. The question had been before the Bombay Government for about a year. I wrote to Jawaharlalji that if he had consulted us in the matter we could have given the Centre many useful suggestions and that relations between the Centre and the States should be reciprocal in such matters. Shri Jawaharlalji accepted my position and introduced the system of previous consultation with the States on such matters.

5

Freedom of the Press

There were some occasions in 1953 when action was contemplated by us against some Bombay newspapers. The English weekly *Blitz* had published two or three defamatory articles about Jawaharlalji. A notice was issued on Jawaharlalji's behalf against the Editor, Shri Rusi Karanjia, asking for an apology and for a donation of Rs. 10,000 to a public charitable fund as penalty. The papers relating to this notice were sent to me and my suggestions were invited regarding the steps to be taken. Before I could send a reply, Shri Karanjia had apologised, but it was not an unqualified apology. He had defended his writings in the letter of regret and had also said that he was not in a position to give any money to any fund. Jawaharlalji's Personal Assistant wrote to him in reply that he had not been asked for any contribution to any fund, but he had been asked to pay the money to a fund as a penalty for the defamation that he had indulged in. The Prime Minister ultimately accepted the apology and gave up the demand for a contribution to a public fund. When I learnt about this, I wrote to Jawaharlalji: 'The apology should have been unconditional, but Shri Karanjia's apology does not fall in that category. As, however, you have already accepted it, I have no further suggestion to make in the matter.'

In the same year, my Government had to consider taking action against *The Times of India.* The editor of this paper was a bitter opponent of the prohibition policy of the Government and this opposition was converted into a personal opposition to me. This paper which had a history of a hundred years and which had never before used any intemperate or discourteous language, howsoever critical it may have been, and which had not till then indulged in personal attacks, changed its policy and began to use intemperate language and make personal attacks. This change in the policy of *The Times of India* was not healthy for the newspaper world. While yellow journalism used such tactics, papers of good reputation and standing should not indulge in it.

It was the policy of the Bombay Government not to give advertisements to communal newspapers or to newspapers which indulged in yellow journalism. Neither the Bombay Government nor I ever objected to criticism of the Government by *The Times of India* or any other newspaper at any time, as such objections would not have been in conformity with democratic traditions. I had never therefore objected to or blamed any editor or journalist for criticising us nor had I asked any newspaper directly or indirectly to make any propaganda for me. When, however, we found that *The Times of India* was adopting a policy of yellow journalism, we had to take action against it and we stopped giving advertisements to that paper. I did so as I was of the opinion that it was not conducive to democratic traditions to lend support to a newspaper adopting such wrong policies.

The Times of India raised a lot of dust in this matter and its editor saw Jawaharlalji and complained to him personally. Jawaharlalji informed me about it, but he supported my action instead of taking any objection to it as the editor wanted. I did not mention Jawaharlalji's support publicly as I did not want Jawaharlalji to be involved in this controversy. I felt very much fortified and happy as a result of his support. Jawaharlalji suggested to me that I might say that the stoppage of advertisements was also due to their excessive tariff. However, I did not make use of this suggestion as the action taken by the Government had no relation to the advertisement rates and I did not think it proper to give an incorrect reason for the action taken. The policy of *The Times of India* changed for the better after some time and advertisements were again given to them.

There was also a change in the proprietorship of this newspaper about this time. Before this change had taken place, the workers in *The Times of India* who had gone on strike requested me to intervene in the dispute. I told them that I could intervene only if *both* sides requested me to do so. They accepted my condition and the manager of the newspaper also asked me to arbitrate. I accepted the request, but before I did so I made both sides accept a condition that if any side did not act according to my decision I would not support that party and would lend my support to the other side. The workers did not like my decision when I gave it and wanted to indulge in some sabotage. I made it very clear to them that Government would not tolerate any sabotage and would not allow them to destroy the institution. This warning had a healthy effect on the workers.

The directors and the manager of this newspaper were very surprised at my helpful attitude in this dispute in view of the earlier inimical attitude of the paper towards me. They did not expect that I would be helpful in this dispute. They expressed their gratefulness and asked me what they should do to express their gratitude concretely. I told them: 'I have done my duty and what I thought was proper for which there is no question of showing any gratefulness to me.'

When the proprietorship of *The Times of India* changed, the new proprietors told me that they would change the editor of the paper if I so desired. I told them, 'It would be highly improper if I made any suggestion for change in the editorship and it is unnecessary to ask me for any suggestion in this matter. I could never think of getting any editor changed because he was criticising me. I believe unequivocally in the freedom of the press.'

A few days later, the then General Manager of *The Times of India*, Shri J. C. Jain, came to me with the editor and discussed several matters. They had come of their own accord. They asked me whether I would suggest any change in the policy of the paper. I told them in clear terms that there was no question of any wishes of mine in this matter. 'It is your duty,' I told them, 'to carry out honestly the policy laid down for your newspaper by the proprietors. I can have nothing more to say than that.' When they pressed me further for suggestions concerning the policy of the paper, I said: 'Whatever policy you may adopt, you should carry it out properly. You will serve the people well only if you point out the faults of the people also as clearly as you point out the faults of the Government. You should base your criticism on policies and not on persons, and the language should be courteous and dignified. I have no other suggestion to make. If you want to know my views on any matter you can certainly ask me and I shall give my views alongwith the necessary facts that may be with me. But I would like to make it very clear to you that I will not expect you to accept my views if you do not agree with them.'

A dispute arose a few days after this meeting between the manager and the editor in the matter of their respective jurisdictions and rights. The editor had demanded that the manager should not interfere in the work of the editor. When they asked for my advice in this dispute, I told them clearly: 'The principle of independence of the editor must be properly observed. The editor alone must have the power of supervision over all the writings in the newspaper and the manager has to confine himself to matters relating to the business management of the paper. While the editor alone should have control over the journalists who are working under him, the manager can draw the attention of the editor if any accepted policy of the newspaper is not properly carried out.' The editor was very much satisfied with these views and the manager also accepted them.

Blitz had made some allegations against my colleague, Shri

Hiray, in the same year in respect of some funds collected by him in Malegaon and other places. The allegations were that Shri Hiray had used a part of the public funds collected by him for his own purpose. A question had been raised in the Bombay Legislative Assembly on this matter and I acquainted myself with the facts from Shri Hiray. I was convinced that, while the accounts were somewhat irregular, Shri Hiray was not in any way dishonest and I considered it proper to reply to this question myself instead of leaving it to Shri Hiray to do it. He liked this decision as he knew that my defence in this matter would be more acceptable to the people than his. I considered it my duty to reply to allegations against my colleagues when such allegations were wrongly made. I explained the facts fully in the Assembly and the matter was closed.

When Jawaharlalji learnt about these charges against Shri Hiray, he inquired from me about the facts as he wanted to know the truth of the matter. He felt that the article in *Blitz* was highly objectionable and defamatory and that such charges should not have been made against an important Minister. I showed the letter to Shri Hiray and sent a reply to Jawaharlalji with his concurrence. Jawaharlalji informed me that he was satisfied by what I had written to him.

I have already referred to Shri Hiray's dissatisfaction with the composition of the Ministry ever since I formed it. It was obvious to everybody that he was not cooperating with me wholeheartedly. In view of this, several friends and Congress workers were surprised at my defence of Shri Hiray. Some of them wished I had not defended him and that I should have let Hiray bear the brunt of the criticism and suffer from it if necessary. I, however, explained to all these friends that even if Shri Hiray was not fully cooperative in his conduct, I had to fully cooperate with him as long as he was number two in my Cabinet and that I had to defend him if his reputation was wrongly attacked. A person who believes in good and proper conduct should not imitate the wrong conduct of another person against him and must continue to behave properly and correctly. As I believe in this principle, I defended Shri Hiray as a part of my duty.

A few months after this incident I discussed with Shri Hiray his relations with me. Even though we were neighbours, our families had not come into any close contact and we too were not meeting frequently. I tried to persuade him to get over his feeling of dissatisfaction or discontent and to cooperate with me as would befit an important colleague. I talked to him also about the

Samyukta Maharashtra agitation which had started at that time and in which he was working very actively, and said, 'Neither Maharashtra nor Gujarat will benefit by separation. On the contrary, both will suffer. The two regions are complementary in their natures and capacities and if they work together the Bombay Government will be the best amongst all the State Governments and will also contribute greatly to the integration of India as a whole. Besides, I do not want to continue as Chief Minister for more than five years and if you cooperate fully and work well you will be my successor as Chief Minister of the State.' But Shri Hiray showed no desire for changing his attitude and told me that he was bound by his promise to take part in the Samyukta Maharashtra agitation and that he could not therefore change his attitude. I did not have any further discussion with him in this matter thereafter and did not hope for any better relations with him in the future.

I thought of Shri Yashwantrao Chavan as my successor after this discussion with Shri Hiray and I recommended him to the Congress members of the Bombay State Legislative Assembly, most of whom respected my view. It was, therefore, Shri Chavan who got far more votes than Shri Hiray and was elected as the leader of the Congress Legislative Party, when the bigger Bombay State was formed with the inclusion of Vidarbha, Marathawada and Saurashtra and the exclusion of Karnatak. Shri Hiray got very few votes in that election.

Shri Hiray passed away about a year and a half after the change in the Bombay State had taken place. He had visited Delhi some time before his death and had met me there. He admitted his mistake to me candidly of his own accord and also asked me to forgive him for it. After that he used to meet me often as I had maintained good relations with him from my side from the very start.

As I have mentioned earlier, the well-known dacoit Bhupat had created great terror in Saurashtra before the elections of 1952. This had created a feeling of discontent and fear in the minds of the people there. Dhebarbhai was the Chief Minister of Saurashtra at the time, but he did not have very cordial relations with two of his Ministers and colleagues, Shri Balwantrai Mehta and Shri Rasiklal Parikh. Shri Balwantrai Mehta had already left the Ministry as a result of the agitation that had taken place on account of an increase in school fees. The responsibility for the raising of fees rested on the whole Cabinet and the Chief Minister, but Shri Balwantrai Mehta sacrificed himself in order to save the Ministry from this opposition and criticism. This was however not helpful in making the relations between him and the Chief Minister better. It even accentuated the want of cordiality between them.

Shri Dhebarbhai placed before me all these circumstances saying, 'I do not want to contest in these elections as I do not very much fancy taking responsibility for forming a Cabinet under such conditions.' In the circumstances which obtained at that time in Saurashtra, it was very important that the Congress should succeed in the elections. Only if this happened could a stable Ministry be formed in Saurashtra. Congressmen would be able to fight the elections efficiently only if Dhebarbhai contested them. Holding this view, I pressed him to contest and also to form the Ministry if the Congress succeeded. Dhebarbhai ultimately agreed. He won the elections and also formed the Ministry.

Even after the elections Dhebarbhai asked me to permit him to give up the Ministry. He again pressed me in this matter at the time of the Congress session at Kalyani in West Bengal in the beginning of 1953 saying, 'You should persuade Jawaharlalji to permit me to get out of the Ministry.' I tried hard to persuade him not to leave the Ministry, but did not succeed. I even said, 'Your colleagues and friends will press you to continue as Chief Minister when you return to Rajkot and I believe you will have to give up your resolve of leaving the Ministry.' He assured me immediately that he would not change his resolve under any conditions and that I should talk to Jawaharlalji as requested by him. I therefore talked to Jawaharlalji about Dhebarbhai's request and explained his viewpoint to him. Jawaharlalji told me that he had no objection to Dhebarbhai's leaving the Ministry if that was his desire.

After his return to Rajkot Dhebarbhai's colleagues pressed him not to resign as Chief Minister and Dhebarbhai acceded to the request. What I had told Dhebarbhai, therefore, came true. Dhebarbhai said publicly, after going to Rajkot, that he had decided as a result of the pressure of his colleagues to continue as Chief Minister. I got the impression from the talk I had with Jawaharlalji that he did not like the turn events had taken. I also felt that I should not have talked to Jawaharlalji about Dhebarbhai's request even though I was pressed to do so by him and should have asked him to talk directly to Jawaharlalji. There was, however, nothing further to be done as Dhebarbhai had already declared his decision.

Sometime after this, Dhebarbhai again desired to work in the constructive field in the Congress organisation if possible and asked me to talk to Jawaharlalji about it. When I did so, Jawaharlalji asked me what possibly could be done in the matter. 'As you are both Prime Minister and President of the Congress,' I said, 'you cannot attend to the constructive programme of the Congress. If you entrust this work to Dhebarbhai, it is possible to make this work more effective.'

Jawaharlalji decided in September or October 1954 not to continue as President of the Congress as he felt that it was only in exceptional circumstances that he had to take up this responsibility in addition to being Prime Minister. It will be recalled that it was under peculiar circumstances, which arose after the resignation of Tandonji as President, that Jawaharlalji had taken his place. He had no doubt in his mind that one person should not occupy both offices. He therefore decided that a new President should be elected for the Congress. He discussed the matter with me. I reminded him about the talk that I had with him about Dhebarbhai in connection with constructive work and suggested his name. I told him that Dhebarbhai was not feeling very comfortable as Chief Minister of Saurashtra, and would perhaps agree to be President of the Congress if asked. Jawaharlalji asked me to consult him. I phoned to him from Bombay and he expressed his reluctance to accept such a big responsibility. I assured him that he would get full cooperation and guidance from Jawaharlalji in his work. He, however, was not satisfied by what I told him and asked me my opinion. I told him that if I was not in favour of his accepting the position I would not have asked him to take it on. He, however, at the end of the talk told me that he was not willing to undertake this responsibility. This ended our talk. An hour after this, Dhebarbhai rang me up and told me that he had changed his mind and that he would accept the position if he was pressed to do so. I told him that I would talk to Jawaharlalji accordingly. After I talked to Jawaharlalji about it, he pressed Dhebarbhai to accept the Presidentship of the Congress and he accepted it. The Working Committee then decided to recommend Dhebarbhai to be elected as President of the Congress and so he was elected to that post in December 1954 for a two-year term.

6

Diu, Daman and Goa

THE FRENCH settlements of Pondicherry and Chandernagore and the Portuguese settlements of Diu, Daman and Goa were still under foreign rule even though the rest of India had got freedom. The French Government agreed to negotiate about the French settlements and to hand them over to India. They transferred their authority over these settlements completely within about two years, i.e. by the end of 1954.

The Portuguese Government, however, was, from the very beginning, not prepared to negotiate and claimed that Diu, Daman and Goa were parts of Portugal not parts of India. It was the policy of the Indian Government from the very beginning to settle international disputes peacefully as far as possible. According to this policy, such disputes were not to be settled by war, but through negotiations and agreements. This was why the Government of India decided not to use force to take possession of Diu, Daman and Goa, even though it could have been done in that manner. The Government of India hoped that even though Portugal might initially display a rigid attitude, it would ultimately have to accept reality and that other countries also would persuade her to accept it.

Some young people were carrying on an agitation in Goa for freeing it from Portuguese rule and some of them were penalised, as a result, and were undergoing long terms of imprisonment. But this agitation could not gather strength on account of the weakness of the people of Goa. Some public workers of India were making strenuous efforts to strengthen the agitation. Shri Peter Alvares, a PSP leader, was taking a particularly keen interest in this matter. Dr. Ram Manohar Lohia was also trying to strengthen the agitation.

Dadra and Nagar-Haveli, the two small Portuguese-controlled enclaves near Daman, were situated within the territory of Bombay State in 1953–54. As Daman is situated on the coast, the Portuguese administration in Goa could control it with the access via the sea. They had, however, to pass through Bombay Government territory to administer Dadra and Nagar-Haveli. Some leaders of Goa wanted to launch a movement for liberating

Dadra and Nagar-Haveli, taking advantage of this geographical situation and saw me in this connection. They felt that they would succeed in their movement if I would help them. I sympathised with their aim, but I felt that whatever was done must be done in consonance with the policy of the Government of India and should be done in a proper manner. I told these friends from Goa, 'You can take possession of these enclaves by entering them as the Portuguese authorities will not be able to send their men there. I can take care to see that they do not pass through our jurisdiction.' I told them this only after consulting the Central Government.

It was clear that it was not possible to help these satyagrahis if they were terrorised after their entry into Dadra and Nagar-Haveli. It was, however, possible to help them indirectly and I planned accordingly. As I have said earlier, the enclaves of Dadra and Nagar-Haveli were within the territory of Bombay State. I posted Reserve Police batches in the territory surrounding these enclaves. These Reserve Police companies were similar to military forces, both in appearance and in training. The satyagrahis entered Dadra and Nagar-Haveli only after I had made these arrangements. The police and other Portuguese officials who were in Dadra and Nagar-Haveli at the time must have mistaken our Reserve Police for a military force. For, soon after spotting them, they ran away to the adjacent forest and hid themselves there. This enabled the satyagrahis to take possession of these enclaves without any difficulty.

It was necessary then to take into custody, the armed personnel of the Portuguese Government who had taken shelter in the adjacent forest. A very difficult situation would have been created if they were not arrested. I had therefore to make arrangements to see that they surrendered to the Reserve Police. This is how Dadra and Nagar-Haveli were freed from Portuguese jurisdiction. For this I received congratulatory letters from several people of those places. I also gave them the assistance of some retired Bombay State officials to help them to run the administration properly. The Portuguese Government wanted to send its forces to recover possession of these enclaves and asked for the permission of the Government of India for their forces to pass through our territory. The Government of India refused, and the Portuguese were unable to recover possession of these enclaves. The Portuguese Government then lodged a complaint in the World Court. When the case was heard India deputed Shri M. C. Chagla to present its case. The decision of the World Court went against the Portuguese.

The movement to free Goa began to gather strength after

Dadra and Nagar-Haveli had been freed. Some people thought of making a similar plan for freeing Goa. This was, however, very improper and impractical. There were two kinds of people in the committees which were formed for running the Goa freedom movement. One committee was formed on behalf of the Praja Socialist Party and was run under the direction of Shri Peter Alvares. The other committee that was formed was led by some communists. Dr. Ram Manohar Lohia was also carrying on a movement through some local people. I had to keep contact with all these people as the Chief Minister of Bombay State, and the Central Government had also to maintain their contacts with them. I was firmly of the opinion that the Goan movement for freedom could be strengthened only if it was carried on non-violently and tried to persuade the persons in charge of the movement there to act accordingly. The Central Government agreed with my view.

Several people wanted to send satyagrahis to Goa from Bombay State as Goa was adjacent to it. I explained to them that such an action would be very harmful as it would invite terrorism from the Portuguese Government and we would not be able to afford any protection. I told them that it would create a very difficult situation. If any individuals wanted to go to Goa and offer satyagraha there, they should be residents of Goa. The violent acts which were taking place in Goa in the course of the freedom movement invited violent retaliatory action from the Portuguese Government which terrorised the people and weakened their resistance. That the majority of the people of Goa wanted to be free from Portuguese rule was clear from the freedom movement in Goa, but they had not the capacity to carry on a sustained and organised freedom movement. The people of Goa had been suppressed under the Portuguese rule for the last 400 years and it was the policy of the Portuguese Government not to allow them to carry on any agitation or movement for freedom. The Congress organisation did not take any part in this freedom movement, though individual Congressmen were supporting it.

Concern at the situation in Goa was growing in this atmosphere and in 1955 there was an increasing demand in the Congress that satyagrahis should be sent to Goa from India to struggle for freedom. The Congress was particularly pressed to undertake it as other organisations had no such capacity. When the Working Committee discussed this question, I opposed the suggestion for running a satyagraha movement in Goa by sending satyagrahis through the Bombay territory. I considered that even if it was a non-violent assault on Goa, it was a war against Goa and we would be helpless if the Portuguese government used violence to suppress the movement. A great feeling of dissatisfaction would be created against the Congress and the Government of India as a result of satyagrahis being killed in Goa. There was no possibility of any gain from such a movement which would only end in harming us. I also drew the attention of my colleagues to the fact that we would have to take strong action against satyagrahis if they were sent by Pakistan to snatch Kashmir from our jurisdiction in a similar manner. We ought, therefore, to realise that the Portuguese Government would take strong and violent steps against our satyagrahis in these circumstances. But as feelings ran very high in this matter, there was a general feeling that such a movement should not be opposed. As a result, several satyagrahis went to Goa and to Daman from India in August 1955.

As soon as those batches of satyagrahis entered Portugal territory, the authorities there attacked them violently and some satyagrahis died as a result, while some others were wounded. As a result, the movement came to a stop. The people of Goa and many others outside Goa felt that Government of India should liberate Goa by force as there was no other way of solving this problem. It was, however, our accepted policy that we must not solve such problems by violent methods. We therefore took no such steps until 1961. The Portuguese Government had declared its determination not to make any compromise and not to give up its hold on Goa under any circumstances. The Government of India ultimately cut off diplomatic relations with Portugal. It was convinced in 1960–61 that there was no possibility of a peaceful settlement with the Portuguese Government and decided to send armed forces to Goa for its liberation and free Goa from Portuguese jurisdiction. I shall deal with this later in another chapter.

The President of Yugoslavia, Marshal Tito, visited India in 1954 and disembarked at the port of Bombay. It was suggested to us that we should have a bullet-proof motor car for him, but as we had no such car, I made arrangements to take him in an open car from the port to the Raj Bhavan.

Some of the guests who had accompanied Marshal Tito were apprehensive about his security and were hesitating to go in an open car. I, however, explained to them that there was no risk in such travel and that it was the responsibility of the Bombay Government and myself to see that Marshal Tito's safety was ensured. We had made the arrangements very carefully and this should convince everybody about their adequacy. Marshal Tito accompanied me in an open car up to the Government House without any hesitation, and the people of Bombay gave him a very enthusiastic and affectionate welcome.

The Prime Minister of Canada, Mr. St. Laurent, also came to India in the same year. He came to Bombay from Delhi. He was a fine gentleman and was very friendly towards India. The friendship between Canada and India is closer and better than that between many other countries. The two countries have identical views on most political matters and respect each other. I felt that Mr. St. Laurent was also of the same view.

Also about this time, Mr. Foster Dulles, the then US Secretary of State, entered into a military alliance with Pakistan after returning to America from his visit to India and agreed to give Pakistan very substantial military aid in the form of equipment. President Eisenhower had offered military aid to India as well, but Jawaharlalji refused to accept it and protested strongly against the USA's decision to give military aid to Pakistan.

On the advent of freedom, the Government of India had discontinued the system of conferring titles which the British Government had adopted. The availability of such titles led people to flatter those in power and harmed both Government and society a great deal. Most governments in the world have some system of giving such inducements to people. The Government of India, however, decided in 1954 to give awards ranging from Bharat Ratna to Padma Shri, and such awards are being given to various persons since then.

I did not agree with this decision of the Government of India and have not recommended any person for such an award. Even though it has been specified that these awards are not titles, many people who have received them have used them as titles by prefixing them to their names. The Bharat Ratna has been awarded to very few persons, but the other titles like Padma Bhushan and Padma Shri are given every year to many. Many entertain a desire to get such awards and also make efforts to get them. Those for whom the awards have some attraction, flatter persons in power in order to get them. Such titles do not uplift their recipients but they tend to bring them down.

Shri Govind Vallabh Pant who was Chief Minister of Uttar Pradesh at that time, was invited by Jawaharlalji to join the Central Cabinet at the end of 1954. Jawaharlalji had asked me to join the Central Cabinet before he sent this proposal to Pantji. But as the States Reorganisation Commission had already been appointed, I could not leave Bombay before its report was received. Jawaharlalji dropped his suggestion about me when he was convinced about the correctness of the view and asked me to persuade Pantji to accept his invitation to join the Central Cabinet.

Pantji accepted the invitation after much consideration. He gave up his office of Chief Minister of Uttar Pradesh at the end of December and joined the Central Cabinet at the end of January 1955. Jawaharlalji had not made up his mind about the Ministry to be assigned to Pantji. He had at first thought of appointing him as a Minister without portfolio, but later on decided to assign to him the Defence Ministry. When I learnt about this decision Pantji had already agreed to accept it. I tried to persuade Pantji not to accept this Ministry. While Pantji had the capacity to run any Ministry effectively, it was my view that he should not undertake the responsibility for defence on account of his physical handicaps. Pantji replied, 'I cannot say anything to Jawaharlalji in this matter. I shall accept his suggestion even though I do not much like this Ministry.' I then discussed this matter with Jawaharlalji and told him that the arrangement was not proper and that he should reconsider his decision. He replied that there was no other ministry vacant and asked me what other ministry Pandit Pant could be given. I suggested giving him the Home Ministry. This Ministry was held by Dr. Katju at that time. I suggested to Jawaharlalji that he should entrust the Defence Ministry to Dr. Katju and the Home Ministry to Pantji. Jawaharlalji accepted my suggestion. Pantji was very satisfied with this arrangement and said, 'You should have come to the Central Ministry in my place as I am not able to talk to Jawaharlalji as you are able to do and persuade him. My relations with Jawaharlalji are such that I cannot press him to accept my view at any time.'

7

The Struggle for Samyukta Maharashtra

SHRIRAMULU OF Andhra went on a hunger strike making a demand for the formation of a separate State of Andhra, and died as a result of his fast. Many violent acts were committed in Andhra after his death. Either as a result of the death of Shriramulu or on a consideration of the merits of the demand, it was ultimately decided by the Central Government to create a separate State of Andhra. Jawaharlalji made this declaration in the beginning of 1953 and also declared that Andhra State would come into existence from October that year. I wrote to Jawaharlalji in this connection that the step taken by him would encourage similar agitations in other areas and that difficulties would be created in the task of integrating the country. But Jawaharlalji used to submit to the kind of pressures mentioned above and my appeal had no effect on him. Even when he did not approve of a certain course of action, he would agree to it as a result of pressures put on him as is illustrated by some other incidents in his life.

After the decision to form a separate Andhra State had been announced, Jawaharlalji thought of appointing a States Reorganisation Commission and discussed his idea with me. He discussed it soon after with the Working Committee also. I had urged upon him as strongly as I could not to appoint such a Commission and tried to explain to him that there was a great risk in taking such a step for at least the next ten years. This step would result in the formation of linguistic states and the reactions would be very adverse. The formation of linguistic states at that stage would present difficulties and create instability in the country. The task of the formation of linguistic states would be easier if it was undertaken after political and economic stability had been established in the country. I therefore tried hard to explain to Jawaharlalji that the step which he was contemplating was very untimely. But he could not be persuaded to see the force of my arguments and his proposal was accepted by the Working Committee of the Congress after discussion. He thus appointed the States Reorganisation Commission under the Chairmanship of Shri Saiyid Fazl Ali who was at first a Judge of the Supreme Court and then Governor of Orissa. It was a three-member commission, including the President, with Shri Hriday Nath Kunzru and Shri K. M. Panikkar as members. The appointment of the Commission encouraged the agitation for the formation of separate States in the different areas of the country. The most violent agitation took place in Bombay city and several areas of Maharashtra.

There was an agitation for quite some time for the formation of Samyukta Maharashtra with Bombay as a part of it. This agitation became more active and stronger with the appointment of the States Reorganisation Commission. The demand of this agitation was the formation of the State of Samyukta Maharashtra including the Marathawada area of the Hyderabad State, Vidarbha and other adjacent Marathi areas. This agitation intensified in 1953 and soon took a violent shape. Shri Shanker Rao Deo formed a Samyukta Maharashtra Samiti consisting of a number of political parties to carry on the agitation. The Praja Socialist Party and the Communist Party who joined this committee took a most aggressive attitude which was responsible for encouraging violent tendencies in the movement.

There was a general feeling in Bombay city in favour of keeping Bombay city separate if Bombay State was to be divided into different states. Bombay city had always been cosmopolitan, without any linguistic group forming a majority of its population. This cosmopolitan nature of Bombay city would be vitiated if it was attached to a linguistic area and the city would lose its established reputation. A large number of people in Bombay believed that this would be detrimental to the country. As against this, the Samyukta Maharashtra Samiti demanded that Bombay city must be a part of the linguistic State of Maharashtra. As this was not accepted by those in authority, the agitation took a violent turn. The people who talked of arson and dacoities for running the movement, were the greatest supporters of this move. There was a general unanimity of opinion in Maharashtra in favour of the formation of a separate State of Maharashtra with Bombay city as a part of it.

Shri D. K. Kunte was the Speaker of the Bombay Legislative Assembly at the time. As I have mentioned earlier, Bhausaheb Hiray had pressed me to include him in the Cabinet, but as I could not accept his suggestion I had proposed that he should become the Speaker. It was necessary under the circumstances which obtained at the time to appoint Shri Kunte as the Speaker. Shri Kunte accepted the Speakership on condition that he would continue as an active member of the Congress and a member of the AICC. I accepted this condition, but never meant that as a member of a political party the Speaker could take part in any political agitation. According to the generally accepted convention of democracy, the Speaker must always be above all parties and should not take part in any agitations. Even though I had accepted the condition of Shri Kunte to continue as an active member of the Congress and a member of the AICC, I had done so under duress. It was not proper to have done so.

Shri Kunte started taking part in the Samyukta Maharashtra movement and delivered a speech in a public meeting while presiding over a meeting in support of the agitation. When Jawaharlalji learnt about it, he objected and asked Shri Kunte for an explanation. Shri Kunte replied that he remained an active member of the Congress with my consent. When Jawaharlalji asked me about it, I informed him about the facts of the situation and also that I had not consented to his taking actual part in any agitation and that I felt he should not have taken part in any controversial activity. Soon after, Shri Kunte agreed to resign from the AICC and I informed Jawaharlalji accordingly.

Shri S. K. Patil who was the President of the Bombay Congress Committee was against the Samyukta Maharashtra movement and wanted the composite Bombay State to remain. He wanted Bombay city to remain a separate entity if Bombay State did not remain composite. He had, however, not been vehement or aggressive in his speeches and actions. Somebody had complained to Jawaharlalji that Shri S. K. Patil's speeches were giving incitement to violence in Maharashtra, and requested him to prevent Shri Patil from acting in this manner. When Jawaharlalji wrote to me about it, asking for the facts, I informed him that while Shri Patil did oppose the Samyukta Maharashtra movement, the leaders of the Samyukta Maharashtra Samiti were so intolerant that they wanted to suppress all opposition and had therefore made this false complaint against Shri Patil. I believed in large State units, as in my view such units would make State Governments strong and also add to the strength of the Centre. Moreover, linguistic States were not conducive to the achievement and maintenance of the integration of India. I was, therefore, of the opinion that States should not be formed on a linguistic basis. There were, however, many in Gujarat and in the Congress who were of the opinion that there should be separate States of Maharashtra and Gujarat.

The Samyukta Maharashtra movement became even more active and aggressive in 1955. Its leaders presented their case before the Commission which also had long discussions with me. In my talks with the Commission, I stressed the importance of the integration and unity of India and told the Commission that the reorganisation must be done in such a manner that it helped in forging this unity. I told the Commission clearly that if States were formed on a linguistic basis, the forging of the unity of India would meet with impediments and handicaps. It would be better and more advantageous if two or three states joined together and formed a group of two or three language states. I told them that I could not foresee where this tendency for the formation of linguistic States would end if linguistic states were formed.

The Fazl Ali Commission handed over their report to the Central Government in September 1955 and it was made public in October.

The Fazl Ali Commission studied this question very thoroughly. They had received 2,000 memoranda and had visited 104 different places, seeing more than 9,000 persons during these visits. The Commission had recommended the formation of the following 16 States. Madras, Kerala, Karnatak (or Mysore), Hyderabad, Andhra, Bombay, Vidarbha, Madhya Pradesh, Rajasthan, Punjab, Uttar Pradesh, Bihar, West Bengal, Assam, Orissa and Jammu and Kashmir. The new Bombay State was to be formed from the then State *minus* Abu and the Kannada-speaking areas and *plus* Saurashtra, Kutch and the Marathawada area of Hyderabad State. Besides, the Commission recommended Delhi, Manipur and Andaman and Nicobar Islands to be made centrally administered areas.

Jawaharlalji did not react favourably to this report and publicly expressed his dissatisfaction with some of its recommendations. As a result, those who were dissatisfied with the report in different States got an opportunity to express their dissatisfaction very strongly in public. Some friends in Maharashtra went to the extent of saying publicly that they would get the matter decided in the streets if they did not get the justice they demanded. This showed that they were determined to get their demand accepted even by resorting to riots which did take place in some places on the publication of the Commission's report.

I have been of the view that if Jawaharlalji had accepted without any reservation the recommendations of the Commission and appealed to the country to accept them, the country would perhaps have been saved from some of the undesirable incidents that took place in the wake of the report. Jawaharlalji's dissatisfaction with the report related only to the recommendation of the Commission for the formation of the present Madhya Pradesh. It is, however, a fact that when the Central Government took its decision on the Commission's report, they accepted fully the recommendation for the formation of Madhya Pradesh. Thus

Jawaharlalji, sometimes, looking at some questions superficially, got emotionally excited and expressed his feelings in public. But on cooler consideration of the question later on, he would accept the position against which he had expressed his opposition earlier. This had some harmful effects on public life and some people did publicly express their disapproval of this tendency.

The Samyukta Maharashtra movement took a much more aggressive turn when it was seen that the Commission's report was not in accordance with their demand. The leaders of the movement were bitterly dissatisfied with the recommendations of the Commission. When they violently demanded the formation of Samyukta Maharashtra, there was a reaction in Gujarat. The Gujarat Pradesh Congress Committee which met in Mehmadabad passed a resolution in favour of dividing Bombay State into three parts—Maharashtra, Gujarat and Bombay city, the last to be a union territory.

We came to this conclusion in Gujarat as we felt no useful purpose would be served by keeping Maharashtra and Gujarat together when Maharashtra did not want it. The Congress Working Committee met in November to discuss the recommendations of the Commission and, after a full discussion, decided on the division of Bombay State into three parts. All the members of the Working Committee, except the member from Maharashtra, were in favour of the resolution. The President of the Maharashtra Pradesh Congress Committee, Shri Deogirikar tried to explain the Samyukta Maharashtra case to the Committee, but it was not accepted.

Riots had broken out in Bombay against this decision and there was very violent opposition throughout Maharashtra. We held a mass meeting at Chowpati beach in Bombay in November in this connection. There was a lot of stone throwing by some people out to create a disturbance. When I was speaking, I was hit by a stone and slightly injured. But some others who were sitting near me were very badly injured. In spite of this continuous stone throwing, the meeting went on. Peace was restored in Bombay within three days.

One day after everything had settled down the Prime Minister of Russia, Mr. Bulganin, and the head of the Soviet Communist Party, Mr. Khrushchev, came to Bombay on a visit. Jawaharlalji had wondered whether it should take place in view of the disturbed conditions but I assured him that it would be successful and should be confirmed. They did come and there was no trouble.

The Gujarat Pradesh Congress Committee had passed a

unanimous resolution in favour of dividing the Bombay State into three parts only as a result of the attitude taken by Shri Shanker Rao Deo and others in Poona. Soon afterwards, Shri Yashwantrao Chavan severely criticised the resolution of the Gujarat Pradesh Committee in a speech in Poona and said that the resolution of the Gujarat Committee breathed imperialism. The relations between me and Shri Yashwantrao had been very close since 1946 and I did not expect this kind of criticism or abuse from him. It, therefore, did pain me. Within a few days, however, Shri Yashwantrao realised his mistake, saw me and expressed his regret. He also expressed his deep anguish at this mistake and again clarified the position by writing a letter to me. The letter reads as under:

Winter Road,
Bombay,
10.11.55

My dear Morarjibhai,

In these last few days since my talk with you, I have been facing an inner conflict within me which tends to destroy unwittingly the bonds of affection and sympathy that we have had all these years inasmuch as that a sudden unpremeditated impulse motivated solely to do ultimately a greater good could have caused you a deep sense of pain.

As I have already told you, that has never been in my thoughts for how can I who has borne for you such personal regards and affection create a situation that can embarrass you or even partly destroy the high ideals of fellowship dinned into us above all other considerations.

I have never been able under this deep strain to really express in words what my feelings are and I have therefore attempted to write this with the hope that you will believe the sincere motives (which unfortunately did not fructify into what they were meant to be) ; and my long talk with Maneckji last night has given me the moral courage to write this to you.

We shall even rise to higher heights when inspired and guided by those like you; and in these last few years my own public life has been moulded on a pattern set by you. This has not been easy; but I have tried honestly and scrupulously and if I have not always succeeded, it is because I have not yet reached the same maturity as you have done.

The decision of the High Command is known to us finally today. In writing this to you I implore you to believe as truth all I have said so far. If in spite of that you feel that what I did was not correct, I hereby resolve to give up all that I have achieved and fade away completely from the political scene.

In these dark shadows that loom before me, I pray to you to show the light as a father to his son so that in some way I may once again endeavour to fulfil the hopes, the faith and the trust that you have had in me all these years.

With my respects and affection,
Yashwantrao

I had gone to Juhu beach to rest for a few days after an attack of pilitis in December 1955. There I received a long letter from Jawaharlalji in connection with the reorganisation of states. He had mentioned in that letter his worries on this question. He also asked me in that letter to consider how Gandhiji would have tackled this question and informed me that he would see me at Juhu on his way back to Delhi via Bombay from the tour on which he was engaged at that time. He accordingly came by plane to Santa Cruz and arrived at Juhu in a helicopter. He discussed the matter personally with me and asked me to discuss it further with him at Delhi in January. The Central Government announced in January 1956 its decision on the recommendations of the States Reorganisation Commission. According to this decision the then composite Bombay State was to be divided into two separate States of Gujarat and Maharashtra and Bombay city was to be a centrally administered area.

It was decided to have the following States in the country: Andhra-Telangana, Assam, Bihar, Gujarat, Kerala, Madhya Pradesh, Madras, Maharashtra, Vidarbha, Mysore, Orissa, Punjab, Rajasthan, Uttar Pradesh, West Bengal and Jammu and Kashmir. It was proposed to have Union Territories also: Bombay, Delhi, Himachal Pradesh, Manipur, Tripura, Andaman, Laccadive, Minicoy and Amindivi.

As I had to go to Delhi to attend an important meeting called by the Prime Minister within four or five days of the declaration of this decision, I left for Delhi and broke my journey, on the way, at Bulsar for the night. Next morning I received a phone call from Bombay that riots had broken out there and that they had assumed a very violent form. I was, therefore, asked to return to Bombay immediately.

As Jawaharlalji had called me to Delhi for an important discussion, I phoned him from Bulsar and asked him, in view of the circumstances that had arisen, whether I should return to

Bombay or whether he considered it more necessary that I should go to Delhi. I told him that I would abide by his decision. Jawaharlalji immediately told me that I must return to Bombay as it was necessary to bring conditions in Bombay under control. I therefore returned immediately to Bombay.

It became clear to me from a study of the situation on my return from Bulsar that these riots had been started by the Samyukta Maharashtra Committee people. Gujaratis were attacked and women were also being harassed. The shops belonging to Gujaratis were being looted and the police force was passing through a very severe test. Ninety-five per cent of the Bombay police were Maharashtrians whose natural sympathy was with Samyukta Maharashtra. The action taken by the police was therefore half-hearted, which gave a fillip to the riots.

Shri Naravane was a Deputy Minister in the Bombay Ministry at the time. As he was in charge of prohibition, he had come into very close contact with the police force. He was a staunch advocate of Samyukta Maharashtra, and his being a Deputy Minister, was affecting the police very adversely as he was also taking active part in the agitation. As the explanation I called for from him in this connection was not satisfactory, I removed him from my Ministry. There were several ministers and deputy ministers from Maharashtra who had sympathy with the Samyukta Maharashtra movement, but they did not encourage riots or violent action and did not approve of them.

My Secretary in the Home Ministry was Shri D. S. Joshi, who had worked under me for many years. He had impressed me as a very able and honest officer. As he was a Maharashtrian, his sympathy was with the demand for Samyukta Maharashtra, but he was a very loyal officer of great integrity and did not alllow his personal views or prejudices to interfere with the performance of his duties. There was complete confidence between us and I discussed the situation very frankly with him. I told him, 'I can have no objection to the demand for Samyukta Maharashtra. But if violence is resorted to in order to get the demand accepted, democracy will be destroyed and anarchy will be created as is happening just now in Bombay. If the police do not perform their duty on such difficult occasions, they will not remain loyal to the Government of Samyukta Maharashtra as well when it is formed, and the violent elements would be strengthened and would get out of control. Government must therefore perform its duty, howsoever unpleasant it may be, of establishing peace and should take whatever steps are necessary under the circumstances.'

Shri Joshi agreed with me entirely and accepted my suggestion. He too was of the view that riots could not be tolerated under any circumstances and that all necessary steps should be taken to suppress them. He said that all questions should be decided only by peaceful and constitutional methods. If that was not done, no democracy could function. I then asked him to issue the necessary instructions and orders to the police officers in the matter. I also discussed with him the steps that were required to be taken and issued orders immediately to all concerned. I called in the Police Commissioner and his deputies and gave them detailed instructions. I explained to them the steps to be taken for getting quick control of the situation and also asked them to see that there was no delay or negligence in taking the necessary steps. I also asked them to see that the steps were not stronger than necessary. The police therefore began to act accordingly and suppressed the riots in a short time. Some looseness was seen in police action during my absence and the riots had assumed serious proportions. A very large number of shops were looted and many people were very badly harassed. The police had therefore to resort to firing in many places.

Jawaharlalji phoned to me at night asking me for details of the riots and I explained the whole situation to him. Jawaharlalji suggested that I should not hesitate to use the military and tanks if necessary. I believed in using only the police force ordinarily for maintaining law and order. The use of military force would cause more loss of life. Moreover, if the police force lost their morale and was freed from its responsibility to control the riots, it would create a very dangerous situation for the future. I therefore decided to use only the police force. I explained this to Jawaharlalji and he agreed with me entirely. I succeeded in suppressing the riots without any help from the military.

I was extremely unhappy at the death of some 70 or 80 persons as a result of police firing during these riots. This was, however, inescapable in view of the necessity for keeping peace in Bombay city and to ensure the safety of its citizens. I had to take very strong steps in order to suppress the riots and I considered it my duty to do so. If I had so ordered, the police would not have resorted to firing. If, however, I had tried to save myself from a difficult situation in this wrong manner and had not taken the strong steps that I had taken, many innocent people would have been killed. It would have also been very difficult then to bring the situation under control. I had therefore no doubt then, and have none now, that I had to take strong steps for suppressing the riots by using the minimum force that was necessary in the performance of my duty.

The leaders of the Samyukta Maharashtra movement, particularly the Communists, had severely criticised me for taking these steps. I, however, did not enter into any controversy with them and maintained silence on the matter. I had no feeling of vindictiveness or dislike against anybody and had shown no partiality whatsoever in any of my actions. I was sure in my mind that all the critics must be realising within themselves that I had no other option before me.

These people also made a demand for a judicial enquiry into the riots and the police action thereon. I, however, refused to accept their demand as I was sure that such an enquiry would inhibit the police from taking effective action with confidence under similar circumstances in the future and that violent people would be encouraged thereby. Jawaharlalji supported me in this view on this occasion. I was examining the situation continuously and took all the care necessary to see that the police did not use more force than was absolutely necessary. The persons who were killed in police firing were engaged in looting. There was therefore no legitimate reason for making any judicial enquiry.

If the very Communists who criticised me for my actions on this occasion would look at the history of communist countries, they are bound to be convinced that the violence that was used by the governments of those countries to suppress opposition against them was far greater than what was used in Bombay. One could recall recent historical events in which Russia suppressed the government of Czechoslovakia by the use of military force and naked violence and prevented that Government from straying from the communist philosophy.

I believe in non-violence, but I also believe in the duty of Government to defend society and the country. We have not yet created conditions under which a country or a government can defend itself by non-violent means. Very few people in our society have faith in non-violence and many people are drawn to violent actions. There is no other course for the government except to prevent and counter violent acts by force.

A question naturally arises as to how a person who has faith in truth and non-violence can take part in running a government. One has to consider in this connection whether such a person should save his ideals merely by keeping out of government or whether he should offer his services for the protection of society through government and take the risk of compromising his ideals when involved in such a course. Governments will always be run, and if those who run government do not believe in truth and non-violence, there is no possibility of truth and non-violence being ever adopted by society. An average person respects and reveres a non-violent person or a saint, or a man of truth, but does not follow him. He imitates only those persons who are in power or who have wealth. It is not therefore possible for an average man to be attracted to truth and non-violence as long as men of power and wealth do not make full efforts to follow the path of truth and non-violence. If those who believe in truth and non-violence do not accept the responsibility of running governments, the latter will go into the hands of those who do not believe in them, with the result that under such governments there will be more violence and untruth than in governments run by people who believe in truth and non-violence.

There is a risk for a person who believes in non-violence and truth that once he accepts office he might have to compromise with his principles in running a government in the public interest. But if he believes that his welfare lies in the welfare of all, he should brave the risk and serve government. When there is a very unpleasant or difficult duty to perform, he has to accept it and must constantly be vigilant in his actions. He must not compromise his principles for the sake of easy popularity or wealth or power. He must not waver in doing his duty, in promoting public welfare. I have undertaken to do public service believing in non-violence and truth and have undertaken to serve through Government, whenever required to do so, only with this determination. I therefore believe that force must be used by Government if there is no non-violent way to restrain violent people in their actions. In the present circumstances, there is no other way to protect society and safeguard public interest. In taking such action, there must be no consideration or motivation of continuing in power or benefiting oneself personally in any way. I have always consciously tried to be vigilant in this respect. I cannot claim that I have succeeded completely in carrying out this determination. But I have taken sufficient care to be as cautious as I can be and not to be swayed by temptation in any way. It is for others to judge how far I have succeeded in my aims. I therefore constantly consult in this matter men of religion who are in constant search of God all their lives and correct myself whenever I find it is necessary to do so.

Soon after the decision of the States Reorganisation Commission was declared in January 1956, I went to the Congress session at Amritsar. Dhebarbhai was President of the Congress then. He had called a meeting of five or six selected persons at the instance of Jawaharlalji and Pantji. Jawaharlalji, Maulana Azad, Pantji and myself were present. Pantji suggested to me that, considering the intensity of the Samyukta Maharashtra agitation, the difficult situation in Bombay State would be resolved and a peaceful solution arrived at if I agreed to the formation of a multi-lingual Bombay State. 'It is not possible for me to undertake this responsibility,' I replied, 'in view of the decision of the Central Government and the opinion which is generally prevalent in Maharashtra and Gujarat on this question. It is not necessary to take my consent in the matter and you all can take a decision as you think proper. If the Working Committee accepts your suggestion and the Central Government also agrees, I shall not oppose it, but I cannot take the responsibility of sponsoring the suggestion which you have made. You ought not to saddle me with the responsibility of persuading Gujarat to accept the suggestion and to take the initiative in the matter. I have no doubt in my mind that it is neither possible nor proper for me to undertake this responsibility.'

But Dhebarbhai pressed me and told me that if I undertook the responsibility to persuade the people of Gujarat to accept this proposition, he was sure the people would accept it. I asked him why he as Congress President did not undertake the responsibility himself and why he was putting this burden on me. He replied that people would accept my suggestion and not his. I told him that he was trying to escape the responsibility himself and to put it on someone else. Jawaharlalji also said that if any such action could be taken, it would be good and that if I undertook to make the effort it might succeed. My reply was: 'If I faced the people of Gujarat with an ultimatum that if they did not accept my suggestion I would take to political *sanyas* or that I would have to sacrifice my life, then the people of Gujarat might accept my suggestion. It would, however, be monstrous on my part to impose myself on the people of Gujarat in this manner. I have no doubt that this would not do any credit to me. You should not, therefore, try to put such an improper responsibility on me.' The matter was then dropped.

In an attempt to achieve some progress in the direction of finding a solution, Shri Bidhan Chandra Roy of West Bengal and Shri Sri Krishna Sinha of Bihar were asked to consider whether it would be possible to make a composite state of the two States of Bihar and Bengal. They agreed to consider this suggestion but could not come to an agreement as the suggestion was rather an unnatural one in my view. All these important matters were discussed during the Amritsar Congress Session and an appeal was made to the people in general to consider the situation in this direction.

The Samyukta Maharashtra Samiti had kept up its agitation and there were more riots in some parts of Maharashtra. But the Government had taken proper steps to control them and the situation was soon under control. I moved a resolution in the Bombay Legislative Assembly suggesting the formation of the new States out of Bombay State as decided by the Central Government.

The Samyukta Maharashtra Samiti registered a strong protest against this resolution. The Maharashtra Pradesh Congress Committee first asked for the resignation of the members of the Samiti from the Assembly. But later on it was decided by them that as that would be a step against the Congress organisation, resignations should not be resorted to. A few members from Maharashtra voted against the resolution in the Assembly, and Shri Hiray made a statement in the matter. Shri Shankar Rao Deo and Shri Deogirikar thereafter wrote a long letter to Jawaharlalji making some complaints against me. In their letter they had also demanded my resignation. Jawaharlalji sent me a copy of that letter. I replied to Jawaharlalji that Shri Deogirikar did not express his views fully and clearly in public and said different things to different people. I also explained clearly in my letter that there was no truth in the complaint.

Shri Prabhakar Kunte had issued a public statement in which he explained why a bilingual Bombay State should not be formed and what damage was likely to be caused to Maharashtra as a result. I placed the true facts in this connection before the Legislative Assembly and made it clear that several assertions made in the statement were not in accordance with truth. I also sent my detailed statement in this matter to Jawaharlalji. The draft bill for the reorganisation of the states was thereafter presented in Parliament and evoked a great deal of discussion amongst the members. Efforts were also made in those discussions to find a solution. Maharashtrians used to blame me for the decision which was taken for the formation of three separate States of Maharashtra, Gujarat and Bombay, but that was not in accordance with truth. The Working Committee had unanimously taken this decision, and Jawaharlalji particularly had given his clear view in favour of the decision. The then Finance Minister of India, Shri C. D. Deshmukh, protested against the decision of the Central Government when it was taken, but all the other ministers in the Central Cabinet had agreed to it. Shri Deshmukh resigned from the Ministry in protest against the decision.

When the draft bill was being discussed in the Lok Sabha,

some leading members of Parliament were taking signatures of members on a resolution framed by them. The resolution asked for the formation of a bigger State of Bombay which would comprise Maharashtra area of Bombay State, Gujarat, Saurashtra, Vidarbha and Marathawada. I learnt at the time that this resolution had the support of Pantji. Pantji had made a similar suggestion to me at the time of the Amritsar Congress as I have mentioned earlier. At that time I had refused to undertake to sponsor this scheme though I had told him that, if the Working Committee and the Central Government decided in favour of it, I would not protest. Jawaharlalji also supported the statement prepared by the Lok Sabha members.

When I went to Ahmedabad in May of that year, the people there were full of enthusiasm for the formation of three different States. On my way from the station to my residence, they showered flowers on me all the way in their joy at the decision. I had refused to accept Pantji's suggestion as I knew this was how the people of Gujarat felt. When the people were showering flowers on me, I told my companions in the car that if these very people who were showering flowers now might throw stones at me in a few months, I would not be surprised. This fear was proved true soon.

About two months after this incident, it was decided to change the decision and to form a bigger Bombay bilingual State. Shri Dhebarbhai phoned to me from Delhi at the end of June and asked me to go to Delhi for a discussion of the proposal for a bigger Bombay State which was under consideration there. He wanted my consent. I replied that it was not possible for me to go to Delhi then, but that I would go there for the Working Committee meeting in July. At this meeting which I attended this resolution was brought in. Jawaharlalji, Maulana Azad, Pantji, Dhebarbhai, Lal Bahadur Shastri and myself had met before the meeting of the Working Committee and I was asked to accept the proposal. I repeated what I had said in Amritsar and added that if the Working Committee passed the resolution I would not offer any opposition to it. I said that I could not sponsor the resolution. I preferred the formation of a bigger Bombay State, but looking to the agitation in Maharashtra and the opinion of many people in Gujarat I had agreed to a division of Bombay State into three parts. Therefore, I did not consider it proper now, under the new circumstances that had arisen, to support the formation of a bigger Bombay State.

But Jawaharlalji was in great distress and gave expression to it when he talked to me. As there was no other alternative, I agreed to the new proposal, but I added that if this bigger Bombay State was formed it should not be subsequently divided and that they should all guarantee this. They accepted this condition orally, but they found it difficult to give a written undertaking. I also asked them to obtain the agreement of the members from Maharashtra in Parliament, which was done.

I met the Parliament members from Gujarat and placed the proposal before them. Considering the circumstances, they accepted it, even though they did not have their hearts in it. The Working Committee and the Central Government formally accepted this new proposal soon after.

Before this resolution was accepted by the Working Committee, I had also made it a condition that I would not remain the Chief Minister of the bigger Bombay State when it was formed. I had said that it was necessary in order to make such a government successful that the Chief Minister should be from Maharashtra. Considering the storm of opposition against me in Maharashtra, I should not become its Chief Minister. Jawaharlalji and Pantji were pressing me to be the Chief Minister of the new State as they felt that otherwise it would be difficult to manage it well. When they told me this, I told them, 'I do not understand why you are pressing me in this manner. If you have a feeling that I have a desire to come to the Central Government after leaving Bombay, please remove it from your minds as I have no such desire. You should not therefore press me to be the Chief Minister of the new Bombay State.' Pantji then asked me whether I would agree to be the Chief Minister if all concerned asked me unanimously to do so. They knew that I had always believed in accepting whatever the party asked me to do unanimously. I, however, requested him and Jawaharlalji to assure me that they would not make any attempt to get unanimity of opinion in this matter. They accepted my request. This is how it was decided to form the bigger Bombay bilingual State consisting of Gujarat, Saurashtra, Kutch, Bombay, Maharashtra, Marathawada and Vidarbha. The Working Committee and the Central Government accepted this proposition and a law was also enacted in Parliament accordingly.

8

The Maha Gujarat Movement

I HAD FELT that there would be a great deal of protest and agitation in Gujarat as a result of the decision to form a bigger Bombay State. The day after I reached Bombay from Delhi, I learnt that riots had taken place in Ahmedabad. The leaders of Maha Gujarat Samiti had incited some students who went to Congress House where they indulged in some sabotage and the police had to fire at them. Some five students died as a result of that firing. This aggravated the tension and the riots spread in the city. When I received this news, I felt that I must immediately go to Ahmedabad. I talked to Dhebarbhai on the phone and told him that I felt it was difficult to suppress the riots merely by police force as that would result in much loss of life. I added that I would therefore have to go on an indefinite fast and asked him to let me know whether Jawaharlalji would agree to such an action by me. He, however did not give me an immediate reply.

I went to attend the meeting of the Gujarat Pradesh Congress Committee which was called within about two days of this occurrence. I had gone there convinced that there was no remedy except an indefinite fast by me, and that if Jawaharlalji did not agree to such a course, I should resign the Chief Ministership and undertake the fast. Dhebarbhai too came to Ahmedabad and told me that Jawaharlalji did not very much like my contemplated action, but would not oppose it if I decided to fast. Dhebarbhai agreed with Jawaharlalji.

Those who led the Maha Gujarat Samiti were forcing people to stop work and were forcibly preventing them from attending our meetings. I had no doubt in my mind that democracy would be a mockery in the country if people were prevented from exercising their rights and enjoying their privileges by such violent actions. I could see no other effective way except an indefinite fast to bring the people back to sanity and wean them away from the path of destruction in which they were involved by the communist-minded leaders of the Maha Gujarat Samiti. I therefore decided to go on an indefinite fast till the people generally gave up violent actions and accepted the right of ordinary citizens to hold meetings. I made this statement in the meeting of the Pradesh Committee.

I was staying at that time with my younger brother Ambelal in the Ellis Bridge area of Ahmedabad, and I immediately started my fast there. Dhebarbhai was very much worried and stayed on in Ahmedabad. He was trying to persuade the leaders of Ahmedabad city to do something to enable me to give up the fast. 'You should not make an effort to get my fast ended or to enable me to end my fast,' I told him, 'efforts should be made only to see that people give up violence. I have undertaken the fast in order to change the hearts of the people. No pressure or influence should be used in these matters. Good results can come out of this step only if the people accept my stand voluntarily. If you are not able to bear this situation, it would be much better if you left Ahmedabad. I consider your efforts harmful to the cause.' Dhebarbhai did not leave Ahmedabad and continued his talks with the leaders. Some of them met me on the eighth day of the fast and requested me to give it up and assured me that a meeting would be held.

Many people saw me during these eight days and discussed the problem with me. As I had done my duty I had great peace of mind. I was, however, not very happy with the efforts being made for the ending of my fast as that would not bring about a proper result. I had made it very clear that my fast was not directed against the agitation for Maha Gujarat. I said that people could carry on their agitation peacefully and were welcome to obtain Maha Gujarat in a peaceful manner. But if they obtained it in a violent manner it would cause great harm to Gujarat itself. My fast was therefore undertaken only to make the people give up violent actions.

As I have said earlier, I was against the formation of linguistic states at the time as I felt that this would make the forging of the unity of the country very difficult. If it was accepted in one place, the agitation would spread to other parts of the country for one reason or another. This fear of mine was proved correct by later events. I, however, believed that those who wanted the formation of linguistic states had a right to propagate their views and I considered it improper to make them give up their propaganda by the weapon of fast. I even felt that it would be against my concept of religion to do so. This is why I had made it clear that my fast was not against the agitation for Maha Gujarat, but was undertaken only to wean away the masses from violent actions.

When the leaders of the city told me on the eighth day of my fast that a meeting had been arranged, I told them that I would decide about the continuance or ending of the fast only after attending the meeting and speaking there. A meeting was held in the Bhadra area in the evening. It was attended by six to seven thousand people in spite of the hostile propaganda indulged in by several people. There were several others also standing round about and watching the proceedings of the meeting. When I reached the meeting, there was a group of young people led by Communists who were raising cries of protest and condemnation and were indulging in stone throwing. I explained to the people in the meeting their duty and also how much harm was caused by violent actions. The stone throwing went on continuously while I was speaking. Six or seven co-workers of mine were standing around me and catching the stones thrown at me, so that they would not hurt me. But men and women attending the meeting were hit by stones. My wife was among those so hurt. The people who were protecting me from the stones did their work so efficiently that I was not hurt at all. The people in the audience sat very quietly and listened to my speech attentively in spite of the continuous stone throwing. None of them moved from their places, even though I spoke for 45 minutes. I had instructed the police not to take action against the mischief-mongers. The police accordingly did not take any steps and this was why that small group of young men could keep on throwing stones right through the meeting.

The question facing me after the meeting was whether I should give up the fast or continue it. All the leaders of the city and my co-workers were of the firm view that the meeting was properly held and that there were only a few who were throwing stones. They said that the meeting proved that the bulk of the citizens had refrained from violent acts, and therefore asked me to give up the fast. While on the one hand I felt that I should continue my fast as long as even the few people who were throwing stones did not desist from their activity, and that my fast, if it ended in death, would be an act of pure sacrifice and would be an assurance against violence in the future; on the other hand I saw clearly that six or seven thousand men and women at the meeting had fearlessly and heroically faced the stones thrown at them and heard me attentively. I also saw that these people by their fearlessness and courage did not allow the activity of the violent group to succeed. It was therefore my duty to respect their wishes and if I did not give up the fast it would be evident that I had no appreciation for their bravery and sacrifice. I, therefore, broke my fast a short time after the meeting was over as a result of the persistent requests of colleagues and leaders of the people. I have, however, a feeling since then that my giving up of the fast was somewhat premature. It was because I did not want a premature ending of the fast that I had requested Dhebarbhai to leave

Ahmedabad from the beginning of the fast, but he did not heed my request as he felt that it was his duty to stay there. I could not therefore quarrel with him. It is a fact that peace was established as a result of this fast and violent actions did stop after this meeting. There was therefore a good public response to the fast. As I felt somewhat weak as a result of the fast, I rested for a few days thereafter.

If I had not fasted, riots would have broken out throughout Gujarat as the feeling in favour of Maha Gujarat was gathering strength, and if riots had spread to many places, the police would have had to fire and there would have been a terrible loss of lives. Peace could not have been restored in Gujarat in that case without at least three to four hundred people being killed as a result of firing in several areas of Gujarat.

It is my belief that a fast unto death should not be undertaken in order to get something from somebody or to pressurise somebody to take some definite action. But my fast was neither directed against any individual nor was it undertaken in order to make somebody do something particularly. The aim of my fast was only to wean away the citizens from violent actions. The fruitful result of the fast was that the people refrained from violent actions thereafter. As people generally kept away from all violent actions after my fast the riots ended completely. I have no doubt that rioting would not have taken place if the mass of the people had no sympathy with the persons who instigated violence. I am therefore sure that the fast I undertook was in accordance with the principles of satyagraha.

Several people raised a question whether I should have undertaken such a fast as a Chief Minister. It is the duty of the chief minister and the home minister to establish and maintain peace. Ordinarily, peace is maintained through the use of the police, but if the chief minister or the home minister felt that it was his duty to fast in order to establish peace and maintain it, instead of resorting to police firing, it would be in accordance with proper religious concepts if he goes on a fast. This is not against the duty involved in his authority. I have no doubt in my mind that nobody should undertake such a fast for any personal advantage. If a person feels that fasting is his duty at a critical moment in his life and that he cannot but fast, he should undertake it. Those who have no faith in such methods should not undertake fasts.

As I have mentioned, the police had to fire in order to stop violent actions and restore peace when the agitation for Maha Gujarat started in Ahmedabad. There was a very strong feeling of indignation amongst the people of Ahmedabad at the death of some young men in that firing. They considered the people who took part in the riots as martyrs instead of holding them responsible for the rioting. I cannot consider people resorting to violent actions of this kind as martyrs as it is against the traditions and principles of democracy that anybody should try to get anything by violent actions. The police have to fire and kill some people for the protection of the general public; those killed cannot be said to have performed an act of national service. In the enquiry I had made into the first riot, I was convinced that the police had resorted to firing very properly and legitimately and that those who had died had taken part in violent actions. I therefore refused to grant the demand for a judicial enquiry and also refused to consider those who were killed in police firing as martyrs.

Jawaharlalji wanted to speak to the citizens of Ahmedabad in the second week of October when he went there. He addressed a meeting of the citizens and a meeting of the students. Several students shouted hostile slogans as the leaders of Maha Gujarat had incited them to do so. Jawaharlalji tried to persuade them to be quiet and to see reason. But these young people did not stop shouting until the meeting ended.

Jawaharlalji had come to the Bombay State earlier in April 1956 to visit some of the districts of Karnatak. At that time I took him to see some interesting sights amongst which was the well-known Gersappa falls also. I took him to Sirsi after the visit to the falls. He was to return to Delhi in his plane from Belgaum after visiting Sirsi which is 150 miles from Belgaum. It was arranged at first to take him to Sirsi and back by car. Before however, finalising the programme, I said to him, 'You will have to suffer a lot of dust on the 150 mile motor journey as the road is not tarred. It will also be very hot. It is not possible to land a Dakota or any other such plane at Sirsi as there are no landing facilities there. If, however, you agree, I can suggest a better way of returning from Sirsi. The Bombay Flying Club has small planes called Tiger Moths which carry two passengers. It is a one-engine plane and can be taken to Sirsi from Bombay. It requires a very small landing place which can be easily prepared. Such a journey would, however, be opposed by security officials and others as it would be considered very risky for a VIP, particularly the Prime Minister, to travel in such a small one-engine plane. If, therefore, you do not inform the Defence Ministry or any other officials concerned with security about this, I shall make the arrangements.'

Jawaharlalji had a love for adventure and did not hesitate to take risks of any kind. He in fact took delight in such adventures. So he readily agreed. This trip was really an adventure. I undertook great risks myself, but hesitated to involve Jawaharlalji. As, however, my faith in God is absolute, I was not worried. I was very happy to receive the consent of Jawaharlalji to my proposal.

I called for three Tiger Moths from the Bombay Flying Club. Jawaharlalji, Indiraji and I travelled in these three planes each with a pilot, and reached Belgaum safely. This arrangement could be carried out as it was kept secret. The Defence Ministry people and some other official learnt about this afterwards and protested, but as the act had already been done, the protest had no meaning.

Jawaharlalji came on a tour to Gujarat and Saurashtra in May of that year, when a programme for seeing lions in the Gir forest was arranged, and I accompanied him there. We were sitting on a platform erected on a tree at night when two lions passed quickly under the tree, but as they passed by the place with great speed we could not observe them properly. We could only see them running away for a few seconds. To give us a closer look at a lion, another arrangement was made to lure a lion to a place where a young buffalo calf was tied to a post. We went there in a jeep and shutting off the jeep lights we stood at a distance of 25 or 30 feet behind a bush from the place where the young buffalo calf was tied. We saw a lion coming there and pouncing upon the young animal. He started eating it leisurely. He could not take it away as it was very firmly tied. The lion had not seen us till we boarded the jeep and put on the lights. This surprised the lion who tried to run away, taking the animal with it. As the bait was tied with a very strong rope the lion could not break it. But he dragged it with such force that while the rope did not break, the young animal broke into two. This demonstrated the extraordinary strength of the lion who then left the place carrying a part of the young animal with it.

We went from there to our camp and when we left that camp for our next destination it was about 6.30 a.m. As we were passing in a car we again saw a pair of lions with their cub walking through a field at a distance of about 75 yards from us. They were walking leisurely in a parallel line to our road. They did not, however, run away on seeing our car. We must have gone side by side in this manner for about a furlong or more. Then our paths diverged and the lion family disappeared in the forest. We were thus able to see three or four lions from close quarters.

The formation of the bigger Bombay State was to take effect from the 1st of November 1956, and as I had decided not to continue as Chief Minister of the new State, the members of the Bombay State

Congress Party had to choose a new leader. Shri Bhausaheb Hiray was a candidate for the post. But I felt that Shri Hiray would not be able to manage the new State efficiently and impartially, considering my experience of his working and knowing his attitude as I did. I therefore asked Shri Yashwantrao Chavan to undertake the new responsibility. He pressed me a great deal to continue as the leader, but I did not agree. Dr. Jivaraj Mehta was then the Finance Minister and a senior member of my Cabinet. His assistance would be very valuable to Shri Chavan, and if Dr. Jivaraj did not agree to continue in the Ministry Shri Chavan's task would have been very difficult. I therefore undertook the responsibility of persuading Dr. Jivaraj to assist Yashwantrao.

One or two months prior to this, Rajkumari Amrit Kaur had pressingly requested Dr. Jivaraj to be the Director of the newly established Medical Institute in Delhi. Dr. Jivaraj told me that he had a desire to accept that offer and asked for my consent. I told him that he would be requested to work for the new bigger Bombay State and it was desirable that he did not go to Delhi. I felt that Dr. Jivaraj desired to go to Delhi at that time because it was not certain how conditions in the new Bombay State would develop, and if he did not go at that time someone else would be appointed to that post immediately. I explained to him the necessity of helping Shri Chavan in his work by continuing in Bombay State and told him that that would be far more useful for the State and the country. He accepted my request. I then told him that if he served as no. 2 and as Finance Minister in Yashwantrao's Cabinet he would be doing a valuable service to the country. He agreed with my suggestion. This facilitated the task of Shri Chavan in administering the bigger Bombay State.

Shri Chavan was the juniormost Minister in the Cabinet at that time, but if Shri Hiray was not to be selected from Maharashtra, Shri Chavan was the only other choice, in my view. This was why I asked him to be my successor. I did not talk to all the members in the Party, but I talked with the important ones who had great regard for me and they accepted my suggestion. Shri Chavan had also talked to some people and taken their consent. Some members from Vidarbha, particularly Shri P.K. Deshmukh, however, persisted until the end in asking me to continue as Chief Minister. Shri Deshmukh told me that it was necessary for me to take the responsibility to make a success of the bigger Bombay State. I told him, 'If I was elected unanimously by the whole party, I would have to consider it, but there is no such possibility as Shri Hiray has already declared his candidature and has already informed me about it. I cannot therefore agree with you as there is no possibility of unanimity in the party.' The friends from Vidarbha saw Jawaharlalji and Pantji and pressed them to ask me to continue in Bombay. Jawaharlalji then told them, 'We have promised him that we shall not make any effort to arrange a unanimous election and we have undertaken not to persuade anybody in this matter. It is therefore not possible for us to do anything further.' Jawaharlalji, however, told Shri Deshmukh that if they could arrange to keep me in Bombay he would be very happy.

Shri Chavan told me that he would propose my name as the leader and I replied to him that if he proposed me I would not be able to accept and would withdraw. When the Party meeting took place, my name was proposed by Shri Chavan. Shri Hiray and Shri Chavan were then proposed for the post. I withdrew my name immediately. When votes were informally taken by the members of the party, if my memory is right, Shri Chavan got 333 votes and Shri Hiray got only 110 or 111 votes. Shri Chavan was then formally elected unanimously as the leader of the party.

This is how Shri Chavan was elected as the first Chief Minister of the bigger Bombay State. This arrangement was to come into effect from the 1st of November. I therefore vacated the government bungalow that I was occupying on 31 October and went to stay in Oceana in a flat on the Marine Drive which had been rented by my son on his own without any help from the Government.

When I completed 60 years of my life on 29 February 1956, some of my colleagues and friends thought of celebrating my diamond jubilee and spoke to me about it. But as I had made it a rule long ago that I should not even celebrate my birthday, there was no question of celebrating the diamond jubilee. So I did not give my consent and told my friends that I would not take part in any such celebration. Shri S. K. Patil told me that he had already made arrangements for a public reception on that day and that I should be present on the occasion. If I did not do so, he said, he would be placed in a difficult situation, I told him I could not break my rule. Because of this rule, I added, I was not taking part in such celebrations of anyone else's birthdays. So the idea of a public reception was dropped. However, my friends came to my residence on the morning of the 29th to personally congratulate me on this day and hand over a purse of more than a lakh of rupees which they had already collected for the occasion. I donated this money to several non-political social service organisations the very next day.

I had also made it a rule for myself since I entered public life, not to let my name be given to any institution, road, place etc., and I have not made any exception to it so far.

The sole purpose behind these rules was to free myself from my ego. I believe that so long as one does not free oneself of one's ego, the realisation of truth is not possible. And I have never cherished any desire in my life save that of realising the truth. As public receptions and memorials like those mentioned above nourish the ego in man, I have made these rules for myself.

On my sixtieth birthday I received telegrams and letters from many friends and wellwishers conveying their congratulations. A telegram and a letter also were received from Shri Jawaharlalji expressing his warm feelings for me (see also the chapter on Jawaharlal Nehru: As I Knew Him).

9

Discussions with Vinobaji

I HAD HARDLY any contact with Acharya Vinobaji until 1954. Vinobaji and I both attended a meeting at Sevagram after the passing away of Bapu. I however only saw and heard him there. I did not meet him or discuss anything with him personally. I had, however, always respected Vinobaji as an ascetic pursuing the path of God realisation.

When Bapu started individual satyagraha in 1940 he selected Vinobaji as the first satyagrahi. Vinobaji's *bhoodan* (land-donation) movement and the fine work he did in educating the people of Telangana had madc a very deep impression on me. I had therefore for long wanted to meet him and discuss several questions with him.

I arranged to meet him and talk with him when I went to take part in the meeting of the AICC at Berhampore in Orissa State in May 1955. I had understood that he also desired to have a talk with me. Before the two of us met separately, we had some discussions with Vinobaji in the Congress Working Committee. There was a discussion about the suggestion which Bapu had made for the conversion of Congress into a Lok Sevak Sangh. I told Vinobaji that if the Government had not been in the hands of the Congress and if the people did not have more respect for the Congress than other parties, I doubted if any of his programmes could ever be implemented. So no progress would be made in any Gandhian programme for the welfare of the people if the Congress was weakened. Vinobaji accepted some of my arguments at that time.

When I was going to Vinobaji for a discussion, one or two disciples of his asked me not to say anything which would make Vinobaji angry. I told them that I did not want to provoke Vinobaji in any way, but it would be difficult to talk only in a manner which would be pleasant to Vinobaji. If, therefore, nothing unpleasant should be said by me, it was better that I did not meet him. Those friends then withdrew their suggestion.

When I felt that Vinobaji was irritated by my arguments during the discussion, I told him very politely, 'If you get angry at what I say, it only means that my view is contrary to yours. This will happen in a discussion between any two people. Both of us want to understand each other and it is our purpose to arrive at truth as a result of the discussion. If one of us becomes angry during the discussion, our talks will be futile. If you tell me not to discuss a matter further where you differ from my view, I shall drop that subject on your telling me so. But if any one of us gets angry we shall not be able to have a useful discussion. In that case it is best we do not discuss anything.' I also added, 'I know you are very much advanced in your pursuit of truth, while I am very much behind in this matter. All the same, both of us are pursuing truth. It is clear that I have not yet acquired truth, but you will also not be able to say that you have acquired the final truth. If you had acquired it, it would naturally follow that I would accept whatever you told me. But as I am not able to do so in some matters, it is clear that you have not yet mastered truth. This is the test which the Yoga Shastras have given us.' He did not claim to have acquired truth and agreed with me that the discussions should be carried on without any irritation or excitement. We then discussed many questions for eight or nine hours in the course of two or three days. The whole discussion was without any excitement or irritation and we understood each other much better as a result.

Vinobaji sometimes urged the establishment of a society without any government. I could not agree with this dictum and asked him: 'Do you consider that it is possible any day to achieve a society without any government? The world is governed by a kind of government, which is a perfect one because it is run by God who is perfect. There are rules for the Sangh which you are conducting and also for any movement that you carry on. This is also a kind of government. No government will be necessary when every person acts in such a manner that he does not interfere with another, does his duty without any flaw, and does not come in conflict with anybody. I do not, however, consider it possible that human society can ever be composed of such perfect men and women. Only a few people in any period can be perfect, but their number will be very small. It is therefore not possible that government can disappear at any time. I do not therefore consider it possible to establish a society without any government.' Vinobaji replied, 'I only want to emphasise that the government should govern the least.' I pleaded with him that if that was the meaning of what he said, he should not talk of a society without government. I told him that I agreed with him that that government was the best which governed least. Vinobaji then said, 'Even if our ideal cannot be achieved, we must keep it before us so that we can work more and more to reach it.' I said, 'I am of the view that if the ideal which cannot be achieved is kept before us it would weaken our enthusiasm or urge for working as there will be no hope of achieving it at any time. This is the risk in keeping an impossible ideal before oneself. If, however, the ideal which while it cannot be achieved by all men, can be realised even by a few, is kept before us, it would enthuse and enable human society to work for reaching that ideal.'

We discussed many other questions and many of our mutual doubts were clarified to a great extent. When I met Vinobaji a few times afterwards, I found that he did not start any discussion on any subject himself and that a discussion would take place only if I had to ask something or say something. I had nothing more to discuss with him after the exhaustive discussions I had at Berhampore. I was also not going to him as a disciple and I had no desire to start any discussion myself. I therefore felt that it was not useful for me to meet him as long as he did not desire to discuss something. We therefore scarcely meet now.

Sometime after the above-mentioned discussion Vinobaji had arranged for a meeting of the leaders of all parties at Mysore. It was attended by Jawaharlalji and I had accompanied him. We discussed the bhoodan movement there. Most of those present felt that maximum cooperation should be given in this work. However I got the impression that the propaganda that was going on was one-sided or what could be called a bit rigid. Many people had donated large areas of land in several states, but the work of redistribution of those lands was not proceeding at sufficient speed.

When Vinobaji started the movement of *gramdan* (donation of villages) I did not consider it very practical and advantageous. I lost my faith in the movement when gramdan was converted into *jilladan* (donation of districts) as I felt that no useful purpose would be served by such donations which were more unreal than real. If I could see two or three villages donated and the aims of the movement carried out successfully in those villages, my faith would be restored, but nobody has yet been able to take me to such villages. Perhaps they do not exist. I have no doubt that *jilladan,* would be only a paper donation.

Vinobaji considers his movement most essential. I discussed this matter with him but could not persuade him to see my point of view. I understood that Vinobaji is carrying on the bhoodan movement in order to increase the spirit of sacrifice amongst the people. If the spirit of sacrifice becomes general and the desire for material enjoyment becomes secondary, human society would be developed in the true sense in my view. The spirit of sacrifice must, however, be real and voluntary. There is a spirit of sacrifice in donating land. But the same cannot be said about *gramdan* and *jilladan*. Any movement for generating the spirit of sacrifice is beneficial in my view, but such a movement must be one that can be easily understood or digested by the common man, otherwise it will encourage hypocritical behaviour and will not strengthen the sentiment of sacrifice. (A detailed note on the discussions with Vinobaji at Berhampore is given in Appendix 3.)

10

Bombay to Delhi

JAWAHARLALJI WANTED to take me to Delhi a year after I took over as Chief Minister of Bombay State in 1952. Shri Gopalaswami Ayyangar who was a very capable Minister in the Central Cabinet died in 1953. In him Jawaharlalji lost a very valuable colleague in whom he had great confidence. He wrote to me in the first week of February of the same year that I should go to Delhi to help him by joining the Central Cabinet and asked me to think over his suggestion and give him a considered reply.

New Delhi
February 2, 1953

My dear Morarji,

Since Gopalaswami's death the burden of work has been very heavy on me. It was bad enough before. So naturally I have been thinking of some one or more than one coming here and sharing it with me. Your name and Pantji's came to my mind. I feel we must strengthen the Centre. At the same time the States are difficult charges. I am writing to you now so that you might think about it and let me have your reaction.

We shall of course meet for the wc. Please try to come a day ahead—on the 7th March.

Yours sincerely,
Jawaharlal Nehru

I replied:

I am extremely grateful to you for the confidence you have shown in me, but looking to the circumstances prevailing in Bombay State I feel that my leaving Bombay for Delhi is likely to harm the Bombay State and it is possible that it might be in some way harmful to the country also. While I have no particular desire to go to a larger field of activity, I have no doubt in my mind that you have to decide ultimately what use should be made of me and how. You are shouldering a very heavy responsibility for the whole country, and I must help you in whatever way I can. I shall accept whatever decision you may take in the present difficult circumstances.

Jawaharlalji wrote to me that he would discuss this matter with me when I went to Delhi for the Working Committee meeting in a few days. I had this discussion with him at New Delhi in March. As a result of that discussion, Jawaharlalji also felt that it might be harmful to Bombay State if I left Bombay at that stage.

I had written about this offer to Shri Balasaheb Kher who was in London, as both of us used to take each other's advice in almost all important matters. He also was of the view that it would be better if I did not go to Delhi, but he suggested that if I had to go to Delhi I should take charge of the Home Ministry and not of Defence. As, however, I had decided not to go to Delhi, there was no question of choosing a Ministry for myself.

The Samyukta Maharashtra agitation and riots soon followed. The States Reorganisation Commission submitted its report to the Central Government in September 1955. The Centre had accepted the recommendations of the Commission for separate States of Gujarat and Maharashtra and a centrally governed Bombay city. This, however, led to an intensification of the Samyukta Maharashtra agitation. As a result, the Central Government changed its decision and decided to form the bigger Bombay State consisting of Maharashtra, including the city of Bombay, Vidarbha, Marathawada and Gujarat. I had decided to give up the Chief Ministership of Bombay State on the formation of the bilingual Bombay State, and to engage myself in constructive work. When I talked about this to Jawaharlalji, he pressed me to join the Central Cabinet. On the day after the decision for the bigger Bombay State was taken by the Congress Working Committee, Jawaharlalji called me to his residence and said: 'As you have decided to relinquish the Chief Ministership of Bombay State, you should join the Central Cabinet and take up the responsibility of the Finance Ministry as Shri C. D. Deshmukh has resigned.' I replied: 'I have already completed sixty years of my life and it is my view that it would be better for me not to remain in any position of power. I have, therefore, no desire to take up any position of authority. I shall continue to serve the people as a non-official through the Congress.' Jawaharlalji said: 'You can be the President of the Congress also, but it will be better if you come to the Centre.' 'The Presidentship of the Congress is also a position of authority,' I said, 'and I have no desire to take it.' Jawaharlalji then pressed me again to take up the responsibility of the Finance Ministry. I hesitated, saying, 'It will be difficult for me to take up administration of the Finance Ministry as I have not studied economics and have never prepared my own budget. I have no attraction for money and it is therefore difficult for me to look after the Finance Ministry.'

I had forgotten the talk that I had with Jawaharlalji in connection with the Finance Ministership some months earlier, and he reminded me of it on this occasion. Shri Deshmukh had resigned the Finance Ministership when Jawaharlalji consulted me about it. I had then told him that if any minister resigned he should accept the resignation immediately, as otherwise resignation would be used as a threat by some people and would develop into a wrong practice. 'The members of our party,' he said, 'are pressing me to appoint a full party man as finance minister, as so far only non-Congressmen had been made finance ministers. They argue that many difficulties are created as a result of a non-party man becoming a finance minister. I find, however, that there is nobody in the Congress party who is an expert in financial matters and who can take up this responsibility.' I replied that it was not necessary to have an expert as a finance minister, but the man must be a full party man. He asked me to tell him what considerations should be borne in mind, in my view, for the appointment of a finance minister. My reply was: 'Four conditions may be kept in mind while selecting the finance minister:

'1. The person whom you select must be a person in whom you have full confidence, so that he can work with confidence and you also will have the confidence that whatever he does will be done well;

'2. The person so selected must be a full-fledged party man, believing in the ideals and programmes of the party and also in implementing them;

'3. The country must have full confidence in his integrity; and

'4. He should have sufficient intelligence and commonsense to utilise the capacity of experts, so that after consulting several experts he is able to come to a proper decision and implement it properly.'

Jawaharlalji agreed with these criteria and reminded me of it on this occasion, and said: 'You satisfy all these conditions and should therefore accept my suggestion. There is none at present in my Cabinet whom I could select for the Finance Ministry for more than three or four months, as none would be able to carry it on longer. You should therefore accept the Finance Ministership at the Centre.' As he would not take a 'no' from me, I accepted his offer, but added that it was not possible for me to go to Delhi until

I was relieved from Bombay State on the formation of the bigger Bombay State. He then told me that he would retain the Ministry and look after it until 1st of November, when I could take it over. This is how he settled this appointment.

I talked about this only to Dhebarbhai who was the President of the Congress and to none else as I did not consider it proper that such matters should go out prematurely for public consumption. Dhebarbhai told me that the Finance Ministry would put me into difficulty. 'Jawaharlalji would not take a "no" from me and made me agree to accept his offer.' I told Dhebarbhai, 'I have therefore now to work and depend upon God. I have always believed that things will happen according to God's Law.'

Some days later I got a phone call from Jawaharlalji at 9.30 p.m. He told me on the phone: 'I had told you that I would keep the Finance Ministry with me and look after it until you come to Delhi, but difficulties have arisen here in relation to foreign exchange and also internal resources and it is not possible for me to look after the work. I have therefore decided to entrust this responsibility to Shri T. T. Krishnamachari, though this arrangement is temporary. I have also to consider the Commerce and Industry Ministry which is at present with T. T. Krishnamachari. When you come to Delhi we shall think of this and make permanent arrangements.' I told him: 'I had no particular desire in this matter then, nor have I any now. You can therefore make permanent arrangements even now.'

When Jawaharlalji met me in Ahmedabad after this in October, he asked me when I was going to Delhi and told me that he would make an announcement about my appointment as a Minister in the Centre at the end of the month. He asked me which Ministry I would like to take and seemed to have forgotten about the Finance Ministry which he had asked me to take up earlier. I inferred from this that he had entrusted the Finance Ministry to Shri T. T. Krishnamachari not on a temporary basis but permanently. I therefore did not remind him about the earlier decision as I had no desire to ask for any particular Ministry.

Jawaharlalji told me that I could take up the Commerce and Industry Ministry which was vacant at the time or, as an alternative, I could take up the Defence Ministry if I so desired. I had then learnt from a friend who held an important position that T. T. Krishnamachari had advised Jawaharlalji not to entrust the Commerce and Industry Ministry to me and to instead give me the Defence Ministry. I did not know why this suggestion was made or whether he had really given such an advice. I did not say anything about this to Jawaharlalji. When he asked me to choose between the two Ministries, I told him: 'You can put me in charge of whatever Ministry you consider proper and I have no desire to make any selection. But I must make my position clear that if I am entrusted with the Defence Ministry I shall not be able to take an active part in day-to-day party politics. If I am at the head of the Defence Forces, I must keep them out of politics and it would therefore be necessary for me not to take a very active part in party politics.' Jawaharlalji immediately told me that that would not do and that I must take a very active part in party politics and the Congress Working Committee. He therefore ultimately decided to put me in charge of the Commerce and Industry Ministry. It was thus decided that I should join the Central Cabinet in this capacity.

Preparations were being made about this time for the general elections that were to take place in February 1957. Shri T. T. Krishnamachari and Shri G. D. Birla had told me in 1955 that I must undertake the responsibility of collecting funds for the election and that that was the desire of Jawaharlalji. It is possible that this suggestion was made to me as I was the Treasurer of the Congress at that time.

I had seldom collected funds for the organisation. I had only once collected some funds in the names of the different Congress committees in the Bombay State during the 1952 elections. When I was asked to collect funds, I wanted to assure myself about Jawaharlalji's wishes in the matter and talked to him directly, so that nobody could blame me or make any allegations later on against me. Jawaharlalji also told me that I must undertake this responsibility and that that was his suggestion. I therefore undertook the responsibility and told Jawaharlalji that whatever funds were collected would be credited to a bank account in the joint names of himself and me. I opened an account accordingly. Shri T. T. Krishnamachari had promised to help me in this work, but he could do so only indirectly.

I asked a few rich people in Bombay to see me. There were about fifteen or twenty important industrialists and businessmen in Bombay city. I had also talked to some business people of Calcutta as I decided to collect funds from these two cities. I talked to these gentlemen very frankly and told them, 'I am talking to you for the purpose of collecting funds for the elections. You can take the help of others as you consider proper, but I do not want to talk to many people individaully in this matter myself. You can talk to the people who are likely to contribute and whatever money is collected will be credited in a joint account in a bank on your giving me a list of persons contributing to the Fund. If you honestly feel that the country's Government would be run properly and with stability if the Congress gets a majority, you should contribute to this Fund and make arrangements for collection from others. If you do not have that confidence in the Congress, I cannot ask for any contributions from you. My dealings will be the same with all, whether they contribute to the Fund or not. I shall not be able to help more the person who contributes nor will I do injustice to a person who does not contribute to the Fund. You can rest assured that everyone will be treated fairly and properly. I do not therefore want to know the names of the persons who refuse to contribute to the Fund. You should give a list only of those who contribute to the Fund with details of the amounts given by each, so that the accounts can be kept properly and receipts can be sent to the persons concerned.'

I did not apply any pressure on anybody. Shri J. R. D. Tata and one or two other industrialists told me that they would have to take permission from the High Court for giving contributions to the party as there was no provision in their Articles of Association for making contributions to such funds. I told them, 'You can go to a court and ask for permission. I do not want to do anything in a secretive manner and it will be better that you help me openly.' These people then obtained the necessary permission from the High Court.

As far as I remember, I collected about one crore and twenty lakhs of rupees in two years. A sum of Rs. 25 lakhs to 30 lakhs was saved from this amount after meeting the expenses of the 1957 elections. This saving was very useful for the subsequent elections. I received contributions of Rs. 20 lakhs after the elections were over and without my having to remind the persons concerned about it.

There were no complaints in the matter of these collections and no allegations were made while it was known to everybody that these collections were made purely on a voluntary basis. I did not spend a rupee from the fund thus collected by me and the work of distribution of amounts during the elections was done by the President of the Congress and those to whom he had entrusted this work. I only signed the cheques after Jawaharlalji had signed them. I did not recommend anybody for help from this fund. The Gujarat Pradesh Congress Committee had collected funds for itself as also some other State Committees. Only those were helped from this central fund who belonged to States which were very poor and could not collect sufficient funds for themselves.

The Central Congress Parliamentary Board had decided to send a member of the Working Committee as an observer to each Pradesh for the selection of candidates for the general elections of

1957, in order to ensure that the selections were made without any group considerations and that proper candidates were selected. It was also decided by the Board that the person to be deputed to a Pradesh Committee must not belong to that Pradesh. I was entrusted with the task of assisting the Bihar Pradesh Congress Committee. I had shown no preference for any particular State. I had no connection with Bihar at the time except that I knew Shri Sri Krishna Sinha and Shri Anugraha Narain Singh since 1952. I went to Patna in the first week of November. While in all the States, except U.P., outsiders were sent as observers, Pantji and Shri Lal Bahadur Shastri were deputed to U.P. When I learnt about this, I talked to the Congress President Dhebarbhai and told him that the arrangement made by him for U.P. was improper and was contrary to our decision. He told me that Pantji was insistent on his being sent to U.P. and he could not displease him. He also did not know who else could be sent to U.P. I replied that he could have sent me to U.P. and Pantji to Bihar. But he told me clearly that he could not displease Pantji. I then told him that he should not keep both U.P. men for U.P. and he should therefore send some outsider with Pantji to U.P. He then sent Khandubhai Desai in place of Lal Bahadur Shastri to U.P. alongwith Pantji. As I had anticipated, Pantji was displeased by my protest and yet I had to insist on the observance of proprieties.

I was not a Minister when I went to Bihar in the first week of November 1956 as I had given up charge of Bombay State on 1 November and was to take charge of my office in Delhi on 14 November.

I stayed with Shri Babu at Patna. Shri Babu was the next most important leader after Rajendra Babu in Bihar. Anugraha Babu was also one of the prominent leaders there and would have liked to be the Chief Minister also. There was thus some rivalry between the two, which had created group politics to some extent there. I had decided to keep clear of group considerations and had decided to select the best men and women without being influenced in any way. I discussed the matter with all concerned with this object in view and heard all people fully.

The Central Parliamentary Board had suggested the election of 15 per cent women candidates in every state. There was not, however, a favourable climate in Bihar for this purpose. I stuck to my determination to select more women as candidates and in spite of the strong local opposition, I could select some 35 women candidates. Many of the people there expressed their apprehension that most of these women would be defeated. I, however, told them that I could not consider their apprehension valid as the persons who would be voting for the Congress would not refuse to vote for women Congress candidates because they were women. As a matter of fact, I felt that women candidates would get more votes than male candidates, as the women voters would be more enthusiastic to vote for a female rather than a male candidate. I was happy to see that my expectations came true and all but four or five of the women candidates were declared elected.

I had to be very careful in the selection of candidates as the leaders of the two groups were displeased when some of their followers were not selected. I felt that if a candidate had a bad reputation or was unpopular amongst the people, it would be difficult to get him elected. I therefore adhered to my decision not to select such persons. Both sides were unhappy about my decision. Fortunately, they could not make any allegations that I had taken sides with any particular group. Dissatisfaction was expressed about the selection when the Central Parliamentary Party met for making final decisions. In this meeting, Shri Lal Bahadur Shastri pleaded strongly, for including more followers of Anugraha Babu in the list. Six or seven names were changed from the original list of the selection which was done entirely on a non-group basis. I, however, did not consider it proper or useful to raise a dispute in this matter at that stage and did not oppose the amendments. As a result of the changes made, however, some of the candidates lost badly.

11

Union Minister for Commerce and Industry

I TOOK CHARGE of the Union Ministry for Commerce and Industry on the forenoon of 14 November 1956, after being sworn in as Minister by the President. I was given the fourth rank in the Cabinet after the Prime Minister, Maulana Azad and Pantji. I had not talked to Jawaharlalji about this matter at all and he too had not asked me about it.

I was quite new to the work of this Ministry but I had the good fortune of being assisted by two State Ministers, Shri Manubhai Shah and Shri Nityanand Kanungo, both of whom were my friends and gave me full cooperation. Shri S. Ranganathan was the Secretary in the Ministry and Shri L. K. Jha was the Special Secretary for the Industries Department. Soon after taking charge, we framed the new import-export policy as our foreign exchange position was not good.

We had a good reserve of foreign exchange when we attained freedom. A large part of this was used to import consumer goods in the first few years. We had to work out a new policy as I felt that the previous policy had not taken a long-range view. We imposed restrictions on imports and made efforts to increase exports. Exports consisted at that time of the traditional raw materials such as tea, cotton and jute. Ground-nut oil was also exported a great deal, but as the conditions of the people began to improve, ground-nut oil began to be consumed more and more internally, with the result that its price began to go up and the export of this item became more difficult. As we had an adverse balance of payment in the initial years we had to make arrangements for supplies of foreign exchange with other countries. These arrangements used to be made by the Finance Ministry. We had previously made arrangements for Short-term loans, i.e. for periods of 5, 7 or 10 years only, and very little thought was given to getting loans for longer periods. We therefore decided in the new policy to get loans for not less than 15 years. In the beginning, however, we were burdened with heavy repayment responsibilities as the loans were for short periods.

The industrialisation of the country is vital for the removal of poverty in this country. Without industrialisation, it is not possible to provide employment for everybody. There have been two views in this country on this subject. Some people are totally against the establishment of heavy industries and plead that we must have only small and village industries, as very large sums have to be invested for heavy industries which would result in an increasing demand on national finance. On the other hand, many economists hold the view that we must concentrate more on heavy and large industries and that we should not depend on cottage and small industries, as the latter would not employ many people. Both these are extreme views.

It is very vital in India to develop agriculture fully and attention was paid to this from the beginning. In the earlier years we could not make rapid progress in this field as our resources were inadequate and we did not have sufficient expertise and experience. I believe, however, that whatever could be done for agricultural development at that time was done.

The Congress and the Government had decided from the very beginning to adopt a system of planned development for the country. The Congress had accepted this policy even before the advent of swaraj and had undertaken the task of preliminary planning even at that time. As however, the Congress then had no governmental power and the information necessary for planning was not fully available to it, this preliminary planning could not be very realistic or effective. All the same, we made a beginning and this came in handy in our work later on.

After the advent of freedom, the First Five Year Plan was prepared for the years 1951—56. However, one or two years passed before the Plan could be formally sanctioned and implementation was therefore taken up a little late. The first Plan consisted of getting together all the projects that were then on hand or contemplated, with improvements or additions. There was little provision for large-scale industries as we did not have the necessary data for considering such projects.

Special attention was paid to the establishment of heavy and large industries in the Second Five-Year Plan which was prepared for the period 1956-61. This, however, did not mean that this was done at the cost of agricultural development. Some people have been complaining that agricultural development was neglected in the early stages of planning. I cannot agree with this view. Agricultural development cannot be effected merely by spending money or making large plans on paper. More than eighty per cent of our people live in villages and maintain themselves by agriculture in one way or another. More than sixty million families are engaged in it. This number includes agricultural labourers. It was not easy, in a short time, to supply the latest agricultural implements and methods, improved seeds and the necessary training to such a large number of people in this huge country where the means of transport and communications are not adequate. Only the peasants themselves can produce more; Government can only give them facilities. Government cannot undertake agricultural operations itself. It is difficult to increase production as long as the large number of peasants living in our five and a half lakhs of villages do not put in an effort and utilise all the facilities provided by the Government. Our average agicultural production per acre was, at the time of independence, less than one-third that obtaining in developed countries. Even today, the average production has not increased substantially, though there has been some increase.

This country has always had peasants who can compare in diligence and ingenuity with the best of the developed countries, but their number is small and their example was not followed by the bulk of agriculturists.

Agriculture was neglected during the British regime and sufficient means for irrigation and water supply were not created. The Government used to undertake agricultural research on government farms. Some of the experiments conducted were not very useful as they were applicable to methods that were so expensive that an ordinary Indian peasant could not adopt them. Land laws also varied in different parts of the country and many of the agriculturists were tenants. Landlords who held large areas under zamindari, inamdari and jagirdari tenures, did not themselves cultivate their lands but got them cultivated by their tenants. The landlords used to take away half the produce from the tenants and did not supply the tenants with improved seeds or implements. The tenants, the real producers, were thus in a very vulnerable situation and even if they produced more, very little would be left to them. Also production could not be increased without modern implements. The peasants in these circumstances always felt frustrated and had no enthusiasm to work harder. The Congress therefore gave priority to the amendment of land laws. The zamindari system was abolished in U.P., Bihar and other states where it was in vogue. In Bombay State, we passed laws about land ceilings and tenancy but these were not fully implemented.

The policy of fixing a ceiling for agricultural land holdings was not taken up merely to restrict individual ownership of land. Ours is an agricultural country and our prosperity depends largely on the prosperity of our agriculture. There can therefore be no two opinions about the necessity of increasing agricultural production per acre. Grain prices can be controlled only if agricultural production increases sufficiently. Peasants must get the full benefit of their efforts and can do so only if their toil becomes increasingly productive. If production does not increase and only prices go up, the present vicious circle will persist. We must have a low cost economy, that is, the prices of our consumer goods must be low. A reduction in the prices of our consumer goods is possible only if there is a reduction in the cost of production of these items. Production in many industries depends, among other factors, on agricultural raw materials. The prices of agricultural produce can be maintained at a reasonable level only if agricultural productivity is raised to three times what it is today. The peasants can get adequate returns and prices can be fixed reasonably only if there is an increase in production. This is the only way of strengthening our economy.

If prices go on increasing alongwith increasing incomes there cannot be a change for better in the living standards of the large masses of our people. If the units of cultivation are not large, methods of intensive agriculture can be applied and production can be increased and the conditions of the peasants improved. If the units are very large, an individual farmer cannot extract the maximum production from his area, howsoever hard-working he may be; it will be very difficult for him to apply intensive agricultural methods over the whole of his holding.

Agriculture in Japan is a very good example in this connection. There were very large agricultural units in Japan before the last war. At that time, rice production was inadequate. When the country came under the influence of the Americans after the war, Japan changed the land system in the country and distributed the land amongst actual cultivators. The units of agricultural land there now average from 2.5 to 10 acres. This led to a substantial increase in agricultural production and Japan has now become almost self-sufficient in rice. They do, of course, have the advantage of having plenty of water for irrigation. They also use organic and inorganic manure including human urine and excreta fully and scientifically. Agricultural production per acre in Japan is, as a result higher than anywhere else in the world.

In India, we have been able to provide facilities for irrigation for only about 25 per cent of our cultivated lands. These means of irrigation include large canals, tanks, wells and tube-wells. We must make arrangements as soon as possible for increasing all these facilities to such an extent that at least 50 to 60 per cent of our cultivated lands get water for irrigation. We are, of course, making efforts in this direction, but it is necessary to extend them much further and make them more real and extensive. Tube-wells should be provided after making proper geological surveys and assessing the underground water properly. If such surveys are not undertaken, there is danger that many tube-wells will be wrongly located and will run dry in a few years.

Good efforts have been made for the improvement of seeds in our country and they should be continued further. We can increase our average production three times if improved seeds are made available to all peasants, irrigation is supplied wherever possible and a proper and good use is made of natural and artificial manures. If this is done there will be no danger of scarcity of foodgrains or raw materials in this country as a result of increase in population. We should therefore make more intensive efforts in this direction.

It is not possible to give everybody a good standard of living as long as nearly 80 per cent of our population depends on agriculture for its maintenance. If this percentage is reduced to 30 per cent, the problem would be solved. But in order to do this, the surplus population which is at present dependent on agriculture should not be brought to cities, but should be provided with other means of livelihood in their villages. Cottage and village industries are therefore very vital for this purpose.

It is equally clear that the economy of the country cannot become strong without developing large-scale industries also. In the age in which we are living, we cannot do without modern means of transport and communication. Every village must have electricity and the demand for metals will also grow continuously. The production of iron, steel, aluminium, copper and other metals will have to go on increasing. If we do not produce these materials ourselves, we will have to import them, which would make us economically dependent. We have therefore to put up factories to produce these materials and unless we do it we cannot supply cheap electricity to our people or put up large fertilizer factories which are very essential for our development. Cement and steel are used in large quantities in modern buildings and it is, therefore, also necessary to greatly increase the production of cement. To enable these factories to work properly, efficiently and economically, it is essential to produce the necessary machinery in our country as well. It becomes imperative, therefore, to manufacture all these items ourselves if we are to increase agricultural production. Large-scale and heavy industries are, therefore, as necessary as village and cottage industries. If we do not have proper coordination of development in these three directions, our difficulties in the economic field will go on increasing.

We could not think about all these matters when we started our planned development as we then did not have the necessary experience. We gained much of it in the implementation of the Second Five Year Plan, and the need for utilising this experience fully was felt since then. If sound economic policies are consistently pursued, without vacillations, we can make economic progress more speedily.

I began to think of all these problems when I joined the Central Government as I had had no experience in these directions earlier.

As we do not, in all cases, have the necessary technical knowledge and technicians, it is necessary to provide facilities for the establishment of some industries in partnership with foreign investors. We are still backward in some directions. We require technical knowledge for the production of different kinds of machinery which we are not yet able to make here, and if we establish such industries in partnership with foreigners on proper terms, it will be easier to get technical knowledge and technicians and also to train our own technicians. At the same time, we must establish those industries about which we have sufficient knowledge and which we can run ourselves without any outside help. We should not have any partnership with foreigners for such industries.

I had a controversy with two foreign firms after the 1957 elections, after which the Commerce and Industry Ministry continued to be in my charge. These firms were Lever Brothers and the Singer Sewing Machine Company. Both of them wanted to expand their operations in this country. Lever Brothers wanted to extend their production of soap on a large scale, and the Singer Sewing Company wanted to establish a factory in this country.

The soap industry had developed very well in this country but half the production was made by Lever Brothers while the other half was distributed amongst Indian producers like Godrej, Tata and other smaller units. The soap produced by Godrej, Tata and others was in no way inferior to that produced by Lever Brothers. Some of the items were even better. Lever Brothers had their factories spread all over the world and controlled large resources. If they were allowed to extend their operations in this country, Indian producers would suffer a great deal and the competition would be one-sided. I therefore told the President of Lever Brothers with whom I had a discussion that they could not be given permission for expanding their production of soap. He felt very unhappy and asked me whether I did not want to allow foreigners to continue their operations in this country. I told him, 'Your inference is not correct. We do want foreign participation, but not at the cost of our indigenous development. Our relations can be strengthened only if there is benefit to both sides. But where we would suffer by such relations we cannot have them. I hope you will appreciate our point of view. If you desire to increase your production or extend your activities in this country, we would give you permission only if you undertake the production of goods which are not produced here at present.'

The Singer Sewing Company also wanted to establish a factory here and had selected an Indian industrialist as a partner who came to see me. The Singer Sewing Company people did not come. The Indian industrialist tried to persuade me to accept his proposal and told me that the country would be very much benefited if this factory was established here. Our indigenous production of sewing machines like Usha and others had developed very well and produced enough for our requirements. The production was such that it even enabled us to export some machines after meeting our requirements. I therefore told the industrialist, 'If you are given permission for establishing this factory, as proposed by you, our indigenous producers will not be able to compete as the resources of Singer Sewing Company are vast in comparison to those of our producers. We do not require further production by a foreign company. It is not therefore possible to give permission for this project.' The industrialist was very much displeased and told me somewhat excitedly that my attitude only meant that foreigners were not to be allowed to work in this country. I told him, 'You are not considering the interest of our country and are thinking only of your own interest. You would like to benefit yourself even at the cost of the country. I do not see why you are not able to appreciate this simple matter.' He took it ill. I, however, told him very clearly that I could not accept this proposition. He felt that I was against him personally which was not correct. When this gentleman came to see me for some other work after some time, I did help him and he was convinced that I had nothing against him personally.

I remained in charge of the Commerce and Industry Ministry for a year and four months, until March 1958, and obtained very valuable experience during this period.

Efforts were being made at that time to modernise the textile industry and there were demands for the introduction of automatic looms in textile mills. It was necessary to do so as such a step would lessen the cost of production and would enable us to export more cloth. But labour unions opposed these demands on the plea that it would lessen the employment of textile labour. Even though they were assured that modernisation would be done only on condition that there was no loss in employment, the labour union people did not agree. It was therefore not possible to make any effective progress in this direction.

Some time back the Khadi and Village Industries Board was established for encouraging small cottage and village industries. This was converted in 1957 into the Khadi and Village Industries Commission. Shri Vaikuntbhai Mehta who was the Chairman of this Commission had great faith in the development of khadi and village industries. I was always ready to assist him in his work and helped him as much as I could.

In the course of my tours in different parts of India for the elections of 1957, some people threw stones in a meeting at Godhra in Gujarat, and efforts were made to disturb my meetings in Ahmednagar and other places in Maharashtra also. The followers of the Janata Parishad in Gujarat resorted to violent methods and the followers of Samyukta Maharashtra Parishad were indulging in similar activities in Maharashtra. Persistent efforts were made to disturb my meetings at Ahmednagar one night, but the people quietly attended to my speech when I faced the disrupters with patience and calmness. The meeting continued till 11.30 in the night and the audience did not move from the meeting till the end. All my meetings in Maharashtra were very well attended and I got the impression that they created a good effect on the voters. This inference was justified by the results of the elections. Many of the candidates from the constituencies I visited were successful, even though the Congress lost in many places in Maharashtra as a whole.

As I had to devote a good deal of time to the task of facing the disturbances created by the Samyukta Maharashtra movement in Bombay in 1956, I could not carry on my daily spinning. I started spinning again in April 1957 and have continued it since then. I had first started spinning in 1929 and was unahppy when this activity was interrupted.

Shri Raghunathji Naik, who was my Additional Private Secretary, used to accompany me on my tours after I went to Delhi, and in the course of a discussion with him during a tour on my practice of spinning one whole hank on one spindle, Raghunathji said that this required patience which was not easy to keep.

He also said that the practice might also be a display of personal vanity. There was some substance in this last argument. On the other hand, however, I told him that this personal vanity increased my capacity for spinning and was therefore not harmful.

I had toured for seven days in June 1957 to see some of the public sector factories. I found a great deal of evidence of bureaucratic working in these factories and gave necessary instructions to change that atmosphere. I believed that these factories could be worked profitably only if they were run in a businesslike manner and that they would not be successful if bureaucratic methods were employed. The factories which I visited were located at Bangalore, Vishakhapatnam, Bhopal, Ranchi, Sindri and Calcutta.

I had visited the Gujarati Association in Madras when I went there at the end of 1956 and in the beginning of 1957. There were some quarrels amongst the workers of the Association. They informed me about the disputes, and I tried to settle them and persuade them to forget their differences and to work together. This advice had good results as I was informed after some time that the disputes had been resolved and the work of the Association was being carried on smoothly.

I had a difference with the Finance Ministry in the middle of 1957, but was able to resolve it after a patient and persuasive discussion. Shri Ranganathan, the Secretary of my Ministry at that time was very helpful in settling the dispute. He was a very able civil servant. He is the nephew-in-law of the then Finance Minister, Shri T. T. Krishnamachari, and they were on very cordial terms. He contributed very objectively to the resolving of the dispute and helped very much in making smooth working arrangements. My personal relations with him were very happy and continued to be so even after I left the Commerce Ministry and went to the Finance Ministry.

I stayed with Shri Ramnath Goenka when I visited Madras in August 1957. There I suffered from food poisoning. I had eaten some over-ripe fruit when I left Bombay and got diarrhoea by the time I reached Madras and the full effects of food poisoning were seen by the evening. I had to stay in Madras for seven days as the attack was very severe. The doctor who treated me told me that the attack was so severe that it would have been fatal if my constitution had been weaker. I could successfully withstand this attack only on account of my strong physique. This was my first experience of food poisoning and I became careful in the future about eating over-ripe fruit. Shri Ramnath Goenka was very worried as I was his guest. I, however, tried to persuade him not to upset himself. However, he continued to be most concerned till I recovered after four or five days.

I became very weak as a result of this illness and had to stay in Madras for two days after I recovered. Ramnathji, his son Bhagwan Das, and daughter-in-law, Sarojben, served me in my illness with very great attention and affection and did everything they could to give me relief from the pain that I was suffering.

When I went to inaugurate the Phalton Sugar Factory in Maharashtra in October 1957, the followers of the Samyukta Maharashtra movement held a black flag demonstration against me, but there was very little strength in that demonstration as the people in general did not cooperate with them. The leaders of the Samyukta Maharashtra Parishad had made many allegations against me in order to create ill feeling against me in Maharashtra, but did not succeed as I had visited all the areas of Maharashtra and served the people of Maharashtra as well as I could from 1937 to 1939 and again from 1946 to 1956. The Samyukta Maharashtra leaders felt that their demand was not accepted only because of my opposition to it and that if they could frighten me somehow and make me agree to their demand, their purpose would be served. Those of the Samyukta Maharashtra people who held communist views were opposed to me on ideological grounds. They believed that I was their determined opponent. Really, I was not the opponent of anybody personally. I, however, certainly opposed the violent and authoritarian methods which were implicit in communist activities. I took all constitutional steps against them very firmly and checked their activities. This is why they disliked me and considered me their enemy. They took advantage of the Samyukta Maharashtra movement to make virulent propaganda against me because of this feeling.

Actually, the demand for Samyukta Maharashtra was not accepted by the Congress Working Committee as all the members opposed it and not because of my opposition. It is true I did not believe in the creation of linguistic states and was in favour of a bilingual Bombay State. I had no doubt that many leaders of the Samyukta Maharashtra movement knew this fact and yet created this opposition against me amongst the people out of political considerations. It was because of all these facts that there was not much strength in the demonstrations staged against me at Phalton.

I attended the Vegetarian Congress held at Banaras in November 1957 as I had been invited to address it. In my address there I explained why I believed that man should be a vegetarian. I, however, made it clear that nobody should be forcibly converted into being a vegetarian and that vegetarians should make propaganda about their beliefs only by their conduct. Vegetarians must not, however, claim that they are better men than non-vegetarians as the choice of food depended upon the ideals and taste of each person.

I delivered the annual address at the Kashi Vidyapith during this visit to Banaras. The Kashi Vidyapith was started in 1920 at the same time as the Gujarat Vidyapith and to serve the same ideals. But I saw in 1957 that Kashi Vidyapith was not governed by those ideals any longer. I saw very little use of khadi there and did not also see the observance of the ideals adopted by the Vidyapith when it was started. I referred to this change in my speech.

I visited Gandhigram in Tamil Nadu at the end of 1957. Shri G. Ramachandran has been conducting a very fine educational institution there based on the ideals of Mahatma Gandhi. I spent some time in the institution and addressed the students. Shri G. Ramachandran in his introduction at that time referred to me as the future Prime Minister. If I had had any idea that he intended to say this, I would have prevented him, as it created antipathy against me in some quarters.

The decimal system began to be introduced in India from April 1957. As this work related to my Ministry I took part in all the discussions relating to it. We decided to introduce the system gradually, as an immediate wholesale introduction of the system would have disrupted the work of many people and it would not have been possible to cope with the difficulties thus created. It was not easy for the people who were not accustomed to the decimal system to adopt it at one stroke. There was no difficulty for the younger generation, but most of the people who were accustomed to the other system had to be given time to get used to it. This was why we decided to introduce this system by instalments. The system had been current in many countries of the world. The adoption of this system in India therefore, was undertaken as it was felt that it would facilitate international transactions. The decimal system makes calculation very easy and once the people are used to it they will forget the other system of work and accounts work would become simpler and easier. This is why this new system was adopted by the Government of India.

12

With Khrushchev and Bulganin

I HAD THE opportunity of welcoming several prominent foreign guests and discussing with them matters of mutual interest while I was Chief Minister in Bombay State and also during the time I was a Minister in the Central Cabinet. I have already referred to my meeting the President of Yugoslavia, Marshal Tito, and the Prime Minister of Canada, Mr. St. Laurent, in 1954 when they visited Bombay.

As I have stated earlier, when there were disturbances in Bombay in November 1955, on account of the Samyukta Maharashtra agitation, the Prime Minister of Russia, Mr. Bulganin, and the Head of the Communist Party of that country, Mr. Khrushchev, were visiting India and visited Bombay also. In view of the disturbed conditions in Bombay city, Jawaharlalji was worried about this visit, but I had assured him that there would be no disturbance while they were in Bombay.

I took the two guests in an open car from the airport to Raj Bhavan and thousands of people had assembled on both sides of the road to welcome them. In spite of this large gathering, there was no disturbance of any kind. In the car I was sitting in the middle and Mr. Bulganin and Mr. Khrushchev were on my two sides. When the people tried to shake hands with them as the car was moving, the two guests were a bit hesitant to respond as they knew about the disturbances on the previous days and were not sure of the temper of the people. When I saw them hesitate, I requested them to sit behind me on the rear seats and I shook hands on their behalf with the people. When I was shaking hands with the people en route, the two guests realised that the people wanted to welcome them by shaking hands and that there was no cause for alarm and they began to shake hands with them without any hesitation.

When the car reached Malabar Hill, there were no groups of people there as there were no residential houses in that locality, and we were free from the crowds. Mr. Khrushchev asked me how this peaceful welcome had become possible when there had been disturbances in the city only two days earlier. I replied that that was due to there being democratic functioning in the country. I felt that he did not like my reply very much and he did not ask me any further questions.

After taking the guests to Raj Bhavan, I handed over to them liquor permits saying that this was necessary as there was prohibition in Bombay City. But Mr. Khrushchev told me, 'You have done well in introducing prohibition. We shall abide by this law and shall not use the permits. We would be very happy if we could introduce prohibition in Russia, but looking to the circumstances prevailing there it is unfortunately not possible to do so.'

When I met him the next day and had a discussion with him, he told me that their policy was to keep good relations with those who were good to them and go against those who did not behave well with them. I told him, 'There is a difference between your policies and ours. It is natural and easy to be good to those who are good to us and such behaviour is expected from every human being. There is no great merit in being good to those who are good to us, but we can claim goodness truthfully only if we return good for evil. That is the policy which we try to follow and that is the difference between our policies.' He did not particularly like what I told him and did not carry on the discussion further.

Mr. Bulganin was the Prime Minister of Russia, whilst Mr. Khrushchev, was the Secretary and Head of the Communist Party. But Mr. Khrushchev constantly impressed upon us that his position was of greater importance than that of the Prime Minister as I could see this also from his behaviour during the visit. We had received instructions from Delhi to treat both of them with equal respect and I carried them out as well as I could.

I took these guests on a visit to the Aarey Colony where we have a dairy established by the Bombay Government and gave them a vegetarian lunch there. It was vegetarian as I did not offer non-vegetarian food to any of my guests. The different items were cooked so well that both guests enjoyed the lunch and expressed their satisfaction. When I was taking them round the Aarey Colony, Mr. Khrushchev was making remarks to the effect that the progress was not satisfactory, referring especially to the programme of artificial insemination which we had just then begun. He also made some critical remarks about the construction operations in the colony.

'You have been developing your country for the last forty years,' I told him, 'whereas we have been working for our development only for the last eight years. We are more advanced today in our development than when we had begun after the advent of freedom. Is it your view, taking into consideration these factors, that we have not made sufficient progress in these few years we have been engaged in the task of development? Do you not think that it would be more useful to us if you expressed your opinion after comparing the conditions in your country and taking into consideration how much you could do in the first ten years of your regime?' Mr. Khrushchev grasped what I was trying to convey and immediately said, 'I did not mean by my remarks that you have made less progress than you could have done. I only wanted to suggest that you should make even quicker progress.' I then said, 'We have adopted a democratic way of life after taking into consideration the progress that has been made in the different countries of the world. We hope and trust that we shall be able to make faster progress in the next forty years than you have done in your country. The progress will appear slow in the beginning, but it will become faster after sound foundations have been laid in the first few years.' Mr. Khrushchev replied that he could not say anything about it. I told him that that was what we thought would be possible.

I saw the effect of the frank views which I had expressed to these two guests when they departed from Bombay City. Amongst those who were bidding goodbye to them were the Governor, the Mayor, Ministers and myself and some prominent citizens. Mr. Khrushchev invited the Governor, the Mayor and other friends who were there, to Russia but he did not invite me. This clearly indicated that the differences of view which I had expressed in our discussions had prejudiced him against me. The citizens of Bombay had welcomed both these guests very warmly and the reception was absolutely voluntary. The Government had made no particular arrangements for it. As these two leaders had left Russia for the first time and were visiting India, the citizens of Bombay had naturally a great curiosity to see them. This was why there was so much enthusiasm and warmth in the magnificent reception that was given to them by the citizens of Bombay.

Mr. Aneurin Bevan, one of the important Ministers of the Labour Cabinet in England, came on a visit to India in 1958 when I was Finance Minister at the Centre. He expressed a desire to discuss with me the prohibition policy that we had adopted and told me in his talks with me that he wanted to persuade me to give up prohibition so that we could get good revenue from liquor taxes.

He came to my place in Delhi for a discussion and we discussed the question for more than an hour. I explained to him why it was extremely essential to have prohibition in this country for raising the standards of the poor and for the regeneration of

India, particularly for the welfare of the poor. He argued with me very frankly and I did the same.

As the arguments in favour and against prohibition are well known, I do not want to give them at length here. But when I gave some facts I found that Mr. Bevan was very much struck by them. I told him, 'There is great difference in the conditions of India and other countries. The majority of the people in India are ordinarily vegetarians; while those believing in vegetarianism and observing it as a rule would be only twenty to twenty-five per cent of the population, the percentage of the people who actually take vegetarian diet on account of economic conditions and circumstances would be about 80 per cent. From a study of the effects of liquor on human beings, I have come to the conclusion that liquor has a far more adverse effect on vegetarians than on non-vegetarians. Liquor generally affects first the food generally taken and as a result in the case of non-vegetarians it has a less adverse effect on their bodies, whereas its effect on the vegetarians is very severe and it also affects their minds. While the majority of non-vegetarians are able to save themselves from becoming addicts, the vegetarians are so badly affected by liquor that they are not able to keep control over themselves and many of them, especially the poor, become addicts. In order, therefore, to strengthen the poor people mentally, physically and economically, it is necessary to save them from the temptation of this evil habit. This is why it is necessary to have prohibition in this country and it is for this reason that prohibition has been provided in the Constitution of India. There is no such provision in the Constitution of any other country in the world.'

Mr. Bevan learnt these facts for the first time when I told him about them and told me at the end of the long discussion that he did not want to press me further to give up prohibition as there was much substance in my arguments.

Mr. Bevan, a Labour Leader, was a brilliant and capable servant of the people. He was a Cabinet Minister in England and a friend of India. Our relations became stronger as a result of the discussion I had with him.

13

Union Finance Minister

A QUESTION ABOUT the Mundhra episode was raised in the Lok Sabha at the end of 1957 by Shri Feroze Gandhi There were serious allegations against the companies run by Shri Haridas Mundhra concerning forged share certificates. Shri Mundhra had been given loans by the LIC. Allegations were made against Shri T. T. Krishnamachari that he was responsible for giving these loans to Shri Mundhra. This created a storm in Parliament and Shri Chagla, who was then the Chief Justice of the Bombay High Court, was appointed to make an enquiry into this episode. Shri G. R. Kamat was the Chairman of the Life Insurance Corporation at that time, and Shri H. M. Patel was the Principal Secretary in the Finance Ministry. They had discussed the question of loans and some instructions were given to Shri Kamat at the end of the discussion. The loans were given to Shri Mundhra by the LIC as a result of those instructions.

When this enquiry was going on, at the end of 1957 or the beginning of 1958, Shri T. T. Krishnamachari offered his resignation to Jawaharlalji who discussed this matter with Shri T. T. Krishnamachari and me together. I said to Shri Krishnamachari, 'If this resignation is tendered before the enquiry is over it will mean that you have accepted the allegations. You have said very specifically that the loan was not advanced on account of any pressure or on improper grounds. The resignation therefore should not be offered.' Jawaharlalji accepted my suggestion. I think this episode took this serious shape as the reply given by Shri Krishnamachari in the Lok Sabha on this question was not very specific and was not considered satisfactory.

Shri Chagla in his enquiry, examined Shri Krishnamachari, Shri H. M. Patel and Shri Kamat and all the other connected with the loan. Some members of the Congress Parliamentary Party had helped the lawyers who were working against Shri T. T. Krishnamachari as they felt that his action was wrong. Shri Chagla completed his enquiry and handed over his report to Shri T. T. Krishnamachari as the latter had appointed the Enquiry Commission. He had criticised Shri T. T. Krishnamachari in the report.

Shri T. T. Krishnamachari went to Jawaharlalji as soon as he received the report and pressed him to accept his resignation. Jawharlalji accordingly accepted it. Shri T. T. Krishnamachari relinquished charge at the end of the first week of February 1958. I had heard at that time from some friends that Shri T. T. Krishnamachari had a feeling that I had some hand in the way the enquiry went. I therefore had a talk with Shri Krishnamachari on the matter and asked him whether he had any such doubts about me. He immediately told me that he had none and that some people were circulating such rumours in order to create bad feelings between us. I had absolutely no idea about this matter before this question was raised in Parliament and did not take any interest in it or in the enquiry after I learnt about it. I had not even a suspicion in my mind that Shri T. T. Krishnamachari had done anything improper. Therefore, when Maulana Saheb told me at the Republic Day Party that Shri T. T. Krishnamachari should immediately resign, I told him that I did not agree with him. I feel Maulana Saheb was prejudiced against Shri T. T. Krishnamachari. I explained to the Maulana why I did not agree with him in this matter. Shri T. T. Krishnamachari left for Madras immediately after handing over charge of office. This happened, as far as I remember, in the first ten days of February 1958.

Maulana Saheb passed away on 22 February and the country lost one of its greatest nationalist Muslim leaders. The loss was an irreparable one.

Jawaharlalji encountered no difficulty in presenting the budget on the last day of February as Shri T. T. Krishnamachari had already prepared it before he left. A few days after the presentation of the budget, Jawaharlalji called me and Pantji to his office and discussed with us the future of the Finance Ministry. I had had no discussion with Jawaharlalji or anybody else in this matter before this. When the three of us met, Jawaharlalji told me that I must take charge of the Finance Ministry as he had decided, after considering all the sides of the question, that I should be given this responsibility. To this I replied: 'I am not willing to undertake this responsibility as I feel that if you entrust me with it, Shri Krishnamachari will be confirmed in his prejudice against me. Looking to the past history, the rumour which has been circulated by some people that I had a hand in the enquiry against him would also be confirmed.' Jawaharlalji did not accept this. 'You should not be affected by such false rumours,' he said, 'Everybody knows that you have had no hand in it.' I then suggested to Jawaharlalji that he should hand over this charge to Pantji as he had been considered a great financial expert when he was in the old Central Legislative Assembly and even now had a deep knowledge of this subject. But Pantji refused to accept this responsibility and told me that I was equally fit for it. He also said that he was not prepared to travel abroad, which would be necessary if he became Finance Minister. It was also very clear that Pantji did not want to give up the Home Ministry. I felt that Jawaharlalji also did not want to shift him from that Ministry. Both of them thus did not accept my suggestion, and I had to accept the responsibility. I thus took charge of the Finance Ministry on 22/23 March 1958.

Though Jawaharlalji had presented the budget to the Lok Sabha, I had to pilot the Finance Bill and had also to reply to the debate. Thanks to my long administrative experience and knowledge of practical economics and thanks also to the help of experts, even though this was quite a new subject for me, I did not have much difficulty either in replying in the House or in administering the Ministry. Several difficult questions had cropped up and deficit financing was on the high side. Sufficient resources for expenditure could not be provided by additional revenue in the budget and there was also a deficit in the foreign exchange availability. All these factors put the Second Five Year Plan into a very difficult situation. I had to find a way out of these difficulties.

Soon after I took charge of the Finance Ministry in March 1958, Jawaharlalji appointed Shri B. Gopala Reddy as a Minister of State in the Finance Ministry. He had first thought of giving Shri Gopala Reddy independent charge of a department from the Finance Ministry, but when I told him that that was not possible, Jawaharlalji agreed and left to me the decision about the allotment of work to Shri Gopala Reddy. Shri B. R. Bhagat had been Deputy Minister in the Finance Ministry since the Cabinet had been formed and continued in that position. Jawaharlalji then expressed a desire to appoint Shrimati Tarakeshwari Sinha as a Deputy Minister in the Finance Ministry and asked for my agreement. I told him that there was no need to ask me about it, and I agreed. Shrimati Tarakeshwari Sinha was quite suited to the work which was entrusted to her. I allotted responsibilities to these three colleagues and passed orders enabling them to take decisions themselves on subjects allotted to them, without consulting me, except when questions of policy were involved or when they considered it necessary to take my advice. I had also directed that if there was a difference of opinion between them and the Secretaries of the Ministry, I should be consulted. But such occasions were very rare. Whenever there was any difference, I generally accepted the view of my colleagues. If I did not agree with their view, I discussed the matter with them and if they agreed with my view at the end of the discussion I used to decide matters accordingly.

The Secretaries worked very well under this arrangement, and there was cooperation amongst all concerned. I had also given instructions to the Secretaries that they should record their honest opinions without any hesitation. If the minister differed from their view, he could pass orders accordingly, giving reasons for his different view, but it was always insisted that the Secretaries should give their independent opinion on every matter.

I went to Montreal in Canada to attend the Conference of Commonwealth Finance Ministers in September/October 1958. I will deal with this visit later on.

I returned for the annual meeting of the World Bank which was held in India that year. Its meeting was held in Vigyan Bhavan which, alongwith the Ashoka Hotel, had been constructed some time earlier for such international conferences and meetings. If these two had not been constructed, it would have been difficult to hold such international meetings or conferences in this country. It was at first thought that Ashoka Hotel should be set up as a joint venture of private and State capital, and the Jam Saheb of Nawanagar was a large shareholder in the venture. But as he withdrew from the arrangement later on, government undertook the whole construction and, as far as I remember, the construction of the hotel was completed in nine or ten months.

A large number of people attended the World Bank meeting, and arrangements for accommodation were made very carefully from the very start. Our foreign guests were happy with the arrangements made and expressed their satisfaction publicly.

Mr. Eugene Black was the President of the World Bank at that time and Mr. Per Jacobson was the Managing Director of the International Monetary Fund. I had got acquainted with them on my visit to Washington before this meeting. I came in closer contact with them after the meeting in Delhi of these two bodies, and I got very close cooperation from them whenever the questions relating to India were discussed in the World Bank meeting and we were able to sort out things satisfactorily. After discussions Mr. Black organised a consortium of the countries which wanted to help India for its development. This included USA, England, Germany, France, Italy, Japan and Canada. This arrangement proved very useful in arranging international help for India whenever required. It lessened some of the difficulties we encountered in the execution of the Second Five Year Plan and continues even now. A similar consortium was arranged also for Pakistan sometime later.

We also received help from Russia and its allies and we made several agreements with them. We had made special trade arrangements with these countries and trade with them expanded steadily. Transactions with these countries were not in foreign exchange but in rupees. These trade relations expanded a great deal in subsequent years. As our imports from these countries were larger than our exports to them, the imports cost us more and our exports to them were sometimes at less than the appropriate market rates. Some of the goods exported to these countries were therefore sold by them to other countries. Such transactions, however, were very few and Russia never did this. Our trade relations with Russia therefore went on developing year by year.

As I have said earlier, handling the Finance Ministry was quite a new experience for me. Even though I had not been willing to undertake it, I was not diffident about being able to do so. I have always been confident that all administrative work can be done efficiently with commonsense, understanding and close study. I had to administer the Finance Ministry and to mobilise the necessary resources for the developing economy of the country. While I had no direct contact with this subject when I was Chief Minister in Bombay State, I did maintain very close contact with the Finance Ministry there. Even though the Finance Department of the Bombay State was much smaller than the Finance Ministry at the Centre, and its work was much more limited, the principles which governed the husbanding of resources in both cases and other financial considerations were similar. So the work of the Finance Ministry was not quite new to me. Nevertheless, I did face a difficult task as, when I took over the Finance Ministry at the Centre, the position concerning internal and external resources was difficult.

The First Five Year Plan was completed in 1956 and the Second Five Year Plan began from 1956-57. While the First Five Year Plan was a beginning and was not a result of a comprehensive consideration of all factors, it was executed very successfully. The goals of the First Plan were fulfilled to a large extent. Bombay State had not only carried out its obligations fully but had even exceeded its targets, though the State had received minimum help from the Centre. Bombay State is generally considered economically strong, and rightly too. It has more resources than other

States and is therefore ahead of them both politically and economically. Its administrative machinery also is considered better than that of other States in the country.

As the First Five Year Plan ending in 1956 was executed efficiently and successfully, India had earned a good reputation internationally. A very favourable world opinion was created as regards the administrative efficiency of the Indian Government and those in charge of it. International institutions and experts were therefore recommending the example of India to other undeveloped countries as worth emulating.

The Second Five Year Plan was conceived on a much larger scale. It was almost double the size of the first and new targets were set. Emphasis was laid on physical planning alongwith financial planning and provisions were made for developing large-scale industries. The manufacture of iron and steel was particularly included in the Plan. This also added to the reputation of India in foreign countries.

The Second Five Year Plan was more ambitious than the first, but sufficient thought had not been given to the question of resources required. A difficult situation had therefore arisen in the first two years of the plan, when I took charge of the Finance Ministry. Great difficulties were experienced in husbanding internal financial resources and even greater difficulties were encountered in providing external resources in the form of foreign exchange. Our foreign exchange reserves were depleted by 200 million dollars in the very first two years. We had, besides, spent the loan which we had taken from the International Monetary Fund. A very serious question was therefore posed about the successful implementation of this Plan. It was in these circumstances that I became the Finance Minister. Shri B. K. Nehru was the Secretary in the Economic Affairs Department, Shri N. N. Wanchoo was the Secretary, Expenditure, while Shri A. K. Roy was the Chairman of the Revenue Board. Shri M. V. Rangachari was Special Secretary in charge of budget preparation. Shri H. M. Patel was the Principal Secretary in the Ministry, but he had left it when he came under a cloud in the Mundhra episode, and I did not fill that vacancy. Prof. J. J. Anjaria was the Economic Adviser, and Dr. I. G. Patel was his deputy. All these officers were very capable and efficient and were also very good administrators. I did not therefore have much difficulty in understanding and solving the difficulties that I faced in the Finance Ministry.

It was decided to collect the necessary internal resources through loans and also to curtail unnecessary Government expenditure. There was a Special Staff Inspection Unit working in my

Ministry at that time, which was examining possible measures of economy and pruning of unnecessary expenditure. This unit was under the charge of Shri Inderjit Singh who was also a very capable officer.

Long and protracted negotiations in foreign countries proved necessary for making arrangements for our foreign exchange requirements. This required constant action by us in those countries. As we got into difficulties in India in these matters, the confidence that the other countries had in India was somewhat shaken. It had to be regained and increased. Therefore, with the agreement of Jawaharlalji, I decided to create a special office of Commissioner-General in Washington for looking after this work. I selected Shri B. K. Nehru for this post as he had very wide and useful experience of foreign countries. He had a deep knowledge of economic matters and was also very prompt in his work. We also had confidence in each other and he had the capacity of thinking independently and suggesting new schemes.

When Shri B. K. Nehru took up this post at Washington, I did not fill in the resultant vacancy in the Ministry as I did not feel the necessity of having more than three Secretaries. I thus reduced the number of Secretaries from 5 to 3, and entrusted both the Economic Affairs and the Revenue Department to Shri A. K. Roy.

I had instructed the Staff Inspection Unit to first look into the Finance Ministry and particularly its Economic Division. The Unit suggested substantial economy measures after inspecting it. When the Economic Division would not agree to the suggestions for effecting economy in expenditure, I discussed the question with them and persuaded them to accept them. This made the work of persuading other Ministries to effect economy in their expenditure easier. There is a saying, 'Charity begins at home', which means that as long as a person does not begin to act himself he cannot expect others to act. This was why I started with the Finance Ministry when taking measures to effect economy in Government expenditure.

We were convinced that it would not be possible to mobilise all the required resources for the successful completion of the Second Five Year Plan and realised the danger of failure in achieving the Plan targets if necessary changes were not made in the Plan after proper consideration. I therefore discussed these matters with the Planning Commission and Jawaharlalji. All agreed to consider the whole thing fully and to take necessary action in order to ensure that the core of the Plan was implemented. We accordingly considered the whole matter, fixed the targets anew and decided to mobilise the necessary resources. The Planning Commission was extremely helpful in these considerations and decisions. The work was satisfactorily done in cooperation between the officers of the Planning Commission and the Finance Ministry.

After sending Shri B. K. Nehru to Washington as Commissioner-General I sent Shri T. Swaminathan to Europe and his headquarters was kept at Brussels. He was to work under the general supervision of Shri B. K. Nehru. They were also given the necessary assistance of other officers. The consortium that I have referred to earlier was formed a few months after these arrangements had been made. I had very frank and useful discussions with the members of the consortium and the Managing Director of the International Monetary Fund and was able to create confidence in them that India would be able to overcome the crisis and advance speedily with its development programme.

We had curtailed the Second Five Year Plan to some extent, as a result of which foreign exchange requirements had lessened. Whatever was then required was provided by the consortium.

Besides this, we also received help from the PL 480 loans of the USA in the form of grain, cotton and other agricultural raw materials. This facilitated the work of implementing the revised Second Five Year Plan fully. We also got substantial help from Russia and its allies.

The Second Five Year Plan was completed in 1961 when the Third Five Year Plan came into operation. On account of the good relations that had been created between us and the Aid India Consortium, they had, before its commencement, assured us of giving the necessary help for the Third Five Year Plan. Russia had assured us of help to the extent of 1,500 million roubles (roughly 1,600 million dollars) for the Third Five Year Plan. When we asked Russia to make a provision in the agreement for the Third Five Year Plan for an increase in the amount, Russia flatly refused and said that nothing more than 1,500 million roubles could be given by them for the Third Five Year Plan. We had to accept this position at that time, but later this amount was increased, after my visit to Russia in 1960.

The World Bank and the consortium sent out a deputation of three wise men in 1960 to assess our condition. The deputation consisted of Sir Oliver Franks of the UK, Dr. Herman Abs of West Germany and Mr. Allen Proul of the USA. This deputation had long talks with many of us, as a result of which they were convinced about the efficiency of the Indian Government and they sent a very favourable report about India to the World Bank and the consortium. This facilitated our task of getting the required foreign exchange. Another deputation under the leadership of Mr. Hoffman visited us after the Oliver Franks Mission had gone. They too made a very favourable report about India.

While we encountered difficulties in implementing the Second Five Year Plan, we started well with the Third Five Year Plan owing to these arrangements and reports. This became possible because of the confidence created in the heads of the international institutions and in the foreign governments concerned about the political honesty and efficiency of India. The help rendered in this task by the officers of the Finance Ministry was notable. These arrangements could not have been successfully made without them.

The Third Five Year Plan which was drawn up in 1960 was much larger than the second. There was pressure for making it even larger, but I firmly said that there was a danger of more harm than good being done if we drew up a larger plan than was warranted by the resources that we could mobilise, as we had actually experienced in the Second Five Year Plan. But the pressure continued. Professor Anjaria, Economic Adviser both to the Finance Ministry and the Planning Commission, had given full estimates of the maximum resources that we could mobilise, and the Third Five Year Plan was based on these estimates. Pressures then began to be applied for mobilising even more resources than those assessed. This worried Professor Anjaria and he felt that he would have been wiser if he had given a figure less than the maximum that could be mobilised, and would thus have saved himself from the trouble that was now created for him.

I tried to explain to Jawaharlalji in this connection that the strategy of our Plan should be such that we should accomplish more than we plan for and not less. 'If we are able to accomplish more than we plan,' I said, 'greater enthusiasm and hope would be created in the country and the self-confidence of our countrymen will be enhanced and it will also create a healthy impression on foreign countries. If, however, we accomplish less than what we have planned for, the opposition parties will utilise this failure against us. The people will be frustrated and foreign countries also may have less confidence in our capacity. We must not repeat the mistakes of the Second Five Year Plan. It is true that our needs are very great and the demands of the people are even greater. This is very natural under our circumstances. But if we do not keep our limitations in mind and plan only on the basis of our desires and hopes, we shall not be able to develop speedily and will also lessen our capacity.' Jawaharlalji accepted my viewpoint and the line of action, and yet, as he did not have a very deep understanding of financial problems and was also an optimist, he was always trying for more ambitious plans. In spite of accepting the efficacy of my strategy, he did not give up his pressure for expanding the Plan. While he accepted the Plan put before the Cabinet by the Planning Commission, he made a very clever move in the National Development Council when the Third Plan was discussed there, being influenced by the pressure of some colleagues to make a last-minute effort to provide for the mobilising of more resources than were assessed. When he spoke about the proposed Third Five Year Plan in the meeting, he referred to the necessity for raising our targets and encouraged other members to take up that line. This added to my difficulties. He asked me soon after he had finished his speech whether I wanted to speak immediately after him. I felt, from the way he asked this, that he was afraid that if I spoke soon after him the members of the Council might not have enough couragc to make proposals for expanding the Plan after my presentation of the facts about financial resources. He thought, I felt, that he might succeed in getting the targets raised if other members of the Council pressurised me for expanding the provision of resources before I spoke. I myself did not want to speak immediately as I felt that if I replied to the arguments advanced and the questions raised by the other members after they had spoken, it would be easier for me to check their pressure. I therefore decided to speak after all had spoken. This suited Jawaharlalji.

Jawaharlalji had appointed a committee consisting of Shri Y.B. Chavan, Shri C. Subramaniam, Shri Mohanlal Sukhadia and one or two others, before the meeting of the National Development Council, to consider the proposed Third Five-Year Plan and to submit a report to the Council. I did not take part in the deliberations of this Committee as I did not want to be bound by the conclusions of the Committee concerning mobilising more resources. I was prepared to accept their proposals if they were capable of being implemented, but I was particularly anxious to see that the mistakes committed in the Second Five Year Plan were not repeated in the third, as a result of an assessment based on hopes rather than realities.

Jawaharlalji then asked Shri Y. B. Chavan who was then Chief Minister of Maharashtra to speak about the Committee's report. Shri Chavan made some introductory remarks and left it to Shri Subramaniam, then Finance Minister of Madras State to speak at length. Shri Subramaniam argued for expanding the Plan and urged that the question should be tackled in a courageous manner. Among other things, he argued that steps should be taken to get larger profits from public sector undertakings for increasing resources, so that the Plan could be expanded. He argued that it was necessary to do so for making speedier development of the country possible. He then gave a call : 'We must dare and do.' Jawaharlalji complimented Shri Subramaniam on his speech and said that it was very specific, lucid and full of vigour. Jawaharlalji thus gave him a certificate for effective presentation.

The other members took the cue from Shri Subramaniam. When all of them had finished their presentations, Jawaharlalji asked me to give my views. I clarified in the very beginning that I did not know whether I would be able to speak with as much clarity and lucidity as Shri Subramaniam, but that whatever I said would have relation to facts and not to emotions. Whatever I presented would be done with practical realism, keeping our limitations in mind.

I presented all the facts about resources to the Council. I described in detail how we passed through difficulties in the Second Five Year Plan and how it had to be curtailed as a result. I conceded that, perhaps, there would be some more profits from the public sector projects, but I added that I would not be surprised if there were more losses. I emphasised the necessity of approaching the problem of mobilising resources on the basis of facts rather than on the basis of speculation. I said that the Finance Ministry could not adopt the methods of the Stock and Share Brokers Association, but must think of mobilising maximum resources by taking due precautions against pitfalls. If the Finance Ministry adopted a speculative line of action the country would be ruined. I then showed that the arguments made for expanding the Plan were not based on realities. In reply to the call given by Shri Subramaniam 'to dare and do', I said that it would be better if he applied that call to himself. I pointed out to him that he had made no provisions for raising extra resources in the budget that he had just at that time presented to the Madras Assembly. I could not see any courage therefore in what he had done. I had, on the contrary, imposed many taxes in the Central budget that was presented, even though it was election year. This made clear who was capable of showing courage. I did not believe in being courageous beyond one's limit and then retreating from one's position. When I presented the whole matter thus, very firmly and clearly, all the members accepted my arguments and Professor Anjaria was relieved of his worry.

14

My First Foreign Tour

Sometime after I became Finance Minister in the Central Cabinet in March 1958, it became necessary for me to go abroad. Shrimati Vijaya Laxmi Pandit, who was High Commissioner for India in London at that time, sent me a message and also asked me, when she came to India, whether I would visit the UK as the British Prime Minister, Mr. Harold Macmillan, wanted to invite me there. The annual meeting of the World Bank was to be held in India that year and it was not necessary for me to go abroad, but Mr. Macmillan wanted me to visit Britain. I replied to Smt. Vijaya Laxmi Pandit that if my Prime Minister so desired and I was exempted from vaccination, I had no objection to going to the United Kingdom.

Soon after my talk with Smt. Pandit, Mr. Macmillan came on a visit to India. When I met him, he invited me personally to visit England. I repeated to him what I had told Smt. Pandit. Mr. Macmillan told me that necessary arrangements would be made as regards exemption from vaccination, but added humorously, 'When some of our people who share your views have to get themselves vaccinated in this manner, they get it done but immediately wipe the vaccine off.' I told him that I did not want to do anything wrong and if an exemption was not possible, I had rather not visit the UK. Some years earlier, the American Consul General at Bombay had told me that I would be exempted from vaccination if I visited America. I told Mr. Macmillan this. After Mr. Macmillan's return to England, he wrote to me to say: 'We shall exempt you completely and you can come here without any hesitation. If there is any objection in your country, I would not be able to do anything in the matter.' There was no question of any objection being raised in India. I therefore accepted the invitation to attend the Commonwealth Finance Ministers' Conference at Montreal in Canada in September 1958, and also to visit England and the USA at that time. I went first to England. This was the first time I left India's shores.

I firmly believe that one should not take another life to save one's own. I also believe in nature cure and therefore do not believe in vaccination and I had decided never to be vaccinated. It was therefore not possible for me to go abroad before 1958. I could go abroad only when the countries which I was to visit exempted me from the vaccination rule. I had decided not to go abroad if I was not exempted. As those governments wanted me to visit them, they exempted me from this rule. If, however, I had had a strong desire to visit these countries and if I had not been exempted, my resolve not to get vaccinated might have weakened. I have always been particular about observing the principles in which I believe at the cost of everything else. I was therefore happy that my foreign trip became possible as a result of exemption from vaccination.

Jawaharlalji asked me about the problem of vaccination, and he was somewhat surprised when I told him that I had got a written exemption from Mr. Macmillan, the British Prime Minister.

I reached London in the beginning of September 1958. At London airport, the press people met me and asked me several questions about my refusal to be vaccinated. They specially asked me : 'Don't you feel that you are exposing this country to the danger of infection by coming here without vaccination ? Why do you not get vaccinated ? Do you think you are doing right in acting in this manner ?' I answered : 'I believe in nature cure and also consider vaccination harmful. I also consider that it is wrong morally. I have read the opinions of several people in England who have the same belief. A healthy person has no need of vaccination. It is only the unhealthy who require it. It is therefore not I who am exposing you to danger, but if there is any infection prevailing here, I would be put to danger. Your fear therefore has no basis.' Thereupon they gave up asking me further questions on this subject, and asked me general questions about economic conditions in India.

Mr. Heathcote Emery was the Chancellor of Exchequer in England at that time. He was a fine gentleman of great discretion. I had many discussions with him. One of the suggestions that was made during the discussions he and his colleagues had with me related to charging a higher rate of interest on the loans they would advance. They had held these discussions mainly to make this suggestion. They also wanted to charge 0.75 per cent extra as administrative expenditure on the loans to be given to us.

'I am sorry I do not consider your suggestion proper,' I told Mr. Emery. 'This is not how we dealt with you. When you were in difficlt circumstances, we had £750 million of our reserves with you. When we became free, you were not giving us any interest on these balances. When we proposed to transfer the balances elsewhere so that we could get proper interest, you refused to release them and later on decided to give us interest at only 2.5 per cent. We accepted all this, considering your difficult circumstances and did not quarrel about it. It is not therefore proper that you today put this larger burden on us in the name of administrative expenditure.' The Chancellor saw the point and agreed with my suggestion.

I met the British Prime Minister over a lunch to which he invited me. I was interviewed on television on India's economic problems by four editors of their principal daily papers, one of whom was Mr. John Freeman who later on became the British High Commissioner. The interview lasted half an hour and I was not informed beforehand about the questions they wanted to ask. Mrs. John Freeman, who was then known as Mrs. Katherine Dove, was working in the BBC at that time, and she was entrusted with the task of preparing me for the interview, i.e. to ensure that I would be at ease during the interview. Mrs. Dove first had a trial interview with me and told me frankly that the questions put in the real interview would be quite different. However, the trial interview soon convinced Mrs. Dove that it was not necessary to give me any suggestions as I was quite at ease and that that was my natural temperament. She told me so later on.

The four editors questioned me alternately. They asked me many questions about India and its economic conditions. I gave them clear and specific replies and they had then no more questions to ask. One of the questions asked was : 'You had a large sterling balance here. All that has been used up and you are now asking for loans. Don't you consider that you are now in difficulties because you were not very wise in spending those balances ?' I said in reply: 'I feel there is some ignorance of facts which is responsible for this question. We got this large balance in England as a result of the British Government buying large quantities of raw materials from India during the war. India was not engaged in industrial development at that time. We have now begun to develop our country in a planned manner. We are convinced that it is not possible to remove the poverty in India without industrialising it and it will also not become economically strong without industrialisation. We have therefore to import machinery and even raw materials for the purpose of industrialisation. This is how the sterling balances have been used. We have only started on the development programme and will need to go on making development efforts for years. Looking to the terrific poverty which is, without any comparison, in such a large country, economic experts like you will easily appreciate that the developmental expenditure will go on increasing. If you will consider these facts you will be convinced of the fact that we have made a good use of the sterling balances.

'We are asking for loans from friendly countries who want to help us for our planned development programme, and not in order to become dependent on others. We consider that we should take loans for development purposes if any friendly country is willing to help us in that manner. No country in the world has ever been developed without getting help from outside, and if you all desire that India should develop economically, as you all say you do, you ought to advance the necessary loans. If, however, we do not get such loans, we shall not have any quarrel with or prejudice against anyone. We shall also not accept any conditional loans. It is certain that we shall repay fully whatever loans we take, and we will be able to return all the loans that we have already taken or that we are going to take. There are countries in the world which have not returned loans taken by them, but we do not want to be in that company. It has been an old tradition of India, for more than a thousand years, that anybody who takes a loan returns it and if he is not able to return it before his death his heirs return it. This tradition has continued and nobody need have any doubts about it.'

When I explained to them frankly all these matters, they understood the basic facts and our requirements. They also realised that it was their duty as the principal member of the Commonwealth to help us.

This interview was very well received in England and several people wrote congratulating me on it. The questioners proved more uneasy than the person who was answering their questions. Lord Mountbatten told me afterwards that I had become a television hero. I had a long talk with him and could see that he had a deep interest in the development of India.

I had discussions with the Prime Minister, Mr. Macmillan, about relations between our two countries and the Commonwealth. Lord Home who was one of his Ministers and who later on became the Prime Minister, was also there, and I had a long talk with him too. He gave up his peerage later on when he became Prime Minister. A toast was raised when the Chancellor gave me a dinner and there were some speeches. The Chancellor was known for his great sense of humour and made a very fine speech. Lord Home told me that he had returned from Scotland only for this occasion. I told him in my speech: 'I hope you have found no difficulty in treating a guest like me, as being a vegetarian I did not deprive you of any food which you like.' As Lord Home had returned from Scotland where he had gone for shooting game, I added, 'The birds which must have been saved from your shooting must be thanking me, and you also have therefore to be happy.' He was happy with my humour, and our relations became friendly.

I saw the places worth seeing in England and met the press. There was a press conference in the Indian High Commissioner's Office, where many questions were asked regarding the economic conditions of India, especially because our Second Five Year Plan had got into some difficulties. I informed the press about the assurance that the British Minister had given me regarding helping India after my talks with them.

After completing my visit to London, I flew to America. My journey to Washington from London provided some unusual experiences. I boarded a BOAC plane at night in London. We were to fly straight to New York. This was my first journey to America and I had reserved a sleeping berth as this convenience was available on that plane. I went to sleep at about 10 or 10.30 p.m. and when my sleep was broken at 1.30 a.m. there was complete silence in the plane. This surprised me. When I left my berth, I was surprised to see that the plane was empty and was grounded. There were no other passengers on the plane. There was only a caretaker around whom I asked where we were. He informed me that we had landed at Shannon and that we would be leaving soon afterwards. He did not tell me anything more and I did not ask him for any further information and went to sleep again. When I got up in the morning at about 7 a.m. I again found the plane where it was the previous night. When I enquired about what had happened, the person who was in charge told me that something had gone wrong with the plane and that all the passengers had gone to the airport as this plane would not be able to go further. We would be able to go further only after another plane came from London. I also therefore left the plane and went to the airport where all my co-passengers were sitting. When I asked them what had happened they told me that one of the engines of the plane went out of order when the plane had gone some distance beyond Shannon. It therefore became impossible for it to cross the Atlantic and had to return to Shannon. As one engine had been damaged they had to empty all petrol before landing at Shannon as otherwise there was a danger of an accident. All the passengers were informed about it and the plane went on circling in the air until it emptied all the petrol after which it alighted at Shannon airport. When the passengers were informed about it, it did not disturb my sleep and nobody awakened me either. Many passengers must have felt worried as a result of this incident and might also have been afraid. As I was asleep and nobody waked me I was saved from all worries. I must have been in very deep sleep at that time.

We left Shannon at 11.30 a.m. and reached New York at about 5 p.m. There we had to catch a plane immediately for Washington. Soon after I took my seat in that plane, I was told that that plane would not fly and I had to board another. As there was very little time left, we had to run to the other plane and take our seats there. We thus reached Washington twelve hours late.

This type of travelling was quite a new experience for me. The United States Secretary of the Treasury was to leave Washington soon after seeing me in the morning if I had reached there at the correct time in accordance with his previously fixed programme. But when he learnt that I was to reach late at night, he changed his programme and stayed over in Washington. He met me the next morning and then went out.

I met the President of the World Bank, Mr. Eugene Black, and the Managing Director of the International Monetary Fund, Mr. Per Jacobson, in Washington. I also met Mr. Dulles who was US Secretary of State and Mr. Dillon who was his Under Secretary and later on became Secretary of the Treasury.

My talks with Mr. Dulles were friendly and he showed much interest in the development of India. He appeared to be a simple man with a religious bent of mind; but I also got the impression that he had some prejudice against India.

Mr. Dillon took a deep interest in India and its development. The Singer Sewing Company people must have complained to him that we were not allowing them to establish a factory in India. Mr. Dillon asked me about it during our discussion. 'We readily permit foreign people to establish industries which have not been developed in India,' I explained, 'but the sewing machine industry has developed very well in our country. If we allow a Singer factory in India at this stage, it would be a great blow to the Indian industry. We welcome help from other countries for the development of India, but this help can be taken only on conditions which are of mutual benefit. Where Indian interests are endangered we cannot take such help as you can very easily understand.' Mr. Dillon agreed with me and dropped the matter.

I saw the Lincoln Memorial and other memorials in Washington, including that of George Washington. I also visited some very ancient caves which were situated 70 or 80 miles away from Washington and which were perhaps more than a million years old. I had never seen such caves before. I went to New York from

Washington where I met some leading citizens and from there I went to Montreal.

The conference of the Commonwealth Finance Ministers was held in Montreal and I had to stay there for a fortnight. We were all put up in a very fine hotel on the Railway Station where our conference was to be held. This was a long conference and many questions relating to the Commonwealth were discussed there. The communique which was issued at the end of it specifically stated that the Commonwealth meant that there should be common wealth or prosperity and all should get the advantage of it. No country in the Commonwealth should remain poor, and the Commonwealth should accept that responsibility. This was particularly emphasised.

The Secretary for the Commonwealth, Lord Home, who was also present at this conference, invited me to dinner. He wanted to discuss the Kashmir problem with me during that engagement. Nobody had raised the question of Kashmir in my talks with the British Ministers in London and I did not refer to it myself either. I adopted the practice of not raising any discussion on any subject myself and to give my views only on questions raised by those whom. I met. After we had dined, Lord Home started on the topic of Kashmir. There was nobody else present. He asked me: 'Is it proper that you should refuse to hold a plebiscite to solve the Kashmir question ? There is a great deal of misunderstanding about you in the Western countries in this matter and they have formed an adverse opinion of you.'

He raised this question particularly because Pantji had declared at the end of 1956 that the question of plebiscite did not survive in Kashmir. I had had a discussion with Jawaharlalji two weeks before this declaration during a visit to Delhi. The Kashmir question was being constantly raised and I felt that this matter remained in suspense all the while. Some people even feared that Jawaharlalji might be prepared to give up Kashmir in order to make a compromise if he was pressurised a great deal. I had no such fear or doubt about him and I was sure that, whatever the pressure, Jawaharlalji would never agree to give up Kashmir. But in order to be sure about this matter I asked Jawaharlalji a direct question : 'If circumstances arise when a great deal of pressure is put on you by some people, would you be willing to reach a compromise with Pakistan by handing over the Kashmir Valley to them ?' Jawaharlalji immediately replied: 'I can never agree to accept such a compromise, whatever may be the circumstances.' He asked me why I had such a doubt in my mind. I then told him that I personally had no doubt in my mind since I believe that if Kashmir was handed over to Pakistan, great harm would be caused to India, and the conditions which had been created by Pakistan by driving out a few million Hindus from East Pakistan would be repeated in reverse. If such an arrangement is accepted, there will be great anger against the Muslims in India and they will not be able then to remain in India. That would make the Hindu Mahasabha and Jan Sangh much stronger than the Congress because the latter will not be able then to keep the confidence of the people of India. Pakistan has no claim on Kashmir whatsoever. If a plebiscite is taken now, Pakistan can pressurise or tempt the Kashmiris to decide in their favour. If Kashmir goes to Pakistan because it has a majority population of Muslims, a great danger would be created for the 50 or 60 million Muslims who are residents of India, and the culture of India which is based on showing equal respect to all religions would be destroyed.'

The Congress never accepted the two-nation theory of Mr. Jinnah and 55 million Muslims had remained in India even after partition, and they had stayed voluntarily and with our consent. If Kashmir now went to Pakistan, the whole position would be reversed. It was therefore not possible to hand over Kashmir to Pakistan.

The movement started by Sheikh Abdullah in 1953 for making Kashmir independent was also an impossible proposition for if that happened Kashmir would be blackmailing both India and Pakistan. The people of Kashmir had understood very well that they were not able to defend themselves against Pakistan at the time when Pakistan had invaded the State. This was why Kashmir merged with India at its own request. The development of Kashmir also depends more on its remaining in India. It will not be able to develop properly if it goes to Pakistan. I have therefore no doubt in my mind that it is in the interest of both India and Kashmir that the merger of Kashmir with India should be permanent. This is also very essential in my view for defence reasons. I was therefore very happy when Jawaharlalji assured me that he would never make any compromise on Kashmir.

I then asked him: 'Why should this question of a plebiscite still continue to be raised? There have been two elections in Jammu and Kashmir by now and on both the occasions the people there have decided by a very large majority that the merger of Kashmir with India is permanent and final. The question of plebiscite does not also survive as a result of the conditions which Pakistan has now created. The UN had made it a condition for plebiscite that Pakistan must vacate its forces from "Azad Kashmir", which it has not done for the last eight years. There is, therefore, no necessity of waiting any longer for Pakistan to carry out this condition. You should consider and decide this matter.'

Only a few days after this talk, Pantji made the declaration that the question of plebiscite did not survive. I inferred that this declaration was in consequence of the talk between me and Jawaharlalji. If I had had an idea that such a decision was to be taken by Jawaharlalji after my talk with him, I would have suggested to him to give six months notice to the UN, America and Pakistan, that if Pakistan did not fulfil its obligations within six months, the question of plebiscite would not survive and we would have to take back Pakistan-occupied Kashmir. Of course, if this notice had been given, Pakistan would not have carried out its obligation, and even if it had done so, the plebiscite would have gone in favour of India. Under both the contingencies, no misunderstanding would have been created about India in England, America and other countries, as it happened.

I explained these facts to Lord Home in my discussions. When he started the topic, I told him that he might give all the facts about Kashmir and I might correct him if necessary, or that I might recount the story and he might correct me if necessary. He asked me to recount the whole history myself and I did so from 1947 onwards. I described the invasion of Kashmir by Pakistan and told him how Kashmir merged with India of its own accord at the last moment. I also pointed out to him that many young men had shed their blood in defence of Kashmir. I told him how a very serious situation had arisen in India as a result of Pakistan's driving away more than four million Hindus from East Pakistan in 1951–52.

I then said: 'Do you not think that the misunderstanding or prejudice shown by other Western countries against India, to which you referred, is a result of your propaganda?' After telling him all the facts I asked him to point out any error of fact in my narrative. He accepted the facts as I had recounted. He asked me why I said that the prejudice of the other Western countries against India was due to them. I asked him whether he would not agree that they (the British) were responsible for the partition of India, and gave him the whole history of partition and their relations with India.

The British Government favoured the Hindus as against the Muslims after the mutiny of 1857. But when the Indian National Congress was established and it began to protest against the British Government, they began to encourage the Muslim League and incited the Muslims against the Hindus. The Britishers encouraged the Aga Khan and others to ask for separate electorates for Muslims and thus created a wall between Hindus and Muslims. Hindus were taking part in the struggle against the British Government in very large numbers compared to the Muslims. This, therefore, created enmity in their minds against the Hindus, and the Britishers encouraged the Muslims in order to prevent Hindus from carrying on the freedom struggle. The Britishers could not have close social relations with Hindus, but they could easily have such relations with the Muslims. Thus the British Government encouraged the Muslim League. One of the former principals of the Aligarh University, Mr. Beck had incited the Muslims. Britishers constantly incited the Muslim League against the Congress, as I specifically pointed out to him.

I then asked a direct question: 'Do you not consider yourself responsible for the partition of the country ?' As he could not deny the facts which I had given him, he replied, 'I must admit that we could have saved India from being partitioned.' Thus, there remained no difference of opinion between us.

He asked me, 'How should the Kashmir question be resolved? I ask for suggestions as to how you could make friends with Pakistan.' I told him: 'You must first give up taking the side of Pakistan in every matter and should give your impartial view in disputes between Pakistan and India, considering the merits of each dispute. Whenever there is a dispute between Pakistan and India you invariably side with Pakistan. This encourages Pakistan and an adverse atmosphere is created against India even in the United Nations on this question. It is therefore you who should find a way out; you should accept the position that India cannot give up Kashmir.'

'This appears to be appropriate from your point of view,' Lord Home said, 'The only solution of Kashmir question can be that Pakistan might retain Azad Kashmir which is in its possession at present and give up all claims to the rest of Kashmir and Jammu. If this is agreed upon, there can be a compromise. I do not see any other solution in this matter.'

'I cannot make such a proposal,' I replied, 'India cannot do it because if India made such an offer, Pakistan would immediately utilise it to strengthen its claim on Kashmir and our case will be weakened. It will also be difficult to persuade our people to accept it. But if Pakistan made such an offer or proposal, and you tell them directly to do so without taking any sides, and if permanent friendship can be achieved between Pakistan and India as a result of such a compromise, it might be possible to persuade the people of India to accept it. India cannot therefore take an initiative in this matter. If you consider it proper, you should take the initiative.' I think he accepted the position and also accepted that it was their duty to take up the question. This is the point on which our discussion on this question ended.

The Canadian Government took us to see several places of interest. One particular centre, where they generated electricity on a large scale, was worth seeing.

Canada is a vast country. It is perhaps two and a half times bigger than India in size. The population of India is 546 million whereas their population is less than 20 million. It is because of this that they are very prosperous. It can be said without exaggeration that they have natural resources of all kinds in abundance. They have large reservoirs of water and large rivers and yet they are such that there is no possibility of any damage being done to the country by floods. There is intense cold in that country and the people are very industrious. The prosperity of Canada will go on increasing as their population is small and the resources are very large.

Mr. Diefenbaker was the Prime Minister of Canada at that time. He welcomed us warmly. Mr. Donald Fleming was the Finance Minister and we became good friends as we often came in contact. The USA has much influence in Canada. Canadian currency is also in dollars, though there is some difference in the value of the two dollars. Americans have invested large amounts of money in Canada, and Canada has as close relations with America as it has with the United Kingdom. As a matter of fact, Canada is getting closer and closer to the USA. Even so, the then Prime Minister of Canada did not like the growing investment and influence of Americans in Canada, and used sometimes to express this publicly.

A communique was issued at the end of the Commonwealth Finance Ministers' Conference, summing up our discussions, and the Indian team was very helpful in the drafting of that communique. This was particularly taken note of. It has been my experience that in such conferences the Indian team often plays a notable part which has always been welcomed. It is so because the Indian team always tries to be helpful without pushing itself forward and without claiming any credit for it. This is why its help is welcomed everywhere.

It was accepted at the end of the Conference that the Commonwealth meant common wealth, that is the wealth must be common to all countries. It is therefore necessary to remove the differences in prosperity between the rich and the poor countries in the Commonwealth and it is the duty of the more prosperous partners in the Commonwealth to help the poor partners. All of us emphasised this aspect which was accepted.

This was a very good opportunity for the delegates of the Commonwealth countries to stay together in one place and to meet one another and to come in closer contact. Our discussions were very friendly and useful and there was no unpleasant incident during the meeting. The British Chancellor of the Exchequer went to Canada as High Commissioner after a few years.

Canada's population is divided into two language groups, English and French. At times there are disputes between the two and some jealousies also. The French portion wants to maintain its individuality, but on the whole I felt then that the two groups were cooperating with each other.

From Montreal I went to Toronto and gave a television interview there. This interview also had a good effect. From Toronto I went to see the Niagara Falls and saw with my own eyes what I had so far read about. This is not a very deep fall, but it is very extensive and the whole sight is very beautiful.

The relations between Canada and India are very friendly. There is a great deal that is common in their position in the international as well as other fields. Canada is always willing and eager to help India, and it has consistently helped India without making any show, considering it a duty. Their help has been on favourable terms. As its population is small, it cannot give as much help as the USA, but the Canadian help is more liberal. We have had hardly any difference of opinion with Canada all these years. The Canadian government allots immigration quotas to different countries and many have migrated there and settled down. Many have gone from India also and are happy there.

I found living in Canada more expensive than in the USA. This was my first visit to all three countries—the UK, USA, and Canada—all of which had exempted me from vaccination. Canada had first specified that their doctor would visit me during my stay, but after I went there, they gave up the idea.

I could not go to many places in the USA when I first went there, but during my subsequent visits I went to places like California and saw many places of natural beauty there. The USA has made much greater progress than any other country in the world in the last two hundred years. They are therefore conscious of their success and feel that they know better than anybody else how to succeed in life. Because of this when they advise others they feel that their advice is better than that of others.

I found the people in the USA generally liberal-minded. There would be no exaggeration in saying that the way the Americans helped western Europe, particularly through the Marshall Plan after the Second World War, to recover from the ravages of war, is an unprecedented example of aid and a liberal mind. They produce more foodgrains, cotton and other raw materials than they require for themselves. The USA is more than two and a half times bigger than India in size and its population is less than half of India's. They have vast natural resources and have developed them very greatly. If they had not helped western Europe so liberally through the Marshall Plan, things would have been very difficult for Europe and there would have been extreme political instability there. The US contribution to the United Nations is also the largest. She has continued to help developing countries directly as well as through the United Nations. I believe it is as a result of their example that the other developed countries also consider it a duty to help undeveloped or underdeveloped countries.

Even though the USA gives help to many countries, some of these countries are sharp critics of the USA. This appears rather strange, but it is also a fact of life that ordinarily very few people are grateful for the help given to them. Bernard Shaw made a very telling remark in this connection once. One day a friend told him that somebody was criticising him very severely and abusing him too. Bernard Shaw replied: 'I have never helped that gentleman. Why does he speak ill of me in spite of that?' The reason why the USA is being criticised by those whom it helps has been given by an American author. He has explained that this is due to the fact that the representatives whom USA sends to the countries it helps behave at times in an arrogant and impudent manner. One section of the Americans is getting very sensitive about this adverse criticism and they are wondering why they should give help just to be abused.

It is necessary to spend large sums of money to help the Negroes in America. These people say that in order to meet that expenditure the help to other countries should be sliced. This indicates that they are becoming less liberal and are becoming more self-centred. This is not healthy for the American people, in my view. If a prosperous country uses its wealth only for its own benefit, the prosperity will not last long, just as the prosperity of an individual does not last long if he uses his wealth only for himself. We learn from the history of the world that prosperity lasts only when it is used for others in a liberal manner and as a duty. This not only maintains prosperity, but also strengthens it and adds nobility to it.

I also saw that while there is abundant wealth in the USA and abundant means of satisfaction of material wants, there is not much mental satisfaction in evidence. People there are beginning to realise that happiness does not lie in wealth alone. This is a welcome augury. They are beginning to think of the necessity of spiritual advancement in order to get real happiness, and this is why they are attracted to India and its culture. They generally mistake socialism for communism. But I see that the ideals contained in their Constitution are those of democracy and socialism, as their purpose is to see that every American becomes happy.

On my way back to India from Montreal, I stopped for a day each at Brussels, Paris and Rome, and had meetings and talks with the leaders of those countries. However, I had more substantial discussions with our representatives there, particularly about our relations with these countries.

15

Indira Gandhi as Congress President

I USED TO get chronic renal colic pains as a result of a stone in my kidney in the latter part of 1958 and got myself operated upon to remove it. I therefore could not attend the annual Congress session at Nagpur in January 1959. I could not postpone the operation further because if I did I would not have been in a position to prepare the budget.

It had been decided before the Nagpur session was held that Dhebarbhai, who had been Congress President from 1955 and whose period of office was extended on account of the 1957 elections, should retire and another President should be elected. The question of a successor was being discussed for some time, but Jawaharlalji did not give his view and remained silent when several names were suggested to him. Most of the members were agreed on the nomination of Shri Nijalingappa but Jawaharlalji would not give his views. This implied that he did not agree. I was not present in Nagpur myself, but I learnt later that Dhebarbhai suggested the name of Indiraji for the Presidentship during the discussions between the leaders, and Jawaharlalji immediately agreed. I had also heard that Pantji had expressed some doubts as to whether Indiraji would be able to bear the burden of the office on account of her delicate health. I was told that Jawaharlalji was very displeased at this and said that her health was not so poor that she could not bear the burden of that office. All then agreed with that suggestion and Indiraji was accordingly elected President of the Congress in February 1959. Dhebarbhai had nominated her on the Working Committee two or three years before this and that was the first time she took a prominent place in the Congress organisation.

Indiraji continued as Congress President till December 1959 and was not willing to continue further. Several colleagues pressed her to continue but she told me that she did not want to continue as there were many impediments in her way and she could not work as she wanted to. She therefore asked me to help her in giving up the Presidentship. When I found that she had decided to resign I asked other colleagues not to press her. So the question arose about choosing her successor. Jawaharlalji and other Congress members discussed this matter. During these discussions I suggested that somebody from the South should be elected as the Congress President as no one had been selected for that office from that area for some years. Others agreed with this suggestion. Several names were discussed. I suggested the name of Shri Sanjiva Reddy, but I did not know whether he would be willing to accept this office and give up the Chief Ministership of Andhra Pradesh. I offered to persuade him to accept the proposal and Jawaharlalji also promised to help in persuading Shri Sanjiva Reddy to be the Congress President.

I discussed this matter with Shri Sanjiva Reddy when he came to Delhi in November 1959 and asked him to accept the offer as it was necessary that some leader from the South should become the Congress President. It was also necessary to strengthen Congress leadership in the South. I also mentioned that Dhebarbhai also had given up the Chief Ministership of Saurashtra to become Congress President, and that it would therefore be a good thing if he accepted this offer. I assured him that all of us would help him in his work. He finally accepted after a discussion with Jawaharlalji and was elected unanimously as Congress President in December that year. He gave up the charge of Chief Ministership of Andhra Pradesh after the Congress session where he presided.

A controversy had then arisen as regards the election of Shri Reddy's successor as Chief Minister of Andhra Pradesh. One section preferred Shri Satyanarayan Raju, a very close colleague of Shri Sanjiva Reddy but the latter, however, did not agree with that choice. He wanted Shri Brahmananda Reddy to succeed him but the majority of the Congress Legislators in Andhra were not in his favour, and Shri Sanjiva Reddy did not want Shri Satyanarayan Raju to be the Chief Minister. After a good deal of discussion, a compromise was made and Shri D. Sanjivayya was elected as Chief Minister of Andhra Pradesh.

I would like to refer to one or two incidents which took place about this time. Some people had created a storm against Shri M. O. Mathai then Special Assistant to Jawaharlalji, in the early months of 1959. Serious allegations were made against Shri Mathai. Jawaharlalji had the fullest trust in Shri Mathai who was completely loyal to him. He used to get some work done through Shri Mathai who used to carry out those assignments very loyally and many people therefore used to flatter Shri Mathai. Even some ministers used to wait upon him, as I could see. Shri Mathai had become Private Secretary to Jawaharlalji when the latter was

Prime Minister and then became Jawaharlalji's Special Assistant.

The controversy was raised even in Parliament. Jawaharlalji asked me to make an enquiry into this matter and give my view. After examining all the facts I gave my view that Shri Mathai had not acquired any money improperly and had not misused the trust which Jawaharlalji had placed in him. Jawaharlalji gave a reply accordingly in Parliament. Shri Mathai resigned from his office as a result of this storm, and the chapter ended.

Communists and fellow-travellers were opposed to Shri Mathai. Shri Mathai has been, since then, leading a private life, and he is perhaps engaged in writing though he has not yet published any work.

Even though there was a Congress Ministry functioning in Orissa since 1956, it was not in a majority. The Congress Party in Orissa therefore considered having a coalition with the Ganatantra Party in order to strengthen its position. Shri Hare Krishna Mahtab and Shri Biju Patnaik were very insistent about making this coalition. As a result of the strong views held by these two friends and on account of the possibility that the members of the Ganatantra Party might join the Congress after working with it for some time, I agreed to the proposal for coalition and persuaded Jawaharlalji also to accept it. Pantji did not agree at first, but ultimately he also gave up his opposition and the AICC accepted the coalition proposal.

The possibility of some of the members of the Ganatantra joining the Congress disappeared a few months after the coalition had come into effect. This created a serious difference of opinion between Shri Mahtab and Shri Patnaik, in spite of the fact that they were very close friends. Shri Mahtab was of the view, that when fresh elections were held, the Congress would not get a majority in Orissa and a coalition government would have to be formed. He therefore wanted to continue the present coalition and considered that a coalition would be necessary even after the elections. If the coalition continued up to and during the elections and did not continue thereafter, there was little possibility of the Congress getting a majority. If the coalition continued, Shri Mahtab would be the Chief Minister. This was why Shri Mahtab wanted the coalition to continue. Shri Biju Patnaik was an ardent supporter of the coalition, but he wanted the coalition to end before the election if the members of the Ganatantra Party did not meanwhile join the Congress in good numbers. This is how differences arose between these two friends and their relations were estranged.

The Central Parliamentary Board ultimately decided to terminate the coalition. The Ministry in Orissa therefore resigned in the beginning of 1961, and elections to the Legislative Assembly of Orissa were held in June, before the General Elections of 1962. If I remember rightly, these elections took place in the beginning of June 1961. The differences between Shri Patnaik and Shri Mahtab continued and I tried to reconcile Shri Mahtab to the position before the elections. I assured him that he would be the Chief Minister if the Congress got a majority and asked him to give his cooperation in the elections. Shri Mahtab felt that Shri Biju Patnaik was his competitor and if he accepted the Chief Ministership he would have to work under pressure from Shri Patnaik. He also was afraid that ultimately, Congress would not get a majority. Shri Mahtab did not agree and Shri Biju Patnaik took over the leadership in fighting the election and worked very hard to get a majority. The Congress did get a majority and Shri Patnaik was elected the leader of the Congress Party and became the Chief Minister of Orissa.

16

India-Pakistan Relations

THE INDUS basin waters dispute between India and Pakistan became more and more intractable with the passage of time after partition. It related to the volume of flow of water of Indian rivers to Pakistan after Pakistan became an independent country. The stoppage or drastic reduction in the flow of these waters would cause great loss to Pakistan. India appreciated this and both countries had accepted the mediation of the World Bank for a solution of this dispute.

Mr. Black, President of the World Bank, was the mediator. The first solution which Mr. Black suggested was accepted by India but not by Pakistan. Mr. Black then suggested another solution which was accepted by Pakistan, as promises of substantial help in providing facilities for more irrigation in Pakistan were made by some friendly countries. According to this solution, India had to give a substantial sum in foreign exchange to Pakistan towards the expenditure that Pakistan would have to incur for making alternative arrangements for water when Indian waters stopped flowing to Pakistan. Friendly countries had promised to give Pakistan an additional 300 million dollars or so for the same purpose.

Mr. Black came to India in the middle of 1959 to discuss this matter. He saw Jawaharlalji and then met me. Mr. Black made for the first time the suggestion that India should give the amount suggested by him to Pakistan for the replacement of the waters. The sum was a very large one and was not justified in my view. Jawaharlalji agreed and asked me to persuade Mr. Black to see our point of view. He hesitated to discuss this matter with Mr. Black himself as he was not sure that Mr. Black would agree with him. I suggested that he ask Mr. Black to discuss the matter with me. Mr. Black accordingly met me alongwith one of his old colleagues who also had very good relations with me. By this time, very friendly relations had developed between Mr. Black and myself. He gave me the details of his proposal and asked for my views. 'Do you want my frank view or only a formal view ?' I asked, 'If I give you my frank view, you may not appreciate it, and I would not like to undertake the risk of doing so, as that would strain our relations, causing a lot of harm. I would like to give you my view, but if you are not going to like it, I had rather not mention it.'

'I shall not take it amiss,' Mr. Black replied, 'Please tell me whatever you would like to tell me, frankly.'

'Pakistan cannot claim any right over any waters from the rivers which belong to India after the old India has been partitioned and an independent Pakistan created,' I said, 'It is our right to stop those waters from flowing to Pakistan if we so wish, and we are not obliged to give any compensation to Pakistan for it. But as they have been using these waters so long and as we are their neighbours, we are prepared to help them in making alternative arrangements. This is how this question ought to be considered. I have the impression that the solution you have thought of has been made with a view to appease Pakistan. I see that the sum that you have proposed to be given by India to Pakistan is very large and India cannot afford it. It is also not justifiable in my view. We had agreed to the solution you had first suggested, but as Pakistan did not accept it, you dropped it. Now the new solution that you have suggested is more favourable for Pakistan and puts a very large burden on India. Do you think this shows an equally friendly attitude to both the countries? The expenditure which Pakistan would have to incur for making alternative arrangements to replace the waters stopped from going from India would be very much less than the sum you have proposed to be given by India to Pakistan. I consider that, from this point of view also, the sum that you have suggested to be given by India does not appear to be in accordance with justice.'

I saw that Mr. Black did not like what I told him.

'If you feel I am partial, I should not be the mediator and I should give up this assignment,' he said.

'You had promised that you would not misunderstand me, whatever I told you and yet you are displeased,' I said, 'It is obvious that you are angry. If that is so, it only means that you expect that I should accept your proposal totally, whereas you had told me that you wanted to take a final decision after discussion with me.'

Mr. Black regained his composure and said: 'It was my mistake. Please tell me what you think should be done in the matter. I shall consider it very objectively.'

'I shall convey to Jawaharlalji,' I said, 'the amount which I consider can properly be given by us and he will talk to you in the matter finally.'

I then talked to Jawaharlalji about it and conveyed to him the amount which I considered appropriate. Mr. Black accepted the suggestion. This is how the final compromise was made with the agreement of both countries.

I realised from this experience that mediation in such disputes becomes arbitration ultimately, and I came to the conclusion that it would be better to resort frankly to arbitration than to so-called mediation in such matters. Actually I believe there should be no mediation or arbitration between two countries in such matters. Direct negotiations are best.

India had very good relations with the World Bank and being the largest developing country, it received more aid from the World Bank than other countries. But, if population is taken into account, the aid received by India from the World Bank is much less per capita than that granted to other countries. Considering all the circumstances, however, one must gratefully accept that the World Bank has given substantial aid to India for its development. A great risk would have been involved if the proposals of the President of such an institution were not accepted after mediation had been entrusted to him. As Mr. Black had confidence in my objectivity and integrity, I put my views before him very frankly. Though his first reaction was one of displeasure and annoyance, his honesty and objectivity came to my aid and he ultimately adopted a just attitude. He was convinced of the correctness of India's stand. I had explained to him that injustice should not be caused to India as a result of the obstinacy of Pakistan. It thus became possible to arrive at a solution acceptable to both the countries. Later events, however, have shown that this was not a final settlement.

It was decided at the end of 1959 that the representatives of India and Pakistan should meet to solve the financial disputes that were pending between them. These talks had been shelved after 1948 and Pakistan was not prepared to reopen them. But after the compromise on the Indus basin waters dispute had been achieved and some correspondence had taken place between us, Pakistan agreed to have a discussion on the financial disputes. Mr. Shoeb, Finance Minister of Pakistan, came to Delhi in December 1959. I had met him before this in the meeting of the World Bank and was therefore well acquainted with him.

Pakistan owed large sums to India as part of the partition division of assets and liabilities and made all kinds of wrong claims against India to avoid having to discharge its liabilities to India. This was why they were not prepared to discuss these matters. This question of the financial outstandings between the two countries should have been entrusted to the World Bank alongwith the

Indus basin water dispute, but Pakistan was not willing to accept such a move, and India did not press the matter. I felt that this was wrong. I was not then in the Central Cabinet. Had I been in it, I would have pressed for sticking to our stand and would have pressed for refusing to submit the waters dispute to mediation by Mr. Black unless Pakistan agreed to the simultaneous submission to Mr. Black for mediation of the financial outstandings. It was always Jawaharlalji's view, which all of us shared, that we should maintain good relations with Pakistan. It was therefore felt that if compromises were made on some questions, a suitable atmosphere would be created. This was the only consideration in agreeing to submit to mediation the Indus basin waters dispute.

I came to the conclusion, from the talks I had with him in Delhi, that Mr. Shoeb did not want to come to an agreement. He therefore put up many wrong claims against India. These claims were prima facie wrong. As he was not prepared to come to a decision in these matters, the talks remained inconclusive at that stage. It was then decided that I should go to Pakistan in 1960 and resume the negotiations there.

17

Division of Bilingual Bombay State

IN SEPTEMBER 1959 Indiraji raised the question of dividing the bigger bilingual Bombay State, created in 1956, into two linguistic States of Maharashtra and Gujarat and discussions were being held in that connection. The then Governor of Bombay, Shri Sri Prakasha, wrote to the President Dr. Rajendra Prasad, suggesting such a division. When I discussed this matter with the President I explained to him all the facts and the circumstances saying, 'If this proposal is accepted, several other linguistic states will have to be created. This will result in the weakening not only of the two States formed out of the bigger Bombay State, but also of the country. I would therefore request a very careful consideration of the whole matter.'

I had learnt at that time that Jawaharlalji, Pantji, Indiraji and Yashwantrao Chavan had had some talks and had also reached a consensus at the time of the Nagpur Congress which was held in the beginning of 1959 and which I could not attend. I was convinced about the correctness of this information when Jawaharlalji, Pantji, Indiraji, Yashwantrao Chavan and I met at Pantji's residence in September 1959 to discuss this matter. I do not remember whether Shri Lal Bahadur Shastri was present at this discussion or not. I could gather that the others must have discussed this matter in my absence earlier, but none of them had discussed it with me. Pantji started the discussion. I intervened to say, 'You decided to form the bigger bilingual Bombay State after the Working Committee and the Central Government had previously decided to make three different States out of Bombay, i.e. Gujarat, Maharashtra and Bombay. I agreed to your proposal then, and yet you are now proposing a division of the State into two. Do you consider it proper?'

I understood at that time that Indiraji was definitely of the view that two separate States of Maharashtra and Gujarat should be created out of the then bigger bilingual State of Bombay and also realised that her view had influenced Jawaharlalji to some extent. Jawaharlalji said: 'It is in the interest of the country that the bigger Bombay State should continue as it is, but we have to consider the views of Shri Yashwantrao Chavan in the matter.

What can we do if he is of the opinion that it will not be possible for him to manage the bigger State and to maintain it as it was. In these circumstances, we will ultimately be forced to divide Bombay into two States.' When he asked Shri Yashwantrao Chavan to comment, the latter said that he had no confidence that he would be able to manage the bigger state. I got the impression that the manner in which this discussion should be held had been already decided in my absence. This impression was confirmed when I found that no real arguments were being advanced.

When I said that I had no doubt that the proposed division would harm the country, all the four leaders said that if the division was not made, the conditions which were obtaining then would worsen and the country would be harmed. I then said: 'My opinion differs from the opinion which all the four of you hold. I cannot inflict my view on you. You can, therefore, take the decision to divide Bombay State, but you should understand that I have not given my consent to it.' They did not object to my dissent and decided to divide the Bombay State.

I met Jawaharlalji after this decision was taken and asked if it was proper to have got the earlier decision taken by the Congress Working Committee and the Union Government and then to change it after having made me a scapegoat for the earlier decision and placing me in a false position in the eyes of the Maharashtrians. I also asked him why he did not defend me against those attacks. He very mildly replied that things had become very difficult both for himself and the country and so he was forced to be a party to the changed decision. When he accepted my feelings I told him that I was satisfied that he realised my predicament and so I had nothing more to complain about.

The decision taken by the leaders was confirmed in the meetings of the Congress Working Committee and the AICC. As I was abroad at that time, I took no part in these party discussions. I had, however, told the leaders that when they were dividing Bombay State I would do everything I could to see that the division took place peacefully even though I was not in agreement with it. It was then settled that Yashwantrao and I should discuss the matter and arrive at an agreed arrangement.

Both of us then met and effected the partition of the Bombay State peacefully and without any difficulty. During our talks, I asked Yashwantrao: 'When you had already discussed this matter earlier, why did you not tell me about it? If you had, I would have thought over the matter from the very beginning.' He replied that he was afraid I would not agree with the proposal. He expressed his regret that he kept me in the dark on this matter. I therefore did not say anything more about this at that time.

It cannot be said that the formation of linguistic states is in principle improper. On the contrary, formation of linguistic states should enable the State Governments to function with greater harmony and uniformity and the people also should derive greater satisfaction from them. This is the main consideration behind the principle of formation of linguistic states. But, as I have said earlier, there was a possibility of regional disputes arising out of the formation of linguistic states in the conditions prevailing in the country, in a situation in which the necessary intensity of patriotism had not been created, owing to historical reasons and the circumstances in which the country had become independent. In this situation, linguistic states would create obstacles in the way of forging the unity of the country. The country had to face many problems and they were so difficult that we had got to be careful to see that more obstacles and problems were not created until the existing ones had been solved. This was my line of thinking in the matter. I therefore believed that it was not desirable to have linguistic states until we were able to solve the basic problems the country was facing and until we were fully integrated.

The bigger Bombay State was considered an efficient, and model State and was contributing greatly to the forging of national unity. Maharashtra and Gujarat are temperamentally complementary and if they had remained together for some time it would have benefited the country and would also have made an effective contribution to its integration. These are the reasons that had prompted me to agree to the formation of the bigger Bombay State in accordance with the Working Committee's decision and to agree with Jawaharlalji at that time.

I had felt that the difficulties facing the country would increase and its unity be endangered if Bombay was divided, and that the bigger Bombay State would work much better. At one time, therefore, I had decided in my mind that if any division was proposed I must protest very strongly against it and try to stop it and even retire from public life, if I failed. I had talked in this way to some friends also. I have said earlier that during the discussions the five of us had, four felt very strongly that the country would be harmed if a partition was not made, and the conditions were such that almost all the people in Maharashtra wanted a separate Maharashtra State and a very large majority of the people of Gujarat also wanted a separate Gujarat State. In the circumstances I felt I should not inflict my views on others. I, therefore, decided to give up my previous intention to publicly and actively oppose any decision to divide Bombay State.

It is necessary that one should not compromise with falsehood in a democracy, but every difference of opinion is not one of principle. Many differences of opinion arise out of different viewpoints. I had no opposition to linguistic states in principle. Mahatma Gandhi had even suggested them earlier. I felt that the formation of linguistic states was harmful in the conditions through which the country was then passing. This was my view and when I found that the majority did not accept it, I considered it my duty to bow to the majority view. I felt that open and active opposition to it would be against my concept of democracy. Having come to this conclusion I decided that the division should be achieved peacefully and smoothly, which was achieved.

This is how the separate Maharashtra and Gujarat States came into existence out of the bigger Bombay State on 1 May 1960.

18

Visit to Europe, America and Japan

The World Bank and the International Monetary Fund meetings were to be held towards the end of 1959 at Washington and the Commonwealth Finance Ministers' Conference was also to be held in London at that time. I, therefore, went abroad for the second time to attend these two conferences.

I first went to London, but made flying visits to Geneva and Paris on my way. As the headquarters of the Swiss Government was at Berne, I went there from Geneva and discussed mutual relations with the Head of the Government of Switzerland. This was a very friendly and useful discussion and the trade relations between the two countries received a fillip as a result.

From Geneva I went to Paris where I had been invited by the French Government. I met the President of France, General De Gaulle, whose personality made a deep impression on me. He struck me as a serious thinker with a very strong mind. He seemed to believe that it was his personal mission to make France prosperous and strong and to promote its glory. He contributed a great deal to making France very strong internally and externally, and wanted to have good relations with India.

I also met the French Prime Minister and Finance Minister and several other public leaders and visited their Central Bank. I visited a village and found that they had made very good progress in the development of agriculture. I went up the Eiffel Tower, the tallest and one of the most famous monuments of Paris. The sight of Paris from the top was very beautiful. Japan has erected a similar tower, taller than the Eiffel Tower, in Tokyo. I saw it when I visited Japan later.

I then went to New York. As usual, I had a television interview there which was arranged by a private television company. I had some preliminary discussions with the person in charge before actually appearing on television. He told me that he would first introduce me and wanted to do so by saying that I was the future Prime Minister of India. I considered this very improper and that it would create avoidable prejudices against me, and said so. The interviewer's reply was that it was his privilege and right to freely express his views and that I could not stop him from exercising this right. I made clear that while I did not want to come in the way of his exercising his independence, I hoped that he would not interfere with mine. When he accepted this position, I told him: 'I am free to give you an interview or to refuse it. In the circumstances which I see now I do not want to give you an interview and I am therefore taking leave of you.' Saying so, I started to leave when the gentlemen relented and agreed to give up the objectionable portion of his proposed introduction.

My interview was recorded after this. Though the duration had first been fixed at fifteen minutes, the interview continued for forty minutes. This gave me the impression that the interviewer was very interested in what I said.

Representatives of several societies in New York had discussions with me on various problems relating to India.

After leaving New York and going to Washington, I attended the World Bank and International Monetary Fund meetings. I also met the different secretaries to Government on that occasion, as also some of the under secretaries, and had long talks with them. Mr. Dillon was then Under Secretary of State. My discussions with him established very friendly relations between us which have continued till today. He had very friendly feelings for India and was ready to be helpful.

After these meetings, I visited the western part of the USA—Los Angeles, San Francisco and Seattle. On the way there, I visited some farms. I was told that only 9 per cent of the US population was engaged in agriculture at that time. The USA is about two and a half times the size of India and its population is less than half that of India. Thus the number of persons engaged in agriculture is very small and most agricultural and dairy operations are mechanised and units of cultivation are very large. No farmer has less than 150 acres of land, and several persons have far larger areas in their possession. Comparatively few people are thus engaged in agricultural occupation and they are all prosperous. US industries and business operations are so highly developed that the greater portion of the US population is engaged in these fields and the Government gives subsidies to farmers to ensure that they do not suffer when the prices of agricultural produce fall. Agricultural produce is also purchased by the State which maintains a stock of their requirements for one or two years, from which they give aid to other countries. They have enacted Public Law 480 for this purpose. India has received substantial aid under PL 480 and has found this aid very useful, as our agricultural production is less than our requirements. We have not to pay them for this aid in dollars but in Indian rupees and in long-term instalments. A large part of this aid was given as a grant, which was very helpful in managing our economy.

On the east coast, I first went to Los Angeles which is a very large centre for film production. I addressed the Foreign Affairs Committee there. Such non-official Committees exist in many of their cities. I had earlier spoken to two or three such bodies in New York. Whenever I went to USA I met such bodies and spoke to them. I had established a practice of having some question-answer time after finishing my speeches at such meetings. This helped me to gauge how my audience were thinking and could clear points that arose.

At Los Angeles, a gentleman asked me: 'You have stated that America has helped India a great deal for which India is grateful. Why, therefore, does the Indian Government oppose our foreign policy? Don't you think you must give up such opposition and support us?' This question had particular reference to relations with China. We were supporting the admission of China to the United Nations and America was opposing it. I answered:

'You have raised a useful question which will enable me to remove several doubts. America and India are independent countries. The help which America gives to India is unconditional and it is useful only if it is unconditional. It is not true that we are opposing the foreign policy of America, but where our views differ, India gives expression to its view very clearly. India is free to do this and it has its own independent view.

'China has been kept out of the United Nations. As we consider this unjust, we do not consider the opposition of America to this proposal proper. The United Nations is an association of all countries, irrespective of their systems of government. Democratic, dictatorial and communist countries are all members of this body, wherein lies its real usefulness. When a communist country like Soviet Russia is a member, it is against the ideals of the United Nations to prevent the admission of China to that body. Formosa cannot represent China. It is in view of these facts that India presents its own view in the United Nations. If, however, it is your view that, because the USA helps India financially, the latter should give up its correct position and support the American one, you are welcome to hold it; but we do not consider that view proper. If you object to our holding an independent view, you ought to persuade your President not to help India. We do not want to have any conditional aid. If American opinion is in favour of giving conditional aid, we are not willing to take it.'

When I explained the position so frankly, it had a very salutary effect on the audience. Others present told the questioner that they did not agree with him.

From Los Angeles I went to San Francisco, met many people there and discussed our mutual relations with them. I also met Indians who have settled down there. I went to Seattle next and saw the very large aeroplane factory there. Previously California was a desert but they found underground water in this area at a depth of 1,000 to 1,500 feet several years ago and the provision of tubewells has now made this area very fertile. This part of USA is now very prosperous and beautiful.

The most vivid and abiding memory that I carry of this visit to America is that of the Grand Canyon. The Grand Canyon is very beautiful and attracts many visitors. I went there on my way to California. Though I had seen this place before in a film, I had a very inadequate idea of its size and beauty. When I went there and actually saw it, I got a vivid idea of its vast size, glory and beauty. A valley, about a mile and a half or two miles deep, has been formed by the constant erosion by running water for fifteen million years. The river Colorado flows through the valley. There are footpaths to go down the valley, but I did not go down. I observed the whole scene from the top. This valley seems to have been formed out of large rocks. Names have been given to some of the over-hanging rocks, some of which are American Indian names. Some of these rocks have taken definite shapes and forms which strike a visitor very deeply. This is an amazing example of how nature creates various formations with the passage of time. I was told that this was the creation of fifteen million years. Many visitors had come to the place from several countries and were enjoying the scenic beauty there. I stopped in the hotel there for a few hours and carried a permanent memory in my mind when I left the place for Los Angeles. Only a poet can describe this place adequately. It is difficult for people like me to give an adequate description. Nobody can get an adequate idea of the beauty and glory of this natural monument without seeing it personally.

The idea which one gets from reading literature about the Taj Mahal is quite different from the one which one gets by actually seeing it. One can realise only after seeing the Taj that it is an incomparably wonderful creation. It cannot be adequately described in words or pictures. This also applies to the Grand Canyon.

From San Francisco I went to Japan, and one date was totally lost during this journey. There is so much difference in time while going from East to West that one day is missed. There is a difference of 5 hours in the time between England and India, i.e. English time is 5 hours behind. There is another 5 hours difference going to New York, and there is again a similar time difference going from San Francisco to Japan. One day therefore gets lost completely. We are given a card on the plane in token of this occurrence.

In Tokyo, I stayed with the Indian Ambassador, Shri C.P.N. Singh. I met the Japanese Prime Minister, Mr. Kishi, while I was in Tokyo. I had met him first in India. His brother, Mr. Sato, who later became the Prime Minister, was the Finance Minister in 1958—59. I met him too. India's connection with Japan is very ancient and I emphasised during my talk that these relations must become closer. I met other ministers of the Government and also the Emperor of Japan. The Emperor in Japan was supreme in authority and status before the war and there was a tradition that when he moved in the city, people could not look at his face. They had to look down. This tradition was an indication of his exalted position and hold over the people. This tradition has completely changed and Japan is now a democratic country. The Emperor is now the constitutional head of Government.

I went to several other cities in Japan. This was my first visit. I saw that Japan had developed very fast after the last war. It had developed greatly before the war also, and had achieved remarkable progress in eighty years. Its development in the forties had reached the level of the Western countries and it had become a strong nation. At that point, it allied itself with Hitler in the Second World War hoping to become the leader of South East Asia. It, however, lost its courage after Hiroshima and Nagasaki were bombed with atom bombs and lost the war like Germany and Italy. Japan had to suffer a great deal of loss in this war and suffered from a lot of destruction. Industry and business were ruined. But possessing great technical capacity and knowledge and a burning sense of patriotism, with a tremendous capacity for working hard, they have achieved the present wonderful stage of progress after the war. Japan received a lot of help from America after the war and utilised it magnificently. It has become economically very prosperous. Its economic condition is much stronger today than it was before the war. It has made great advances in agricultural development also. I saw this development when I visited a village some distance from Tokyo.

There were big landlords in Japan before the war. This system was changed under the influence of America after the war and there is now no unit larger than 8 or 9 acres. The units varied in size from 2.5 acres to 8 or 9 acres. Japan's agriculture has developed very greatly. The Japanese people are very industrious and achieve large production even from a unit of 2.5 acres. They also have side occupations like poultry breeding and village industries. Their living standard is therefore very high. They have the natural advantage of a perennial water supply as it rains throughout the year. They utilise natural manure and human excreta and urine are also fully utilised as manure for their agriculture, with the result that it has become very productive and prosperous. They derive large benefits from the combination of fertilizers, i.e. chemical manure, with the natural manure mentioned above. All the human excreta is carried by peasants to the fields and they even pay for it. If this system is adopted in India, it will benefit us greatly and the liberation of the sweepers would also become easy. The production and protection of fruit orchards and horticulture is as successful as their production of foodgrains. If any fruits which come to the market are found to be rotten, they are immediately reported, and the persons from the relevant agricultural department visit the field concerned and apply necessary remedies immediately. Every citizen of Japan works very honestly and with a great sense of responsibility.

There is a practice in Japan that if the head of any department of Government is not able to detect the wrong action of his subordinates, he considers himself very inefficient and commits suicide, which is called *hara-kiri*. This is an old practice in Japan, and shows what a great sense of honesty and responsibility they have. If one visits a factory in Japan, one will see that the workers do their work without looking at the visitors. This shows their sense of responsibility. Whatever machines they import from outside are copied by them and are then manufactured in the country. It is on account of this sense of responsibility and capacity that their industries have developed greatly and their annual production has risen at a higher rate than in other countries. India has got a great deal to learn from Japan.

I went to Yokohama which is the second port of Japan at a short distance from Tokyo. Going to Yokohama gave me a feeling that it had developed in such a manner that it had almost become a part of Tokyo. Tokyo has the largest population among all the cities of the world and is very modern.

I saw several industrial units in Japan. The devotion with which the workers work and their sense of responsibility made a very deep impression on me. Their salaries are not large and the standard of living is more or less the same for all people. This is also a very peculiar feature of Japan. Japan has adopted Western dress for day-to-day working, but they have maintained their national dress and way of life in their homes. Their houses are very clean with very sparse furniture. They have thus preserved their own culture while taking full advantage of the Western industrial system.

19

In Pakistan

I HAVE ALREADY mentioned Mr. Shoeb, Finance Minister of Pakistan's visit to India towards the end of 1959 for discussions with me relating to the financial disputes between the two countries. He invited me, before leaving India, to go to Pakistan and continue the talks as we could not find any solution in Delhi. I did not entertain any hope of reaching a settlement in view of the attitude he had adopted in Delhi. But I considered it necessary to make all possible efforts to solve the dispute and went to Pakistan in the third week of March 1960 and stayed there for six days. I first went to Karachi by air where I was received by Mr. Shoeb and our High Commissioner, Shri Rajeshwar Dayal. The next day, I went to Mr. Jinnah's grave and placed a wreath on it. The Minister for Industries took me round their industrial estates in Karachi, and one of the Muslims of Godhra, who had gone to Pakistan and settled there, took me round his woollen mills. I met some prominent citizens of Karachi at the reception and dinner given by our High Commissioner and had talks with them on different matters. The National Day of Pakistan was also being celebrated on that day and I attended a function held to celebrate it. Mr. Shoeb also took me round the Karachi port which I found of great interest.

I then went to Rawalpindi where Mr. Rehman a Minister in the Government gave me a dinner. It was attended by the President of Pakistan, Field Marshal Ayub Khan, with whom I had a talk. Before talking with him I had discussions with Mr. Shoeb and the Foreign Minister of Pakistan. The talks between us went on till the last day of my visit, but the Pakistanis stalled a solution by raising a new point every day and did not show any willingness to compromise. As I have said earlier, I did not expect any solution to be arrived at while I was in Pakistan.

I had sent a message to the President of Pakistan when my visit to Rawalpindi was fixed that I would very much like to meet Khan Abdul Ghaffar Khan as I was visiting Pakistan for the first time. I also said in that message that I would be grateful if he would arrange for me to go and meet him at his place if he had no objection. My request was granted.

Actually I met Badshah Khan at the airport when I reached Peshawar. I had intended to go and meet him at his place. When I asked Badshah Khan why he took the trouble of coming to Peshawar, he said that this was because of the wrong attitude of the Government. They had told him that I would like to meet him at Peshawar. I told him that I would accompany him to his place on his return journey. We went together to the place where I was to stay and had a long talk about all that he had suffered in Pakistan. We were alone when we talked about these matters. He was very angry with the Pakistan administration and described to me how they were persecuting him. He was also bitter about the manner in which the partition of India took place. 'India threw us to the wolves without consulting us,' he said, 'Gandhiji had told us that India would send us help if we were harassed in Pakistan, but this promise was not honoured and even now no steps are taken by India in this direction.'

'Facilities were given to the people of North West Frontier Province,' I told him, 'to decide by plebiscite whether they wanted to remain in India or Pakistan. When this plebiscite was taken, the people opted for Pakistan. You and your brother, Dr. Khan Saheb, boycotted the plebiscite. If you had not done so, you would have got the majority of votes in your favour and you would not have then had to remain in Pakistan.'

'We did not take part in the plebiscite,' he said, 'because we wanted to avoid disputes amongst ourselves.'

'How then can you find fault with India?' I asked, 'It is true that Gandhiji himself wanted to come to Pakistan to help you, but he was murdered. If you are thinking of military help, I cannot understand how Gandhiji could have promised it. It is very clear that India could not have invaded Pakistan in this manner as it was against the established policy of India. Do you not, therefore, think that there is some misunderstanding in what you say?'

I tried to persuade Badshah Khan to see my point in a very polite manner but I could not satisfy him.

I accompanied him on his return to his village. We went by car and on the way he talked to me about many things. A Pakistan Government representative was accompanying us, but his presence did not in any way deter Badshah Khan from talking to me very frankly. Throughout the whole journey he continued to make very bitter remarks against Pakistan and said that he was sure that that Government did not want to allow him to do any work and therefore there was no alternative for him except to go to jail. He was in fact imprisoned a short time after my visit as I learnt after my return to India.

On the way he showed me how his institution was destroyed by Pakistan. When I went to his place, I visited the grave of Dr. Khan Saheb and laid a wreath on it. After leaving him at his place, I returned to Peshawar. When I went to see the Khyber Pass, I observed how the tribesmen there lived on the hills. I also saw one or two of their military posts on the way. All that I had read about the Khyber Pass came before my vision when I actually saw it. It is a very beautiful spot. I also saw how the Moghuls and other Muslims from beyond the frontier invaded India through this pass when modern means for defending it were not available.

From Rawalpindi I also went to Takshasila, the site of a very great university in ancient times. Some relics of the Buddhist times were preserved there which I saw.

I met the Pakistani press at Rawalpindi and they asked me many questions about the possibility of friendship between India and Pakistan. I told them: 'India is very eager to forge friendship with Pakistan, but until Pakistan reciprocates such a sentiment, India will have to wait with patience for achieving it.' They also asked many questions about Kashmir. I told them frankly and clearly that the merger of Kashmir with India was final. This annoyed them to some extent, but it is my conviction, as a result of long experience, that it is always useful to talk frankly and clearly in such matters.

In the talks which I had with Mr. Shoeb and the Foreign Minister, they told me that they did not expect as much help from Jawaharlalji as from me for making peace between the two countries. I immediately saw that they wanted to create some rift between Jawaharlalji and myself and said: 'Many people in India consider Pandit Jawaharlal Nehru as the only nationalist Muslim. How could you have more confidence in me than in him? You ought not to talk to me in this manner as our relations, instead of being better, would worsen as a result.' They understood my point immediately and did not proceed further in that vein.

Several Muslim friends who had migrated from India to Pakistan at the time of partition met me in Karachi and Rawalpindi. During my talks with them, some said, 'You are the elder brother and we are the younger brother. You ought to deal with us magnanimously.'

'If you really believe India to be your elder brother,' I said, 'the younger brother should accept the advice of the elder when it is given and should improve his conduct. If the younger brother does this, the elder brother can deal with him magnanimously. But if the younger brother is only waiting for an opportunity to pick the pocket of the elder brother and calls him elder brother with only that in view, India cannot agree to be such an elder brother.'

I also talked to President Ayub Khan and his Ministers frankly in the same manner. I told them: 'The National Congress had been very liberal and magnanimous to the Muslim League, even more than necessary, before we obtained freedom and before India was partitioned. The Muslim League took undue advantage of this magnanimous behaviour and an impression was created in the Muslim mind that the Congress was afraid of the League and that they could take anything from us by threatening us. It was clear that if both the communities worked together for winning swaraj for India, freedom would have been achieved earlier and more easily. This was why the Congress made many concessions to please the Muslim League and accepted separate electorates also. It also accepted separate Urdu schools, but the leaders of the Muslim League misrepresented all this to the Muslim masses and spread such poison amongst them that ultimately India had to be partitioned.'

I added: 'You would be very much mistaken if you think you can get something from India by threatening and frightening it; and if you will not change this attitude we will both suffer great harm. We are convinced that such a policy of threat and blackmail is very wrong. We have decided not to submit to such a policy under any circumstances. If, therefore, you behave with us in a friendly manner and want us to help you, not as a matter of your right but as friends, our relations can become very cordial. But as long as you go on threatening us, it will be difficult to forge friendship between us. I would therefore submit that you should change the attitude and strong feelings that have been aroused in Pakistan against India. The interests of both countries lie in their good relations and they should become very good friends. Only this will make both the countries prosperous and strong, and no other country will then be able to raise a finger against us.

'If your young people raise such slogans as "We have taken Pakistan by sport and we will conquer Hindustan by war", how can we trust you? You should realise that you will not be able to frighten India in this manner. The earlier you realise this truth, the better for both countries. India will go on getting stronger and it is able to defend itself fully against anybody.'

They did not attempt to counter what I said and I got an impression that they understood correctly what I wanted to convey. But they did not admit in words the truth of what I said. I got the feeling that Pakistan would be friendly with us only when they were convinced that India was a very strong country and could not be bullied by anybody in any way. It was also clear in my mind that India had constantly to make efforts to forge friendship with Pakistan and that such friendship could not be achieved by pampering our neighbours or by making concessions to them. If they were pampered they would be encouraged to be more aggressive.

During the discussions on the economic disputes between us I told them: 'If you persist in making unjustifiable demands in these matters, I am not able to understand how you will be able to contribute to the improvement of our relations.' I explained to them that we had accepted the solution suggested by the World Bank in the dispute about the river waters between the two countries, even though it was favourable to Pakistan. We accepted it in the hope that a beginning would be made towards bringing about an understanding between the two countries. When they told me that they wanted Pandit Jawaharlal Nehru to visit Pakistan to sign the agreement and that I should persuade him to accept the invitation, I felt that they were making an effort, till this agreement was signed, to show that they were in a mood for compromise. I also felt that after the agreement was signed the attitude of Pakistan would again become stiff. Even so, I thought we had to do our duty without any fear. I therefore requested Jawaharlalji to accept the invitation and he went. But, as I had anticipated, soon after the waters agreement was signed, Pakistan returned to its stiff and aggressive attitude.

From Rawalpindi I went to Lahore and after seeing some sights in that city I came by car to Amritsar. This completed my visit to Pakistan.

20

Shri Krishna Menon

SHRI KRISHNA MENON is known as a shrewd but controversial politician. I would like to give here my impressions of him, formed after I had worked with him.

Shri Krishna Menon had made propaganda for India in London where he was then living during the freedom struggle. Jawaharlalji, therefore, had been in very close contact with him. When India became free, Shri Menon was appointed as Indian High Commissioner in London.

In 1951-52, while he held his London post, a great controversy arose around him, which came to be known as the 'jeep scandal'. An order had been placed in London for the purchase of jeeps required for our defence forces with a company which consisted of two individuals with a very nominal capital. These persons had alleged that Shri Krishna Menon had some interest in the transaction with them. This episode was discussed a great deal in Parliament, but Jawaharlalji was able to quieten the controversy by the force of his personality. As a result of this episode, however, Shri Krishna Menon had ultimately to resign his post in London and the order for jeeps was cancelled. Shri Balasaheb Kher was appointed High Commissioner in London.

The people forming the company that had got the order for the jeeps sued the Indian Government for breach of contract. This suit went on for quite a few years. The lawyer who represented us in that suit was engaged on the advice of Shri Krishna Menon. The Company had sued the Indian Government for £ 10,000. The Indian Government had sued that Company for damages of £200,000 to £300,000. When the suit came up for hearing in 1960, our lawyer in London advised us to compromise and some negotiations were going on in this direction. The respondents did not want to give us anything in the compromise.

This matter was discussed by Shri Jawaharlalji, Pantji, myself, the Law Minister Shri Asoke Sen and Shri Krishna Menon, and we decided that Shri Krishna Menon should give evidence in the suit as he was the principal person concerned and that we would win the suit only if he appeared as a witness. Shri Krishna Menon was reluctant to do this and argued that it was not proper that he should go to a court as a witness while he held the office of a Minister at the Centre.

Both Pantji and I told Shri Menon that his argument was not correct as there were instances in which the Prime Minister as well as other ministers had given evidence in several cases. If Shri Krishna Menon did not give evidence and the suit was decided against us, the Indian Government and the Cabinet would suffer very badly in their reputation. We therefore felt that Shri Krishna Menon should give evidence. Jawaharlalji agreed with us and Shri Krishna Menon had ultimately to agree to go to London to give evidence.

The negotiations that were going on for a compromise before these discussions amongst us required that we give up our claim and pay £ 10,000 to the Company. We had refused to accept this. I said that the suit for £ 10,000 which the opponents had launched against us was based on their rights and there was every possibility of a decree being passed against India. If the Company withdrew their suit for £ 10000 damages, we would not lose our reputation. Pantji, Shri Asoke Sen and myself were of this view, and Jawaharlalji agreed with it. When we sent this condition to the opponents, they refused to accept such a compromise. Our lawyer in London then informed us that the suit would go on and, if Shri Krishna Menon did not give evidence, our case would not be proved. However, later on, when the date for the hearing of the suit was fixed, our opponents accepted our conditions of compromise just before Shri Krishna Menon was to go to London to give evidence, and the matter ended there.

In my talks with Pantiji, I had told him that I was sure that if we stuck to our conditions and Shri Krishna Menon was pressed to go to London to give evidence, he was bound to get a compromise and thus save himself from giving evidence. What I said turned out to be true. If we had not remained firm in our attitude in this matter, it would have been very difficult for us to face Parliament. Shri Menon might not have lost anything, but the Cabinet would have lost its reputation. Pantji, Shri Sen and I were of the same view and we conveyed it clearly to Jawaharlalji. He appreciated the position and, accepting our stand, pressed Shri Krishna Menon to give evidence, which the latter could not refuse to do.

It was my experience that Jawaharlalji could make Shri Krishna Menon accept his point of view whenever he thought it necessary, and Shri Menon always agreed to do what he was asked to by Jawaharlalji.

After being relieved of the High Commissioner's post in London, Shri Krishna Menon functioned as a roving ambassador on behlf of India in other countries, and also attended meetings of the United Nations in that capacity. But his desire was to work in India as a minister, as I could gather from my talks with Jawaharlalji. When I had once gone to Delhi for a meeting of the Congress Working Committee in 1953-54, Jawaharlalji asked me about the propriety and usefulness of including Shri Krishna Menon in the Central Cabinet. 'Shri Krishna Menon is a very intelligent and capable person,' I said, 'but he has been used to working alone and he is temperamentally individualistic. It is not possible for him to work in cooperation with others, as I have been able to observe. He will, therefore, do very useful work if you entrust him with a responsibility in which he has to work by himself. I feel that he might create controversies in the Cabinet if he is taken in as a Minister.' I got the impression then that Jawaharlalji had accepted my advice and had given up the idea of taking Shri Menon into the Cabinet.

However, Jawaharlalji ultimately decided in 1956 to include Shri Krishna Menon in his Cabinet. Pantji agreed but Maulana Saheb opposed the proposal. Jawaharlalji wrote to the President of India requesting him to appoint Shri Krishna Menon as a Minister. When Maulana Saheb received a copy of the letter, he opposed it very strongly and threatened to resign if the appointment was made.

I had gone to Delhi at about this time and Maulana Saheb talked to me about this development and this is how I came to know about the incident. Jawaharlalji did not talk to me about this particular matter at that time. Maulana Saheb told me the facts and asked me whether or not his attitude was proper. My answer was: 'If it is your view that the jeep scandal has not yet subsided and if you feel that he should not be taken into the Cabinet as he would not be able to work in cooperation with the other colleagues of the Cabinet, the attitude that you have taken is quite proper and correct.' Jawaharlalji did not succeed in his efforts to persuade Maulana Saheb to change his mind.

After a meeting of the Working Committee, Jawaharlalji, Pantji, Shri Bidhan Chandra Roy and I were discussing some matters when Pantji sopke to Bidhanbabu about the inclusion of Shri Krishna Menon in the Cabinet and asked for our help in persuading Maulana Saheb to agree. I answered for both of us: 'Shri Bidhanbabu and I will not be able to persuade Maulana Saheb to change his attitude in this matter because we consider his attitude to be justified and you would have to face opposition if Shri Krishna Menon is taken in the Cabinet.' Pantji also was not favourably inclined to the appointment, but he could not say no to

Jawaharlalji and continued his efforts to persuade Maulana Saheb to agree. Ultimately, Maulana Saheb gave in and agreed to the appointment of Shri Krishna Menon in the Cabinet as a Minister without Portfolio. He was appointed Defence Minister in the new Cabinet after the General Elections of 1957.

By that time I had also joined the Central Cabinet as a Minister, and I saw that whereas previously the relations between Maulana Saheb and Jawaharlalji were very close and Jawaharlalji used to take his advice in every matter and would accept his advice many a time, these relations had got estranged ever since Maulana Saheb had opposed the entry of Shri Krishna Menon into the Cabinet. This estrangement was not very obvious, but I saw that after this incident Jawaharlalji did not consult Maulana Saheb as before and used to even criticise him at times. This had never happened before this incident. This was the first indication I had of this side of Jawaharlalji's temperament.

It had been my view before this that Jawahalalji did not hold any prejudice against those who opposed him and even welcomed opposition. But when I saw his relations with Maulana Saheb estranged in this manner, I realised that Jawaharlalji was not able to reconcile himself to any opposition in any matter where he wanted to act in a particular manner. He did not make this prejudice obvious, but one could see its indirect effects.

Shri Krishna Menon insisted on opening a medical college at Poona on behalf of the Defence Ministry, which I opposed as I was of the view that the Defence Ministry must not take on this kind of responsibility. Shri Krishna Menon had undertaken the production of many articles for civilian consumption in defence undertakings, which also I did not think proper. I had no doubt that, if he had not done so, the country would have been benefited far more. Shri Krishna Menon persisted in asking for the medical college for two or three years, and Jawaharlalji ultimately supported him. I then gave up my opposition, especially since Jawaharlalji had declared his firm decision in the matter. I did not consider it proper to persist in opposition and leave the Cabinet because such a step would have been of no advantage to the country.

During the General Elections of 1957, Shri Krishna Menon was a candidate on behalf of the Congress from the suburban parliamentary constituency of Bombay city. Many people had opposed his candidature. Shri S. K. Patil gave his consent and helped him greatly. Shri Krishna Menon was elected as a member of the Lok Sabha from that constituency. If Shri Patil had not agreed to his candidature, it would have been very difficult for Shri Krishna Menon to find another constituency and if Shri Patil had not helped him in the election it would also have not been possible for him to win.

Shri Krishna Menon rewarded Shri Patil for this help by creating opposition against him after the election and by creating intrigues against him in Bombay, as was generally known in that city. The relations between Shri Patil and Shri Krishna Menon were thus spoiled. Shri Krishna Menon had earned the respect of the Indian people by his powerful advocacy of the Indian cause in the United Nations and in refuting Pakistani lies there, but people got very upset with him when he showed weakness in our relations with China later on. Ultimately he had to resign his Ministership on account of popular demand and pressure after the shameless aggression made against us by China in 1962. Before this happened, Shri Krishna Menon again fought the election for the Lok Sabha from Bombay city in the General Elections of 1962 and was elected. But in the elections of 1967, he was not given a Congress ticket by Shri Patil and Shri Krishna Menon contested that election against the Congress, after leaving it, as an independent candidate. This was a very telling indication of the measure of loyalty which Shri Krishna Menon had for the Congress. Shri Krishna Menon lost in the elections in 1967 and Shri S. G. Barve who defeated him as a Congress candidate died a short time later. Shri Krishna Menon contested the election again, but Shri Barve's sister, the Congress candidate, even though she was quite new to politics, defeated him. Shri Krishna Menon was then elected to the Lok Sabha in a by-election from West Bengal with the help of the Communists. He holds rather extreme political views and there is a feeling amongst the people that he is a supporter of the Communists.

At the end of 1956, before Shri Krishna Menon joined the Cabinet, Shri Lal Bahadur Shastri had resigned his Railway Ministership as several accidents had taken place on the railways at that time. Such accidents had occurred before and have occurred again since, not only in India, but in all countries. But Shri Lal Bahadur Shastri felt that the Railway Ministry must accept the blame for not preventing the accidents and that he must resign as the Minister in charge. Jawaharlalji accepted his resignation. It did increase the reputation of Shri Lal Bahadur Shastri and I felt at that time that he took this step only to enhance his reputation and prestige. He was not responsible for the accidents and if ministers have to resign in this manner and if it became a rule, hardly any minister would be able to work for any length of time. Shri Lal Bahadur Shastri was a skilled political tactician, and I therefore felt that he had taken this step to enhance his political prestige.

21

My Russian Tour

THE RUSSIAN Ambassador, Mr. Benedictov, met me at the end of 1959 and during his talk with me, asked me why I did not go via the USSR when I went to meetings of the World Bank. He also said that there was an air service from India to London via Moscow and there was also one to Washington. 'I have no desire to visit any country indirectly in this manner,' I told him, 'and I do not go to any country without an invitation from the government of that country. I am not fond of merely seeing the world or places of interest. If, however, my visit adds to the friendship between the two countries, I consider it my duty to go. I cannot therefore go to USSR unless I am invited by your Government.' He immediately said that that would be easily arranged. 'This depends upon your desire, but I do not want to invite any invitation,' I told him. When, soon after, the Foreign Minister of the USSR visited India, he invited me to visit his country.

When Mr. Khrushchev visited India early in 1960, he pressed me to visit Russia. When I had met him at the end of 1955 in Bombay, he did not invite me, as I have mentioned earlier, even though he invited several people in my presence to visit Russia. His attitude at that time was, therefore, somewhat different. When I met him this time again, he pressingly invited me to go to Russia. When we were together at lunch with Jawaharlalji, he asked Jawaharlalji also to send me to Moscow as I was the only person who had not gone there. Before flying back home from the Delhi airport, he again pressed me to go to Russia and requested Jawaharlalji to send me there soon. But I did not immediately make any plans for going there.

It was my practice to visit countries according to my convenience when I went to attend the meetings of the World Bank and I did not, therefore, want to make a special visit to Russia at that time. Then, in the month of April, Mr. Benedictov asked my Economic Secretary when he met him why I was not fixing a programme for visiting Moscow and why I was indifferent about it. The Economic Secretary told him that the Minister would not arrange a visit to any country until he was convinced that such a visit would benefit India. Mr. Benedictov assured him that my visit to Russia would certainly be profitable. When I saw that he was so eager about my visit to Russia, I considered it advisable to make a special visit to Russia and arranged accordingly a programme for visiting Yugoslavia, Poland, Czechoslovakia, West Germany, the UAR and the USSR, as they had all invited me to visit them. Jawaharlalji gave his consent to this programme.

As I had to go to Yugoslavia through the UAR, I first stopped in Egypt where I met President Nasser and his Finance Minister. I had very friendly talks with President Nasser and discussed with him how we could make our economic relations stronger. I had similar talks with some of his ministers also. I visited the pyramids and the site of the high Aswan Dam. I visited archeological sites and did some boating on the Nile. From Cairo, I went to Alexandria and saw a modern textile mill and some other factories. President Nasser was very popular in Egypt and led a very simple life. He was thinking all the while of how Egypt could be made more prosperous and strong and used his energies towards achieving that end. President Nasser passed away suddenly as a result of a heart attack in 1970.

From Egypt I went to Yugoslavia where I met President Tito at his residence on an island. I had very frank talks with him and also with some of his ministers. They showed me some of their factories and the way they were managing them. I was shown some cooperative farms. When I visited one such cooperative farm I had some discussion with some peasants there and was convinced that the cooperative farm was working very well and had increased its production a great deal. I could see easily that their factories were working with full autonomy and there was no interference from Government in their day-to-day working. The Government judged them on the basis of their efficiency and the annual results. I also observed how this Communist country was carrying on its Government in its own way, in a pragmatic manner, and how they were constantly working for getting cooperation from the people in all that they did. This was not my first meeting with President Tito. I had first met him in Bombay. Relations between Yugoslavia and India were very friendly and efforts were constantly being made to see that these relations became closer and more profitable to both the countries. My visit helped in strengthening these relations. From Belgrade I went to Poland. I met the Prime Minister who was also the head of his party. I could see in my short visit that Poland had made very good progress in all directions. They had accommodated me in a Guest House which had many conveniences and had made very good arrangements for my comforts. They took me to see a Nazi concentration camp which had been the scene of numerous atrocities during the war. I felt extremely unhappy at what I saw. They showed me how the prisoners were induced to remove their clothes by telling them that they were being taken for a bath and were then taken to a chamber where they were gassed and killed. I also saw how they used to cut the hair from the dead bodies of these prisoners and how this hair was woven into cloth. The Nazis even extracted teeth from the bodies to collect whatever gold there was in some of the teeth. They described to me how inhuman and abominable were the atrocities perpetrated by the Nazis and graphically described how terribly the Jews and others suffered at their hands. This made me so unhappy and made me feel so nauseated that I could not eat that day. If I had not seen all this it would have been difficult for me to believe that people can be so cruel.

From Poland I went to Prague in Czechoslovakia where I was put up in a special very well furnished villa. I had long and frank talks with the Czech President, Prime Minister and others at Prague. I told them that there were some differences in the methods of our working and beliefs, as we had chosen the democratic way of life, but we believed in peaceful coexistence and we appreciated the policies which different countries adopted for themselves, according to their requirements. We had, therefore, to cooperate without interfering with each other. I had to make this clear as the President asked me some significant questions on these matters. But our discussions were very frank and friendly on the whole. They related also to our mutual economic relations and interests.

I observed that the people of Czechoslovakia are very much advanced. Their youth movement has developed a great deal but I also saw that there was a feeling of suppression amongst the people. Some of the persons I met were not prepared to talk frankly. I could gather from my talks with several people that only about 7 to 8 per cent of the population believed in communism while the rest believed in democracy. But the hold of the Communist dictatorship was very strong. They had to behave as Moscow directed them to do and those who carried on the Government were all Communists. The people therefore very naturally felt suppressed.

From Prague I went to see the famous Skoda factory. I was deeply impressed by the efficiency which I saw in the working of this factory. I also saw the main centre of hot springs of Czechoslovakia. It is a beautiful place and is visited by many people. Then I saw their famous glass works and the different articles of fine glass, some of which are not produced elsewhere.

From Czechoslovakia I went to Bonn, the capital of West Germany. From there I went to the Black Forest and the hot springs sanatoria. They also took me to see their port, Hamburg. I also went to Berlin for a day. The present Chancellor of West Germany, Mr. Willy Brandt, was the Mayor of Berlin at that time. When I met him there I had long talks with him about the partition of Berlin and Germany. Our views on many subjects coincided. West Germany encountered many difficulties as Berlin was partitioned and was also cut off from it. I saw some of the cities of West Germany and also the part of Berlin which belongs to East Germany. The destruction in Berlin and West Germany as a result of the last war was immense. Though they had constructed many new buildings, the ravages of the last war could still be seen. I, however, was impressed by the fine recovery which Berlin had made after the war, and their prosperity was such that no sign of the war damages could be particularly noticed.

Economic conditions in East Germany did not appear to be as good as in West Germany and many people from East Germany used to migrate to West Germany every day. Later on, East Germany built a high wall between the two Berlins to stop this. I saw Chancellor Adenaur in Bonn. He stood straight as a rod and was very healthy, even at the age of 85 or 86. He was very alert and impressive in his talks. I had good many discussions with him about the economic aid that they were giving. We had also some discussion on why developed countries should contribute to the development of underdeveloped countries. I told him that Germany could not have revived so well from the ravages of the war if they had not received vast aid from America. I made a polite suggestion that Germany could justify the help received by it from America by helping other countries to develop. Chancellor Adenaur appeared to agree with this. He was a very strong opponent of Nazism and accepted the general feeling that the strength and freedom of Germany depended on the care taken by it to see that Nazi conditions did not arise again in Germany. He was also of the opinion that other countries would have faith in Germany's professions of peace only if it could nip in the bud any revival of Nazism.

I had gone to Bonn at the invitation of Dr. Ludwig Erhard who was the Vice-Chancellor of West Germany at that time. My colleagues and I had discussions with him. Shri B. K. Nehru who was India's Commissioner General at Washington at that time had joined me in Bonn. During these discussions on economic relations between India and Germany, Shri B. K. Nehru suggested that it was very necessary that developed countries should help undeveloped or underdeveloped countries and that the loans that were given must be long-term loans. He also suggested that half the loans should be converted into grants and the rate of interest should also be very low. Dr. Erhard gave a very unsatisfactory rejoinder to Shri B. K. Nehru's suggestions. There was some harshness in his replies. He said: 'Foreign exchange is not a fruit which can be plucked from a tree, and it is therefore not possible to give aid as you have suggested. If the conditions on which Germany gives aid to India are not acceptable and are considered hard, it is for India to decide whether they should take the aid or not.' When I heard Dr. Erhard speaking in this manner, I got a feeling that it would not be possible to have good relations with them. I did not, however, say anything at that time and went on listening for about ten minutes in silence to the exchange between him and Shri B. K. Nehru. I remained completely at ease and quiet even though I was shocked to some extent by Dr. Erhard's reactions. Dr. Erhard addressed me after ten minutes and asked me to give my views. I then said very quietly: 'I have heard all that you have said with great attention and have got a complete idea of the position. I have come here only on your special invitation and also because I was given to understand that the conditions of aid would be made more liberal. This is why I was discussing these matters. I did not volunteer to come here and hold discussions.'

'The poorest man,' I added, 'also has his self-respect. I have realised that no country or institution can become prosperous without incurring debts and this is why India is ready to take help from other countries which are desirous of advancing that aid. But I feel from the manner in which you have spoken that I should not have come here and shall be more careful in this matter in future. We are very grateful to you for all the help that you have given us so far and thank you for it, but I do not want to put myself in this position in future, after this talk.'

When I talked to him so frankly and quietly, it seemed to have a substantial effect on him and he said immediately: 'It is not our intention not to help. It is also not our desire not to think fully about your requirements. As a matter of fact, we want to help you and are ready to do so. I hope, therefore, you will not misunderstand me in any way. It was my intention in saying what I said to explain to you the difficulties which I encounter in persuading my Government in this matter.' He then added he was sorry for any misunderstanding that might have arisen and asked me to forget it. When he thus reinterpreted his attitude and expressed regret for what he said, I accepted his explanation gladly.

Our Ambassador at Bonn gave a reception that very evening

which Dr. Erhard attended. He took me aside and assured me again of his good intentions. He also assured me that he would do all that was possible to explain to his colleagues the necessity of making the conditions of aid more liberal and again asked me to forget what he had said in the morning. I assured him again that I had forgotten the whole incident.

Germany made the conditions, under which she gave aid, lighter and more liberal, after my talks with them and more aid was also promised. I am sure that if I had not talked to them in the manner in which I did and with such frankness, India would have lost its self-respect and would have suffered a lot of damage. The result of talking with firmness and with self-respect was very happy and our relations were also strengthened.

When I visited other parts of Germany outside Bonn, they sent police pilot cars with me, so that I could move swiftly.

From Germany I had to go to Russia. As there was no direct flight from West Germany to Russia and the flight was via Denmark and Sweden, I travelled that way. I stopped for the night at Stockholm, the capital of Sweden. The nights had daylight at that time and I actually experienced what I had read in books about the midnight sun, and had to sleep with all the curtains closed.

The Swedish Prime Minister invited me to dinner at Stockholm, and I discussed many matters with him and his Ministers after dinner. I also obtained useful information about their economic arrangements. Sweden is a socialist country where socialism has made very great progress. There is a difference of only five to six times between the highest and lowest incomes in that country. There is no difficulty in getting employment and everybody gets wages or salaries according to their merit and working capacity. Every man and woman receives an old age pension after a certain age. Children get their education free and Government meets all the expenditure. Everybody has a house and a vehicle, and health services are provided by the state. While there is so much prosperity and socialist management on the one hand, on the other this country has a very high rate of suicides and madness. I also learnt that the number of illegitimate children was very large and that they had quite different notions to ours about relations between man and woman. Promiscuity seemed to be very common. The State provided for illegitimate children and nobody feels that anything wrong was being done in these matters.

I left Stockholm the next morning and reached Moscow within a short time. It was the beginning of July. The Finance Minister and some other officials received me at the airport and I was put up in a villa. Several people told me then that Jawaharlalji was put up in the same villa when he had visited Russia a few years earlier. Mr. Khrushchev placed his interpreter at my disposal, and the arrangements made for me were very comfortable. They had also made very careful arrangements for my food as I am a vegetarian.

I realised from one incident that nobody could come to my house to meet me without their knowledge. An Indian official who was then in Russia came to see me. He arrived somewhat earlier than the appointed time and, as he was not accompanied by any Russian official, he was not allowed entry into the house. The sentries had some talk with their officer over the telephone, and the Indian official was admitted into the house after fifteen or twenty minutes. I was therefore convinced that there was no possibility of my meeting anybody I liked in that place. I had no such intention either, as I knew about these arrangements in Russia, which was very natural with the kind of administration that was functioning there.

The President of India, Dr. Rajendra Prasad, was also in Russia at that time as a State guest. Mr. Khrushchev was not present in Moscow when Dr. Rajendra Prasad arrived there. I reached Moscow the day after Dr. Rajendra Prasad arrived and Mr. Khrushchev met me before he saw Dr. Rajendra Prasad.

I once saw Mr. Khrushchev returning to Moscow from tour. There were eight or ten similar cars in procession in one of which, I was told, Mr. Khrushchev was travelling. It was not possible for anybody to find out in which car he was travelling. I understood that this was done as a security precaution. Moscow roads are very broad—broader than those in other cities.

I was taken to see a play in a theatre. Even though I did not understand the language I could see that it was very well played. I went to see the university which was very near my residence. They also showed me the new houses that they were constructing. Four-storeyed houses were being erected in different parts of the city. They were all made out of prefabricated material and the construction was completed in a month. I saw one or two blocks of the new houses. They had two or three rooms and a kitchen and the arrangements were quite convenient, even though the rooms were not large. The old houses were demolished and the population in that area was shifted to these new housing blocks. Housing facilities were thus provided speedily but there was nothing amazing in such arrangements as they had obtained their freedom more than forty-three years ago. While I was shown all these arrangements in the city I was not shown any rural areas.

When I met Mr. Khrushchev, the Finance Minister and several other officials were also with him. I was accompanied by Shri B. K. Nehru, the Economic Secretary, and two or three other officials, including an Indian interpreter. Mr. Khrushchev initiated the discussions in his own characteristic style. I had got an impression during his visit to Bombay that he was a very frank person. He was also a very capable and well-informed person. He had a great aptitude for discussions and had the capacity of making quick repartees. He started by saying: 'Mr. Desai, you are an enemy of communism and as such it will be better if you see what the devils of communism are doing here.' This was his style of humour, but I also got the impression that he wanted to make a hit of some kind in talking to me in this humorous manner. I replied: 'Mr. Khrushchev, you are known as a very well-informed person, and yet I see that you are not so well-informed by the manner in which you have addressed me. I am not an enemy of any person or theory and I have no interest in enmity of any kind as I do not believe in it. I am not an enemy even of the person who is inimical to me. I would certainly defend myself against such a person, but I would not attack anyone. While I am not in favour of communism as its programme does not attract me and I have no faith in its principles, I have and can have no quarrel with those who believe in communism in other countries. I believe in peaceful coexistence and in freedom of action. I have not come here for any inspection and it is not my business to find out what the Communists are doing here. I would not even consider it proper. But I have much interest in finding out what useful work is done for human welfare and benefit by it, and this is why I have responded to your invitation to come here. I hope therefore that you will not consider me an enemy of communism.' Khrushchev hastened to say that he had spoken in a humorous vein.

He began to discuss religion and God. I had to express my views, and when, after some discussion, he could not counter my arguments, he said with a smile that God had asked him not to believe in Him. When he made this reference to God, I said: 'I am quite satisfied with your statement because you are accepting the existence of God in this manner.' He realised that he had lost his argument and closed that subject.

He then began to criticise America severely and said: 'We help you in order that the Americans might give you more aid. They will give you more aid as soon as we give you aid.'

I replied: 'For me both are friendly countries. How would you feel if I tell you that you help us because the Americans help us? I would not consider it proper to do so. It would not be right to criticise countries helping us in this manner and I, therefore, cannot agree with what you say.'

'Americans are war-minded,' he said, 'You and we are peace-loving people. The Americans want to destroy us in war.'

'It is not proper, in my view,' I said, 'to say that Americans are warmongers. If anybody makes such a charge against us, we would not like it. But supposing Americans are warmongers, and you and we are peace-loving people, is it not our duty to preserve peace? If two persons are driving their cars from opposite directions and if one of them drives carefully in order to avoid an accident and the other is driving in a reckless manner, do you not think that it is necessary for the person who wants to take care to be more careful in order to avoid an accident? If he is careful enough to see that an accident is avoided, even if the other man is reckless, will you not agree that an accident can be avoided? Even if, therefore, America is war-minded, do you not think that it is our duty to make them peace-minded? If this is our duty, will we be able to convert them by making such charges against them? We can convert them only by friendly behaviour with them.'

He replied: 'I agree with you, but they say that they want to destroy communism.'

I told him: 'You say that they want to destroy communism, but they have not made any such public statements to others. But you specifically said in a speech in New York that you would bury America. If you can tell them this in their own country in this manner, and if they retaliate, it is but natural. Peace-loving countries must therefore be more careful and you will agree that it is not wise to criticise Americans in this manner.'

He accepted the truth of my arguments and then told me: 'Communism is so good that it will spread in your country also.' I replied to him: 'If our people are impressed by your work or are convinced that you are doing very good work and voluntarily prefer communism, it is another matter. But if you consider it proper to take steps to spread communism in my country, would you permit us to propagate democracy in your country or would you allow us to do so? If you are not willing to do so, how can you expect a different kind of behaviour in our country and how would you justify it? It is, therefore, better that there should be healthy competition between the two systems, and it would be appropriate if people accept communism if it has good results. Would you not agree that this should not be achieved by force or aggressive propaganda?" He accepted what I said with a smile, but again asserted that 'people in India will accept communism', to which I retorted, 'It is my faith that you will be converted to democracy as democracy always functions better in my view.'

We closed the discussion about political matters at this stage. This discussion made our relations very friendly and, after discussing some matters about our country, he asked me where I was going in Russia. I told him: 'My programme could not have been arranged without your knowledge. Why then do you ask me about it? I myself do not know anything about it.' He immediately sent for the programme that had been arranged and examined it.

It was arranged that I should go to Leningrad and see some places in Moscow. After seeing the programme Mr. Khrushchev said: 'This is a very inadequate programme. We are not living in a bullock cart age; in this jet age when one can travel to many places in a short time, the programme should have been drawn up accordingly.' He then rearranged my programme. He made arrangements for my visiting an industrial city in the Ural mountains, Stalingrad, Baku and other places. He placed at my disposal his turbo-jet aeroplane which could carry sixty to eighty passengers. He also arranged for a smaller plane to go to places where a bigger plane could not land. I visited all these places in three or four days. I also visited Leningrad where I went by a night train which was airconditioned. I could not see anything outside as it was night and the windows were closed. I was put up in very beautiful houses and modern hotels in all these places. I saw that in Leningrad very nice arrangements had been made for marriages of many couples in an old palace. These marriages were performed at very small expenditure. I also saw their arts museum where I saw specimens of their art both before and after the revolution. I got the impression that pre-revolutionary art was superior to the post-revolutionary art. The Russians have made much progress in science as the persons engaged in scientific research had full freedom to work in their field. Workers in the fields of art and literature did not have such freedom and, as a result, there was not as much progress in these two fields as there was before the revolution. It is peculiarly true of art that an artist must be completely free if he is to develop fully. If he is bound down by any social or government control, his capacity for art gets circumscribed, and I saw this illustrated in that museum.

I also saw the splendid arrangements that had been made for the entertainment of children and their development in Soviet Russia through very nice institutions and I was deeply impressed by what I saw. I saw that they had provided similar institutions for the welfare and development of workers.

At Baku I visited the place where off-shore drilling was going on for oil exploration. I went to a platform that had been constructed in the sea for this purpose and saw what great risks were being taken by the people who were working there on high platforms, in the midst of very severe winds, large waves and bright sunshine. Their courage and efficiency impressed me very greatly.

Several pressmen had accompanied Dr. Rajendra Prasad on his visit to Russia. Some of these met me and asked me how much more help Russia was going to give us. They wanted to know what I had discussed with the Russian authorities in this connection. I told them: 'I have not come here to ask for anything. Do you want me to ask them for something? Why don't you ask them instead of asking me this question.' Some of them then met Mr. Mikoyan who was then Vice-Premier. When our Press correspondents asked him what help they were going to give us, he told them: 'Your Finance Minister has not made any request in this connection.' He said nothing more.

I happened to meet Mr. Mikoyan after this talk and my discussions with him were held in a very friendly atmosphere. He told me: 'We like to hit at people who behave with us with arrogance and in a wrong manner.' I then related to him the following story.

Gautama Buddha was once giving a discourse to his disciples when a learned Brahmin came to the spot. He was very angry with the Buddha as the latter was making propaganda against the wrong rituals which were indulged in by Brahmins in that age. The learned Brahmin criticised and abused the Buddha in a very bitter language. But the Buddha heard all that outburst patiently and with a smile and said nothing. When the Brahmin abused him for half an hour and got tired of it, he asked the Buddha, 'Oh Buddha, give some reply.' Then the Buddha asked him with a smile: 'Supposing I give you something now and you don't accept it, what would happen to it?' The Brahmin replied: 'It will remain with you.' The Buddha told him that that was what had happened to him and as he had not accepted his abuses they remained with him. When the Buddha talked to him in this quiet manner, without any excitement, the Brahmin was put to shame and after some time became his disciple.

Thus relating the story, I told Mr. Mikoyan, 'This is the special characteristic of India and we utilised this method also for obtaining our freedom. This is how we succeeded in obtaining freedom early and why we are able to achieve development very peacefully.' Mr. Mikoyan understood what I wanted to convey to him and appeared happy even though he did not make any remark.

When my talks were ending, I referred to what our pressmen had told me and asked Mr. Mikoyan: 'You have told my pressmen that I have not made any request to you. This means that I should make some request to you. Last year, you had fixed the amount of aid that you were going to give us for the Third Five-Year Plan, at 1,500 million roubles. When Jawaharlalji suggested that the agreement should specify that 1,500 million roubles was the sum fixed in the first instance and was the first instalemnt of help, you objected and said that the help will not be increased at all in future. You said that it was not possible to increase that sum, looking to your economic conditions and you had even said that if we did not agree with this arrangement, you were not prepared to make an agreement. We then accepted the agreement for the fixed grant of aid of 1,500 million roubles according to your desire. In view of this I did not want to embarrass you by talking further on this matter, and this is my attitude today. But if you feel that your economic condition is now much stronger and that you can give more aid, and would like to do so, and you desire that I should make a request for it, I shall be very glad to make one. I am therefore asking for clarification in this matter.' Mr. Mikoyan replied with a smile: 'I have understood what you want to convey and we shall let you know our decision after considering it.'

A few days after this talk, Russia made an addition of 500 million roubles to the aid of 1,500 million roubles which they had promised for the Third Five Year Plan. I got the impression that they had thought over this matter even much earlier, especially because their Ambassador, Mr. Benedictov, had assured us, before my visit to Russia had been fixed, that my visit would be profitable.

The Russian Government also held a reception in my honour. The reception was arranged in two adjoining rooms, one of which was smaller than the other. There were some selected people in the smaller room while the adjacent room had all the rest of the invitees. I inferred that such an arrangement was deliberately made. They also have a peculiar system of dining. They consume large quantities of vodka and drink frequent toasts during dinner. Vodka resembles water in appearance and does not have any particular smell. Some guests therefore mistook it for water. I knew about it and they also knew my views in the matter. They were, therefore, very careful so far as I was concerned and also made the position very clear somewhat humorously. The interpreter who accompanied me during my visit to Soviet Russia was Mr.

Khrushchev's personal interpreter. Particular care was taken about my convenience at the residence where I was put up and I thanked them for it.

I returned to India after a ten-day visit to Russia. Mr. Khrushchev wrote a very warm letter to Jawaharlalji about my visit. Jawaharlalji told me about it and said that Mr. Khrushchev had expressed great satisfaction about my visit and had even used very complimentary words for me. But Jawaharlalji did not show me the letter and I did not ask him to do so.

22

The Ten-year Rule and Gujarat

THERE WERE heavy floods in the river Tapti near Surat during the monsoon of 1960 and many areas in Surat were inundated. There was heavy damage in some parts of the city and several houses collapsed in nearby villages. There was loss of human and animal lives and crops were also damaged. I was then abroad and on returning home I went to the flood-affected areas. I was very happy to see that the people had faced this natural calamity very courageously and that good arrangements had been made for giving them relief. I was, however, very unhappy that I could not be in Surat, my constituency, at the time of the floods.

Shri Kanjibhai Desai had been ill for some time and had received some injuries as a result of a fall in the house. He passed away at the end of 1960. I could not be present at his death bed as I was then in Delhi. I, however, went immediately to Surat and met all the family members and shared their grief and loss. Kanjibhai and I were great friends and I considered him my elder brother. Our approach to life was so similar that if anybody asked us questions, even when we were separated by large distances, our replies would be almost the same. He had served Surat district and particularly the backward people of Olpad taluka. He made a substantial contribution towards making the Gujarat Pradesh Congress Committee strong and effective. He was President of this Committee from 1946 to 1960, for about fifteen years, and was very popular. I lost my only friend by his death. He was ten years older than me, and my relations with him and his whole family were those of a family member and have continued as such till today.

Kanjibhai's son, Shri Hitendra Desai, became Education Minister in the bilingual Bombay State in 1957 and Revenue Minister in the Gujarat Ministry after Gujarat became a separate State. Shri Balwantrai Mehta who was then Chief Minister of Gujarat died tragically on 19 September 1965 when the plane in which he was travelling was shot down by Pakistani fighters. Shri Hitendra Desai succeeded him as Chief Minister.

The annual Congress session was held under the Presidentship of

Shri Sanjiva Reddy at Bhavnagar in the beginning of 1961 and Shri Balwantrai Mehta was the Chairman of the Reception Committee on that occasion. Arrangements had been made at that time for the stay of the delegates and leaders together in one camp. Members of the Reception Committee were enrolled in very large numbers and many of them attended the sessions. Arrangements had to be made for housing them. It was winter and the cold at Bhavnagar at that time was more severe than usual. We all stayed in the camp, but Jawaharlalji for whom we had prepared a suitable hut in the camp, stayed at the palace of the Maharaja of Bhavnagar for security reasons.

There was a discussion in the Working Committee at Bhavnagar as to how long ministers should continue in their posts. Shri Sanjiva Reddy suggested that no minister should continue as a minister for more than ten years at a time. No resolution was passed to this effect, but the opinion of nearly all those present at the meeting was in favour of establishing such a convention. This was subsequently discussed in a meeting of the Gujarat Pradesh Congress Committee, when Dr. Jivaraj Mehta the Chief Minister, Rasikbhai Parikh, Shri Ratubhai and a few others opposed the proposal. But a very large majority of the delegates present agreed with the suggested ten-year rule and wanted that this should be implemented in Gujarat. I too supported it. If this rule was implemented, all the three colleagues whom I have mentioned above would have had to retire from ministership after election. As far as I could see, it was because of this that they were opposed to the rule. Shri Dhebarbhai had agreed with the proposal and even challenged me for its implementation, saying that this was the real test of my leadership. He was very keen on the implementation of this rule. To give effect to this rule, it was necessary that these three friends should not contest the elections. If they did, it would create difficulties if they were not appointed ministers, and it would create an awkward situation. When the time came for selecting candidates for elections, Dhebarbhai asked me on the phone from Rajkot what objection I had if these friends contested in the elections. They might not become ministers, but they could stand for election as members of the assembly. I was somewhat surprised by this suggestion of Dhebarbhai, but if I had objected to the suggestion, my objection would be interpreted as my personal opposition to these friends. I therefore did not oppose their candidature, and this created bitterness later on.

When Gujarat was formed as a separate State on 1 May 1960, I had discussed the question as to who should be the first Chief Minister with Dhebarbhai, Khandubhai and some other leaders. A large number of the Gujarat members of the Bombay Assembly did not favour Jivarajbhai; some favoured Khandubhai, while some others favoured Shri Balwantrai Mehta. The last two were not members of the Assembly, and general elections were to take place only after a year and a half. It was, therefore, difficult to choose a non-member as a Chief Minister and such a step might have created some bitterness in the party also. We, therefore, decided that those who were in the Bombay Ministry from Gujarat should be the members of the new Gujarat Cabinet and that it should not be expanded. A Cabinet of five was therefore formed. This arrangement was also considered helpful in ensuring that the new State started with simplicity. Jivarajbhai was seniormost amongst all the Ministers and I suggested that he should remain Chief Minister until the elections of 1962. The proposed arrangement was agreed to by friends on condition that the arrangement should continue only for two years and that he should not thereafter continue as Chief Minister. In order to avoid any misunderstandings with Jivarajbhai in future in this connection, I conveyed to him a message through Shri Shantilal Shah asking him whether he was willing to be Chief Minister for two years only. When Shantibhai told me that he was so willing, the Congress legislators of Gujarat elected Jivarajbhai as the leader at my suggestion.

When the 1962 elections were approaching and the time came for his retirement, Jivarajbhai forgot the previous talk with Shantibhai and advanced his claim to be the Chief Minister for a further period. He had opposed the ten-year rule in the Gujarat Pradesh Congress Committee meeting, and Shri Rasikbhai and Shri Ratubhai Adani had joined him in that opposition. When it was decided to elect Dr. Jivaraj as Chief Minister in 1960, Dhebarbhai told me with some insistence that I should make it clear at that time that Shri Balwantrai Mehta would be the Chief Minister after the 1962 elections. I personally did not like to make such a declaration in advance, but on account of Dhebarbhai's insistence in this matter, I made this very clear in the presence of some colleagues. Any one amongst the other three leaders—Shri Balwantrai Mehta, Babubhai Patel and Thakorebhai Desai—would normally have been the Chief Minister of Gujarat. But efforts had been made to get them defeated in the elections and all the three were defeated. When this happened, I felt that in their absence it was better that Jivarajbhai, who had been elected as a member, should continue to be Chief Minister, and I told him so over the telephone from Delhi. He appreciated my suggestion. He did not have a majority in the Congress Legislature Party.

Only 15 to 20 per cent of the members supported him. As, however, the three candidates who could have been considered for chief ministership were defeated, I suggested this arrangement.

Jivarajbhai accordingly became Chief Minister again after the 1962 elections, and he included in his Cabinet Rasikbhai Parikh and Ratubhai Adani as Ministers with my concurrence. The implementation of the ten-year rule was thus given up.

All those involved were my friends, but the way things developed they got very much annoyed with me and have continued to be so till today.

Group photograph of the Union Ministers (1956).

The President, Dr. Rajendra Prasad, administering the oath of office and secrecy to Shri Morarji Desai as Minister for Commerce and Industries, at Rashtrapati Bhavan, New Delhi, on 14th November 1956.

The author with Acharya Vinobha Bhave.

The author taking a stroll in his garden.

The Union Ministers pulling their weight.

The President, Dr. Radhakrishnan, with the Prime Minister, Shrimati Indira Gandhi, the Deputy Prime Minister, Shri Morarji Desai, and various members of the Cabinet (1966).

The author with Shrimati Indira Gandhi.

The author with the West German Federal Minister of Foreign Affairs, Willy Brandt (1969).

Morarji Desai, Indian Deputy Prime Minister and Minister of Finance, pictured with Britain's Prime Minister, Mr. Harold Wilson (1967).

The author with American President John F. Kennedy.

The author entertaining Mr. Nicolai Bulganin and Mr. Nikita Khrushchev on their first visit to India (1955).

The author addressing a World Bank Conference.

The author at work.

23

The Question of Deputy Leadership

PANTJI TOOK seriously ill in 1961. He had had a heart attack two or three years earlier also, and in this second attack he remained in coma for a little more than two weeks. Death, however, did not spare him a second time even though all possible medical aid was given to him. The Congress and the country lost a very capable leader.

Pantji was then the Deputy Leader of the Congress Party in Parliament. Ever since it was formed in 1946, whoever was No. 2 in the majority party, became the Deputy Leader without any contest. Sardar Patel was thus the first Deputy Leader and was also the Deputy Prime Minister. After the passing away of the Sardar, Maulana Azad became the Deputy Leader as No. 2 in the Party. He occupied that post from 1951 to 1958. After his passing away, Pantji became No. 2 in the Cabinet and was Deputy Leader from 1958 to 1961, in which year he passed away. When I joined the Cabinet in 1956 I was given the fourth place. I became No. 2 in the Cabinet after the Maulana and Pantji passed away. I should, therefore, have naturally become the Deputy Leader according to the established convention. I, however, understood that Jawaharlalji had some other intention.

As long as I was in Bombay Jawaharlalji used to consult me on most of the important problems, even in the formation of his Cabinet. I did not notice any change immediately after I joined the Cabinet at Delhi but I saw some change in his attitude in 1960. One of the reasons for this might have been the propaganda being carried on by some people and in some newspapers that I would succeed Jawaharlalji. I did not like such discussion but I was helpless as I could not prevent it. I knew that this would create jealousies. My name was mentioned as Jawaharlalji's successor even during the life-time of Maulana Saheb and Pantji and I considered it very improper. I had felt at that time that this had created some doubts in Pantji's mind too. But when once some members asked me about it, I told them that if Jawaharlalji stepped aside Pantji alone could succeed him. There could be no question about this as he was the seniormost and most reliable Congress leader. He was also a most capable and experienced administrator. There could, therefore, be no other consideration in this matter. When Pantji heard about my views his doubts about me disappeared as I could understand from his subsequent talks with me. But it is probable that some misunderstanding might have prejudiced Jawaharlalji. I observed that it was Jawaharlalji's practice not to have anybody as an adviser for more than three years. He was thus taking precuations to see that nobody would create difficulties for him. I observed this only after I joined the Central Cabinet at Delhi.

Jawaharlalji encouraged ministers to argue independently in Cabinet discussions and did not discourage anybody from putting forward his own point of view. Sometimes he did persuade some ministers to accept his view before a meeting. But he never tried to persuade me in advance in this manner. He knew I would not compromise in matters of principle and there was an unspoken understanding between us that whenever a question of principle was involved, he would not pressurise me to make a compromise and would not even argue in the matter. Where there was no question of principle I would give my view, but ultimately accepted his decision. We had, therefore, no difference of opinion in our discussions inside or outside the Cabinet and our relations were very cordial. But he knew that I would not approve of everything he would want to do, and I saw that he had some reservations in his dealings with me after I joined his Cabinet.

Jawaharlalji did not believe in God and, while adhering to truth generally, he had no objection to resorting to an occasional untruth. He, however, avoided being directly associated with untruth personally and turned a blind eye when colleagues resorted to falsehood, either of their own accord in order to please him or at his instance. I realised, after coming to Delhi, that I was not useful to him in such matters. He must, therefore, have decided that I should not be made the Deputy Leader. If he had not supported their proposal, Shri Krishna Menon and some other members would not have supported Shri Jagjivanramji in the election for the post of Deputy Leader.

When I learnt about the candidature of Shri Jagjivanram, I saw Jawaharlalji and conveyed to him my point of view. I said: 'According to the present convention, the No. 2 Minister in the Cabinet becomes the Deputy Leader. I do not, therefore, consider it proper that you should allow a contest to take place. If it does take place it will mean that you have no confidence in me and that I should therefore leave the Cabinet.'

Jawaharlalji then proposed electing two Deputy Leaders, one from the Lok Sabha and the other from the Rajya Sabha. He told me that he had felt, from the very beginning, that there should be two Deputy Leaders and had been thinking of introducing this even when Sardar Patel was alive. I told him that if he had made such a proposal to the Sardar, the latter would have left the Cabinet and that was why he had not made it till today. 'I have so far observed the rule,' I added, 'that I should accept a position in the party only if I am unanimously elected to it. If, therefore, there is a contest for Deputy Leadership, I will not stand for election and I feel that I must resign from the Cabinet.'

Jawaharlalji asked me how he could persuade the other contestant to withdraw, saying I should be prepared to contest an election in a democracy. I replied that if that was his desire, I was ready to contest the election. I also said that if I was defeated it would mean that the party had no confidence in me and that I would in that case also resign from the Cabinet.

When I declared my candidature in the election, the general atmosphere was such that I would have been elected and Jawaharlalji changed his tactics and asked me whether I had any objection if no minister became Deputy Leader and one ordinary member from the Lok Sabha and another from the Rajya Sabha were elected as Deputy Leaders.

'I am not obsessed by the desire to be the Deputy Leader,' I replied, 'but I would lose my self-respect if any minister who is lower in rank than me becomes the Deputy Leader. I can have no objection if ordinary members become Deputy Leaders as my self-respect is not involved in such an arrangement. When somebody has to speak in the Lok Sabha in your absence, I will have to do so as an ordinary member will not be able to speak on behalf of the Government. The question of any loss of my self-respect would therefore not arise. If, therefore, you want to make such a new arrangement, you may do so.'

He then took that decision and I was convinced that all these plans were made only for preventing me from becoming a Deputy Leader.

When Jawaharlalji proposed the resolution for changing the constitution of the Congress Parliamentary Party for this purpose, there was no unanimity and when votes were taken some of us felt that the majority was not in favour of the resolution from the hands that were raised. But Jawaharlalji declared that the resolution was passed. One of the members had asked for a division, but he paid no heed. Nobody then pressed for a division. If a division had been made and if the resolution had been defeated as a result, Jawaharlalji would have had to resign from the leadership of the party. If under those circumstances I or anybody else had been elected leader, there would have been a split in the party and Jawaharlalji would never have tolerated this. Neither I, nor anybody else had even half the popularity which Jawaharlalji enjoyed amongst the masses. If I, therefore, took his place under those circumstances, Jawaharlalji could have created a situation where it would have been impossible for me to work. This would have destroyed the Congress and the country would have suffered a great deal. I had no desire for office but I was determined to see that the unity of the Congress party was maintained. I have always tried to see that no harm is caused to the country as a result of my actions. A division was not therefore insisted upon and we accepted Jawaharlalji's decision. I felt that Jawaharlalji, by this step, wanted to lower my position in the party and adopted this plan to ensure that I did not succeed him in office. I must, however, make it clear that in spite of all this he never behaved with me in any improper manner and he never interfered in my work.

There was a talk in some quarters that I would not be included in the new Ministry to be formed after the elections of 1962. I would not have been in any way dissatisfied or unhappy if I had not been included and I did not, therefore, see Jawaharlalji at all until he sent for me at that time. When he called me he was lying ill in bed. There was talk that he would bifurcate the Finance Ministry in order to weaken that office and only one part would be entrusted to me. When I met him he made a reference to this proposal, but I told him that it was not practicable and that I was opposed to it as the work of the Ministry would be greatly hampered as a result. When I spoke to him like this, he gave up that proposal and did not make any change, but I saw that he had been seriously considering it.

Some people had felt, after the passing away of Pantji in 1961, that the Home Ministry should be entrusted to me. Many people felt that I would be able to manage the Home Ministry even better than the Finance Ministry, but I did not think that Jawaharlalji would accept such an arrangement. I felt that he was afraid that if the Home Ministry was entrusted to me, it would increase my political importance a great deal. This was why, when Shri T. T. Krishnamachari resigned and he asked me to take up the Finance Ministry and I suggested that it should be entrusted to Pantji, he did not accept my proposal. If he had, he would naturally have had to put me in charge of the Home Ministry. I, therefore, did not expect that the Home Ministry would be entrusted to me after Pantji's departure. Ultimately it was entrusted to Shri Lal

Bahadur Shastri who always carried out Jawaharlalji's wishes and did not do anything which he did not like. I did not talk about the matter at all with Jawaharlalji and when some friends wanted to discuss it with me I asked them not to raise it and not to come in the way of Jawaharlalji making whatever arrangements he wanted to make.

24

Talks with President Kennedy

IT HAD been decided to hold the annual meetings of the World Bank and the Monetary Fund at Vienna in September 1961. I had to attend these meetings as well as the annual conference of the Commonwealth Finance Ministers which was to be held at Accra, the capital of Ghana. I thought I should also visit the countries neighbouring Ghana as I had been invited by some of them. But I could not do so as I did not have the time.

In the Finance Ministers' Conference at Accra there was a long discussion as to whether England should join the European Common Market. Australia, New Zealand and some other countries were opposed to this. I told the conference that England's joining the Common Market would not benefit her and that it might damage the Commonwealth very seriously. I, however, made it clear that we did not want to come in the way of England's deciding whatever it wanted to do in its own interest. I also warned that it was not easy for England to get admission to the Common Market and, if their request for admission was not accepted, it would hurt their self-respect. It was, therefore, necessary for them to ascertain the views of France in this matter. From the views that he had expressed indirectly on some matters I felt, at that time, that President De Gaulle of France would not allow England to enter the Commom Market. The British Ministers did not, however, see this at that time. The discussion in the conference was rather heated in the beginning, but ended on a quiet note. I was, to some extent, helpful in persuading England to take a reasonable attitude.

While going from Accra to Vienna, I touched the airport in Nigeria, but I could not break my journey there. I had good relations with the Finance Minister of Nigeria who was a very fine gentleman. He was very able and full of humour. He was pressing me to stop in Nigeria for some time, but as I had no time to spare on that occasion I could not comply with his desire. He was murdered in the revolution that took place in Nigeria some time later.

As this was my first visit to Austria, I made enquiries about the arrangements for vegetarian diet in the hotel where I was putting up. I had learnt by experience that if a vegetarian was not careful about the arrangements for food, he might get non-vegetarian food mixed in his meals. This happens particularly in soups. I found that what they called vegetarian soup also got stock put into it. If one, therefore, was not careful, the soup that one would get would not be vegetarian. When I enquired from those in charge of the kitchen of the hotel, they promised to give me vegetarian soup. When I asked them whether they would put stock into it or not, they told me that it would not be possible to prepare soup without stock as it would remain very thin without it. They could not appreciate that stock was non-vegetarian. I told them that whatever soup was given to me should be without stock. I added that if they wanted to make it a bit thicker they could add rice water. They acted on my suggestion and told me that they had learnt a new recipe, and I got pure vegetarian soup.

I met some Ministers of the Austrian Government and discussed our economic relations with them. They gave me the impression that they wanted to help us according to their capacity. From Vienna I want to see several beautiful and delightful places in Austria. I also went to the headquarters of the Atomic Research Council and met its Directors. I learnt from them several facts about their latest researches.

After the meetings of the World Bank at Vienna were over I went to Hungary which is a neighbouring country. I had been invited by the Hungarian Government. Some years before I went there, the Hungarian people had revolted against Soviet influence but their revolt was suppressed with a heavy hand by the Soviet army and I saw several remnants of the firings that had taken place on that occasion. In Budapest I was put up in a hotel which was located on an island. It was an old hotel but full of modern conveniences and facilities.

Hungary is a unique country which has often had to suffer foreign rule and had often revolted against it. I remembered at that time the non-violent revolution and non-cooperation that the people of Hungary had successfully launched about a hundred years ago. Hungary was at that time under the Austrian Government and the people had revolted. They first made an armed revolt but they failed. They then consulted a very popular leader known as Mr. Deak. Mr. Deak was a very silent worker and believed in peaceful methods. He told them that if they did not pay taxes to the Government, the Austrian rulers would not be able to govern them. If they did not buy any property in auction after the Government had confiscated their properties for nonpayment of taxes, the Government would have to take them to Vienna to sell them which would be very burdensome to the Government. He told them that they should work with courage and determination and if nobody bought the forfeited property, they would surely succeed. The people respected him very greatly and had great confidence in his wisdom. They therefore followed his advice.

When the Hungarians refused to pay taxes, their movable properties were attached as expected. As none in Hungary would buy that property, the Austrians tried to take it to Vienna. But as they found this too costly, they gave up the attempt. The Austrian Government then quartered the military on the population in order to defeat the people's revolt. As the Hungarian people had remained non-violent, it was not possible for Government to use force against them. The Hungarians again took the advice of Mr. Deak who told them that they should not offer any opposition to the persons quartered in their houses. They should give them whatever food they required, but they should not talk with them and should not have any social relations with them. If they asked them for anything, they should answer them in monosyllables and not enter into argument. Mr. Deak said that if they behaved in that manner, the military would be frustrated.

The people acted on this advice and the military people who were quartered in their houses felt disgusted in a short time and frustrated too. They informed the Austrian Government that they would not be able to continue living in those houses for long. The Austrian Government was thus ultimately defeated and asked the Hungarian leaders what they wanted. The leaders asked the Government to consult Mr. Deak. When Mr. Deak was consulted he told them that they only wanted their own Government. The Austrian Government had realised from the determined behaviour of the Hungarian people that they would not be able to govern them any longer. They therefore accepted the demand for freedom. Mr. Deak refused to take any office after the attainment of freedom and said that he did not want any mausoleum to be put up on his grave. There should be only a stone bearing his name. This illustrated how simple and humble he was. He was a servant of the country expecting nothing in return. As he was resourceful and wise, the people succeeded in their aims by following him.

Although the Hungarian people have had to fight foreign rulers for centuries they have not lost their morale. They are a brave people and I have great respect for them. They are very cheerful and very fond of boating and other outdoor sports, as I could see while I stayed there. They took me to see two or three places which were at some distance from the Hungarian capital. One of these was the place where Rabindranath Tagore had stayed for improving his health many years ago. For the short time I was in that place, I stayed in the house in which Tagore had lived and I was told of his activities during his sojourn there.

From Hungary, I went to Washington to have discussions with the leaders of the American Government. I met President Kennedy at that time. The elder daughter of Gandhiji's son, Ramdasbhai, was at that time in Worcester University. Her brother Kanubhai was also in America at that time as he had gone there for further studies. As he was to be married at Worcester, I went there to attend the marriage. He was to be married to the daughter of Shri Madhavji Thakkar of Calcutta who was one of the 80 persons who marched with Gandhiji to Dandi in 1930. The marriage ceremonies were performed by Shri Satish Kalelkar.

I had to go by car to catch a train at the railway station which was 100 to 125 miles away, the same night, after the marriage ceremonies had been performed, as I had to see President Kennedy at Washington the next day. As I was somewhat late in starting, the car had to be driven at a very great speed. The driver told me when I reached the station that he had driven at a speed of 120 miles per hour. He had to drive at that speed as the police pilot car ahead of us was going at that speed. He would have been hauled up by the police if he had driven his car at this speed on his own. The road was very wide and as there was very little traffic it was not difficult to go at such a high speed. As it was a very large car, I did not feel the speed: I learnt about it only when the driver informed me about it.

I met President Kennedy at Washington the next day. I had a long talk with him. The Indian Ambassador, Shri B. K. Nehru, was also present.

I learnt from the talks which I had with President Kennedy that he was very well informed about the Indian political situation and was very well inclined towards India. He had proposed a resolution in favour of India in the Congress when he was not the President and had got that resolution passed. I had therefore known about his good feelings for India. He asked:

'You follow a policy of non-alignment and you have friendly relations with all countries. Do you not consider that you are more inclined towards Soviet Russia or somewhat partial to it ?'

I asked him why he put that question. He answered :

'Whenever you consider that we are erring, you criticise us in very strong language, but when you find Soviet Russia erring in some matter, you talk to them in very polite language and hesitate to find fault with them. Do you not consider this a partial attitude?'

'Soviet Russia,' I said, 'is a communist country with a dictatorial government, while you and we are democratic countries. It is clear that Soviet Russia cannot behave like a democratic government. It is, therefore, not possible to convert them by finding fault with them or by censuring them if they do something wrong. But there is a possibility of converting them to some extent if the method of friendly persuasion is adopted. Do you not consider it necessary and proper to persuade them in this manner? If you or we err in our behaviour in maintaining democratic traditions, we would be able to improve ourselves only if we look at it in a severely critical manner, and it is only then that we would be justified in talking to Soviet Russia in such a manner. Do you not consider this a very practical attitude? The first country outside the communist bloc which Mr. Khrushchev visited was India. He then began to visit other democratic countries, and his policies became somewhat liberal. Do you not agree that this would not have happened if he had not visited India first? If we wish that their government should also be democratic, we cannot effect a change by violent methods. If we are successful in our democratic governments and if the results are happy and if they feel that our behaviour with them is friendly, they might get converted. Do you not consider that this is a proper way of dealing with them? We should keep our contacts with them as long as there is hope for change, but we should not give up our own traditions or positions. If we act honestly, according to our policies and standards, we will increase our capacity to convert them.'

Mr. Kennedy heard my arguments with great attention and asked me whether we should not have informed him about this policy. I told him that this was more a matter of understanding than one of speaking publicly. We had to allow our actual behaviour to have its action on Soviet Russia. We therefore did not consider it proper to discuss this policy publicly. I got the impression that Mr. Kennedy accepted the wisdom of this stand.

Mr. Kennedy impressed me as a statesman of very liberal and broad views who was very eager to do whatever he could to establish world peace. This is how his talks impressed me. He did not want to utilise the great strength of America to suppress other countries. He wanted to utilize it for the protection of other countries and desired that all countries should remain in friendly relations with one another. I told him when the discussion shifted to the topic of China:

'I feel that it has been a great error that China has not been admitted to the United Nations. The United Nations is a league of *all* independent and civilised countries. China is also an independent nation. Formosa (Taiwan) was a part of China, but it has now an independent government. It is a small island. It is not proper to hold that independent China cannot be a member of the United Nations because it is a communist country. There are several member nations in the United Nations like Russia, which are communist. Moreover, China gets encouraged to work in an indisciplined manner by being kept out of the United Nations. It is a great danger to world peace. America has been so rigid in its attitude about China that it is not able to get out of it. American public opinion has therefore gone against China as I have observed during my visit.'

President Kennedy had engaged several capable advisers. He used to consult them often, but his personality and capacity were of an order which enabled him to take a decision according to his own judgement after taking the necessary advice. He was also very clever in arguments. The language of his speeches was very effective and his control over the language was evident in them.

From Washington I went to Princeton University on 2 October, Gandhi Jayanti Day, to deliver a speech on Gandhiji there. This university is an institution with a very great reputation. I had to deliver a speech in the chapel, where I was given a reception. I thanked those in charge of the university for this. It was a very impressive gathering and the whole chapel was full. I had to speak for twenty minutes, but I had not prepared a written speech. I was going to deliver it extempore. The persons in charge of the function were worried, for if I exceeded my time their whole programme would be upset. They did not say anything about this direct to me, but I could sense their worry and immediately assured them that I would finish my speech in eighteen minutes instead of twenty, and I did. They were all very happy about it. In my speech I said :

'America has produced great truthful politicians like Abraham Lincoln. Many people in the world today have great expectations from America for the establishment of world peace. Spiritualism is not the monopoly of India. All countries have spiritual influence, but as the spiritual philosophy of India is thousands of years old, it has made a deeper impression in this field than that of others. This was why Mahatma Gandhi was successful in spreading his message in India.'

I inaugurated the Indian Investment Centre in New York during this visit. This was a branch of the Indian Investment Centre in India. It was necessary to make available in New York all necessary information to those considering establishing industries in India in partnership with Indian industrialists. It was necessary to see that this was done systematically. It was with this in view that the Indian Investment Centre was established in India in February 1961. This was a society registered under the Societies Registration Act. It was necessary that this institution should work in close cooperation with the Government of India, and the Government therefore supported it fully and supplied the necessary finances. It was, however, not possible to get this work done with ease and speed by a Government department.

The Centre was expected to propagate the policies of Indian Government and its rules and also give the necessary information to those who wanted it. It was also the function of this institution to ascertain in what industries foreign capital could be invested and was required, and also to issue different publications to attract foreigners for this purpose. This would enable the investors to know the rules, regulations and policies of our Government. A governing body was appointed with a Chairman and ten members who were all appointed by the Government. Shri Gaganvihari Mehta was appointed its President. None was better fitted for this work at that time. He had had a very long experience of industries and been Indian Ambassador in the USA for several years and was very popular there. He developed this centre very well and performed very valuable services for the country. He continues to be its President till today.

I inaugurated this centre's branch in New York and held discussions with several industrialists there and got them interested in this activity. A branch was also opened in Brussels in 1964. This work is done through the High Commissioner in London where the work is looked after by a technical adviser.

I spoke to several societies and committees, like the Foreign Affairs Committee in New York, and explained the economic and political policies of our Government. I succeeded in removing some prevailing misunderstandings about India in these talks.

I returned to India from New York.

25

The Liberation of Goa

THERE WAS conference of the delegates of the Indo-African Association after I returned from my tour abroad in the beginning of October 1961. The problems of the apartheid policy of South Africa and of freeing some African countries were discussed. When I was invited to speak at the conference, I made it clear, while accepting the invitation, that it was my conviction that the opposition to the apartheid policy and the freedom movement must be carried on in a non-violent manner, as otherwise it would create many problems and difficulties. The African delegates were advocating removal of Portuguese rule by violent action. I had told them that I was against that policy and would give expression to my view in the conference. The policy of the Government of India was also for the solution of these problems in a peaceful manner. Some friends had sent me a message that I should not advocate non-violent methods when I spoke in the conference. I told them that I would specifically mention non-violent methods if I were to speak in the conference and that, therefore they should consult Jawaharlalji and if he agreed to my speaking in that manner I would speak; otherwise I would not go to the conference. I received his agreement and I gave expression to my views at the conference.

Soon after this, when the annual Governors' meeting took place, the President, while referring to Goa said that our policy was to free the territory in a peaceful manner. I heard at the end of November or beginning of December that our troops were concentrating on the border of Goa at Belgaum and that a force of about 30,000 men had camped there. It was, therefore, very strongly rumoured that Goa would be taken possession of by military action. Jawaharlalji did not consult the Cabinet in this matter and had not discussed this problem with anybody except Shri Krishna Menon. The Railway Minister might also have been consulted as the military forces had to be taken to Belgaum by train. Special trains were running to Belgaum, which led to the leakage of the information that military forces were concentrating at Belgaum. Jawaharlalji informed the Defence Committee about this in its meeting held at the end of December and said that the meeting of the Committee was called in order to fix a date for marching into Goa. I opposed the proposed step but as I was alone in this opposition, my opposition had no effect. I advanced many arguments without any result.

Our forces then entered Goa and took possession of it. The Portuguese could not put up any effective resistance and I had never expected any resistance from them. I was of the view that one or two thousand policemen could have taken possession of Goa, but the Defence Ministry was misled by its sources of information that the Portuguese were very strong and this was why they sent such a large force there.

As a result of these military operations, there were complaints that several unlawful and atrocious acts were indulged in by some of the military men and that they had taken away many things from the people. I learnt from reliable sources that there was a good deal of truth in those complaints. History has always witnessed the occurrence of such incidents in military operations of this kind. This should have been kept in mind by those who sent the army in and they should have taken precautionary measures against such occurrences. It was very unfortunate that this was not done. The people of India generally supported the military operation and my attitude was generally criticised in the newspapers. There was an intense feeling amongst the people that Goa should be freed quickly and this feeling was natural, but the step taken was against our professions and established policies. We have declared in our Constitution that it is our policy to solve international disputes peacefully and by negotiations, and yet this step was taken all of a sudden. Fourteen years of patience ended in this manner, and the moral respect which India commanded in the international field was destroyed. There could be no doubt that this lessened the influence of India in international affairs a great deal. If I had been consulted earlier, I would have advised the Prime Minister to give twelve months' notice to the USA, the UK and the United Nations for solving the problem as we were convinced that the Portuguese authorities did not want to make any compromise on the issue and the Portugal Government had made a public declaration to that effect. We should have informed the United Nations and others that if the Portuguese Government was not ready to arrive at a compromise and merge Goa in India within twelve months we would take military steps. If we had given such a notice, I am sure the Indian case would have been strengthened and any military steps which India had ultimately to take would have been justified and the moral stature of India would not have suffered. It was argued by some that if a notice had been given to the Portuguese Government they would have made preparations for resisting us and would have made our task very difficult, if not impossible. There were also rumours about the Portuguese Government wanting to sell Goa to Pakistan. If, however, Portugal had taken that step, the military steps taken by India would have been justified and India would not have suffered in its moral reputation as it did on account of the sudden military action it took.

When the Congress session was held in Bihar soon after this incident, this matter was discussed in the Working Committee and a resolution drafted by Shri Krishna Menon was placed before it for consideration. The resolution was to the effect that the steps taken for taking possession of Goa were in conformity with the policy of the Congress and also of the Government. Most of the members did not offer any specific comments on this, but when my turn came I said, 'This resolution is based on untruth as the taking possession of Goa by military force is a violent action and is contrary of our established policy. I have no doubt that this resolution is totally wrong and I cannot support it.'

Krishna Menon argued a great deal in favour of the resolution and said that the violence used by the Government during riots in the country was considered legitimate. Goa was also a part of India. The military action was therefore considered to be legitimate by Krishna Menon. To show that this argument was quite wrong, I said:

'When violence is used by the Government to suppress violent riots within India it was in accordance with the Government's policy. But Goa is a part of India only geographically. It is a historical fact that Goa was in the possession of Portuguese and was governed by the Portuguese Government, and that it was not a part of the territory under the Government of India. It thus was an international dispute. We have a constitutional provision that international disputes should be solved by compromise and peaceful methods and not by violence. We have made such statements from time to time for fourteen years publicly in this country and outside it. Even as late as October-November, Jawaharlalji himself had made such a statement in America. There can therefore be no doubt that this step is against our established policy.'

Shri Krishna Menon was not prepared to accept this position. But Jawaharlalji could not deny the truth of my arguments and he considered them correct. He asked me to suggest changes in the resolution. I told him that I could not make any useful suggestions in view of the attitude taken in the resolution and that my advice would be useful only if he was ready to admit that the step taken was wrong. I did not feel that he was ready to make such an admission and I could not therefore give my advice. Shri Dhebarbhai and one or two other members supported my contention. As a result of this discussion, an amendment was made in the resolution to the effect that the step taken in Goa should not be considered as being against our policy. This amendment did make a change in the previous attitude and there was also a suggestion of an indirect admission of having done wrong. But I did not consider it sufficient from the point of view that I had put forward. I, therefore said that I could not agree with it, but stated that I did not want to create any difficulty for the other members and abstained from voting. It was then suggested that I should move this resolution in the AICC meeting. I did not accept the suggestion. If I was to move the resolution I could do so only after admitting that a wrong step had been taken. As the Committee was not ready for such an admission, I did not move the resolution and remained silent on it.

When I went to Washington for the World Bank meeting in September 1962, I met President Kennedy again and had a discussion with him on this problem. He told me that he was shocked by the steps taken by India in Goa. He told me that when Jawaharlalji visited the USA the previous October or November he had referred to the peaceful policy of India as regards Goa and gave no indication that such a step would be taken within two months. If he wanted to do so, he should have taken him into confidence, so that no misunderstanding could arise. Mr. Kennedy knew my views on the matter. I told him :

'You know my views in the matter, but you ought to consider this matter from another point of view also. You have not yet accepted the policy of solving such matters by peaceful means. The steps that you took in Cuba in the beginning are being defended by you even now. In view of this, is it consistent that you should oppose India's step in Goa? Even though Jawaharlalji believed that such disputes should be settled peacefully, I understood that he had to take military action as there was a very intense feeling amongst the people of India that Goa should merge in India soon. When a person has great responsibilities, as Jawaharlalji has, one cannot say for certain as to how long he can observe principles against public opinion. You should therefore consider this problem from that point of view.'

Mr. Kennedy was impressed by this argument, but his main objection to the step was that he had not been taken into confidence in this matter.

It was the feeling of several people in the political field in

India that Shri Krishna Menon had decided to take this step to win his election from Bombay and to get over the opposition to him in that election. It was my feeling that there was truth in this view. I, therefore, suggested to the Prime Minister that if this step had to be taken, it should be taken after the elections. But the haste with which this step was taken created a justifiable feeling that it was done to win the election. It is natural that people would not believe that it was not so.

ABOUT this time the problem of the Nagas had assumed a very serious form and their leader Shri Phizo had made a persistent and vehement demand that Nagaland should be independent of India. The Nagas were indulging in many violent actions and had also set up an independent rebel government. We used our military force there to keep law and order, but full freedom was not given to our military forces to act effectively and suppress the rebellion. They were therefore not succeeding. The Naga rebels were getting sympathy from other Nagas and many allegations of terrorism were made against the military. Jawaharlalji was very worried about this and was considering very seriously how to solve this problem. He was told that the Nagas would be satisfied if a separate State of Nagaland within India was created. I understood that he was considering such an arrangement and had taken a decision without consulting any of us in this matter. I believe he had consulted some representatives of Nagas. He called a conference of the representatives of the Assam Government in 1960 in which the views of Assamese and the Naga people were presented. Jawaharlalji had already made a suggestion for separating Nagaland from Assam and making it a separate State. I opposed this and said that such a step would not solve the problem and that it would increase the difficulties instead of lessening them. I also said that giving separate statehood to such a small population, would lead to demands for separate states from different parts of the country and the unity of India would be endangered. Others present did not say anything. Jawaharlalji had probably discussed this matter with them before the meeting. Jawaharlalji argued that this question could not be solved by violent action. I then asked him :

'Will the rebel Nagas be satisfied by this step? They want complete independence. You cannot satisfy that demand by this proposal. They would, on the contrary, feel convinced that the Government of India is acting in this manner in its own interest and will feel encouraged in the revolt.'

Jawaharlalji did not like my stand and said that the Nagas considered their culture different from that of India and did not believe that Nagaland was a part of India. He considered that there was some truth in that argument. I then told him:

'If you are convinced that the Nagas are quite different from the Indians and that Nagaland is not a part of India, it would be proper that you declare it an independent country.'

But he refused to consider this proposition and said that it was not possible. I told him that if that was so, he should not advance such an argument and so he gave up that argument. But he did advocate very strongly the formation of a separate State of Nagaland within India. I repeated my argument that 'this would not only not solve the problem, but would expose the weakness of the Government of India and the problem of Nagaland would become more difficult. Moreover, the other Adivasi areas of Assam, Jharkhand, Bihar, Manipur, Tripura, the hilly tracts of Uttar Pradesh, Himachal Pradesh and such other areas would make demands for separate states, as their populations were much larger than that of Nagaland. This will, therefore, create many difficulties and it will be difficult to maintain the unity of India.'

Jawaharlalji said with some irritation: 'If there are demands from other parts for separate states, I will accept them, but I have given hope to these people that a separate Nagaland State will be formed and we must therefore take this decision.'

No one else supported my contention and all the rest agreed with Jawaharlalji. I was, therefore, the sole dissenter and did not say anything more.

After this conference, I talked to Shri Pantji and Shri Lal Bahadur Shastri and told them that this would be very harmful. They replied :

'We also do not like this step. We argued a great deal with Jawaharlalji, but he did not accept our arguments and we could not continue our opposition any further. We therefore remained silent and gave our assent to the decision.'

This convinced me that Jawaharlalji had had prior discussions with them and had taken their consent. The Cabinet also gave its assent to it because, while several colleagues agreed with me, they did not have the courage to differ from Jawaharlalji.

The Assam Government was fed up with the terrorist activities of the Nagas and gave their assent to the formation of a separate State. This also made Jawaharlalji's decision easy. I believe that this was also a result of the fact that the Assam Government did not take any steps to satisfy the Nagas and took no steps to keep up good relations with them.

Several such questions arose later on as a result of the formation of this State, and the fears which I had given expression to proved justified.

26

Britain and the Common Market

THE THIRD general elections took place in 1962. I toured most of the States during the campaign and gave a few days more to Gujarat for this purpose. I gave only six or seven days in all to my constituency of Surat and I was elected with a very good majority.

There was strong opposition to the candidature of Shri Krishna Menon. Shri S. K. Patil had agreed to his standing from a north Bombay constituency in 1957 and had helped him to get elected. But Shri Menon did not maintain good relations with the Bombay Pradesh Congress Committee between 1957 and 1962 and created a separate informal organisation for himself there. Shri Patil therefore opposed his candidature in 1962. Shri Menon was also opposed to Shri Patil in several matters. But it was ultimately decided at the highest level that Shri Menon should contest from Bombay. Acharya Kripalani opposed him in this constituency. I addressed one or two meetings there and explained to the voters that 'the casting of votes should not be on the basis of individuals. Shri Krishna Menon is a Congress candidate and you should elect him if you support the Congress.' Shri Menon won that election with a very good majority. I believe that the action in Goa helped him a great deal.

The Congress succeeded well in almost all the States and won a very large majority at the Centre. Jawaharlalji was ill when he formed the Cabinet. He discussed this matter with me from his sick bed. I found that Jawaharlalji had some prejudice against Shri Manubhai Shah, and he decided to give him the portfolio of Export Trade only. I suggested that he should also be entrusted with looking after textiles, tea and coffee plantations and jute textiles as these were the main items of export, and the Ministry would not be able to function properly if these were not added to it. He accepted my suggestion. He considered the question of dividing the Finance Ministry into two, but he agreed with me that such a step was neither feasible nor proper. Shri T. T. Krishnamachari had been elected to the Lok Sabha and Jawaharlalji proposed to take him in the Cabinet. He had first asked for the Finance Ministry but Jawaharlalji did not agree. He was, therefore, not immediately taken in the Cabinet but later on a new

Ministry was created for economic coordination and Shri Krishnamachari became the Cabinet Minister in charge of that Ministry.

A conference of the Prime Ministers of the Commonwealth countries was fixed in the beginning of July 1962, for considering the question of Great Britain's entry into the Common Market. Jawaharlalji attended that conference and took me with him. When it was the turn of India to speak on the Common Market problem, Jawaharlalji asked me to do so. I persuaded him to speak first as that would be proper. I suggested to him that he should speak generally on the policy and that it would be proper if I followed him with details. He accepted my suggestion. Both of us said in the conference that it was for England to decide whether she should join the Common Market or not and it was not for us to oppose such a step. But Britain must consider the repercussions on the other Commonwealth countries. The responsibility would be that of Britain if, as a result of its entry into the Common Market, the Commonwealth broke up. Britain must see that the Commonwealth countries did not suffer as a result of its joining the Common Market.

I visited some countries of the Common Market after this conference was over. I also attended a meeting of the Economic and Social Council at Geneva and presented India's point of view there. I went to Geneva, Brussels, Amsterdam, Bonn, Paris and Rome. I discussed with all these governments the question of India's relations with the Common Market and also tried to ascertain the attitude of these countries towards Britain's entry into the Common Market. Mr. Heath was carrying on negotiations of behalf of Britain. I had repeated in my discussions with him in London what I had said at Ghana, viz. that there was bound to be opposition to Britain's entry especially from France, and that he should take further steps keeping this fact before him. I got to know the attitude of the Common Market countries better when I visited these countries.

I went from Brussels to Luxembourg which is a very small but very prosperous state with a very large steel industry. I got the impression in my discussions with the persons concerned with the Common Market and the ministers at Bonn, Amsterdam, Brussels and Luxembourg that they were not very favourable to Britain's entry. They were not opposed to it, but they were not very enthusiastic about it.

It was arranged that Mr. Heath should meet me in Paris, so that I could convey to him the impression which I gathered from the Common Market countries. This arrangement was made as I was not to go to London again that time. I told Mr. Heath all that I learnt and said that I had understood that France was very opposed to Britain's entry into the Common Market and that it would not consent to such an entry. I was convinced that they might have long negotiations but they would ultimately say no. The chief consideration for this attitude, as I understood it, was that if Britain joined the Common Market, it would have greater influence on it and France's influence would lessen. The relations between France and Germany in those days were very good and both these countries were firmly in the Common Market from the very beginning. They were very much afraid of British diplomacy and were afraid that Britain's influence would be greater than theirs. The Common Market countries wanted to forge a political union out of the economic union. I understood that it was the policy of France not to allow Britain to enter the Common Market before the political union was achieved.

I conveyed all this in detail to Mr. Heath. He told me that he would bear all this in mind, but I got an impression that he did not want to give up his efforts for joining the Common Market. My information ultimately proved to be correct and France did not allow Britain to enter the Common Market at that time.

From Paris I went to Rome where I met the members of the Government of Italy and discussed our economic relations with them and the steps necessary to strengthen them. I considered the Italian attitude favourable and returned to India from Rome.

The 17th Annual Meeting of the World Bank and the International Monetary Fund was to take place in Washington in September of that year. I therefore went abroad again in that month. I first went to London to attend the Commonwealth Finance Ministers' Conference where we had discussions about the Common Market alongwith some other questions. New Zealand and Australia were very much opposed to Britain's entry into the Common Market as they were afraid that they would suffer a lot of harm as a result.

From London I went to Washington via New York. After attending the World Bank meeting in Washington, I went to Ottawa in Canada on the invitation of the Government there. I met the Canadian Prime Minister and other ministers. The relations between Canada and India had always been very close and cordial, and the conditions of the aid which they have given us have been far more favourable than those of other countries. From Ottawa I returned to New York. As usual I met the press in New York and addressed several institutions. I had some discussions in the Investment Centre too. I have already referred to the talks which I had with President Kennedy at Washington about Goa. We also discussed our mutual relations.

From Washington I went to San Francisco. I had severe pain in a molar tooth for some days during this tour. I had first thought of not getting it treated there and had decided to get it treated after returning to India. But when I was passing through the Redwood Forest in San Francisco, I found the pain had increased. As I could not return to India for seven or eight days more, I felt that I must get the tooth treated there for if the pain went on increasing, there was likelihood of more harm being caused. I therefore, asked one of the members of our Embassy to fix an appointment with a dentist if he knew one in San Francisco. He arranged with a very well-known dentist there. When I requested the dentist to extract the molar tooth, he told me that he would not take that step unless he took an X-ray of it. He then took an X-ray immediately and decided that the tooth had to be removed. He extracted it very skilfully, after giving me the necessary anaesthetic injection. I was bleeding and also had pain. He suggested some pills for easing the pain, but I refused to take them as I believed that such pills ultimately did more harm than good. He, however, gave me two or three pills to be taken if necessary. He did not ask me to gargle and said that it would be better if the wound healed without it. When I asked the dentist what his fees were, he refused to tell me and said that he was treating me as the country's guest. I tried to persuade him to take his fee, but he did not agree.

I had to attend a reception immediately afterwards. From the reception I went to a dinner party. I was bleeding when I went to the dinner and was also suffering from some pain. I did not, however, allow anybody to know about this. The dinner arrangements were very fine and the room was very well decorated. I had also to speak in reply to the speeches made after dinner. It was after the function was over that the bleeding stopped and the pain also disappeared.

From San Francisco I went to Tokyo, where I met the Prime Minister and others. I also met some of the businessmen and their organisations in Tokyo and discussed with them several problems regarding their trade with India. I got the impression that Japan was eager to strengthen our relations in all fields. I visited Hiroshima from Tokyo where I got an idea of the terrible damage done by the atom bomb during the last war. I also launched the ship, which Dr. Dharma Teja had bought for his Shipping Company, in a shipyard at Nagasaki.

I stopped for one night at Hong Kong on my way back to India and got an idea of the prosperity of that place. I also saw how they carried on their business in Hong Kong. I met several Indians there and when I discussed with them the possibility of their investing capital in India, I got the impression that they were not eager to do so unless they got profits from such investments at rates fully satisfactory to them.

27

The Chinese Invasion

WITHIN A FEW days of my return from my foreign tour at the end of September 1962, China started its invasion of India. They had taken possession of a lot of territory in Ladakh in the North of India and then began to invade NEFA. We had had forebodings of this invasion for some time. Before I describe this invasion I should like to give a short account of how China became inimical towards India.

There was a great revolution in the Government of China within two or three years of India becoming free. As a result of the civil war which had been going on in China for years, the Communists defeated the forces of Chiang Kai-shek who, with whatever forces he could save, went to Formosa and established his own independent government there. The mainland of China went completely into the hands of the Communists led by Mao Tse-tung. Chiang Kai-shek's Government had its capital at Taipeh in Formosa. The rest of the world was surprised by the speedy political, economic and social changes that were made by the Communists as a result of their dictatorial and disciplined rule. Those Indians who visited China after this change were very well impressed and slogans of *Hindi-Chini Bhai Bhai* began to be shouted in India. My doubts about them, however, continued from the experience that I had had of communist methods and policies, and I was of the view that we must behave with them with great caution and care. Later events exposed their real intentions.

There is an unpopulated area called Ladakh adjoining Tibet belonging to the Jammu and Kashmir State, where we had not kept any military force because there was friendship between China and India and there had been no wars between the two countries in the past. The adjacent area—Tibet—was an independent kingdom and was situated between China and India. The Chinese boundary was, therefore, not adjacent to the Indian boundary, but China claimed sovereignty over Tibet somewhere around 1950 and began to establish its hold over Tibet in 1954, sending its armed forces there. They took possession of Tibet and began to establish their administration. This created a serious struggle between Tibet and China. India had accepted the sovereignty of China over Tibet in 1950-51 on condition that China would respect the autonomy of Tibet. India did not foresee that China would establish its hold over Tibet by invading it, though Sardar Vallabhbhai had warned Jawaharlalji about this in 1950.

When the Chinese began to commit atrocities on the people of Tibet, Tibet's Dalai Lama and his followers escaped from Tibet into India. They asked for refuge in India which was given to them. This enraged China.

China has a peculiar belief that it is the most superior nation in the world and that if anybody does not accept this he is an enemy. China, therefore, began to make incursions on our borders after we gave refuge to the Dalai Lama and his followers. India thus had a clear warning and began to make military arrangements on the border.

But we were late in making these arrangements as, taking advantage of our ignorance, China had begun to construct a road in 1957 in the Aksai Chin area of Ladakh keeping us in the dark about it, and we could not stop them. When we sent some people to find out facts about this road in 1958, our men were arrested and imprisoned in China. China exposed its real attitude at that time and convinced us and the world that they had adopted an inimical attitude towards India.

The Prime Minister of China, Mr. Chou En-lai had suggested a meeting of the delegates of both the countries in Burma to discuss this dispute, but we did not accept the suggestion. Mr. Chou En-lai then came to India to discuss these matters in 1960. He held discussions with Jawaharlalji, Pantji, Krishna Menon and myself. When he expressed a desire to have a discussion with me, I offered to go to the place where he was staying but Mr. Chou En-lai sent me a message that he wanted to come to my place and meet me and accordingly he came to my residence. The discussion lasted for about seventy-five minutes. I asked him in the beginning to decide whether he should first speak about his case or whether I should do so. He decided to speak first, after which I tried to explain to him our view of the whole matter. While presenting his case, he said:

'We have the right to construct the road which we have built and that region also belongs to us.'

The Chinese had at that time taken possession of the northern part of Ladakh, that is, Aksai Chin, and he therefore argued that India had never established its authority over Ladakh. After he concluded his version, I began to argue our case. I said:

'When nobody supported China, India took your side and put

up your case in the United Naions and forged friendship with you. You accepted the principles of Panchasheela. India accepted your sovereignty over Tibet, but you had accepted the condition that Tibet's autonomy would be respected and that you would not interfere with it. When that understanding was broken and China began to take possession of Tibet and kept its army there, and the Dalai Lama and his followers came to India to save themselves from the oppression of the Chinese army and India gave them refuge, you began to be inimical towards us. We had not raised any disputes about the boundaries before this and we had suggested that we should solve whatever differences there may be about the boundaries by mutual consultation.'

When I gave him these facts, Mr. Chou En-lai got angry. When he began to talk in an angry tone, I said:

'Anger is not going to help us if we want to have any useful discussion. I heard you very quietly, without any excitement, when you talked against us in presenting your case; but when I am presenting my case, it is not proper that you should get angry. We might, therefore, close these discussions if you do not want to discuss the question any further.'

Chou then cooled down and we carried on our discussion for about twenty-five minutes more. The discussions were, however, without any result as they were not prepared to give up their stand, and as they had committed an aggression against India, there was no question of India giving up its stand.

After these discussions in India, Mr. Chou En-lai returned to China and since then they harassed us continuously on the border. They took forcible possession of about 15,000 square miles of Indian territory in Ladakh. When our army went there and saw that China had taken possession of that area, it also camped there and the armies faced each other.

On the north-east side they began to make claims on the NEFA border and claimed about half of NEFA. They claimed also some of the area on the UP boundary. Ultimately they suddenly invaded NEFA without any provocation in the month of October 1962, as I have mentioned earlier. We had sent our forces to that area. Lt.-Gen. B. M. Kaul was in charge of those forces, but he could not defend our area on account of his weakness and want of experience. Our armed forces were ready for a fight and are considered amongst the most efficient in the world. But where the Commander himself is weak and cannot use proper military tactics, even the bravest soldiers become weak. These operations were a standing example of this truth. The Himalayas had been considered an impregnable wall till then, but as proper arrangements for defence were not made it did not remain impregnable and the Chinese forces invaded NEFA crossing the Himalayas through two passes.

When there were rumours of a Chinese invasion, Jawaharlalji, while going abroad, made a statement that if China did invade our territory it would be met very strongly. Shri Krishna Menon must have assured him about our strong defences, which must have been the reason why he made the statement. But it is a fact that we could not withstand the onslaught of the Chinese in NEFA. This defeat created great anger among the people who showed great unity in the face of the threat on our borders. People from every nook and corner voluntarily sent contributions for the Defence Fund amounting to Rs. 500 million. The people of India thus showed their mettle, and China did not consider it safe to march further into India. They left NEFA and went back to their territory at the end of 1962. We have since strengthened our defences in that area.

When the invasion was on, there was a fear that China might occupy the whole of Assam and if they had continued their invasion and advance we could not have stopped them from doing so, considering what had happened in NEFA. This created some panic in Assam. The message which Jawaharlalji broadcast on the radio on that occasion also suggested such a possibility indirectly. This had a very adverse effect on the morale of the people. This defeat in NEFA was a very shameful one and India lost a good deal of its international reputation.

Jawaharlalji was deeply shocked and upset. All his calculations with regard to China went wrong. This affected his health very badly and he broke down physically. Since then he carried on his activities only with the strength of his will. Ultimately he got very ill and passed away in May 1964.

When we were discussing in the Cabinet about the danger from China in 1958, Shri Krishna Menon's attitude appeared a bit peculiar and I got somewhat worried about it. I was of the opinion that we must recover soon the area of Ladakh which China had taken possession of in 1958—59, but I found the attitude of Shri Krishna Menon very lukewarm about it. I, therefore, saw Jawharlalji at his place and told him, 'If we show any weakness in this matter, I have no doubt the country will not forgive us. Whatever may be the circumstances, we must strengthen ourselves and recover the Ladakh area.' Jawaharlalji agreed with me, and both he and Pantji took a very firm attitude.

Soon after China invaded India, a unanimous resolution was passed by Parliament declaring its firm determination to recover the area unlawfully occupied by China at the end of 1962. We have not, however yet been able to recover this area. I had told Jawaharlalji at the time of the invasion in 1962: 'If the bases which China had created in Tibet, which were very few at that time, could be destroyed by bombing, we could easily expel China from our territory.' But Jawaharlalji felt that if we bombed those areas, China could as well bomb Calcutta and some cities of UP and Delhi. This would cause a lot of destruction and there was the danger of the people getting frightened and demoralised. He, therefore, did not agree with the suggestion.

As a result of our defeat, there was a storm of opposition against Shri Krishna Menon in the Congress party. The Secretary of the Congress Parliamentary Party pressed Jawaharlalji to remove Shri Krishna Menon from the Cabinet. Jawaharlalji did not at first agree, but when the Executive Committee continued its pressure and even threatened to take more drastic steps if Jawaharlalji did not agree, he very reluctantly divided the Defence Ministry into two parts, keeping one with Shri Krishna Menon and taking charge of the other himself. But this did not give any satisfacttion to the party. Some of his colleagues had probably told Jawaharlalji, that the step taken by him was not at all adequate, and if Shri Krishna Menon was not removed from Ministership, the storm would become more violent and all of us would have to suffer as a result. I would not be surprised, I told him, if it would lead to violent actions. Some people were even talking of committing murder. I informed Jawaharlalji about all this and impressed upon him my view that Shri Krishna Menon should be immediately relieved of his office. Shri Krishna Menon was relieved of his Ministership a day or two after this talk, but with very great reluctance. I believe that the President of India and other colleagues must also have conveyed the same view as I did to Jawaharlalji. There was such a tense atmosphere that if Jawaharlalji had not relieved Krishna Menon and threatened to resign instead, there were many in the party who were prepared to accept his resignation.

Jawaharlalji then discussed with me the question of a successor to Shri Krishna Menon as Defence Minister. Two names were being considered, one of Shri Biju Patnaik and the other of Shri Yashwantrao Chavan. Jawaharlalji himself felt that Patnaik would not fit in and dropped his name. I told him that Shri Yashwantrao Chavan would be the fittest choice and his appointment would be welcomed. Shri Chavan was thus appointed as Defence Minister. Jawaharlalji had consulted Chavan before appointing him, and he showed his readiness to accept the responsibility.

It became necessary to elect the successor of Yashwantrao as Chief Minister of Maharashtra. There was some manoeuvring about this, but ultimately Shri Kannamwar was selected for the post and he relieved Shri Chavan. Shri Chavan stayed with me for a few days when he took over charge at Delhi. He used to stay with me before this whenever he came to Delhi for any meeting. Some of my other colleagues from Bombay also used similarly to put up with me.

28

1963–64 Budget and the Gold Control Order

WHEN CHINA invaded NEFA at the end of 1962, Jawaharlalji and some colleagues were of the view that a supplementary budget should be presented to get more finances for strengthening our defence forces. After considering the suggestion from all sides, I came to the conclusion that such a step would create difficulties for increasing the revenues of the Government substantially for strengthening our defence forces on a permanent basis. If such a step was taken in December it would be very premature and would create handicaps for the budget to be presented in February 1963. The people of India had voluntarily contributed Rs. 50 crores to fight the Chinese invasion. It was therefore appropriate that such a step should be taken in February. I explained my reasoning to Jawaharlalji who agreed with it. As a result, I presented the budget for 1963-64 on 28 February of that year, imposing new taxes after considering the whole question from all sides.

The Gold Control Order had been introduced in Parliament before the budget. Jawaharlalji, Shri Krishna Menon and other colleagues had been asking me to introduce control on gold ever since I became Finance Minister. I had also been contemplating such a step, but I considered it would be risky to take it before formulating a very effective policy in this matter. I therefore considered all the sides of the problem and formulated a plan. I showed it to Jawaharlalji in July 1962, when I went with him to England, and requested him to make whatever suggestions he considered necessary. He went through the proposal and accepted it. I considered that the time was ripe for introducing gold control when the Chinese invaded India. I thought people would accept the step, even though it was somewhat harsh, to meet the emergency which the country was facing.

The main purpose of gold control was to prevent the smuggling of gold worth crores of rupees into India from outside. As long as the attraction for gold was not lessened and the demand for gold was not reduced, it would be difficult to control the smuggling of gold. It was, therefore, necessary to take steps to lessen the attraction of gold in the public mind. The smuggled gold was refined illegally in some refineries. Nobody could identify it as smuggled gold after it has been refined. The import of gold had been banned for many years, but transactions in gold were taking place freely inside the country. The smuggling of gold would not, therefore, be stopped or reduced to a minimum without controlling its use in India.

There were two reasons for the smuggling of gold into the country. There has been greater attraction for gold ornaments in India than in other countries from ancient times. Very little gold was obtained from the gold mines in the country and as the demand of the people was much larger, the price of gold in India was 50 to 100 per cent higher than that obtaining in world markets. The smugglers of gold, therefore, reaped huge profits from their illegal transactions and the value of the rupee also deteriorated as a result of the money which went out of the country for the payment of smuggled gold. The £ was valued at Rs. 13.65 officially. While the value of the rupee lessened in the market, a £ cost up to Rs. 21 in the black market. Rupees were exchanged in this manner in Hong Kong too. One dollar cost officially Rs. 4.75 while it fetched Rs. 7.50 or Rs. 8 in the black market. Official transactions were at official rates. But as there were large-scale transactions in the black market, the country had to suffer a great loss and it therefore became imperative to control the smuggling of gold. Other goods were also smuggled into India, but the total transactions of other goods amounted to Rs. 5 crores to Rs. 7 crores only while the smuggling of gold amounted to Rs. 50 crores which has now greatly increased. The foreign exchange that was acquired by Government through exports was thus lost to a large extent.

The Gold Control Order was, therefore, issued as an ordinance in January 1963 and the manufacture of gold ornaments of more than 14 ct. purity was banned completely. The other controls that were imposed involved the taking out of licences for those who traded in gold and conducted refineries. The refineries and the gold merchants had to declare their gold stocks and a very strict rule was framed asking all people to make a declaration of the gold that they possessed, other than ornaments, beyond a certain limit. A rule was also made banning the possession of any gold of more than 14 ct. purity by refineries and those who dealt in gold. Gold bonds were also issued, and I broadcast a statement on the radio on 9 January explaining the purposes for which the Gold Control Order had been issued.

I increased the provision for defence expenditure from Rs. 395 crores in 1962—63 to Rs. 868 crores in the budget that I presented at the end of February 1963. The provision of Rs. 1,500 crores for economic development which had been made for five years in the

Third Five Year Plan in the budget of 1962–63 was raised to Rs. 1,750 crores in 1963–64. If adequate economic development did not take place, defences could not be strengthened. This was why this increase was made in the provision for our Five Year Plan. This necessitated the imposition of taxes on a large scale. These amounted to Rs. 280 crores, including increased railway fares and freights and taxes on shares. This enabled the Government to get the necessary financial resources. One of the purposes of this taxation was also to reduce the use by the people of imported goods required by the military and also to reduce other imports. In the direct taxation, the surcharge was increased from 4 to 10 per cent and a special surcharge was also levied. A 10 per cent surcharge was levied on import duties on all imported goods, and a surcharge of 10 to 33.5 per cent was levied on about forty items.

A Compulsory Deposit Scheme was also introduced at the same time. The money which was taken in the form of taxes from the people reduced the income of the people, but the money that came to Government as a result of the Compulsory Deposit Scheme was to be returned to the people at the end of five years with interest which was fixed at 4 per cent. The Compulsory Deposit Scheme was applied to all income-tax payees and also to persons who received annual salaries of between Rs. 1,500 and Rs. 3,000. This scheme was also applied to those who paid land revenue and also to those who were not paying sales tax on annual transactions up to Rs. 1,500 and who did not pay any income tax. It was also applied to people who had immovable properties in cities and who did not pay any income tax. I had discussed this scheme with all State Finance Ministers before introducing it, and it was ultimately accepted by all of them. I had told them that even if one State did not accept the scheme I would not introduce it. But all of them, without any exception, accepted it. I had sent such a proposal to Jawaharlalji from Bombay in 1952–53 after I became the Chief Minister of the State, but the then Central Finance Minister did not accept it. I had confidence that the country would now accept it in view of the dangers that it had to face.

The Gold Control Order was discussed in the Cabinet one or two hours before it was announced. Some of my colleagues pressed me to include control over the possession of ornaments and to make the provisions more rigorous. But I told them that if we introduced all the controls simultaneously there would be a violent opposition from the people as we were proposing to make changes in the centuries-old habits and sentiments of our people. It would not, therefore, be wise to impose all controls in one step, and the other necessary steps could be taken as we succeed in the steps first taken. The scheme that I had proposed was then accepted by the Cabinet. But I found that those colleagues who were pressing me to make it more rigorous became quite lukewarm later on and indirectly supported the opposition to gold control by maintaining silence. They did not defend the step in public.

The main reason for introducing the Compulsory Deposit Scheme was to mobilise more financial resources. Another reason was the necessity of cultivating a saving habit amongst the people which was very essential. Ours is a very poor country and it is natural that the people, as they earn more, will spend more to raise their standard of living. But the economic development of the country is essential and the conditions of the poor will improve only if the country's wealth increases. It is the universal experience of individuals and countries that wealth cannot be increased without increased investment. It would be impossible to raise the necessary capital for investment if the common man did not help in the task.

There are only four sources for raising capital: (*i*) taxes, (*ii*) loans from the people, (*iii*) foreign aid, and (*iv*) profits from public undertakings. The taxes which were considered already high were further raised and it was not possible to raise them any further at that time. In a poor country there is a limitation to taxation. Loans also have their limitations. It was not very advantageous or profitable to take more aid from foreign countries beyond a certain limit. It would not be harmful as long as we obtained 10 to 15 per cent of our requirements from foreign aid. If we took more than that, we would not be able to repay and would ultimately have to suffer heavy economic losses. The public undertakings did not yield any profit on the whole and several were running at a loss. As long as these were not made efficient, there was no possibility of getting substantial profits from them. We had to depend ultimately only on taxation and loans. As I have mentioned earlier, the field for raising public loans in the country is limited on account of the low income of the people of this poor country. The saving habit alone would enable us to raise economic resources, and it was in order to cultivate the saving habit amongst the people that the Compulsory Deposit Scheme was introduced. At first sight, it appears hard, looking at the problem superficially, to expect people having an annual income of between Rs. 1,500 to Rs. 4,000 only to make savings. But if we look at the problem properly, the plan which appeared apparently harsh would clearly benefit the people and the country, and wherever I explained it to the people they accepted it immediately. People with an income of Rs. 1,500 had to deposit about Rs. 50 per year according to this savings scheme. People have to realise that those who earn Rs. 1,500 annually cannot spend more than that amount if they want to improve their economic condition. If a person wants to make progress in his economic condition, he must never spend more than his income. On the contrary, he must try to save something from his income, whatever it may be. It is only then that he can go on improving his economic condition. But the person who does not act accordingly and spends more than his income, becomes indebted and after getting into such spending habits his expenditure goes on increasing as his income increases and he is not able to save himself from indebtedness. His economic condition therefore worsens. But the person who can save even a little from his low income and forms such a useful habit, saves more and more as his income goes on increasing, as he would go on improving his standard of living to some extent and also would better his economic condition by saving more. If a person earning Rs. 125 per month spends Rs. 121 instead of Rs. 125, it does not make any particular difference in his standard of living, but he forms a habit of saving about Rs. 50 a year. This enables him to improve his economic condition as, under the scheme, he would get back his deposits at the end of 5 years with interest. I had also another aim in devising this scheme which I had not specified in Parliament at that time, as I considered that any premature declaration of the scheme would not be useful. It will not be possible to give social security to the people in this country for several years more. When the person who earns for the family dies, the whole family is put in a helpless condition. I have had personal experience in this matter. If every earning member of the family is insured, even if the insurance be for Rs. 500, his family receives Rs. 500 if he suddenly disappears from the world, and gets some security. I, therefore, wanted to introduce a Compulsory Insurance Scheme if this Compulsory Deposit Scheme succeeded. But this could be considered only after three or four years, and I did not therefore mention the scheme at that time.

When I introduced the Compulsory Deposit Scheme several communist and socialist members welcomed the step very warmly. They also welcomed the Gold Control Order and described both the steps as effective socialist measures. They, however, said all this in private and not publicly. They all joined the opposition in public. This is a peculiar feature of public life and politics.

Both these schemes met with opposition in Parliament. The increase in taxation was also opposed. Constitutional objections were raised against the two schemes. I had considered this point very carefully and had discussed it with the legal advisers also. I was clearly told that the order was constitutional and I said so in Parliament. Some members asked that the Attorney General be called to Parliament. I told them that this was not necessary. But when the opponents claimed that it was the right of Parliament to do so, I told them that it was the right of Government to decide whether the Attorney General should be called to speak in Parliament, and even if, therefore, Parliament decided unanimously to call him, it would not be binding on me. This statement of mine was misrepresented by several opponents who made propaganda against me that I did not believe in democracy.

I have as much or more faith in parliamentary democracy than anyone else. I cannot agree to any other system under any circumstances. It was my purpose in saying what I said to convey to the members that a right which parliament did not have could not be imposed on the government and, if its own limitation was not observed by parliament, democracy would be endangered, in my view. I did not then realise that my statement could be misrepresented. Howsoever justified and correct the statement, it ought not to have been made under certain circumstances, as I soon realised. I have been careful since then in such matters. But I know that my opponents utilise this to the maximum and deliberately refused to accept its correct meaning. But I have no ill will against them in this matter. I know that in politics opponents will take such advantage, whether right or wrong, and one should be careful oneself to see that one does not provide such opportunities. I believe that one should not expect opponents not to take a wrong advantage.

Jawaharlalji agreed with me that the Lok Sabha could not force Government to call the Attorney General to Parliament and I had discussed the matter with him before speaking in Parliament. Some members of the opposition began to circulate a story that I did not agree to call the Attorney General as his view would go against Government. I consulted Jawaharlalji and decided to invite the Attorney General to speak in Parliament to prove that the story circulated by the opposition was entirely wrong. The Attorney General then attended the Lok Sabha and supported our contention. Several questions were put to him by some members and he gave effective replies to all of them.

The opposition to the Gold Control Order and to the Compulsory Deposit Scheme continued and became even more intense. Agriculturists used to argue that the Compulsory Deposit Scheme should not apply to them. Goldsmiths had formed their own associations and a lot of propaganda was made that many goldsmiths had committed suicide. When I enquired into those cases, I found that the suicides were not due to the Gold Control Order, but were due to their own difficulties. The goldsmiths were free to carry on their business. They were not free only to make ornaments of gold of more than 14 ct. purity. They could make any ornaments of 14 ct. gold, but there was less gold smuggling and the goldsmiths did not get sufficient stock of gold for making ornaments. The rate of Rs. 21 or Rs. 22 for a £ which prevailed before the introduction of the Gold Control Order was reduced to Rs. 15 within four or five months of the promulgation of the Gold Control Order. This proved the efficacy and success of the order.

Great pressure was brought to bear on Jawaharlalji against both these schemes later on, and he discussed these matters with me twice or thrice. When, however, I explained to him the propriety and usefulness of the measures, he did not persist in asking me to make any changes and he supported me publicly whenever occasion arose.

The minimum limit for income tax payees was Rs. 3,000 at that time. Jawaharlalji pressed me twice to reduce it to Rs. 1,500. But I submitted to him that he would not be able to defend the measure against the strong opposition that we would meet and we would be put in an awkward position. The people, from whom this income tax would be taken up to an income of Rs. 1,500, would have less income as a result. The Compulsory Deposit Scheme which had been introduced for incomes up to Rs. 1,500 was, therefore, more suitable and proper and without any blemish. There was a strong advocacy in Parliament for raising the lower limit of income tax from Rs. 3,000 to Rs. 7,000. There was, therefore, no hope for the acceptance of a limit lower than Rs. 3,000 as suggested by Jawaharlalji and I did not support it. But Jawaharlalji who pressed me to lower the income tax limit agreed later on to give up the Compulsory Deposit Scheme and substitute it by the Annuity Scheme when I left the Cabinet in accordance with the Kamaraj plan. He also agreed to water down the Gold Control Order. Several members had told me in the Lok Sabha very frankly that the step that I was taking was endangering my political life and prospects. I told them that I had to consider whether I should take the step in the interest of the country or not, irrespective of whether it endangered my public life or not. I said that I was not worried if my political life was destroyed as I had no ambitions in that direction. My only aim was to do my duty, whatever might be the risks. As the Finance Minister of the country I had to take all steps to strengthen the country socially and economically and I must cheerfully accept the consequences if

I had to give up political life as a result of taking the necessary steps in that direction. Those Communists who were congratulating me on these steps in private joined the opposition to it inside and outside Parliament. This was their political honesty. I am always of the view that nothing better should be expected from many in political life.

The budget that I introduced for 1963–64 was the heaviest of all the budgets introduced so far. But I had no doubt in my mind that it was vitally necessary for the defence of the country. Jawaharlalji was in favour of imposing even more taxes, but later on he could not maintain even what I had introduced and got passed by Parliament. The country acquired the necessary resources for development and for strengthening our defence forces as a result of the budget which I introduced and got passed by Parliament. If this had not been done at that time, we could not have taken the effective steps that we took for repulsing the aggression of Pakistan in Kashmir in 1965, and the country would have been put in a very dangerous position. With the increased resources at our command we could defend the country successfully against Pakistan's aggression and the reputation that we lost at the time of Chinese invasion in 1962 was recovered to some extent in 1965.

I decided to go to Amarnath in the beginning of July 1963. It was a full moon day of the month of Shravan when I went there. Shri Ghulam Mohammed Bakshi was the Chief Minister of Jammu and Kashmir at that time. He had been pressing me for some time to go to this place of pilgrimage and I undertook this trip with the members of my family, my additional Private Secretary, Raghunathji Naik, and his family. A cousin of mine, Smt. Tarakeshwari Sinha, and one or two other persons joined us in this pilgrimage.

From Srinagar we all went to Pahalgam and from there to Chandanwadi in jeeps. I arranged to get my wife carried on a chair from Chandanwadi as she could not ride a horse and could not walk the distance. All the rest, except Shri Raghunathji Naik and myself, rode on ponies. Both of us walked the whole distance. The path was very steep and difficult in some places. But I had resolved to go to Amarnath on foot. After Chandanwadi we first broke journey at Seshnag and stayed there for the night. The ascent from Chandanwadi was particularly steep and difficult. Chandanwadi is about 9,000 ft. high and we had to climb a further 2,500 to 3,000 ft. to reach Seshnag. On the way one had to go up and down twice or thrice, which also increased the climbing distance.

On reaching Seshnag we were confronted by a very beautiful sight. The arrangements for staying there were very convenient and the bluish lake was a delight to the eye. We left early in the morning and reached Amarnath via Panchtarni by about 11 a. m. We started back after spending about two hours at Amarnath. The whole way was full of natural beauty. The journey on foot was not therefore in any way tedious. I had not, however, walked such a distance for several years and had also not climbed so high. I was then 67 years old. I, therefore, undertook an adventure in deciding to go the whole distance on foot. I was very tired towards the end of the journey to Amarnath and found it very difficult to walk the last mile. I took rest every 200 to 300 yards.

Getting into the Amarnath cave I found that snow was percolating into it from the crevices at the top and that the Shivalinga idol was made of snow. This was a very fine and solemn sight and the shrine is a popular place of worship. Idols of Shankar and Parvati were also formed in the same way. I bowed to all three idols with great reverence.

I gave up the idea of walking down on the return journey as I was tired and considered that if I walked again on the strength of mental determination, it might cause physical injury. I therefore decided to return on horseback and did so. Returning from Amarnath we reached Seshnag in the evening via Panchtarni and stayed there for the night. We reached Chandanwadi the next day before noon. From Chandanwadi we returned to Pahalgam by jeeps. As I rode a pony on the return journey I got relief from the fatigue that I had suffered on the way up and when I returned to Pahalgam and from there to Srinagar, I felt very nearly free from fatigue. The arrangements made by the State for this pilgrimage were very good.

We had very good weather during the pilgrimage. There was no rain and we had good sunshine throughout. Ordinarily there are rains after the three days of pilgrimage and the path becomes very slippery and it becomes very difficult to walk on it. The descent from Seshnag to Chandanwadi is very steep and rocky and going down on horseback is considered somewhat difficult. Several people therefore prefer to walk down. But I did the whole descent on horseback as I saw that the ponies, being very strong and firm-footed, were descending with even greater care than the men. I therefore did not consider it in any way risky to go downhill on horseback. Each pony was accompanied by an attendant who guided it when necessary.

29

The Kamaraj Plan

JAWAHARLALJI WENT to Kashmir in May or June 1963 after the Lok Sabha had been adjourned and Shri Biju Patnaik met him there. Shri Patnaik later told me about the talks he had with Jawaharlalji and said that he had suggested to him a plan which was very much like what was later on known as the Kamaraj plan. In fact, the Kamaraj plan was thus started by Biju Patnaik, but this was not known to the public. Kamaraj suggested this plan at the end of June or the beginning of July 1963. Kamaraj's original plan envisaged the resignation of two or three chief ministers and some state ministers, so that they might apply their energies to the work of the party organisation. There was no reference to the Centre in the plan at that time as far as I knew. But later on, suggestions were made to include central ministers also in the plan and they were accepted.

This plan was discussed by Jawaharlalji first with five or six colleagues. He first suggested that as he was the seniormost person in office he should resign first to make the plan successful. When he said this, Kamaraj and two or three other colleagues said that that was an impossible proposition and if that had to be done, the plan must be dropped. Jawaharlalji did not need much persuasion to give up his suggestion. I got an impression that it was a very formal one and that he had taken no decision at that time. He, therefore, accepted Shri Kamaraj's suggestion without any hesitation. I would not be surprised if they had had some previous talk about it.

I said to Jawaharlalji, 'The aim of the plan is good, but the arrangement that you should decide which ministers from the Centre and the States should resign was not a very happy one. It will lead to many doubts and allegations and you would come in for much criticism.' I suggested an alternative which, if accepted, would not lead to any allegations against anybody. I said, 'The number of ministers is very large in most of the States except Madras and Gujarat, and this is the impression of the people too. It is, therefore, necessary to reduce the number of ministers in the Centre and in several States. It should first of all be decided what number of ministers is required in the cabinets at the Centre and the States, and then the surplus ministers should be relieved. Those who are less efficient and against whom there may be allegations should be first relieved, so that a good impression is created amongst the people and the administration also improves. At the same time, three or four efficient ministers who may be required for the work of the organisation should be asked to give up offices and work for the organisation. I have no doubt that they would agree to do so very willingly. If this arrangement is made, nobody will make any allegations against you.' I also suggested that those who were asked to resign for organisational work should be taken back in the ministries after five years, that is one term, and some other ministers who were in office should take their places in the organisation. By this arrangement, the work of the organisation and the administration would go on efficiently and without much difficulty.

But Jawharlalji and some other colleagues were not prepared to accept this suggestion. Their aims, I believed, were different. Kamaraj's aim was to strengthen the organisation, especially as he found that because he was busy in Tamil Nadu as Chief Minister, party work there had deteriorated. He had devised this plan to enable him to resume the work of the organisation again. This relinquishing of the Chief Ministership for organisation work would raise his prestige. But the plan took quite a different shape.

Jawaharlalji went to Hyderabad soon after the plan was first mooted. There he discussed it with Shri Kamaraj and Shri C. Subramaniam. Nobody had told me anything about these discussions. I suspected some hidden purpose in them. The plan was approved by the AICC and a decision was taken by the Working Committee at the end of the third week of August. Jawaharlalji, Shri Subramaniam, Shri Lal Bahadur Shastri, Shri Gulzarilal Nanda, Smt. Indira Gandhi and Shri Kamaraj had been talking about these matters before the Working Committee meeting, but none of them discussed it with me. All the ministers were asked to resign before the meeting of the Working Committee took place. I wrote a letter to Jawaharlalji saying that I had accepted the plan sanctioned by the AICC and would, therefore, send in my resignation letter as soon as I heard about his decision.

Shri C. B. Gupta who was the Chief Minister in UP did not want to send his resignation as he had assumed office only a little earlier and had been out of government for a long time. But Jawaharlalji explained to him that he should send in his resignation just as others were doing and that there was no question of accepting it.

Two days before the Working Committee meeting, Lal Bahadur Shastri told me when he met me in the lobby of the Lok Sabha that he had pressed for his resignation being accepted and that he would give up office but that it was not necessary for me to give up office. His resignation should not affect me. When he spoke to me in this manner, I suspected that some game was being played behind the scenes. I told him that Jawaharlalji had not talked to me about that matter and that I did not know anything about it. He then told me that Jawaharlalji would meet me the next day and tell me about it. This convinced me that he must have had a talk with Jawaharlalji about me also. But I did not ask him about it and he did not tell me also anything more on this matter.

Jawaharlalji asked me to see him the next day to discuss the plan. He told me that according to the plan he and I were the only two seniors left, and that one of us must give up office. He said that as it was the decision of everybody that he should not give up office, I must be relieved from the ministry for the work of the organisation. He also talked to me about relieving Shri Jagjivan Ram and Shri Lal Bahadur Shastri from office and also Shri Gopala Reddy. I told him: 'I am not at all unwilling to give up office. On the contrary, I am quite happy about it.' When he told me about the acceptance of the resignation of Shri C. B. Gupta, I told him that it would be a great blunder and there would be allegations that he was doing so because he did not like Shri Gupta. I, therefore, advised him to think further about it. I told him in addition that I did not consider it proper that Shri Gopala Reddy should be relieved as he was of no great importance for the work of the organisation. Agreeing to my resignation, I said, 'I have only to tell you that if the budget arrangements and plans which were made with your consent, and to which there is opposition from some quarters, are given up or some undesirable changes are made in them, the country's economy will receive a great blow. I would therefore request you not to yield to any pressure in this matter.' I added: 'As I am giving up office and getting out of the Cabinet, I should like to give you the impressions I have formed of you. There is something missing in the relation which you keep with your colleagues. Nobody is able to know what your view is about any of your colleagues and some of them, therefore, find it difficult to work freely and are afraid of you also. I am personally not afraid or worried in this matter and I can, therefore, tell you many things frankly. Today I am talking to you very specifically and frankly about it. I have not got any specific impression about what you think of me. I am not worried about it, but in such a situation I cannot work with you with the confidence I should have.'

Jawaharlalji replied: 'If there is anything special in my mind I will certainly tell you about it.'

I then said, 'This matter is not so simple. Many people see you and talk to you about many things and you also encourage some people to talk to you behind the scenes and you have encouraged them to do so. You do not ask me or some other colleagues about the impressions given to you by these people and the colleagues concerned may be ignorant about all these matters. All these talks are bound to make some impresssion on you and create some prejudices in your mind too. If you ask those persons about whom you have heard certain things, even in an indirect manner, you would know the facts. But if they do not get any opportunity to explain matters, your prejudice will not be removed.'

On hearing me talk to him in this manner, he told me that there was no such prejudice. I then said that I would illustrate my argument by an example. 'When I talked to you about Shri Krishna Menon's work,' I said, 'you immediately told him about it and even gave him a copy of my letter to you in that connection. But when he talks to you about me, you do not tell me anything at all. Such discrimination in behaviour with colleagues is not proper, in my view. This creates groupings inside the Cabinet and you ought not to encourage it. If you do not act in this manner, the work that you are doing will be more effective and you will succeed much more in achieving your aims and also increase the capacity of your colleagues. I hope and trust you will think about this matter and change your method of work and behaviour.'

While leaving him, I said, 'You need not reconsider the question of my release from the Cabinet. I have not told you all this in order that I may be continued as a minister as a ministership has no attraction for me. I have been a minister for nineteen to twenty years and that is a long period. Giving up ministership, therefore, would be of great benefit to me, I have no doubt.'

The Working Committee met the next day. Jawaharlalji gave his decision, according to which Shri Lal Bahadur Shastri, Shri Jagjivan Ram, Shri S. K. Patil, Shri Gopala Reddy and I were to be relieved from the Central Cabinet. Amongst chief ministers of States, Shri Kamaraj from Tamil Nadu, Shri Mandloi from MP, Shri B. N. Jha from Bihar, and Shri C. B. Gupta from UP had to give up office. Shri Ghulam Mohammad Bakshi who was then Chief Minister of Jammu and Kashmir also expressed his desire to give up office. The decision of the AICC did not apply to him as his party at that time was the National Conference which was not a part of the Congress. Some of the members asked him not to resign, but he remained firm in his decision. I had no previous knowledge about it. He also at that time informed us about his decision to join the Congress. Later on, I asked him why he had taken this decision to resign. He told me that amongst all the persons who were giving up office, there was no Muslim and he felt that if he also joined them it would have a very good effect. I told him that he had taken a thoughtless step and that it would be very harmful in many ways. Conditions in Kashmir would deteriorate. 'Your step will please Jawaharlalji and Indiraben,' I told him, 'because I have learnt that they are against you, especially because you yourself once told me that you had complained very strongly against Indiraben to Jawaharlalji. I had then told you that there was no wisdom in your making such complaints to Jawaharlalji as these complaints would make both of them your enemies'. Jawaharlalji asked Shri Bakshi to make Shri G. M. Sadiq the Chief Minister of Kashmir and Shri Bakshi accepted the suggestion.

Later on I found that the ruling party in Kashmir was not willing to relieve Shri Bakshi and accept Shri Sadiq in his place. Shri Sadiq made allegations against Shri Bakshi in this connection, but from the facts that I learned from Shri Bakshi and others these allegations were not justified. Really speaking, he should have continued as Chief Minister as he alone had the confidence of the ruling party in Kashmir. They all wanted Shri Bakshi and desired that he should withdraw his resignation. This worsened relations between Shri Bakshi and Shri Sadiq, and the latter when he was elected as Chief Minister, ultimately pursued Shri Bakshi and appointed an investigation commission against him.

Either before or during the time the Kamaraj plan was approved, a bye-election was to take place for a seat in the Legislative Assembly of Madhya Pradesh and Shri D. P. Misra had declared his candidature. This matter was considered before the Kamaraj plan had been sanctioned. Jawaharlalji was very much against Shri D. P. Misra who, after he had returned to the Congress in 1953–54 wanted to be elected to the Legislative Assembly or to Parliament. He was not allowed to stand as a candidate. Indiraji had gone out of the country when a meeting of the Paliamentary Board was fixed for deciding the Shri D. P. Misra's candidature. I asked D. P. Misra why he did not press Indiraji to attend the meeting. He told me that as I would be present it was not necessary for her to attend. When the Parliamentary Board's meeting was fixed, it was at very short notice and I had to go to Ahmedabad that day. But at the persistent request of Shri D. P. Misra I postponed my visit to Ahmedabad and decided to attend the meeting.

Shri K. K. Shah who was then one of the General Secretaries of the AICC had also told me that if I did not attend the meeting, Shri D. P. Misra's candidature would not be approved. The Madhya Pradesh representative, Shri Totla, opposed the candidature of Shri D. P. Misra at the meeting. He was supported by Shri Lal Bahadur Shastri, which led me to believe that Jawaharlalji was also opposed to it. Shri Jagjivan Ram did not take a definite stand. I told Jawaharlalji that this attitude was unfair: 'It is very improper that you persistently refuse to give a ticket to a person for so many years.' I was told that Shri D. P. Misra would not win the election. I then said that this argument was totally wrong as I had no doubt that Shri D. P. Misra was a person who would not contest an election from a place where he was likely to be defeated. It was only because of my persistent support that D. P. Misra's candidature was ultimately accepted.

A controversy had arisen in UP as a result of the resignation of Shri C. B. Gupta. He gave up office as a disciplined Congressman, but I was convinced that great injustice had been done to him and to the state of UP. He had been elected Chief Minister of UP only in 1963.

Shri Krishna Ballabh Sahay was elected the Chief Minister of Bihar in place of Shri B. N. Jha. Shri Bhaktavatsalam was elected in place of Shri Kamaraj, and after a lot of controversy, Shri D. P. Misra was elected as Chief Minister of Madhya Pradesh in place of Shri Mandloi.

Shri Gulzarilal Nanda was appointed Home Minister in the Central Cabinet. I was told that Shri C. Subramaniam wanted to be Finance Minister, but Shri T. T. Krishnamachari objected to his appointment and was successful in being appointed as Finance Minister himself. I wrote to Jawaharlalji that I would like to be relieved from office from 1 September at the latest and hoped that I would be so relieved. Shri T. T. Krishnamachari had previously taken charge as Finance Minister on 1 September 1957, but he did not remain long in office at that time. He, therefore, decided to take charge this time on the evening of 31 August instead of 1 September, I therefore, gave up charge of my office on the evening of 31 August.

Shri S. K. Patil was appointed an additional member of the Parliamentary Board. Shri Jagjivan Ram and I were already members of that body. The Kamaraj plan was intended to relieve from office such persons as would be useful in strengthening the Congress organisation. Shri Gopala Reddy, Shri Mandloi and Shri Jha were not useful for this purpose. But Jawaharlalji utilised this plan to relieve them from office.

There was a lot of criticism in the Gujarat Congress Party against Dr. Jivaraj Mehta, but Jawaharlalji did not include him in the Kamaraj plan. It is possible that Jawaharlalji did not know about the feeling against Dr. Jivaraj in Gujarat. He had told Jawaharlalji that he had a very large majority in the Congress Party with him and was receiving encouragement from Jawaharlalji.

Later I fully understood the real purpose of the Kamaraj plan, but I did not raise any controversy about it because I had no hesitation in giving up office. As a matter of fact, I considered my release as the grace of God. Actually this was the second step taken by Jawaharlalji to prevent me from succeeding him whenever such a contingency arose. Earlier he had prevented my being elected Deputy Leader of the Congress Parliamentary Party. It soon became clear that he wanted Indiraji to succeed him. This was not surprising. Pandit Motilalji had requested Gandhiji to see that Jawaharlalji succeeded him as Congress President and he was then elected to the post, as is well known. To show that the Kamaraj plan was not particularly aimed at me, Lal Bahadurji was also included in the plan, but there was an understanding that he would be taken back in the Cabinet after three or four months. This was why he did not give up his official residence and the Government staff working for him when he was a Minister continued to work for him after his resignation. He was taken back into the Cabinet in February 1964. When I attended the last meeting of the Cabinet before I gave up office, an appreciation of my services was recorded. Jawaharlalji at that time expressed the hope that some ministers would return to the Cabinet. This hope was fulfilled in the case of Shri Lal Bahadur Shastri.

A committee consisting of Shri Kamaraj, Shri Jagjivan Ram and myself was appointed under the Kamaraj plan to enquire into allegations made against Congressmen. An important task of the organisation was thus entrusted to this Committee, but it ceased to function after Shri Kamaraj was elected Congress President and he dissolved it soon after.

When the Working Committee met at the end of November 1963, Shri Atulya Ghosh proposed, with the approval of Jawaharlalji, that Shri Kamaraj be elected President of the Congress. I understood that some of the members had earlier discussed this question amongst themselves. I had no knowledge of this and, as far as I was concerned, this proposal was suddenly sprung on the Working Committee. Nobody opposed it. Really, if the purpose of the Kamaraj plan was to be achieved, I should have been asked to be President of the Congress. As early as 1960, Atulya Babu had suggested to me that I should give up my Cabinet post and become President of the Congress. I had then told him that I had no objection to doing so if he obtained the consent of Jawaharlalji and Pantji. Atulya Babu talked to Pantji about it, but he did not accept the suggestion, saying that I could not be spared from the Cabinet. Jawaharlalji had suggested to Shri Lal Bahadur Shastri that he should be the President before Shri Kamaraj was proposed for this office. But as Shri Lal Bahadur Shastri declined, all of them proposed Kamaraj. I understood that Shri Lal Bahadur Shastri was also present in these consultations. I would have opposed this suggestion, but my doing so would have created several complications. I therefore accepted it. The next day, two members of the Inner Council of the Congress, which had latterly come to be known as the Syndicate, met me. They told me that they had proposed Kamaraj in order to prevent Shrimati Indira Gandhi from becoming President and that I should have no misgivings in the matter. I told them that I could not understand their action but did not want to discuss it. Shri Kamaraj was then elected Congress President.

During the period when the Kamaraj plan was being discussed, a resolution of no confidence in the Government was moved in the Lok Sabha by Dr. Ram Manohar Lohia who made many allegations against Jawaharlalji and Indiraji. This was the first time such a motion had been moved and Jawaharlalji desired that I should reply to Dr. Ram Manohar Lohia as he found it embarrassing and difficult to do so himself. I agreed.

I should like to refer here to one or two other incidents which took place during this period.

Shri Pashabhai Patel of Baroda had been dealing in tractors for some time and also had a factory for their manufacture. A Parsi lady was working with him. She had some quarrel with Shri Pashabhai and was relieved from service. She complained to a Member of Parliament, Shri Feroze Gandhi, about tax evasions by Shri Pashabhai Patel and gave him some facts. Shri Feroze Gandhi sent the complaint to the Finance Minister and asked for an enquiry. An enquiry was made and a compromise was arrived at in the matter by the Income Tax Commissioner and Shri Pashabhai Patel. Shri Patel admitted the tax evasion but if he had not admitted it there was no evidence to prove it against him. This was why the Commissioner had to agree to a compromise in the matter. However, the full penalty was levied. The only real compromise was that Shri Patel was not prosecuted. A reward was given to the Parsi lady in proportion to the tax evasion actually discovered on the basis of her information. She had given information about a much larger amount, but there was no evidence to prove it. She wanted a reward on the basis of her estimate of evasion. I informed Jawaharlalji about the result of the investigation and the penalty levied on Shri Pashabhai Patel.

Later on this lady complained to Jawaharlalji that I had favoured Shri Pashabhai Patel on the recommendation of Shri Kunvarji Bhabha and others and had dealt with him leniently. She asked for a large reward than she had been given. Jawaharlalji sent her letter to me and asked me to comment. I immediately replied to him:

'I have sent you all the information in this matter already. The charge of being influenced which has been made by this lady is absolutely untrue and without foundation. I am very much pained that you have given no opinion about the allegation made and have sent me her letter as it is, even though I had sent you all the information about the investigation and the penalty. If you think that I am capable of being influenced in my official work, I must resign my office immediately. No minister can do his work if such false allegations are given credence. It also affects my self-respect. The informant lady is making false allegations only in order to get a larger reward and it is a kind of blackmail. If you find any truth in what she is saying, you should tell me so immediately, so that I may resign my office. Otherwise you should inform her that her complaint is quite wrong.'

Jawaharlalji immediately replied to me that the earlier letter I had written to him had slipped his mind at the time he sent the letter to me. He also told me that he did not believe in the woman's story and that he had told her so specifically. He asked me, in view of his explanation, not to take offence. This is how this chapter ended.

My son, Kantilal, wrote to me at the end of 1963 that, as he had informed me a few years earlier, he wanted to enter public life after doing business for a few years. He did his business accordingly and had saved enough to maintain himself in the future. He did not want to collect more money and had, therefore, decided to enter public life. He wanted to begin by serving me personally for some time. He also said that as I was not a minister at that time, he could work as my private secretary and would leave Bombay and come and stay with me in Delhi. I wrote to him that if he wanted to do so he must get out of business entirely. I could accept him as my private secretary only if he did not do any business. Nobody could take objection to his joining me as private secretary if he did not do any business as nobody could then say that he had any financial motives in taking this step. Kantilal informed me that his wife and children would stay on in Bombay as his wife was doing some business there in partnership with another person and would look after it. Both his sons also would continue their studies in Bombay.

As Kantilal was giving up his business and would stay with me in Delhi, I accepted his offer. He accordingly came to live with me in the beginning of 1964 and began to work as my private secretary. His family continued to live in Bombay. We had to go to Bombay or pass through Bombay often, and could, therefore, be with the family from time to time. The boys used to come to Delhi during the vacations. I was then staying at 7 Thyagaraja Marg. I gave up my official residence, 1 Willingdon Crescent, within seven days of giving up office on 1 September. No appropriate house from the Parliament pool was vacant at that time. 7 Thygaraja Marg belonged to the Presidential Estate. It had been vacant for a few months and the President agreed to release it for my use. It was, therefore, allotted to me by the Government.

30

Storm against Dr. Jivaraj

THE OPPOSITION against Dr. Jivaraj Mehta in Gujarat increased a great deal in September 1963. There was also a strong feeling against two other Ministers, Shri Rasiklal Parikh and Shri Ratubhai Adani, in the Congress Legislature Party. Sometime before this, Shri Balwantrai Mehta had been elected to the Legislative Assembly in a bye-election. Some people tried to see that he was defeated, but as Shri Balwantrai was forewarned, he frustrated those efforts. The main reason for the opposition to Dr. Jivaraj and his two colleagues in the Pradesh Congress Committee related to the fact that these three disregarded the Pradesh Committee and its suggestions and used to harass those who did not fall in line with them. Such complaints were made twice or thrice to the Pradesh Congress Committee and to me too. Every time I told my colleagues in Gujarat, 'You should not take any hasty or strong steps in this matter and you should not start a new tradition of making changes in the Cabinet between general elections.' They did not very much like my advice, but they did not say anything to me.

Dr. Jivaraj Mehta called a meeting of the Congress Legislative Party one night in September. A very large majority of the members in the meeting expressed their want of confidence in his leadership. Shri Rasiklal Parikh and Shri Ratubhai Adani had resigned as Ministers sometime earlier in order to lessen the opposition to Dr. Jivaraj Mehta. If they had taken this step three or four months earlier, this motion of no confidence, would not, perhaps, have been moved. I had advised Dr. Jivaraj Mehta five or six months earlier to change the portfolios of these two Ministers saying, 'If you do so, the opposition to them will disappear. If it is not done, I am afraid there will be very undesirable developments.' This advice was, however, disregarded and I did not press for its acceptance. I have never expected anyone to accept my advice if he did not agree with it. I believe in the policy of allowing those who work on the spot to do so according to their own lights and to help them to do so. As a general rule I give advice only when it is asked for.

When the vote of no confidence was reported to the President of the Congress, the late Shri Sanjivayya, Jawaharlalji was surprised and also got angry. He told me that Dr. Jivaraj had told him that he had a large majority in the Legislative Party. I replied: What I had told you before has now been proved true. But you may send the President of the Congress to Ahmedabad to question every member and find out for himself whether this opposition to Dr. Jivaraj is an honest or an engineered one. If the members who opposed him were honestly doing so on their own, Dr. Jivaraj Mehta has to be relieved, but if the opposition was engineered, it should be disregarded.' Jawaharlalji accepted my suggestion and sent Shri Sanjivayya, in whom he had confidence, and who remained loyal until his death to Smt. Indira Gandhi, to Ahmedabad. I had suggested to Shri Sanjivayya before he went that he should associate Dr. Jivaraj Mehta with all stages of his enquiry, so that he might be convinced about its impartiality and justness.

Shri Sanjivayya went to Ahmedabad and suggested the convening of a meeting of the Congress Legislature Party in Congress House after having a preliminary discussion with Dr. Jivaraj and the President of the Pradesh Congress Committee. Dr. Jivaraj opposed the suggestion and said that the meeting should be held in the office of the Congress Legislative Party in the building where the Legislature met and the meeting was held there. In accordance with my advice, Shri Sanjivayya asked Dr. Jivaraj to sit with him during the enquiry. Dr. Jivaraj, however, refused to do so and sat outside the room to keep a watch on the members who were going in and coming out of it. I understood that he took up this position to ensure that those who saw Shri Sanjivayya did not afterwards meet those who were yet to see him. Shri Sanjivayya met all the members separately, cross-examined them and ascertained their individual views. He questioned even the members of the Cabinet and found that, barring one or two members of the Cabinet, all the rest were opposed to Dr. Jivaraj and his system of dealing with them, and had expressed their want of confidence in him. Shri Sanjivayya had questioned particularly the members from the backward classes more closely and had crossed-examined them. He told me on his return to Delhi that he was convinced that a majority of the members were opposed to Dr. Jivaraj and did not approve of his behaviour and his method of work.

Shri Sanjivayya gave his report to Jawaharlalji on his return to Delhi. It was discussed in a meeting of the Parliamentary Board and it was decided to elect a new leader for the Gujarat Congress Legislature Party. Shri Lal Bahardur Shastri was sent to conduct and supervise the election. The Gujarat Congress Legislature Party met in his presence and unanimously elected Shri Balwantrai Mehta as their leader and Chief Minister.

In the meanwhile, Dr. Jivaraj had addressed a letter to Jawaharlalji suggesting that the reasons for the want of confidence in him should be examined and if the members could not show any valid reasons, the no confidence resolution should be disregarded. He also asked for a hearing in the Parliamentary Board. I was not given a copy of this letter when it came. But when the Parliamentary Board met at Jawaharlalji's residence for some other work, he referred to this letter at the end of the meeting and also supplied us with copies of Dr. Jivaraj's letter. He also said that Dr. Jivaraj was present in the adjacent room and that he might be called for a discussion. I opposed this suggestion very strongly. None of us knew until that time that Dr. Jivaraj was waiting in the adjacent room. I said,

'A very wrong procedure has been adopted. The resolution of no confidence against Dr. Jivaraj has been accepted and it has been decided to elect a new leader after the enquiry made by the Congress President and a discussion in the Parliamentary Board. The question raised by Dr. Jivaraj is not at all proper. It is he who ought to know why there is no confidence in him and there is no meaning in the question why there was no confidence in him. Calling him before the Board and discussing with him will only lead to mutual recriminations, allegations and counter-allegations. This procedure is entirely wrong and against all rules of the Congress. I cannot therefore accept it.'

I then told Jawaharlalji, 'I am leaving the meeting and if you want to discuss anything with Dr. Jivaraj, you can do so in my absence. I shall not be present at the discussion, and if this behaviour of mine is considered against Party discipline, I shall accept any disciplinary action that the Board might take against me, but I would not like to have any discussion with Dr. Jivaraj now.'

As I got up to leave, Jawaharlalji immediately asked the Congress President to inform Dr. Jivaraj that there was no necessity of any discussion with him and that it was not necessary for him to attend the meeting of the Parliamentary Board. This is how this episode ended.

31

Jawaharlalji's Demise

Shri Kamaraj took charge as President of the All India Congress Committee at its session at Bhubaneswar in the beginning of 1964. A resolution was passed on economic policy at that meeting in which several steps were suggested to be taken by the Government. As the Government did not implement these suggestions, much criticism was made later on. I had warned at the time that the steps suggested were very hasty and impracticable. But very little attention was paid to what I said.

Jawaharlalji got very ill during the Congress session and was bedridden. He recovered from that illness, but he found it difficult to walk. He had become so weak that he was carrying on his daily routine only through the strength of his will. He then reappointed Shri Lal Bahadur Shastri to the Cabinet to assist him in his work, but he could not give him the rank in the Cabinet which he wanted to as the senior members of the Cabinet opposed his proposal. I had heard at the time that Jawaharlalji intended to include Indiraji also in his Cabinet. But he was then advised that such a step would not be generally acceptable and would be very severely criticised. He therefore gave up the idea.

The Committee of three, which was appointed by the Working Committee after the Kamaraj plan had been implemented, had ceased to function as no particular work relating to the Congress organisation was entrusted to it. In the meeting of the AICC that was held afterwards, no member defended the Kamaraj plan as I did. As I have mentioned earlier, I had warned Jawaharlalji about what allegations would be made against him as a result of the Kamaraj plan. My strong defence of it in the meeting quietened the opposition.

At the end of March or the beginning of April 1964, two or three friends saw me on behalf of Jawaharlalji and told me that he desired that I should rejoin the Cabinet. I told them that if Jawaharlalji so desired he could certainly call upon me to do so without asking me. I had given up office only at his desire and I did not, therefore, understand the purpose of this consultation. Then those friends suggested that I should give my word that if there was any difference of opinion between Jawaharlalji and myself on any matter, I would carry out Jawaharlalji's decision if differences persisted even after discussion and that I would not oppose Jawaharlalji's decisions even if I disagreed with them. I told them that there had never been any difference of opinion between us in any important matter in the past and I did not understand why this has to be considered now. I made it very clear that I could not give any such undertaking as it involved my self-respect. 'I do not want any office conditionally,' I said, 'If I get any office without any conditions I can certainly accept it. But I cannot accept any office at the cost of my self-respect.' These talks therefore ended there.

Jawaharlalji passed away on 27 May. He had gone to Dehra Dun three or four days earlier and, on being questioned by pressmen, he had said that he was quite healthy and that the day of his passing away was very far. But he took very ill within three days and had to be brought back to Delhi. He passed away within a few hours of his return to the capital.

I went to Jawaharlalji's residence as soon as I learnt of his passing away. I noticed that arrangements were not being properly made. His body was placed in porch in order that the people could come and have his *darshan* and pay their last tributes to him. I, however, saw that the leaders were more worried about what would happen and were busy considering what was to be done later on. As the arrangements for the exposition of his body were not being made properly, I undertook to look after them on my own. Yet several opponents made false allegations against me to the effect that I was at that time trying to succeed Jawaharlalji. There could not be a greater lie than this. In fact these rumours were set afloat only in their own defence by those who were engaged in making arrangements for the succession.

The funeral took place the next day and the funeral procession went to the place which is now known as Shantivan, where the last rites were performed. Thousands of people took part in the funeral procession. The crowds were somewhat less than those in Gandhiji's funeral procession and the general atmosphere of great sorrow which prevailed at that time was not evident. There were several people who were very much grieved and were weeping, while most of the ordinary people did not show any grief on their faces.

Jawaharlalji had desired that his ashes should be spread all over India from aeroplanes after his funeral. This was an extraordinary wish. It was obvious that this wish was a result of his ambition to acquire a reputation of being the greatest man in the world. His ashes were scattered according to his desire in several places in the country from aeroplanes as desired by him.

Shri Gulzarilal Nanda who was No. 2 in the Cabinet was sworn in as the acting Prime Minister on the day Jawaharlalji died. Some Prime Ministers and delegates of foreign countries came to India to attend the funeral.

A great controversy arose as to who should succeed Jawaharlalji after the final rites of his funeral were over. Some months earlier, Shri Kamaraj, Shri Sanjiva Reddy, Shri Nijalingappa, Shri Lal Bahadur Shastri and some others had met at Tirupati. They had considered some arrangements and it is not improbable that some thought was given to such a contingency also. Those leaders who met in this manner at Tirupati were later known as members of the Syndicate. Shri S. K. Patil was also considered to be a member of this Syndicate, but I do not know whether he was present at the meeting or not. It is my presumption that Lal Bahadurji was at the centre of this plan as he had great capacity for such arrangements. I had had very good and close relations with him ever since he became the General Secretary of the Congress in 1951. He used to stay with me whenever he came to Bombay. After he became a Minister and joined the Cabinet, our relations became even closer and more cordial. He had expressed the view in 1962–63, before seven or eight friends, that he would never contest against me for anything. But when he joined the Kamaraj plan, I felt that the ambition of becoming Prime Minister grew in him and it was with this in view that he took part in the consultation mentioned a little earlier. While discussions were continuing for the choice of a successor to Jawaharlalji, a special messenger came to me from Lal Bahadurji and told me that arrangements would be made to make me the Deputy Prime Minister if I accepted Lal Bahadurji as the Prime Minister. I replied: 'I do not approve of making any such bargains. I do not want to give up my self-respect for any post and it is not proper that such an offer should be made to me.'

Some colleagues suggested that the decision of this question be left to the Working Committee. These colleagues wanted to ensure that Lal Bahadurji became the Prime Minister. I did not accept the suggestion and said that the decision must be left to the Congress Legislature Party.

Shri D.P. Mishra met me while these discussions were going on. He had, till then, been telling me that he would support me. However, at the same time, he was telling me that I should support the election of Indiraji as Congress President. I did not accept his suggestion. He then told me that I should propose Indiraji for the office of Prime Minister. I asked him how I could make such a proposition. He replied:

'These are only tactics. When you propose Indiraji for this post, Lal Bahadurji will not accept it. Indiraji will not, therefore, contest the election and will support you. Your position will thus be secured.'

I replied to him that I did not believe in such manoeuvres. His reply was that Sri Krishna believed in such manoeuvres and tactics and that I should adopt that policy. I replied:

'Sri Krishna was God incarnate and is known as Sampoorna Purushottam, while Rama was considered Maryada Purushottam. Rama behaved as an ideal human being and one should, therefore, act as Rama acted. Sri Krishna was, however, acting as God and could act in any manner he liked; but ordinary men cannot imitate him. One should only do what Krishna has advised people to do in the Gita. I do not want to enter into any intrigue whereby if I do not become the Prime Minister, Lal Bahadurji should not become Prime Minister either. I consider Lal Bahadurji more capable and fitter than Indiraji and I cannot, therefore, make a proposal that she be appointed Prime Minister.'

This enraged Shri Mishra and he left my place abruptly. He then supported Lal Bahadurji against me. He used to tell me earlier that he would always oppose Lal Bahadurji, but, as he said, he behaved according to the policy of Sri Krishna as he understood it, and I was not, therefore, surprised by any of his actions.

When the meeting of the Working Committee took place, it was the view of a majority of the members that Shri Kamaraj should take the consensus of the Congress members of Parliament. I expressed myself against this view. But the Committee accepted the proposal for consensus by a majority. Shri Kamaraj took the opinion of the members according to his own particular method and, seeing me one day, told me that the consensus was in favour of Lal Bahadurji. I replied to him that I had no trust in his consensus, but he could do whatever he wanted to. I was told by all those, from both sides, who were making enquiries and calculations that the party was very nearly equally divided between Lal Bahadur Shastri and myself. If there was an election, either of us was likely to win by eight or ten votes. Some supporters of Lal Bahadurji accepted this calculation. If I was elected in such circumstances, it would have been very difficult for me to do my work, and all my time and energy would have to be spent in meeting opponents or a situation might arise when I would have to resign out of sheer disgust.

There was also universal talk both in and outside the country that the Congress would break up after Jawaharlalji. I had no doubt that great damage would be done to the country if the Congress was divided. On account of all these considerations, I withdrew from the contest and accepted the consensus decision of Shri Kamaraj. Shri Lal Bahadur Shastri was thus unanimously elected Prime Minister of India by the Congress Parliamentary Party.

32

Jawaharlal Nehru: in My View

I FIRST MET Jawaharlalji in 1931, but I did not come in close contact with him till 1934–35. Our contacts increased from 1935 when he was elected again as Congress President as I was then the Secretary of the Gujarat Pradesh Congress Committee.

Kumari Mridulaben Sarabhai had spoken about me to Jawaharlalji at length and he had learnt quite a lot about me from her. Similarly it was she who gave me impressions of Jawaharlalji. I believed at that time that he was above intrigue and manoeuvre, that he was a great and fearless intellectual full of courage, and that he had a feeling of intense sympathy for the millions of poor in the country, and that he was a great patriot. He was in the forefront in the struggle for freedom against the Britishers. He had been jailed more often and for longer periods than other Congress leaders. He was impatient by temperament. He also impressed me as a person who wanted to impress the public by his personality and was, therefore, to some extent, an exhibitionist. He liked to be with the crowds and welcomed them and used all his skill to be popular with them. He was the most popular leader after Mahatma Gandhi. He used to get up on the bonnet of a car and attract the attention of the people. He would also ride on the coach-box with a driver in a horse-carriage, and used to mix very easily with crowds, which sometimes became disorderly as a result.

He used to get angry very often but, as I experienced later on, often his anger was assumed. Seven or eight times out of ten he used to feign anger in order to make the other man submit to him. When he was really angry and somebody opposed him, he would not resist the impulse of giving him a push or a blow. He had a keen sense of humour and sometimes made fun of others. He was so popular that even if he behaved wrongly, nobody would tell him so. He behaved in the same way with everybody and this was why the masses were attracted to him and loved him.

Jawaharlalji trusted very few people. I sometimes doubted whether he had total confidence in even one single person. He trusted no person for more than two or three years. Shri Krishna Menon, whom he trusted till the end of his life was the solitary exception. Some people are of the opinion that Jawaharlalji did not assess people properly and, therefore, trusted the wrong people. My experience convinced me that this estimate was wrong. I learnt by experience that he assessed people very well and the way he described their characteristics convinced me that he was a good judge of people. The way he described Shri Krishna Menon's personality to me, his intelligence and his methods of work could not be improved upon by anybody, in my view. I realised after going to Delhi that he believed in Machiavellian tactics and at times made use of some individuals to create differences between people. I was convinced that he had no petty ambitions for wealth or personal power. His patriotism was of the highest order and he constantly thought of the welfare of the poor. But I felt that his only and overpowering ambition was to attain the stature of the greatest man of the world. Sometimes I got an impression that he aspired even to being considered greater than Mahatma Gandhi. He, therefore, never patterned himself on Mahatma Gandhi, but was always careful to make an impression of his distinct personality. Shri Krishna Menon used to make propaganda continuously for creating a greater impression in favour of Jawaharlalji than in favour of Mahatma Gandhi. This was why, in my view, Jawaharlalji felt indebted to him. Jawaharlalji did not hesitate to use political manoeuvre to fulfil his great ambition and used some people to further his ends in those manoeuvres. Those who allow themselves to be used by others do so only for their own self-interest. A selfless person will not allow himself to be utilised by others for any wrong purpose. This is why Jawaharlalji sometimes got involved with undesirable people.

Jawaharlalji used to be taken in by the flattery of those whom he utilised and he was, therefore, often influenced by stories conveyed to him by them. He did not trust anybody whom he considered his opponent, even though his outward behaviour with him was always proper. But when he felt that the person who opposed him, and told him some unpleasant things, was not his enemy, he was not annoyed. If, however, a person whom he considered an enemy said something unpleasant, he used to get very annoyed. He would not give any importance to him. His relations with Maulana Saheb during the last few years of the latter's life were to some extent strained, and it was from watching this relationship that I inferred that he did not forgive those whom he considered to be his enemies. He had very close and cordial relations with Maulana Saheb for years and used to take his advice on many matters, but when Maulana Saheb opposed his taking Krishna Menon in the Cabinet and even offered his resignation on the proposed appointment, Jawaharlalji had to give up the idea of making the appointment. Later on, when Pantji and others persuaded Maulana Saheb to give up his opposition, he did so, and Krishna Menon was appointed as a Cabinet Minister without Portfolio, as I have mentioned earlier. But Jawaharlalji did not forgive Maulana Saheb for his opposition until his death.

Since I joined the Central Cabinet in 1956, I saw that Jawaharlalji did not consult Maulana Saheb very much and even disregarded him to some extent. This position continued until Maulana Saheb's death. It may be as a result of this change in attitude that Maulana Saheb may have felt that Jawaharlalji was a jealous person. I did feel that Jawaharlalji had some jealousy in him but this jealousy did not relate to wealth or power. This related only to his popularity amongst the people.

He behaved ordinarily in such a proper manner that he appeared to be free from prejudice. But I saw after 1956 that he did not easily give up his prejudices. He would never act himself against a person whom he disliked, but if someone else harassed that person, he would connive at it. He was so fond of popularity that he used at times, to give up a correct position in order to please a crowd. Ordinarily, Jawaharlalji was a fearless person so far as money, physical safety or power were concerned. But he was always afraid of being unpopular. If, therefore, a very large crowd offered opposition to him and criticised him, he considered their opinion as real popular opinion. He was not free from small weaknesses of human nature which are there in every human being. But some people used to take advantage of them.

When he was very angry he used unrestrained language, losing control over himself. But he used to cool down very soon and when calm he used to be sorry for his anger and would do something to satisfy the person with whom he was angry, even if his request was not proper. He would sometimes get angry with one person for the fault of another.

When he came to Bombay at the end of 1947 or thereabout, a large crowd had gathered near his plane. Though he often encouraged the gathering of large crowds, he would sometimes get angry at their behaviour. On this occasion he got angry with the crowd and, to show his displeasure, he gave two or three slaps on the back of the Police Commissioner who was standing near him at the time.

While he used to study a great deal and was constantly reading and remained in touch with the latest literature, his knowledge about the Hindu religion was not very deep. It may be that this was so as he had no faith in God or religion until the last few years of his life, as I could understand from my discussions with him. In fact, I noticed a prejudice against Hinduism in his mind.

He ordinarily refrained from doing anything improper or wrong, but he did not mind those whom he utilised, doing something wrong on his behalf. Sometimes he wanted them to act on his behalf but he did not want to take any responsibility for their actions, sometimes making them scapegoats. The way he utilised me as a scapegoat in the separation of Maharashtra and Gujarat States is an illustration. He did not want to divide the Bombay State into Maharashtra and Gujarat States and also did not want to include Bombay city in Maharashtra State. He had talked to me about it specifically and frankly and had even given some very strong arguments in favour of his views, but he used to maintain in public that he was without any prejudice in the matter and he created a feeling in Maharashtra that I was responsible for not allowing Bombay to go to Maharashtra. I have referred to this matter in a previous chapter and have mentioned that he accepted my charge that he had used me as a scapegoat in this connection.

He had been well-disposed towards me ever since I came in contact with him and I believed that he had full trust in me as long as I was in Bombay. But he was very cautious in accepting this in public. I was convinced of this from the letter he wrote to me on my sixtieth birthday. He had earlier sent a telegram which was formal, as he himself mentioned in his later letter. It will be seen from this letter that I am not misrepresenting him in this matter. He had written the address on this letter with his own hand and had sent it in two sealed envelopes, one inside the other as is done only for highly confidential letters. Here is the letter.

New Delhi
28.2.1956

My dear Morarji,

I have sent you a brief telegram—rather formal and rigid. It is difficult to be expansive in a telegram. But may I add to it and say how much I have admired your calm steadfastness of purpose in the face of attack and difficulty. We have had a difficult time and we are likely to have no easy time in the future. In the middle of this turmoil you have stood out without losing your temper or allowing yourself to be swept away. Please remember that you have all our friendship and admiration.

I am afraid most of us have passed or are passing the 60 mark. I am far on the other side and even you have joined this band. We shall carry on of course but the future does not offer an encouraging prospect. However, enough for the day is the work and the evil thereof.

Affectionately yours
Jawaharlal

Jawaharlalji's relations with Mahatma Gandhi were affectionate and close. It is my view that Mahatma Gandhi contributed more towards forging these relations than Jawaharlalji. Gandhiji used to be tolerant towards his opponents. Jawaharlalji sometimes used to oppose Gandhiji in public and then explain his position to him privately. Mahatma Gandhi did not criticise him publicly. I have referred in an earlier chapter to the talk of Jawaharlalji with Mahatma Gandhi at the time of the truce in 1931–32 and also at the time of the Quit India movement in 1942. These incidents convinced me about this trait of Jawaharlalji.

Mahatma Gandhi had great respect and appreciation for Jawaharlalji's patriotism, intelligence and liberality of mind and used to connive at his weaknesses. This is how Mahatma Gandhi groomed many ieaders, but those leaders whom he moulded including Jawaharlalji, did not imbibe this capacity from Mahatma Gandhi. Sometimes Jawaharlalji used to lessen the importance of people and did not thus cultivate the capacity of adding to the stature of people and making them leaders. I did not see any desire in him to acquire that capacity either.

I believe there was some strain in his relations with Shri Feroze Gandhi, his son-in-law. He did not seem to have very great respect for his public conduct. I got this impression from some talks which I had with Jawaharlalji, but I also saw twice or thrice that he was afraid of doing something which would displease Feroze Gandhi.

On the whole, I got an impression that Jwaharlalji used to put forward and utilise some people for increasing his popularity and serving his political ends, and was in turn utilised by these people. I found that he could not prevent them from making an improper use of him. This is a weakness not shown by Sardar Saheb. The Sardar also used people in politics, but he never allowed them to misuse him. The Sardar was thus stronger and more capable in these matters.

Jawaharlalji was deeply impressed by what he saw in Russia when he visited that country before independence and was also deeply impressed by the writing of Marx. He was, therefore, attracted by the economic policies of communism. His sympathy for the poor was of the same intensity as that of Mahatma Gandhi.

This also must have contributed to his attraction towards the economic policies of communism. But he had the greatest attachment and respect for democracy and democratic methods and did not, therefore, approve of the violent methods of communism.

Jawaharlalji's inherent love for democracy was strengthened and confirmed when Mahatma Gandhi entered his life. Mahatma Gandhi was the best and truest representative of democratic behaviour. This also may have saved Jawaharlalji from total communist influence though I cannot deny that, even if he had not come in contact with Mahatma Gandhi, he would have maintained his democratic instincts and methods and would not have become a Communist. He had a great antipathy to conservatism and was to some extent afraid of the strength of conservative forces. He, therefore, always honestly desired that those progressive forces which were working against conservative forces should continue to do so even if their methods were not proper and, while not supporting their programmes, he supported those forces to some extent to see that they were not wiped out. There was no communism in the socialism in which he believed because his faith in democracy was so deep that differences of treatment between man and man used to pain him greatly. He was constantly making efforts to remove such differences. He wanted that everybody should get an equal opportunity for his development and advancement and that there should be a society free of exploitation. He, therefore, did not strongly criticise some so-called progressive programmes even if he did not like them. He sometimes even encouraged them. He had no patience with those whom he considered conservative as he honestly and truly believed that conservatives were the greatest impediment in the development and progress of society. I believe he was correct in this view, but I also believe, in spite of this, that it is the duty of every public worker to prevent wrong things being done in the name of progressivism if these actions are injurious to society. Jawaharlalji could not be objective in this matter as he could not overcome his deep prejudices in this as in certain other matters.

Jawaharlalji fervently desired world peace and opposed all wars. He was afraid of the destruction that is caused by wars, and it was not pure love of peace that made him oppose wars. I believe that wars can never be abolished as long as one wants to maintain peace on account of the fear of war. Every war is the result of fear, and peace can only be a result of fearlessness. It was suggested to Jawaharlalji that if the bases of the Chinese in Tibet had been bombed out when they invaded us in NEFA, we could have defeated the Chinese invasion. But there was a possibility of the Chinese bombing Calcutta and some cities of Bihar, UP and Delhi and Jawaharlalji was afraid of the heavy damage that would be done as a result of such bombing. It is clear that it can be very harmful and damaging if steps are not taken to counter those who start a war, out of fear that damage would be caused. It is only the willingness to take risks that sometimes gives strength to nations which are engaged in defending themselves. Jawaharlalji did not think it proper to bomb Tibet as he was afraid of the losses consequent on the bombing of our cities and had not acquired the necessary fearlessness in this matter.

He had a great love for children, but sometimes this love was also governed by his great passion for gaining popularity. He had a great feeling of respect for women, but he could not translate this feeling into actual practice. Women used to influence him at times and he encouraged them sometimes. This is why women were also attracted to him.

As he had spent many years in England for his education, he was deeply affected by the thought and culture of that country. His thinking, therefore, was more British but his heart was Indian, and this contradiction sometimes came in the way of his taking clear-cut decisions in some matters. This is why he did not succeed in forging real nationalism in the country after the establishment of swaraj. His love for the English language was a handicap in the development of the Hindi language. He had great mastery over English and he was a great writer. If he had not been involved in politics, he would have been one of the great writers of the world.

Jawaharlalji was a thinker but he could not associate others in his thinking. I believe it was because of this trait that he could not sometimes translate his thoughts into action.

33

Lal Bahadur Shastri and War with Pakistan

WHEN SHRI Jawaharlalji passed away, Shri Lal Bahadur Shastri formed his Cabinet after being elected the leader of the Congress Parliamentary Party. One night he invited me to see him when he was forming his Cabinet. When I saw him he requested me to join his Cabinet. When I asked him in what position and for what work he was inviting me to join the Cabinet, he told me that I should join as No. 3 in the Cabinet as Shri Gulzarilal Nanda, having been the Acting Prime Minister, had to be No. 2. I told him that he was my junior and his being an Acting Prime Minister was an accident. I also said that if the Kamaraj plan had not come into effect, I should have continued in the Cabinet and would have become the Acting Prime Minister. I, therefore, told him that his stand was not correct. He said: 'Indiraji is also insisting that Gulzarilalji should be No. 2. You should accept my invitation and join the Cabinet. There will be no difference in your importance as a result of the third position in the Cabinet.' I then told him that it did not behove him to persuade me in that manner and that he should not press me to accept a position which I did not consider proper. When he told me that he was told by others that I would be willing to accept the third position in the Cabinet, I pointed out to him that he had known me for years and that he should not insult me in this manner by believing such stories. I, therefore, requested him to give up his attempt and assured him that, remaining outside the Cabinet, I was not going to oppose him and that I would cooperate with him as much as I could. Our talks ended there and I left his place.

Lal Bahadurji gave me the impression that he was very unhappy at my not accepting his invitation. I was told later on that he did not sleep that night. I could not be certain whether the stand he had taken was taken under pressure or whether it was his own manoeuvre. I would not be surprised if he took the stand on his own in order to lessen my importance, so that his importance might be enhanced. I inferred this from the manner in which he acted. I had assured him I would create no difficulties and that my personal relations with him would continue to be as cordial as before, and that I would not do anything to impair those relations.

Lal Bahadurji took Shri Sanjiva Reddy, who had resigned as Chief Minister of Andhra Pradesh as a result of a judgement in the Andhra High Court against him, in his Ministry. I very rarely met Lal Bahadurji after this.

Lal Bahadurji suffered a heart attack a few days after he became Prime Minister. He had already had a heart attack sometime previously. One day a colleague told me that Lal Bahadurji had told him, with some unhappiness, that I was reported to be saying that he would soon die. This pained me very much as I was not capable of entertaining any such idea. Someone must have started this rumour thinking I would want my way to Prime Ministership cleared by Lal Bahadurji's death. When, therefore, Lal Bahadurji recovered from his illness to some extent, I went to see him and talked to him about this matter, saying, 'If you tell me the name of the person who has told you this, it will be possible for you to verify it by confronting me with him. But how does it befit you to entertain such a terrible idea about me in spite of our close personal relations for so many years ? I wish you had taken this into consideration.' He accepted that the story was false and he did not discuss the matter further. All this, however, revealed one side of his nature.

The sittings of the Lok Sabha had started to be rather stormy from 1963. The dignity of the House was, however, ordinarily maintained as long as Jawaharlalji was alive. But disturbances in meetings of the Lok Sabha began to increase from the second session of 1964 and the Speaker was unable to maintain the dignity of the House. There was no peace in the House in spite of the expulsion of some members and there were improper demonstrations in the meetings of the Lok Sabha. These demonstrations had a very unhealthy effect on the visitors in the gallery.

I did as much Congress organisation work as came my way while I was outside the Government, though it is a fact that very little such work was entrusted to me. But many people used to see me and take my advice, and I continued to be very busy.

I had very seldom written for the press, but Shri Durga Das's press agency, INFA, pressed me to write some articles on different subjects for public education. I accepted the suggestion and wrote several articles in the years I was out of office. I could gather from the newspapers that these articles were well received and were subsequently published in the form of a book under the title, *In My View.* All the money I received for these articles were credited to the Education Trust which I had formed some time earlier. I did so as I had decided much earlier that whatever writing I did and whatever money that I earned from it would be for the benefit of the Trust.

A meeting of the AICC was held at Bangalore from 23 to 25 July 1965. A proposal was brought forward there for the extension of the term of the Congress President. It was proposed to amend the resolution which had been passed on 24 October 1958 on this subject which ran as under :

> This All India Congress Committee decides that the Congress President and the Secretaries of the AICC should not hold their offices for more than two years at a time.

The proposed amendment was discussed in the Working Committee before it was brought up in the AICC. Most of the members of the Working Committee were in favour of extending the Presidentship of Shri Kamaraj for two years as suggested by Lal Bahadurji. I opposed the suggestion. My opposition was not directed against any person but to the amendment of a useful rule to accommodate an individual. If rules were not properly implemented and observed and exceptions were made to accommodate individuals, the organisation would weaken and the people would not have any confidence in its decisions. This was my reason for opposing the amendment. I said:

'What is being done is not proper. I have never opposed any resolution in the Working Committee during the last thirty-five years of my membership of this august body and I believe that the Working Committee should talk with one voice. However, difficult occasions arise in life and one should not suppress the voice of one's conscience. I have had two such previous experiences in my life and this is the third one. You (my colleagues) are advising me to withdraw my opposition. But I oppose this on principle as I am convinced that it will be a great disservice to the organisation if this resolution is accepted. I cannot, therefore, accept this resolution. If we really want to serve the Congress and the nation, we must use only pure means and should not suppress the voice of our conscience. If the voice of our conscience is not suppressed, the atmosphere which we see prevailing here today will be cleared.

'Many colleagues are afraid of giving expression to their real opinions. They show their dislike for this resolution in private, but when they have to speak against persons in authority, they remain silent. I would certainly advise them to speak out the truth whenever it is necessary. I speak with deep anguish when I say that several colleagues are not able to give their views for fear that they will not get tickets as Congress candidates in future. One cannot of course expect man to be perfect, but everybody has to decide for himself to what extent he should compromise with the voice of his conscience. If things are to be decided on political and utilitarian considerations, duty will be forgotten. Congress is the one institution in the world to which we owe our allegiance and pledge our loyalty for our whole life. There is affection and respect for the Congress in the public as this organisation is based on high ideals and principles. It is these which have made the Congress strong and have earned the confidence of the people. But if things are to be carried on in the manner in which it is proposed, the organisation will one day disappear in spite of this rich heritage.

'I would not mind if the Congress disappeared in the interest of the country. There can be differences of opinion, but if the Congress organisation, which is an instrument for leading people on the path of progress, loses the confidence of the people, the country will suffer very greatly. Moral standards have not fallen so low yet, but I would not be surprised if they go down completely in future. Those, therefore, who are in the Congress have a duty to the country, which is to see that pure means are always employed. I am opposing this resolution with great hesitation because I am disregarding the advice of several people for whom I have great respect and affection. I am not indulging in any revolt by offering this opposition, nor do I want to be an opponent. I am against groupism as a matter of principle and have therefore stood up to oppose this resolution. I have been warned that this will end my political career, but I have never attached more importance to my interests than those of the party and the country. Duty to the country is of greater importance than the interest of an individual.

'I was given a similar warning when I presented the budget, which was not an ordinary one, in 1963. I had then made a statement in the Parliament that I have tried throughout my life to understand and live according to truth. I have considered the importance of other things only so far as they helped me in my search for truth. I cannot suppress the voice of my conscience. When I see that the country's interests are being harmed, I cannot remain silent. This is why I am opposing this resolution which gives authority to the Working Committee, even though I do not know what effect it will have on the Working Committee.

'The resolution accepted at Hyderabad was passed after consideration for about seven years. I, therefore, appeal to my colleagues to listen to their inner voices and act accordingly. I do not want them to act as I ask them to, but they should act according to their own conscience.

'When this resolution was proposed at Hyderabad, I had

opposed it and had said that voluntary restraint should be observed in the matter. But my suggestion was considered very idealistic and impractical and it was considered necessary to impose a ban by a rule. This resolution was then passed unanimously in the Working Committee and the AICC.

'If an exception is made for an individual, it would be a disregard of democracy and democratic principles. If such an exception had been made in the case of Shri Sanjivayya who was then the Congress President and who had yet not been able to address the Annual Congress Sessions, I could have appreciated it, and yet no exception was made in his case. The Working Committee will be put in a very awkward position if an exception is now made or authority is given to the Working Committee to make it in the case of rules which have been accepted after long consideration and discussion. If exceptions are made in some cases and not in others, a very difficult situation will be created. This will harm the interest of the country. It is, therefore, wrong to saddle the Working Committee with this kind of responsibility.

'If such a suggestion was made in the Working Committee and accepted unanimously I could have understood an exception being made, but that has not happened. Why then should an exception be made in the case of Shri Kamaraj? The Congress will not suffer any loss in fighting the elections if it is not done. If that is the intention, the Working Committee should elect the President. But if that is not the intention, it will be a dangerous precedent to authorise the Working Committee to make an individual exception. I was shocked to learn that the AICC office had made an exception with regard to this Hyderabad Congress Resolution without the knowledge of the Working Committee. How can things go on in this manner? I do not know how all this will end if such things are connived at. Those who are responsible for it ought to be punished. It is in these circumstances that I am opposing this resolution. I have much more to say but I do not want to say anything which would weaken the Congress. I hope that whatever I have said will strengthen the Congress. My purpose will be served if others will be enabled to raise their voice of protest on such occasions as a result of my voice of dissent today.'

I had made it very clear to my colleagues that I had no personal objection to Shri Kamaraj and that my opposition was one of principle.

Lal Bahadurji appealed to me to withdraw my opposition, but I could not accept his appeal. I said then that I had made it clear that I would oppose this resolution in the meeting of the AICC also. Two or three members then said that the resolution of the

Working Committee was binding on every member and if I spoke against it, it would be a breach of discipline. I replied, 'I have observed discipline more strictly than any other member. There is no question of discipline in this particular matter. This is a matter of principle for me and I cannot, therefore, suppress my voice of dissent. If, however, the Working Committee considers it a breach of discipline, the Committee should take action against me and I shall not protest against it.' The discussion ended there, and I recorded my dissent.

When the resolution was moved in the meeting of the AICC, I opposed it with a very heavy heart as this was the first occasion for me to raise a voice of dissent against the Working Committee. There are, however, occasions in a man's life when he cannot suppress the voice of his conscience without abandoning his principles altogether.

The speech I made to the AICC was not prepared beforehand. It was delivered extempore and I put all my feelings into it. I repeated the arguments which I had advanced in the Working Committee.

Lal Bahadurji then discussed the matter with me saying, 'We shall consider this matter again and I assure you that the resolution will not be implemented without further consideration.' After giving me this assurance, he asked me not to record my voice of dissent. As a result of this, I did not vote on the resolution in the AICC. I could see that my speech had affected many delegates very deeply and I felt almost certain that if votes had been taken immediately, there would have been a majority on my side. Some speeches were made after me putting forward the other point of view. Ultimately the resolution was carried.

In September 1965, Pakistan sent many armed intruders into Kashmir. The purpose of this intrusion was to incite the people to expel the Indian forces and join hands with Pakistan. This was really a direct invasion of India. India warned Pakistan about it and issued orders to the Kashmir Government to arrest the intruders or destroy them. Pakistan disregarded the warning and continued its invasion. At one stage, President Ayub Khan even made a declaration that one day he would take a stroll to Delhi and that he would not be surprised if he reached Delhi without encountering serious opposition. That was their intention. The Indian forces faced this attack with great valour and defeated the Pakistani forces. The Indian army had thought of attacking Lahore and taking possession of it, but did not succeed in doing so. This was an unwise step. Pakistan had erected several defences around

Lahore and the Indian forces did not know about them. They, therefore, suffered great losses at these places.

In the invasion, Pakistan first attacked Jammu and took possession of some parts of the Chhamb area. The Indian forces halted their advance and inflicted heavy losses on their forces. Pakistan suffered reverses on other fronts also. Pakistan used all the military equipment, which it had received from America, in this invasion. America had declared earlier that this equipment would not be used against India. But Pakistan did not observe this condition. Pakistan had thus the latest equipment, including tanks and planes while our equipment was old-fashioned. But the men and officers of the Indian army were very brave and the officers were very capable. They, therefore, attained success with great valour and repulsed the Pakistani forces. Pakistan had attacked us also on the Rajasthan border where also they were successfully resisted.

America and other countries did not say anything in the early days of Pakistan's invasion and did not protest against it. But when Pakistan began to get defeated, they perhaps felt that Pakistan would be destroyed and began to make appeals to both sides to halt the war. This showed their partisan attitude very clearly. The Indian forces had recovered some of the area in Kashmir which Pakistan had illegally occupied. The whole country became alert and helped the Government as one man in repulsing the invasion. All the parties cooperated fully with Government in these operations.

Lal Bahadurji made a declaration in the Working Committee and also in public that we would not return to Pakistan the areas of Kashmir which we had recovered. I tried to persuade him not to make such a declaration as it would put him in a very awkward position. When the war ended and negotiations took place for bringing about peace between the two countries, both sides would have to return the areas which they had conquered during the operations. This is a general rule and when we accepted truce and peace, we would have to return those areas. Such brave declarations, however, bring great popularity to the person who makes them, at least at the moment. Lal Bahadurji did not pay any heed to my advice and repeated his declaration.

Pressure was then brought to bear by the United Nations, America and Russia for the declaration of truce. We said we had no objection as we were not in favour of war, but as an invasion had been launched by Pakistan, we could not stop our military operations unless Pakistan stopped its operations first. Our operations were only in self-defence.

Pakistan was soon convinced that, if the war continued, they would have to suffer terribly and also be put to great shame. They, therefore, accepted the appeal for truce and we then agreed to it. The negotiations after the truce should have really taken place in Delhi but the Prime Minister of Russia, Mr. Kosygin, suggested Tashkent for holding the negotiations and also offered to help in the negotiations. It was not proper, in my view, to go outside the country for negotiations, even though we had won the war. I had given expression to my view publicly also. But Lal Bahadurji accepted the suggestion of Mr. Kosygin and went to Tashkent alongwith the Defence Minister and others. During the negotiations that took place at Tashkent, he agreed to return the areas that we had recovered from Pakistan during the war. This created a very bad impression in India and Lal Bahadurji, who had become very popular during the war, became very unpopular as a result. On the night before his return to India he suffered a serious heart attack and passed away at Tashkent on 10 January 1966. I was told that he had talked over the telephone with the members of his family before he got the heart attack. He was informed about the opposition to the Tashkent decision. This information perhaps gave him a shock and he died within an hour and a half after this talk. He had had two heart attacks before this. Several doubts and suspicions have been expressed in many quarters with regard to his death. But looking to all the circumstances, I do not find any ground for these doubts. I do not believe in the allegations that he did not die a natural death but was murdered.

Lal Bahadurji's body was brought to Delhi the next day and the funeral ceremony took place at the spot which is now known as Vijay Ghat.

I am not in favour of making such special funeral ghats because if such special ghats are made for all Prime Ministers, very little spare area would remain in Delhi city. This also lessens the importance of Raj Ghat.

34

Indira Gandhi becomes Prime Minister

WHEN SHRI Lal Bahadur Shastri passed away, it became necessary to elect a new leader of the Congress Parliamentary Party. Shri Gulzarilal Nanda, who was No. 2 in the Cabinet of Shri Lal Bahadur Shastri, was again sworn in as temporary Prime Minister and a meeting of the Party was called for electing a new leader.

Shri Kamaraj had got prejudiced against me in 1964 and his prejudice continued. He did all that he could to see that not I but Smt. Indira Gandhi was elected leader of the Congress Parliamentary Party. Shri Jagjivan Ram initially supported me, but Shri Kamaraj won him over by promising him a ministership in the new Cabinet. Shri Jagjivan Ram met me and told me that I did not have the support of the majority, and that he would go with the majority. I did not try to persuade him to do otherwise; it would have been futile to do so. He had taken his decision. I told him that he was free to do what he considered proper.

It is possible that if I had made bargains with some members I could have won the election. Some colleagues even told me that it did not pay to be quite straight in politics and that one must resort to manoeuvres and intrigues. But I do not believe in such methods as I am convinced that if one wants to pursue truth one must observe it in every action of one's life. If one wants to pursue truth, one cannot resort to intrigues or manoeuvres. I had also no doubt that even if I succeeded in winning the contest by such means and became the Prime Minister, I could not have served the country well and that if I could not serve the country properly it was better that I did not become the Prime Minister. It was not my ambition to be the Prime Minister, but I did not consider Indiraji to be suitable for this office and considered it my duty to oppose her in the election. Some of my colleagues also pressed me to contest. Indiraji won by a very large majority. I got 169 votes; she got more than double that number. But most people felt that the number of votes I got constituted a moral success. I was not disappointed at being defeated as I knew from the very beginning that I would be.

As I have mentioned earlier, Shri Kamaraj and some of his friends were determined to prevent me from being elected to this office and they had put up Smt. Indira Gandhi only in order to defeat me. They probably thought that nobody except Smt. Indira Gandhi could contest against me successfully. They opposed me because they felt that I was a man with a very strong mind and would not allow myself to be controlled by anybody. This was the main reason for their opposition to me as I understood it. Howsoever firm I may be in my actions, I have never imposed my views on my colleagues at any time. I have always accepted majority decisions. This is one of the main features of my life. I have accepted majority decisions of the Congress invariably and have carried them out cheerfully and with discipline. I considered it wrong to try to mollify Shri Kamaraj and other friends who opposed me and to persuade them to support me. I also felt that such an effort on my part would have been misused. It was also a question of my self-respect and I had no ambition to be Prime Minister at any cost. I, therefore, did not consider it proper to discuss this matter with friends unless they wanted to discuss it with me.

Indiraji had publicly said that Shri Kamaraj was her leader and was also the President of the Congress and that she would do whatever he asked. This is probably why Kamaraj and his friends felt that Indiraji would act on their advice and their influence in the Congress would be maintained. Later events have, however, shown how they went wrong in their calculations. I had warned several colleagues about this in the very beginning.

If Indiraji had stood on her own and these friends had not supported her with one-sided propaganda, she would not have got more than twenty-five votes. At any rate, this was my estimate. I have no doubt she would not have contested under such circumstances. But Shri Kamaraj took the support of several State Chief Ministers and made very one-sided propaganda against me amongst Congress members of Parliament. This is how Indiraji won with a very large majority. I did not go to anybody to canvass support, but I talked to several members of Parliament on the telephone and told them that they should not be influenced by anybody and that they should vote for the person whom they considered the fittest for the office. This was the only appeal I made to them. But when prominent leaders of the party made one-sided propaganda and applied pressure on the members, it was not surprising that the majority of the members voted with them.

After being elected as leader, Indiraji formed her Cabinet in which she did not at first want to include Shri Jagjivan Ram. As I was given to understand, the then President of India, Shri S.

Radhakrishnan, had also advised her similarly. But Indiraji ultimately included Jagjivan Ramji in her Cabinet under pressure from Shri Kamaraj. I was not invited to join the Cabinet; but even if I had been, I would not have accepted.

Lal Bahadurji had decided in the beginning of November 1965 to appoint an Administrative Reforms Commission and had invited me to be its Chairman. Later on, after the death of Lal Bahadurji, Indiraji also asked me to do so. Lal Bahadurji desired that I should accept his invitation as he felt I was the fittest person for the task. I discussed this matter with him and Nandaji and told them that if the other members of the Commission were appointed with my consent and did not exceed five or six in number, I would agree to be the Chairman. My conditions were accepted and Shri Hanumanthaiya, Shri Harish Chandra Mathur, Shri H. V. Kamath and Shri V. Shanker, ICS, were selected as the members of the Commission. Shri V. Shanker was to work on the Commission in addition to carrying on his duties as the Secretary of his department. Shri V. V. Chari was appointed Secretary to the Commission. All this was done on my recommendation. In the meanwhile, it was decided that I should lead the Indian Delegation to the Conference of the Commonwealth Parliamentary Association to be held in New Zealand at the end of November. I had, therefore, hoped that if the Commission was formally appointed before I left for New Zealand I could have made some arrangements to start the work of the Commission before leaving India. But for one reason or another, the announcement of the Commission was not made until January 1966. This did not surprise me as many things are delayed in implementation by the Government, even after decisions are taken.

After I returned from Australia and New Zealand, the appointment of the Administrative Reforms Commission was notified at the end of February or in the beginning of March. I was told that Indiraji was having second thoughts on the matter since she became Prime Minister. There was also a talk of appointing a larger number of members on the Commission, but as I refused to accept the Chairmanship if such a decision was taken, the proposal was dropped.

I discussed with the members of the Commission the question of the position of the members in the government hierarchy according to the warrant of precedence. It was their opinion that the members should have the status of cabinet ministers. I discussed this question with the Prime Minister. She was not inclined to accept the suggestion. I did not bother about status at all. My only purpose in fixing it was to know what places the members would get when they attended government parties or dinners. I, therefore, ultimately told Indiraji that no rank lower than that of a cabinet minister would be acceptable to us. If this could not be assigned, I said, it would be better if no rank was specified as we would not attend any government functions and no difficulty would therefore arise. Fixation of rank would not make any difference to the positions of the members in the public eye. That did not require any government approval. The appointment of the Commission was then notified. The first meeting of the Commission, where we discussed procedure and methods, took place at the end of March. The offices of the Commission were first located in Travancore House where we first met. We were later allotted offices in the Sardar Patel Bhawan which was a new construction.

I wanted to ensure that the Administrative Reforms Commission functioned effectively and told my colleagues that we should have our report and recommendations ready by the end of 1967. The members felt that this was not possible and that the work would take at least three years. I told my colleagues that there was no need to go into great details. We should formulate rules and regulations on major points, so that the work could be continuously revised. If we did this, I felt we would be able to submit our report before the end of 1967. My colleagues accepted this suggestion.

I had known, before I went to New Zealand, that a similar Commission had been appointed there and I made it a point to see the report of that Commission when I went there. They had finished their work in a year, which was also in my mind when we took our decision. A similar Commission had been appointed some years earlier in the USA also. I had gone through their report too. We decided our procedures and methods of work after taking these reports into consideration.

The Commission discussed the appointment of a high authority, as they have in some countries, to enquire into allegations against the ministers, and to report their findings to Parliament. We considered it very necessary to have such an arrangement in this country and we submitted an interim report making this suggestion. The arrangement suggested consisted of two levels. One was to be called Lokpal and the other Lokayukta. The Lokpal would look into complaints against ministers and the Lokayukta into those against secretaries and other high officials. A Bill was framed by Government on this recommendation and was presented to Parliament.

Ever since I undertook this responsibility, I attended the Commission's office for five or six hours a day and regularly discussed various matters with my colleagues and others to ensure that the work of the Commission proceeded on the right lines. We held frequent meetings and appointed several panels to consider the major questions and submit their reports for our consideration. This was done to speed up the Commission's work. I continued as the Chairman of this Commission until March 1967 when I was appointed Deputy Prime Minister by Smt. Indira Gandhi. The Commission was dissolved on 30 June 1970, even though its work had not been completed. I learnt this only through the newspapers.

The Prime Minister decided on the devaluation of the rupee and made a declaration accordingly in July 1966. When this possibility was raised in public from time to time, the Government consistently denied the possibility of any such step, and persons raising this question were criticised. The step was ultimately taken on the advice of the World Bank and the International Monetary Fund and also at the instance of some ministers. Shri Sachin Chaudhury was the Finance Minister at that time. I was not consulted in this matter, but Shri T. T. Krishnamachari was and had opposed the measure. Shri Kamaraj too was against it. In spite of this the devaluation was decided upon. It increased the external debt of the country by 57 per cent overnight and correspondingly increased also the interest to be paid annually on that debt. This step was against the interests of the country. Many people criticised it and said that it had been taken without proper consideration. I agreed with this criticism.

I submitted a note on devaluation to the meeting of the Congress Working Committee held to discuss the matter. I pointed out that if the three ex-Finance Ministers who were present in the country had been consulted before taking this decision, it would have been better. But only one of them was consulted. If the two others viz. Shri C. D. Deshmukh and I had been consulted, the Government would have had a better basis for considering the proposals. Relationship between these three ex-Finance Ministers were such that they could not have colluded in giving their opinion and three independent expert opinions would have been available. It so happened that the view of all three was against devaluation. It was very clear that Government had taken this step out of fright. Devaluation could benefit only that country whose exports were larger than its imports and of which the exports could be increased and imports lessened. If, therefore, a fully industrially developed country decided on devaluation, it could export more of its goods and lessen its imports and benefit by devaluation. But in a country like India, where imports were much larger than exports, it would clearly cause great harm. The price of imports would go up in terms of rupees and we would get larger amounts in rupees for exports. But as more amounts would have to be paid in rupees for imports production costs would increase in the country and this would create difficulties for exports. It was thus very clear that devaluation enhanced the difficulties of the country a great deal.

The Prime Minister had no experience of this sort of problem and naturally acted on the advice of others. If she had taken the advice of those who could have advised her properly, she would not have taken such a step. It is possible that she acted on the advice of just two or three persons who were near her. There was a danger that external aid would not be received if devaluation was not accepted. This, I feel, is why devaluation was resorted to. If the Government had declared that it was willing to face such an eventuality and that by working harder we would produce for ourselves the items which were being imported, the prestige of the country would have gone up, the economy would have been strengthened and the rupee need not have been devalued. All would have been convinced of the determination and the capacity of the country if such a decision had firmly been taken, and we would have got external aid also. At any rate, that was my view, and I spoke accordingly in the Working Committee.

It was indeed unfortunate that, having taken this harmful step, no thought was given to the follow-up action to be taken after devaluation. This should have been thought of beforehand and steps taken to get the maximum advantage from devaluation. When Britain devalued the pound they had first considered the steps to be taken subsequent to devaluation and issued simultaneously a book of 800 pages describing the consequential steps to be taken. No such thought was given to this problem in this country when devaluation was declared. This increased the damage to the economy of the country and also injured its reputation.

Preparations were being made at the end of 1966 for the General Elections to be held in 1967. The Congress Parliamentary Board which met for the selection of candidates adopted a policy of going by the views of Indiraji in the selection. This created a danger of wrong persons being selected. I had pressed for adopting a policy of selection whereby only proper persons would be selected, without any consideration of groups. I did not, however, succeed in my effort, and Indiraji selected some ex-Communists and persons who favoured her, and thus encouraged group politics. This vitiated the election climate and we did not get a majority in several States, and even at the Centre we got a majority of only 21. This is how the Congress was weakened and groupism encouraged within it. It was at this time that Indiraji made a beginning in her plan of taking full control of the Congress.

As I said earlier, I was asked by the Prime Minister, Lal Bahadurji, to lead the Indian delegation to the Conference of the Commonwealth Parliamentary Association at the end of 1965, which was to be held in Wellington, New Zealand. I accepted the invitation. Lal Bahadurji had suggested that I should visit Australia on my way. He wanted me to go to Japan too, but as Shri T. T. Krishnamachari wanted to go there, I dropped Japan from my itinerary.

Visitors to New Zealand and Australia can enter these countries only after being vaccinated and this rule is very rigidly observed in both countries. They do not allow the import of even fruits from outside. I, therefore, asked the Secretary of the Foreign Affairs Ministry to find out whether I would be exempted from the vaccination rule in Australia and New Zealand. He knew that I had been exempted from this rule by all the countries I had visited so far. I informed the Foreign Secretary that I could not go to these countries if I was not exempted. He got into correspondence with the two countries and informed me three days before the date of my departure that I was exempted. I, therefore, left in the third week of November 1965.

I stopped on the way for three or four days at Sydney in Australia. I met the Prime Minister and other Ministers there. I was very well acquainted with Sir Robert Menzies who was the Prime Minister of Australia for a few years. We had regard for each other. He gave a special lunch in my honour and invited all his ministers and the leaders of the parties. He proposed a toast to me and spoke about me in very complimentary terms. I thanked him appropriately.

During his talks with me, Sir Robert told me that he was very friendly with President Ayub Khan of Pakistan, and I found that he had a very high regard for him also. I explained to him our viewpoint regarding relations between India and Pakistan and explained to him that Pakistan had no right over Kashmir which had merged voluntarily with India. He told me that the then Foreign Minister of Pakistan, Mr. Bhutto, was a very aggressive person while President Ayub Khan was a reasonable person. If, therefore, an attitude of compromise and conciliation was adopted towards President Ayub Khan, Mr. Bhutto would be weakened. Otherwise, Mr. Bhutto would be strengthened and great harm would be caused to India. I told him that Mr. Bhutto owed his influence only to President Ayub Khan and could not, therefore, say anything unless he had his approval. If he projected Mr. Bhutto, it only showed the President's clever tactics. I explained to Sir Robert, India's case and also why India could not give up Kashmir. After hearing my arguments, he agreed with me and said that he was convinced that India should not give it up.

My visit to Australia was thus very useful. I went round the Port of Sydney which is a very large one. It is so big that it can contain the largest navy. The people are very fond of boating, and boating competitions are very often arranged. They are very adventurous and are not afraid of the sharks which are seen in the port waters. The sight of a boating competition is a very beautiful one. I also found that the city of Sydney was very beautifully situated and built.

Sir Robert Menzies told me with a smile that his Health Minister had proposed in the Cabinet meeting that I should not be exempted from vaccination, but that he did not accept his opposition and got a resolution passed in the Cabinet exempting me. I was given to understand that this was the very first case of exemption in that country.

I also met Lord Casey who was the Governor-General of Australia at that time, and discussed many problems with him. He was very friendly to India. My talks with him were very useful.

I found Australia to be very prosperous. It is a huge country with a very small population, less than twelve or thirteen million in an area two and a half times that of India. The fact that we make an addition to our population every year equal to the total Australian population shows up the difference between the two countries very graphically.

From Australia I went to Wellington and attended the Commonwealth Parliamentary Conference there. The delegation consisted of Professor N. G. Ranga, Shri Swaminathan, Shri S. M. Krishna and a lady doctor MLA from Bombay. The Government of New Zealand had also exempted me from vaccination, but they sent a doctor to see me every day where I lived. The doctor told me that he had instructions from the Government to visit me daily and hoped I had no objection. I told him immediately that I had none and hoped that he would not ask me to take any medicines. He said that the question did not arise. He thus came every day for four or five days, after which he told me that it was a formal routine and it was not necessary for him to continue it. He did not, therefore, see me during the last three days of my stay there.

There were many discussions in the Conference during which

Pakistan raised the question of Kashmir. I opposed its discussion saying that such questions should not be allowed to be raised in a conference of this nature. If, however, it was not possible to prevent Pakistan from doing so, I had to be given an opportunity to reply. The President of the Conference could not prevent the raising of the question, but he gave me twenty minutes to reply. I made statement in twenty minutes and explained the whole case of Kashmir from India's point of view. Most of the delegates appreciated my statement.

I met the Prime Minister and other Ministers of New Zealand. I saw two or three places away from the capital. I also saw their naval yard and their dairy industry. The country impressed me as a very beautiful one. I met several Indians who had migrated there, some of whom were from my district in Gujarat. I also addressed one of their meetings and once had dinner with them.

There are neither extremely rich people in New Zealand nor any poor people. All have proper houses and there are no slums. New Zealand has made very good progress and is economically strong. It has a very small population which is the reason why they have been able to maintain a very good standard of living. They have to import many things and they export the products of their dairy industry from which they get the necessary foreign exchange.

I returned to India after the Conference.

35

Deputy Prime Minister and Finance Minister

After the general election in 1967, I declared my intention of contesting the election for the leadership of the Congress Parliamentary party. Shri Kamaraj was no longer supporting Indiraji and had admitted to me that he had done me injustice on the previous occasion. Some of Indiraji's staunch supporters threatened the Congress President and some others that forty to fifty members would leave the Congress party if Indiraji was not elected as leader. As the majority was very thin, this threat worried the Congress President. I then told him that I would not allow the Congress to be divided on my account. I would, therefore, not contest the election for the leadership. Indiraji was then unanimously elected leader of the newly elected party.

It was my impression that Indiraji had been prejudiced against me from 1962 and was considering me inimical to her. Her method of work and temperament were such that she wanted her view to be accepted by everybody. This was undemocratic and it was, therefore, very difficult to work with her. I had, therefore, said in the very beginning that I would not join her Cabinet, but Shri Kamaraj and other friends pressed me to do so. The Congress had been considerably weakened in these elections and the opposition had been strengthened. I was, therefore, told that if I did not join the Cabinet the Government might not be able to meet the opposition adequately and that the Congress would be further weakened, which would harm the interests of the country.

It seemed to me that some of the supporters of Indiraji pressurised her to ask for my cooperation and told her that, if she did not do so, she might have difficulties in running her Government. On the second or third day after Indiraji was elected leader of the Congress Party, she phoned asking for my cooperation and expressing a desire to have a discussion with me, for that purpose. I told her that I would not be able to go to her residence for this discussion under the circumstances that existed then as, if I went there, many people would misrepresent my action as showing a desire on my part to join the Cabinet. I, therefore, told her that if she wanted to discuss this matter with me we could discuss it only if she came to my house. She accepted my suggestion and came to my place at about 10 a.m. Both of us had to meet Shri Kamaraj in the evening. The Prime Minister requested me to cooperate with her in running the Government and to join her Cabinet, I answered:

'I have been noticing since 1962 that you are prejudiced against me and I talked to you about it at the end of 1962. If this prejudice still continues, it would be futile for me to join the Cabinet as I would not be able to function usefully under those circumstances. If I am not able to talk to you very frankly and clearly now in this discussion, the discussion is not likely to be of much use. I should, therefore, like to know whether this prejudice still persists and whether, if I talked very frankly and you did not like some of my arguments, you would take it ill. I would not like to take that risk as I do not want to spoil our relations further. I would, therefore, request you to answer me very frankly.'

She asked me to forget the past and assured me that she had no prejudice against me.

I explained to Indiraji that if she wanted me to assist her in her work, I could do so only if I was put in a position where I could help her. If that was not done, it would not be possible for me to give much help. She asked me to tell her what I would suggest. I replied:

'If I can speak with authority in your absence on your behalf, I can help you by hoining your Cabinet. This will be possible only if I am given the position of Deputy Prime Minister. I have no particular ambition for any position and I have no desire to join the Cabinet; but I have no doubt that I cannot be of much assistance to you if I do not get this position. Many capable persons have been returned to the Lok Sabha on behalf of the opposition parties this time and they are very good speakers. As I have more experience, I can meet their arguments better than you. You have not got much experience so far of this work. I can reply more effectively to the opposition. It is, therefore, also necessary that I should be given the Home Ministry.'

Indiraji did not show any eagerness to give me the position of Deputy Prime Minister but she did not refuse to do so. She, however, told me that as the Home Ministry was with Shri Yashwantrao Chavan at that time, he would take it ill if a change was made. I told her:

'It is necessary that this Ministry should be with me if I am to be useful to you in view of the conditions prevailing in the different States. Shri Yashwantrao Chavan has worked under me for several years. I, therefore, believe that he will not take it ill if the Home Ministry is given to me. I also have longer experience than him of this work and I believe that I would be able to do it better.'

Our discussions remained inconclusive at this stage and Indiraji left as she had some other work. We then met in the evening at Shri Kamaraj's residence.

Meanwhile, a Member of Parliament came to me in the afternoon and told me that there was a controversy going on in the Central Hall of Parliament as I was reported to have said that Smt. Indira Gandhi was not fit for her position and that Shri Yashwantrao Chavan was not fit for the Home Ministry. I had not talked with anybody after my discussion with Indiraji and I had met no other person since then. Such a discussion could take place in the Central Hall, therefore, only if such a story had gone out from Indiraji's side. This convinced me that Indiraji still harboured prejudices against me. I did not tell her or even remotely imply that she was not fit to be Prime Minister and Shri Yashwantrao Chavan was not fit to be Home Minister. If Indiraji had not given an indication of such a talk, there would not have been such a discussion in the Central Hall. This information therefore pained me very much.

When we met at Shri Kamaraj's in the evening, I asked Indiraji whether she had talked in that manner to anybody. I also asked her as to when I told her that she was unfit to be the Prime Minister and that Shri Chavan was unfit to be the Home Minister. She immediately denied having said anything like that to anybody and said that she had talked to nobody about our discussion. I then asked her how such a baseless story could go to the Central Hall and that too within two hours of our discussion. But she persisted in her denial and said that she had not said anything in the matter. It has been my experience that she generally gets out of a difficult position by such denials. When she denied the whole thing very strongly, I could not discuss the matter further with her.

During the talks between the three of us, Indiraji pressed me to take the Finance Ministry which she had offered me in the morning. I had decided, long before that, that I should not again take charge of the Finance Ministry and I told her that I was not willing to do so. There was a discussion between Shri Kamaraj and myself on this. He wanted a compromise and suggested that the Prime Minister should agree to appoint me Deputy Prime Minister and I should agree to take up Finance.

We then went to the meeting of the Working Committee where also this matter was discussed. All the members of the Committee were of the view and strongly desired that a compromise be effected and that I join the Cabinet. They wanted us to talk it over. Indiraji said that she was willing to do so.

From the Working Committee meeting we again went to Kamaraj's place and discussed the matter all over again. There I explained my difficulty in accepting the Finance Ministry and said that I was convinced by my experience of 1963 that I should not do so again. We dispersed without coming to any conclusions.

Shri C.B. Gupta saw me at 9 p.m. that night and told me that he had had a discussion with Indiraji and that I should accept the Deputy Prime Ministership and Finance Ministry. I told him that I could take a decision only after Indiraji talked to me direct about it. He then went straight to Indiraji's place. As he did not come back till 10.30 p.m. I went to sleep. Guptaji came back at about midnight and told me that the Prime Minister had accepted the proposal after a long discussion and that I should accept it. He told me that several Members of Parliament, who were supporters of Shri Chavan and Shri Asoka Mehta had gone to Shri Kamaraj to oppose the proposal to ask me to join the Cabinet as Deputy Prime Minister. He also told me that the discussion at Indiraji's took very long as several of her supporters were vehemently opposed to this proposal. He said that both he and Shri D.P. Mishra had asked Indiraji to accept the proposal in the interest of the country and made it clear to her that, if she did not accept it, they would not support her. It was only then that Indiraji agreed. I told Guptaji that I appreciated what he told me, but again made it clear that I would take a decision only after Indiraji told me herself about it. He then told me that Indiraji would talk to me the next morning.

I received a phone call from Indiraji at 10 a.m. the next morning asking me to go to her for a discussion. Soon after, Shri Kamaraj also asked me to see him. I told him that I was going to Indiraji as I had been called by her and would see him after finishing my discussion with her. I then went to see Indiraji. Shri Yashwantrao Chavan and Shri Jagjivan Ram were already sitting in the room in which the Prime Minister was to meet me, and she came in immediately after my arrival. It was clear that these two leaders were also to take part in the discussion. I was a little taken aback at this as Indiraji had not told me anything about it.

Indiraji started the discussion and asked me how I would be able to strengthen the Cabinet, if I joined it, while holding the opinion that she and her colleagues were weak. I replied:

'What you say only supports the story that was circulated in the Central Hall yesterday, even though you have denied it. If this is your view about me; if you feel that I would weaken you by joining the Cabinet and if this is going to be the pattern of our relations, you should not include me in the Cabinet. I have expressed no desire to join it. You are pressing me to do so, and if after thus pressing me you put me such a question, it only means that I must not join the Cabinet.'

To this Indiraji replied that her only intention in asking the question was to remove all misunderstandings.

Shri Chavan and Shri Jagjivan Ram then asked me to give them an idea of what were the duties and the importance of the Deputy Prime Minister. I answered:

'I can only say about the position of the Deputy Prime Minister that Sardar Patel was Deputy Prime Minister and it, therefore, does not require any elucidation. But the position certainly also means that the Deputy Prime Minister is superior in status to the other Ministers of the Cabinet and has greater importance.

They asked me whether this meant that the Deputy Prime Minister could give instructions to other Ministers. I pointed out to Shri Yashwantrao that he had worked with me for many years and that it was very strange that he should question me in this manner. 'The Deputy Prime Minister,' I said, 'cannot issue instructions to other Ministers, but can certainly advise them. It is for them to accept the advice or not to do so. It is clear that the position is higher than that of any other Minister.' Shri Yashwantrao then said that, according to him the Deputy Prime Minister was nothing more or greater than No. 2 in the Cabinet. I told him that his understanding was not correct as the position would be higher in the Warrant of Precedence. He said that that was not a correct statement according to his enquiries. I told him that his information was not correct and that I was right in my statement. He would understand the correctness of my statement, if he made further enquiries.

Jagjivan Ramji then asked me: 'Does the position of Deputy Prime Minister mean that the Prime Minister can form his Cabinet only with the advice and consent of the Deputy Prime Minister?'

I replied that his question was very surprising. 'If I am asked for my advice I shall give it,' I said, 'The Deputy Prime Minister does whatever work is assigned to him by the Prime Minister. He will give his advice if it is asked for. Advice is advice, not an order.'

I was very much pained at this cross-examination and protested agaist it saying 'The Prime Minister has put me in a very insulting situation by calling me for a discussion in this manner. It only means that these two friends are kept here as witnesses as the Prime Minister has no confidence in me. I cannot join the Cabinet under these circumstances and you should not, therefore, press me to do so.' The Prime Minister then said that that was not her intention, and the other two colleagues also expressed their regret. I got up and, asking for leave to go, said that I did not understand what she actually meant. Indiraji then told me that she wanted me to join the Cabinet as Deputy Prime Minister and Finance Minister, and pressed me to do so. I told her Shri Kamaraj also wanted to see me and that I was going there. I asked her whether I could tell him about what had happened here, saying, 'If you agree, I shall inform him, otherwise I will not.' She said she had no objection to my acquainting Shri Kamaraj with the discussion.

I went to Shri Kamaraj and informed him about all that had happened. I asked him why he was putting me in such an awkward and insulting position. He told me that the circumstances were so delicate that, if I did not join the Cabinet, the Government and the Congress Party would not last long. I asked him to have a frank discussion with the Prime Minister and satisfy himself whether the Prime Minister honestly wanted my cooperation. I told him that if he was so convinced and asked me to put myself in an awkward position by joining the Cabinet, I should accept his suggestion as I must respect it. He then had a discussion with Indiraji and told me on the telephone after some time that he had had a discussion with her and I must join the Cabinet. I then agreed.

The next day, I was called by Indiraji for advice on the formation of the Cabinet. When I met her, she gave me a list of the Ministers she proposed to take in her Cabinet. I did not make any suggestions as she did not ask for any. But she asked me for advice about the names in the list which she proposed. She told me that she intended taking Dr. Karan Singh and Dr. V. K. R. V. Rao as Ministers of State. I told her that these friends would not accept State Ministerships. They would agree to join the Government only if they were taken in as Cabinet Ministers. I said that it was also not proper to ask them to be State Ministers. She had not included Shri Sanjiva Reddy and Shri Satya Narayan Sinha in the list. I referred to these omissions and told her that it would be a great mistake from the national point of view not to include Shri Sanjiva Reddy in the Cabinet and much harm would be done. She told me that in her view Shri Sanjiva Reddy had not shown great capacity in his work. I told her that I could not agree with her as I knew that he had shown much efficiency as Chief Minister of Andhra and that he was a good administrator. It would, therefore, be better if she included him in the Cabinet. She said she would reconsider the matter. Referring to Shri Satya Narayan Sinha, I said that if she did not include him he would take it very ill. But I got the impression that she was not prepared to include him either in the Cabinet.

When I got out of the Prime Minister's house, her Personal Secretary, Shri Kapoor, told me that the time for swearing in was fixed at 10.45 or 11.15 a.m. I told him that the list was not yet ready and that intimations would not reach all concerned. If, therefore, a later time was fixed it would be better as all concerned would then receive an intimation. He told me that there was no other auspicious time as he had learnt in his consultations with some pandits, and that the Prime Minister had given her assent to that time. I then said nothing more.

When the swearing-in ceremony took place, on 13 March 1967, I found that Shri Sanjiva Reddy had not been included in the Cabinet and that Shri Satya Narayan Sinha whose name was not in the list had been called for the swearing-in ceremony. But he was not assigned any portfolio. After being sworn in, I went to the Finance Ministry and took charge of my office.

Coalition Ministries had been formed in Kerala and West Bengal, dominated by Communists. The DMK Ministry was formed in Madras. A coalition Ministry of the opposition parties was formed in Bihar, and the Akali Dal and the Jan Sangh had formed a Ministry in Punjab. The Congress did not get a majority in Rajasthan and the opposition parties were jointly claiming a majority. Dr. Sampurnanand, who was the Governor of Rajasthan at that time, refused to go into the claims of the opposition parties and recommended Presidential Rule for the State. This recommendation was accepted by the Central Government. I felt that this was not quite constitutional. Shri Mohanlal Sukhadia, after some time, formed a Congress Ministry by winning over some members from the opposition parties to his side and he went on expanding his Cabinet. This is how the Congress Ministry was formed in Rajasthan and the opposition parties made a strong attack on such tactics. A coalition of the Swatantra and Jan Sangh parties formed a Ministry in Orissa, and the Naga Party formed a Ministry in Nagaland. In the rest of the States, Congress Ministries were formed.

Even though the Congress formed a Ministry in UP, it did not survive very long. A coalition Ministry was then formed there as Shri Charan Singh defected from the Congress with a few colleagues, being tempted by the prospect of becoming Chief Minister. He headed the coalition Ministry.

The Congress Ministry in Haryana did not survive long and there too a Ministry was formed by the opposition parties. But this coalition Ministry also did not last long as the constituents could not work in co-operation. This created instability in several States.

36

Nationalisation of Banks and Abolition of Privy Purses

THERE WAS a proposal before the Working Committee meeting in May 1967 for nationalising some banks and general insurance. There was also a proposal for abolishing the privy purses and privileges of the Princes. Several members advocated nationalisation of banks and general insurance. After most of the speakers had given their views, I gave my own. I said:

'The question of nationalisation of banks is being talked about since 1948 and the proposal has been considered from time to time, but no specific scheme has been accepted so far. I do not personally consider nationalisation a principle; I consider it only an instrument. If the country benefits by nationalisation and the interest of the common man is served, it should be resorted to, but if that purpose is not served, there should be no nationalisation just for the sake of nationalisation. The Congress has accepted the idea of a mixed economy and has made frequent declarations about it. I do not, therefore, approach nationalisation as a principle but I am not against it where it is necessary in national interest.

'Our economic condition has deteriorated during the last two or three years. We have had to face many difficulties as a result of the Chinese aggression in 1962 and have had to incur heavy expenditure as a result. There has been famine for two years consecutively and the Centre and some States had to spend crores of rupees to meet the situation. The prices of grain and other goods have gone up very high. The rise in prices has been greater in the last three years than that in the last eighteen years. On the other hand, industrial production has gone down and there is an economic depression. These are two contradictory conditions, but they exist in our country and we have not yet overcome them. We have not yet been able to make some of our public sector undertakings efficient and profitable and they are incurring losses. If banks are nationalised in these circumstances, the economic structure of our country will be damaged greatly and it will be very difficult for us to find resources for investment and to get out of our economic difficulties.

'If we examine the purpose of nationalisation, there are three main considerations. As most of the banks have been started by industrialists, they are under their influence and are managed by them. They consequently get loans more easily and the smaller entrepreneurs, who may be more adventurous and may have capacity, intelligence and honesty, do not get them as they have no property to offer as security. Agriculturists also do not get loans from commercial banks. The main purpose of nationalisation is to alter these conditions. It has been the policy of Government so far that commercial banks should not give credit to agriculturists. This policy has been framed for giving encouragement to cooperative banks. It is not, therefore, the fault of the banks that they have not provided agricultural loans. We can exercise social control over commercial banks through the Reserve Bank in order to change these conditions and we can make the necessary reforms without nationalisation. We can utilise the banks for making the necessary changes without harming our economic structure. We can bring in legislation for social control with a view to reduce the majority of industrialists on banks' managements into a minority and put other interests in a majority. We can also formulate a credit policy for banks and ask them to implement it. We can then think of taking over those banks which do not implement our policy.

'While it is thought of nationalising five or six major banks only, we can control *all* the banks through social control and can cover also the foreign banks through this method. Such a scheme of social control would be more beneficial to us. Nationalisation of five or six banks will not give us the desired benefits, but will involve us in some difficulties. We will also have to pay compensation of crores of rupees if the banks are nationalised. This will reduce our investable resources. The resources available for investment in economic development will also be reduced. The banks will be involved in red-tapism as a result of nationalisation as we have not yet been able to get rid of it in state-run enterprises.'

I made it clear that I could not take the responsibility and risk of nationalisation under such circumstances.

Referring to the proposed nationalisation of general insurance, I said:

'The position of general insurance is different from that of life insurance. There is a profit of only three to four crores of rupees annually in general insurance. There is, therefore, no possibility of a large increase in our resources with nationalisation of general insurance. The difficulties of management of this business will be very great and corruption will greatly increase. We can make regulations for removing the malpractices that are observed in the working of general insurance companies. We should, therefore, have social control over general insurance also rather than nationalise it.'

When I advanced these arguments, one or two members told me that, in their view, social control would not be sufficiently useful and asked me whether I would be prepared to nationalise banks if social control did not bring the necessary benefits, and also how long we should wait to judge the success of social control. 'Social control,' I told them, 'will be more effective than nationalisation, but if most of my colleagues are not convinced at the end of two years about the success of social control, I shall myself come forward with a scheme for nationalisation without anybody asking for it.'

At the end of these discussions the scheme for social control was accepted by the Working Committee.

When the question of the abolition of the privy purses and privileges of the Princes was discussed, I said:

'We have made promises concerning these privileges and privy purses and if we break these promises in a one-sided manner we will lose our reputation. But we can make new agreements with the Princes to achieve this purpose by discussing the problems with them as we had made the former agreements with them, and I am prepared to take the responsibility for such negotiations. If we do not succeed in these efforts, we can take legal measures to give effect to our intentions and then nobody can object to our doing so.'

I was not, however, asked to take this responsibility. At the end of the discussions it was decided that the privileges should be discontinued and the question of abolition of privy purses was dropped. A resolution was passed for a ten-point programme for the speedier economic development of the country.

A meeting of the AICC was then held in Delhi to consider these questions. Just before the meeting was to conclude, at night when the attendance was very thin, an amendment was proposed calling for the abolition of privy purses and privileges, which was accepted by a majority. There was hardly any quorum at that time, but nobody objected to the proceedings on that count. There were twenty to twenty-five votes in favour of the amendment and five to ten votes against it. This is how this amendment was passed at the fag-end of the meeting.

The question of nationalisation of banks was then considered in the Cabinet where I again explained my point of view. Most members of the Cabinet were in favour of nationalisation of a few banks, but when I firmly and clearly explained my opposition and the scheme of social control, the scheme was accepted. It was also accepted in the AICC meeting at Jabalpur in 1968. There was some opposition from a few members, but a large majority accepted my proposal.

I started work on making changes in the management of banks from the time my proposal was accepted by the AICC, without waiting for an enactment of the necessary law. I called a meeting of the Chairmen of the important banks and discussed my proposals with them. They accepted them and started to implement the changes from May/June 1968 though the necessary law was enacted only in February 1969. By the time the legislation was passed, changes in the Boards of Directors of the banks had also been made. Steps were being taken to see that industrialists did not have a majority voice in the management of the banks.

I appointed a Credit Council under my chairmanship to formulate the credit policy. The Governor of the Reserve Bank and the Deputy Chairman of the Planning Commission, Professor D. R. Gadgil, who fully agreed with my policy in this matter, were members of this Council. The other members included representatives of banks, industrialists, small entrepreneurs, agriculturists and economic experts. The Credit Council met twice and formulated a credit policy which the banks began to implement.

I called a meeting of the representatives of the foreign banks separately. The law of social control would not apply to them as their head offices were in foreign countries and they were governed by the laws of those countries. I told them that they should nevertheless appoint Advisory Boards, implement the policies of the Government and give credit according to these principles. They agreed to appoint a larger number of Indians to the management with the minimum number of foreigners and to have equality in salaries for equal responsibilities. I also suggested that they bring in larger foreign exchange resources for their banks.

However, those people who were wedded to nationalisation and were not prepared to consider any alternative, continued their opposition to social control and frequently criticised it in the Lok Sabha. They included some members of the Congress Party also.

Shri Asoka Mehta became a member of the Cabinet in 1967. Government had accepted the recommendation of the Administrative Reforms Commission that a minister should not be the Deputy Chairman of the Planning Commission. Shri Asoka Mehta who was the Deputy Chairman of the Planning Commission at that time, therefore, proposed that another non-official Deputy Chairman should be appointed. Five or six senior ministers of the Cabinet met at the residence of the Prime Minister to consider this matter. I suggested to the Prime Minister at the time of the formation of the Cabinet that those people who had lost in the elections should not be appointed to important posts by Government, i.e., posts like the Deputy Chairmanship of the Planning Commission or Governors, as such appointments were rightly criticised by the people. The Prime Minister told me that she was of the same view and that this policy would be implemented.

When we met at the Prime Minister's house to consider the appointment of the Deputy Chairman of the Planning Commission, Shri Asoka Mehta proposed the name of Shri C. Subramaniam as the Deputy Chairman of the Planning Commission. He said that he did not find any other fit person. Shri Subramaniam had lost in the Lok Sabha elections of 1967. Other colleagues who were present at the meeting supported that proposal, and the Prime Minister also expressed her willingness to accept the suggestion. When she asked me about it, I said, 'I am not able to understand your stand now, as you have already accepted the principle of not appointing defeated persons to such posts.' She admitted that what I said was correct but as it was said that no other fit person could be found for the post, she had shown willingness to accept the proposal. I then said:

'If the country is reduced to such a condition that only one person can be found fit for such a post, the future of the country is indeed very dark and we shall never be able to make any progress. Shri Subramaniam is a very capable person and can do the work very well, but I cannot accept him, as a matter of principle, as he was defeated in the last elections. There will be severe criticism from the people.'

Two or three colleagues told me that if I supported such an appointment, the opposition from the people would disappear. I told them that I would not deserve to have the confidence of the people if I supported such a wrong proposal and, therefore, it would not be possible for me to support it. I also said that other names could be considered and, if the Prime Minister so desired, I could suggest some.

The proposal was then dropped on account of my strong opposition and we dispersed. I could see immediately that I had incurred the displeasure of the Prime Minister. I came to the conclusion that the other colleagues had previously met and had made this proposal after considering it amongst themselves. Only this could explain their speaking with one voice about it. I saw later that the Prime Minister adopted the same strategy in discussions of some matters in the Cabinet also.

When the Prime Minister asked me to suggest other names, I suggested two: Dr. C. D. Deshmukh and Professor D. R. Gadgil, saying that if she did not approve either of them, I would suggest other names. The Prime Minister accepted Professor Gadgil who was a well-known economist and a man of progressive views who had rendered very valuable services in the cooperative field. He had also helped in the work of the Planning Commission in the past. He was a fearless critic and a frank speaker. I had had great respect for him for several years. Nobody could influence him, but he was always ready to accept others' views if he was convinced about their correctness. This was why I suggested his name. Indiraji agreed and decided to consult him. I told her that it was possible that Dr. Gadgil might not be willing to accept the responsibility and that I would try to persuade him to agree if she so desired. I told her that I had suggested both the names without consulting either of them. She readily agreed to this and said that I should talk to him. I, therefore, invited Professor Gadgil to see me before he saw the Prime Minister, and he met me accordingly.

Professor Gadgil and I knew each other very well since 1937–38 when I had come in very close contact with him. I was at that time the Minister for Cooperation in the Bombay Cabinet and had appointed a Committee under the Chairmanship of the late Shri Vaikuntbhai Mehta for the reorganisation of cooperative work. Professor Gadgil was one of its members and the third member was the Registrar for Cooperatives. Professor Gadgil did very valuable work in that committee. He had also rendered very useful service to the Central Cooperative Bank, Bombay. His services proved to be very valuable and useful when we started cooperative sugar factories in Bombay State. Some years earlier he had been Professor and Principal in a college at Surat and had then started the Gokhale Institute of Politics and Economics in Poona. When he saw me, I told him that the Prime Minister had accepted my proposal for appointing him as Deputy Chairman of the Planning Commission and requested him to accept that proposal. He first hesitated but at the end of our discussion he accepted the proposal. He added that he could take up the responsibility only if the other members to be appointed to the Planning Commission were such as could work with him as a team. He was particularly anxious to have Shri B. Venkatappaiah as a member. I told him that he could make that proposal to the Prime Minister who, I was sure, would have no objection to that appointment.

He met the Prime Minister and accepted the responsibility of the Deputy Chairmanship of the Planning Commission after a talk with her. The Prime Minister also accepted the proposal of appointing Shri Venkatappaiah as a member of the Planning Commission. The other members who were chosen for the Planning Commission at that time were Shri Venkatraman from Tamil Nadu and Shri Pitamber Pant.

When sometime after this Professor Gadgil met me, he said that, by a strange coincidence, all the four members in the Planning Commission were Brahmins. This was not planned by anybody, but as all the four were Brahmins the Prime Minister wanted to change one of them. Professor Gadgil said that he would not be able to continue in the Planning Commission if Shri Venkatappaiah was dropped. I told him that he could suggest to the Prime Minister to drop one of the other two and not to drop Shri Venkatappaiah, and I was sure that the Prime Minister would not do anything against his wishes. Ultimately, all the four members remained and a fifth one was added—Dr. Nag Chaudhury.

37

Battle against Economic Stagnation

THE PRIME MINISTER Shrimati Indira Gandhi, was the Chairman of the Planning Commission and I was one of its members as the Finance Minister. No other minister was a member, but any minister whose assistance was required was invited to discuss matters with the Planning Commission. I always participated in the discussions which took place in the Planning Commission on mobilising financial resources, and I used to give them an indication of the maximum limit up to which the resources could be mobilised. The financial resources which were mobilised were allotted to different Ministries and States by the Planning Commission. I took part in this task also, but I always agreed with the arrangements made by the Planning Commission. I adopted this policy as I wanted to see that it was done objectively. I would decide on the maximum limit of resources that could be mobilised, as this was ultimately my responsibility as Finance Minister. I did discuss with the members of the Planning Commission and especially with the Deputy Chairman as to how the resources could be mobilised and to what extent it was possible to do so, but as I had to finalise the budget and present it, the final decision was left to me by the Planning Commission. This was the understanding under which we worked in the Planning Commission. The work therefore went on very smoothly and without any misunderstandings.

I presented the budget of 1967–68 as Finance Minister in May 1967. The economic conditions at that time were somewhat more difficult than when I had presented the budget of 1959–60. There was depression in many economic areas as a result of two wars imposed on us and the onslaught of scarcity in some States for two consecutive years. The position of foreign exchange reserves was very delicate and caused worry. It was also to some extent dangerous. It was, therefore, felt necessary to present a balanced budget. Resources had been lessened on account of the depression. More expenditure had to be incurred on account of relief works in the scarcity affected areas and prices of food articles were going up rather high. On account of all these difficulties and other reasons, I had to provide for a deficit of Rs. 168 crores in the budget. Several

States were presenting deficit budgets and were spending more than their income, thus transferring their burden to the Central budget. The rate of public savings had gone down in 1967–68. Household savings from the national income were only about eight per cent. The main purpose of the 1967-68 budget was, therefore, to bring about economic stability.

On the one hand, production was lower than capacity in machine-making and other industries and it was necessary to make a larger investment. On the other hand, it was necessary to continue the subsidy for foodgrains and to exercise a great deal of economy in expenditure in order to keep control over prices. All these factors made economic conditions difficult. Greater expenditure was provided for the plan in 1967–68, but more attention was paid to agriculture in the plan. Efforts were made to cut down expenditure and to levy further taxes. The taxation was increased by Rs. 76 crores in the budget of 1967—68 and an increased amount of Rs. 38 crores was obtained from the railway budget by increasing fares and freights. All the measures thus taken enabled us to get some control over the economic situation in 1967–68.

This also made the position somewhat easier at the time of the budget of 1968–69. By then economic conditions had improved and there was some stability in prices. As we got the advantage of larger production in the agricultural sector in the budget of 1968–69, the framework of the plan for 1969–70 was expanded and the prospect was more hopeful. Efforts were made to improve the climate of investment in industries which had become static by reducing the surtax on companies. Dividend tax was given up, and some steps were taken to increase agricultural production and to increase exports. Some concessions were given in income tax on income from dividends, that is the limit of exemption was enhanced, and some of the recommendations of the Bhoothalingam Committee for making the tax structure simpler and easier were accepted.

Steps were taken in the budget of 1968–69 to enlarge the tax structure, particularly in order to prevent tax evasion. A limitation was put on expenditure of companies and enhanced punishments were provided for evasion of income-tax and wealth-tax. One of the steps taken was a provision for the payment of money by cheques by companies for amounts for which they claimed exemption from income-tax.

Further taxes amounting to Rs. 66 crores were levied in the budget of 1968–69 and a further revenue of Rs. 52 crores was raised by enhancing railway fares and freights and the rates of postage and telegrams. Some new schemes were introduced to encourage more savings by the people, including a five-year fixed deposit scheme with income-tax exemption and a Public Provident Fund Scheme. The Public Provident Fund Scheme was introduced specially for those who did not have any opportunity for contributing to an ordinary provident fund scheme and, therefore, could not get exemptions from income-tax.

As the economic conditions had deteriorated at the end of the Third Five Year Plan, the Fourth Five Year Plan could not be prepared in time, but annual plans were being made. The climate was, therefore, prepared in the budgets of 1967–68 and 1968–69 to facilitate the preparation of the Fourth Five Year Plan. Prices stabilised by the time of the budget of 1969–70, and industrial development got out of the depression and took a turn for the better. Larger efforts were made in the budget of 1969–70 for higher capital investment and steps were taken to make the tax structure simpler and practical. It was also so devised that larger tax receipts would be obtained with the same rates as development proceeded. The annual plan expenditure was not increased in 1969–70 from the level of 1968–69, and yet steps were taken to accelerate the pace of development. Thus a provision was made for an expenditure of Rs. 177 crores more than the previous year on development in the budget of 1969–70. The expenditure on subsidy for foodgrains and on account of scarcity relief was lessened.

It was evident that the larger non-development expenditure that took place was due to the expenditure on military and police and overdrafts of States. The main characteristic of the 1969–70 budget was the greater importance given to development works. Steps were taken to lessen export duties and for accelerating the savings scheme. Some fundamental changes were made in the taxation structure in order to meet the requirements of development. The central excise duties which were levied at fixed rates were then related to the prices of goods in several cases. Wealth in agricultural land was included in the wealth of a person for the purpose of wealth tax, and further steps were taken for checking tax evasion.

It was estimated that the Government would get an additional revenue of Rs. 875 crores in the five years of the Fourth Five Year Plan as a result of the extra levy in the first year of the Fourth Five Year Plan. Steps were thus taken to see that the necessary financial resources for the Fourth Five Year Plan were mobilised. The taxation revenue of the Centre and the States, which amounted to 14.2 per cent of the national income in 1965–66, was reduced to 12.4 per cent in 1967–68. It increased by 2 per cent in 1969–70. The atmosphere of depression was overcome to some extent on account of the policy governing these three budgets and economic conditions began to improve. In the industrial field also, there were better hopes of development.

As I have said earlier, it was decided at the end of May 1967 to introduce social control of banks. I had earlier appointed Shri V.A. Pai Panandiker to consider this scheme and submit a report about it. He submitted his first report before I went to Japan during which time I studied it. He submitted his last report when I returned from Japan in the month of September and it was discussed for some time. I had, however, to go abroad soon after for attending the annual meeting of the World Bank and Monetary Fund. Discussion on the final report was thus postponed. It was resumed after I returned from my tour in October, and the social control scheme was sanctioned by the Cabinet.

When the Bill for bringing in social control of banks was introduced in Parliament in December 1968, I made a statement about the credit scheme, the changes in the management and administration of banks, the establishment of the institute for training bankers and the appointment of the Banking Commission. I had appointed the National Credit Council in February 1968. It first met in March and fixed the policy in July. The Bill for social control was passed in Parliament in February 1969. It received the assent of the President and was thus enacted as law. I started the National Institute of Bank Management in March 1969. The National Credit Council met in that month and surveyed the progress made. It was found that deposits had increased by Rs. 150 crores. The number of bank branches had also increased. Greater credit had been given to agriculturists and small industrialists.

The Prime Minister had a meeting with the Deputy Chairman, Planning Commission, two or three other Ministers and myself, to consider the question of giving greater help to one or two States after the budget of 1967–68 had been passed. Great emphasis was laid on the specially larger requirements of these particular States and the Prime Minister tried to persuade me to provide for giving them additional help to the tune of a few crores of rupees. I told her:

'You know under what difficult circumstances we have prepared the budget and the annual plan and that we have mobilised all the resources that we could. If you want to incur a larger expenditure than what has been provided for, it can be done only by increasing deficit financing. It is necessary to halt the rising prices and if deficit financing is increased we shall fail in restraining the rise in prices, and great harm will be done by increasing expenditure.'

When, in spite of what I said, she persisted in pressing me to provide for more aid, I had to say:

'I shall be put in a very awkward position if you insist on asking me to provide more funds. If God had not very kindly given me strong nerves, I would have perhaps lost my balance of mind and even sanity in such circumstances. But God has been very kind to me and I am able to keep my balance and I cannot therefore, submit to your pressure. I would, therefore, request you to give up your demand.'

It was only after this that she gave up her suggestion.

38

Visit to Japan, Trinidad and Brazil

I GOT THE impression in my talk with the Japanese Ambassador at Delhi in June or July 1967 that Japan was somewhat dissatisfied with our relations with them, particularly because no representative of the Government of India had visited Japan for some time. Shri T. T. Krishnamachari was to go to Japan at the end of 1965 when he was Finance Minister, but he cancelled his programme, and there had been some coolness in the relations between the two countries since then. The Japanese Ambassador told me that if I visited Japan at this juncture, relations between the two countries would improve a great deal and some of their leaders would then visit India also.

The Japanese Government had invited me to visit Japan. After discussing the question with the Prime Minister, I accepted the invitation and went to Japan in August 1967. There I met the Foreign Minister, other Ministers and also the Prime Minister, Mr. Sato, in Tokyo. I was well acquinted with Mr. Sato since 1958 when he visited India as the Finance Minister of Japan. I met him twice in Tokyo and had very satisfactory talks with him. I found him desirous of strengthening Indo-Japan relations. He had organised a world exhibition, Expo—70, to be held in 1970 at Osaka, and pressed me to see that India took part. I told him that we would give our earnest consideration to this and added that it would be easier to fix it up if Air India was permitted to go to Osaka and facilities were given to them for that purpose. He told me that he would give this his earnest consideration. There was some sort of rivalry between the Foreign Minister and the Prime Minister. The Prime Minister told me that he wanted to visit India but that he would not be able to do so that year as he had some other important engagements.

From Tokyo I went to northern Japan where I saw places of interest, including some industries and some hot springs. There were three or four hot springs at different temperatures. All had to bathe in the nude. They could keep only a towel with them. It was a special feature of these hot springs that both men and women took baths at the same time. I took a bath in one of the springs for about twenty minutes and found myself considerably refreshed.

The railways of Japan are very efficient and all the trains run to time without any exception. I travelled by a train which went at a speed of 150 miles an hour and saw the efficient and fine arrangements they had made on their railways. I also saw some industries near about Tokyo. I had been there also in 1962 and I found that Japan had made considerable progress in the intervening five years.

Tokyo, the largest city in the world, is very crowded. Yet the traffic arrangements were very good. All places were very clean and the people also appeared to be very clean and neat. I saw that every citizen took great care to maintain cleanliness. No householder put any refuse in any but the fixed places, and they used also to clean the roads in front of their houses. This is how the cleanliness of Tokyo city is so well maintained. They had also a very distinctive arrangement for city lighting. In each locality, the people staying there made the arrangements for street lighting themselves. I, therefore, saw different artistic arrangements for lighting in different areas.

Japanese patriotism is unparalleled. One hardly sees in any other country such close cooperation between the people and the government.

The Japanese are very industrious and disciplined. I saw in the factories that I visited that the workers were doing their work with great care and attention and did not divert their attention to the visitors at all. I saw that in several offices the outer walls were transparent, being made of glass, and one could see from the streets the people working inside those offices. I saw that those working inside did not look outside at people moving on the road. They were constantly engaged in their work with great devotion. It is because of these qualities that Japan's development has gone up by leaps and bounds and it would not be surprising if Japan beats all other nations in prosperity.

Some friends asked me why, when Japan has made so much progress, we, by comparison, have done very little. I told them that it was on account of their unparalleled patriotism and devotion to duty that the Japanese had made such tremendous progress. Moreover, Japan had worked for eighty years before the last war for the development of Japan and had made great progress in scientific and technical fields during this time. It was already one of the developed countries before the war. The Japanese utilised all their skills after the war and also received ample assistance from the USA. It was because of all these factors that Japan has made such amazing progress. In India, there is a lack of such efficiency.

There is also a want of mutual cooperation and we have made much less progress compared to them in technology and science. It was, therefore, natural that we had not been able to develop as well as they had done. We have therefore much to learn from Japan. More particularly their supreme patriotism, great devotion to work, and their discipline and economical habits are worth imitating.

From Japan I returned to India via Hong Kong. I met several Indians in Hong Kong and discussed some matters with them. I also did some sightseeing there.

Soon after, in the month of September, I had to go to Rio de Janeiro in Brazil to attend the annual meeting of the World Bank and the Monetary Fund. I had, at the same time, to attend the Commonwealth Finance Ministers' Conference which was to be held at Port of Spain in Trinidad that year. I, therefore, went out again within a few days of my return from Japan. I first went to London where I met the Chancellor of Exchequer, the Prime Minister and some other ministers and, as usual, discussed several matters of mutual interest and importance.

Prime Minister Wilson had criticised India during Pakistan's 1965 aggression against India. I discussed this matter with him and explained our point of view. Mr. Wilson admitted in the talk that his statement was the result of misunderstanding and was not proper. He invited me to lunch over which I had an opportunity of discussing some matters with the other ministers who were present. This time I visited London as the Government's guest. I, therefore, did not stay with our High Commissioner, Shri Dhawan, but at Claridge's Hotel where the British Government made arrangements.

I had a discussion with some British businessmen and industrialists connected with India. The High Commissioner was present in all these discussions and he was very much impressed by the manner in which I presented India's viewpoint. I felt that some of the people there were dissatisfied with Shri Dhawan's work. They had the feeling that he was against England in his views and that he was somewhat influenced by the communist philosophy. When, later on, Shri Dhawan became the Governor of West Bengal, this impression was strengthened. The speeches which he made in Calcutta after returning to India served to confirm this impression.

I met the Press in London and attended a meeting of Indians with whom I had discussions. They gave me the impression that they were very much satisfied with what I told them.

From London I went to Washington. There I met President

Johnson, Secretary Freeman, and the Defence Secretary Mr. McNamara. I also met the President of the World Bank and the Managing Director of the International Monetary Fund. I had very frank discussions with President Johnson. I had met him first when he came to India in 1961–62 as Vice-President. I already knew Secretary Freeman and I had very friendly talks with him. Our talks related to the necessity of mutual understanding and having more friendly relations.

I met the Vice-President, Mr. Hubert Humphrey, before I met the President. I discussed with him the attitude which India had taken in connection with the Arab-Israel war which was going on at that time. He asked me in a friendly manner whether we had not taken a one-sided attitude against Israel and whether there was not some departure from our non-alignment policy. I told him that his impression was not correct and that we should discuss the matter very fully and frankly. He accepted my suggestion and asked me to explain our viewpoint to him fully. This is what I said:

'A great injustice was done to the Arabs twenty years ago by establishing the new State of Israel. The Jews are an ancient race and the community was scattered over many countries. Great atrocities were perpetrated on them in Germany during Hitler's regime. This was why America, Russia and others decided to rehabilitate them in their original country and they carved out the new country of Israel. This area then belonged to the Arabs. It was taken from the Arabs and handed over to the Israelis—the Jews—because the Arabs were weak and could not resist. We could have no objection to creating a new country for the Jews, but do you think that it was proper to do it at the cost of Arabs? If the USA had given them a part of their own territory for the purpose, it would have been creditable. If Russia had acted similarly, that also would have been creditable. It would have been just if a portion of Germany had been given to them. But even though the Arabs were not responsible for any harassment of the Jews, the new State of Israel was carved out of Arab territory which was a wrong use of strength and was an injustice to the Arabs. This cannot be denied by anybody. We must, therefore, accept that if the Arabs are angry as a result of this new arrangement, they are justified. At the same time, the discontent that is raging as a result of the new arrangements for the rehabilitation of the Arabs who had become refugees on account of the creation of the new State, was also natural. Do you not, therefore, consider that our sympathy with the Arabs is natural as a non-aligned country? It is our duty to have sympathy for those against whom injustice has been done.

'Israel now is an established State and a member of the United Nations. It is not, therefore, possible to undo this fact which can be easily understood and I cannot make any such proposition. But how can Israel be supported if it wants to extend the territory which has been given to them and that too by force? Moreover, Israel attacked even the forces of the United Nations which were stationed in the area. It is a fact that they attacked these forces without any cause. There were also some Indian forces there. If, therefore, India found fault with Israel for this aggressive step, every objective person must admit that it was a proper attitude.'

Mr. Humphrey did not deny the facts which I had placed before him, but said, 'All these quarrels take place because the Arabs are not accepting the accomplished fact of Israel.'

'Arabs do not accept Israel,' I said, 'because injustice has been done to them. But they ought to be persuaded to do so and necessary arrangements should be made for the rehabilitation of Arab refugees by the United Nations. Israel should also not extend its territory. This is the only peaceful remedy in the circumstances. If, instead, Israel attacks Arab countries with your help, how can India justify it. India has to protest.'

Mr. Humphrey then told me with a smile that there was a large population of Jews in the USA to which I countered:

'There must not be more than five million Jews in the USA. If this is considered a very large population and you have to be influenced by this, there are fifty-five million Muslims in India. Would that not be considered as a very strong argument for India?'

He finally told me that there was no answer to my arguments and our discussions ended there. Mr. Humphrey conveyed my views to President Johnson with whom, therefore, I had not to discuss this matter again.

I had to speak on television before I had a talk with the President about Vietnam. I was asked in the television interview about the policy of India with regard to Vietnam. I said:

'In India's view there should be no outside forces in South Vietnam, whether they are of USA, North Vietnam, China or any other country. You are seeing every day that this quarrel cannot be settled by force of war. It is necessary to see that all the outside military forces vacate the area. The USA which is the strongest nation in the world ought to set an example in establishing peace. If it set an example and others did not follow it, then nobody can find fault with the USA.'

I received a message from President Johnson that he had very much appreciated my television interview. When I had a talk with him he asked me to have a discussion with the Defence Secretary Mr. McNamara first, and to meet him again if necessary after my talk with the Defence Secretary. I had an hour's talk with Mr. McNamara and I put our point of view to him with complete frankness. We also discussed nuclear weapons and I put to him India's viewpoint in the matter clearly, and I understood their viewpoint too. He also explained to me what they were thinking about it and what arrangements they were making. As I had already placed our point of view very frankly and clearly to Mr. McNamara, it was not necessary for me to see President Johnson again, and I sent him a message accordingly.

From Washington I went to New York where I met members of several associations whom I used to meet on previous visits. I went to Montreal from there. Expo—67 was on at Montreal at that time. It was a very vast world exhibition, and I spent a day there. The Indian pavilion had impressed visitiors very well as I could gather from my talks with some people. I saw the pavilions of several other countries, including that of Czechoslovakia which struck me as a very fine one. I got very useful information from some other pavilions and added to my knowledge of the countries represented there.

From Montreal I went to Ottawa where I stayed with the Indian High Commissioner, Gen. J. N. Chaudhuri. There I met the Canadian Prime Minister, Finance Minister and other ministers. I understood at that time that the Prime Minister was to retire after a year. His personality made a deep impression on me. I had met him when he was the leader of the Opposition. He discussed with me several matters with great friendliness and sympathy. The relations between Canada and India have been very close and I am sure they will continue to be so in future. These two countries cooperate with each other in international affairs also. Canada has given substantial help to India in atomic research. I went to Canada as the Canadian Government wanted me to visit that country if I went to Washington.

From Canada I had to go to Trinidad and I went there with the Canadian Finance Minister in his plane as arranged previously. As usual, the Commonwealth Finance Ministers' Conference was held there for two days. I stayed there for about three days and met the Prime Minister and other ministers there. Many Indians had settled in Trinidad many years ago and their population was large. The Hindus and Muslims lived there in a very friendly manner and I learnt that there were never any undesirable incidents between them. I met many Muslims and had discussions with them. All the Indians were very happy at my visit and I too was happy to meet all of them.

From Port of Spain I went to Caracas which is the capital of Venezuela in South America. I met there the President and other Ministers and also saw a fine hotel on a mountain top. I went there by a ropeway. The hotel was an up-to-date one, but was vacant. I learnt that the Government had made an agreement with an American Company to run that hotel. It was a very well-equipped one and ideally located.

From there I went to Rio de Janeiro for the World Bank meeting. Rio de Janeiro is a beautiful city situated on the sea coast. It is the largest port of the world. The city is so built that one can go from any part of the city to the seashore within five to fifteen minutes. I found that the citizens there were very fond of the sea. I saw a large number of them lying on the sands, enjoying the sunshine. They enjoyed lying in the sun more than sea bathing. I was also told that some people went there even from their offices for a short time.

There is a very large statue of Jesus Christ on a mountain in Rio de Janeiro which can be seen from a long distance. When it is lit at night, the statue and the sight are so beautiful that it affects everybody very deeply. I went there and saw from the top the beautiful city. Visitors went there continuously. One could go to the top by car. One had to walk up only a few steps to reach the statue. The artist who was responsible for this statue deserves great credit. I also got an idea that it would be a very good thing if a statue of Gandhiji of that size was put up at some suitable place in India. I have not, however, located such a convenient place in India so far. The importance of that place is due to the fact that it is close to a large city. I also saw that Gandhiji's statue had been put up in a prominent locality in Rio de Janeiro and they were going to pay him tributes on the next 2nd of October. The Indian Ambassador was to attend the function. The square where this statue is located is named after Gandhiji. Gandhiji is greatly revered in that country.

From the site of the Christ statue there is a ropeway to some other mountains which I also visited. These were also very delightful and attractive. On the whole, a visitor cannot but be struck by the beauty of Rio de Janeiro.

I met there the President of the World Bank, Mr. George Wood, and his wife. I had had very friendly relations with them for several years. He was to retire from Presidentship that year, and he discussed with me the matter of his successor. He felt from his talks with the US Government authorities that Mr. McNamara would be appointed. In Mr. Wood's last year in the World Bank, he was somewhat tired and was eager to be relieved. The Presidentship of the World Bank is a very important office. It carries heavy responsibilities and heavy work and is connected with many intricate problems. Mr. Wood had worked in that office for five or six years and it was natural that he looked forward to his retirement.

Mr. Schwitzer was the Managing Director of the Monetary Fund. I was told that he was a close relative of the well-known philosopher Dr. Albert Schwitzer. He was very desirous of being helpful to everybody and actually helped many countries. I had long talks with him on many subjects.

I also met the President of Brazil who expressed very friendly sentiments towards India. He talked about extending our trade. There is a great deal of similarity in the export and import items of Brazil and India and, therefore, the possibilities of expansion in our trade are limited

There had been a great deal of inflation in Brazil for several years. I learnt that the inflation was then less than in previous years. If we suffered from the same degree of inflation, India's condition would be very bad, but Brazil is a very extensive country with a very small population. Several areas of Brazil are still uninhabited and are not yet explored. They have the giant Amazon river with an expanse like that of a sea, and steamers can go up it for miles. They have very dense forests also. The population is dominantly Portuguese in origin but it is now very mixed. The original inhabitants of Brazil are seen more amongst the workmen while in some fields one saw more Portuguese working.

I went to see a very fine military centre. There must be hardly any other such place anywhere else for the use of military officers.

I returned to India via Paris and Bonn. As the Finance Minister was ill in Paris, I could not meet him and went on to Bonn. I met the President of West Germany and Chancellor Kissinger, and some of his colleagues. We had very useful discussions about our mutual relations. Chancellor Kissinger visited India within two months of my visit there and I again had long talks with him when he was here. I wanted to go and call on him at his residence in Delhi, but he was so humble that he came and saw me at Parliament House. When I called on him in Germany, he came down from the first floor, where his office was, to see me off. This was the extent of his courtesy. Such courtesy was not necessary according to protocol. It showed his great humility and friendliness.

39

Nepal, Bhutan and Sikkim

I WENT TO Nepal for a few days after my return to India from Trinidad and Rio de Janeiro This was in response to a long-standing invitation from the King and such a visit was necessary for improving the relations between the two countries.

I met the King of Nepal and had frank and friendly talks with him. He gave me the strong impression that he wanted to have friendly relations with India. I also got the impression that the strain in the relations between the two countries which had appeared some time previously still persisted. I saw an exhibition of small-scale industries in Khatmandu in the company of the Maharaja. He impressed me as a very able administrator in his talks with various people in the exhibition and with me. I also met his Prime Minister, his Finance Minister and other prominent people. I spoke about the relations between Nepal and India in a meeting arranged by the Indian-Nepalese Association there.

I saw there one or two projects which were under implementation with the help of India. I visited the Pashupatinath Temple of Nepal in Khatmandu. This temple is in the tradition of India and is one of the twelve Jyotirlinga temples of Shiva in the subcontinent. It is a pilgrimage centre of great importance. There is a long tradition of getting Brahmins from Mysore for worshipping the deity in the temple. I also saw several beautiful places round about Khatmandu.

When I went to Nepal, my plane flew between the mountains amidst which Nepal is situated. I got a beautiful view of Khatmandu from the air. It is a beautiful and pleasant city with a very good climate. I learnt from the people that my visit had improved relations between the two countries a great deal.

When I met the Maharajas of Bhutan and Sikkim in Delhi in 1967, they invited me warmly to visit their states. I, therefore, went to both Bhutan and Sikkim in March 1968. I first went to Bhutan, from where I went to Sikkim. A small but useful airstrip had just then been prepared for planes to land in Bhutan. I went there by helicopter. I went from the airstrip by car to Thimku which is the capital of Bhutan.

The Maharaja of Bhutan called on me, taking me by surprise before I could call on him. I had a long talk with him about the development of Bhutan, which is an independent country. He expressed to me his desire to join the UN. I told him that India could not have any objection to his doing so, but that he should consider the question from the financial point of view. Bhutan is now a member of the United Nations.

There can be very good development of agriculture in Bhutan. The Government there can play an effective role in this development and India can assist in this task effectively. We had discussions on this subject. Both of us agreed that there should be development of small-scale industries for utilising the natural resources of that State.

The Maharaja of Bhutan had very progressive views. He told me during my discussions with him that he wanted to vest his Parliament with full sovereignty, which meant that if the Parliament wanted to remove monarchy, it could do so. He wanted to decentralise authority and took several steps in that direction. There has always been close friendship between Bhutan and India. Their relations have been strengthened after India became free.

I had discussions with the officers of the State also. I saw their power house and some other places nearby. Bhutan is beautifully situated. The people of Bhutan have to go via India if they want to visit any other country. I visited a Buddhist monastery. There are many Buddhists in Bhutan. The Bhutanese are well-disposed towards the people of India. They have always believed that the defence of Bhutan can be secured only with the friendship of India.

From Bhutan I went to Gangtok, the capital of Sikkim, and stayed with the Maharaja of Sikkim. Gangtok struck me as a fine place and is very much like one of the hill stations of India. The Maharaja of Sikkim is called the Chogyal. I sensed that the Chogyal had some bitterness against India when I first met him in 1967 because of the improper behaviour of the Indian representative there. Sikkim is connected with India by an agreement under which she is protected by India. She faces great danger from China. The security of Sikkim includes the security of India also. When India became independent, Sikkim was one of the Indian States, but she was not merged in India and was accepted as a separate country and an agreement was made with her accordingly.

I had heard that the treatment meted out by the Secretary and the Joint Secretary of the Foreign Affairs Ministry to the Chogyal was not proper. I talked to the Prime Minister about this and suggested that there should be a change in this treatment. She agreed with me and took the necessary steps. Such improper behaviour went on without the Prime Minister knowing anything about it. The steps taken in this direction did give some satisfaction to the Chogyal, but he desired that Sikkim should be recognised as an independent country like Bhutan. I explained to him that if Sikkim became an independent country, the Indian army could not guard its borders with China and it was not possible for Sikkim to defend herself against China in any way. I, therefore, suggested to him that he should consider the question of status taking this fact into consideration. India could not prevent her from becoming independent if she wanted. But if Sikkim became independent, India had to withdraw her forces. Sikkim had no strength or resources to defend herself. He accepted this position. I then explained to him that even though technically she was not an independent country the Government of India could have no objection to, or hesitation in, treating her as if she were an independent country. These were the relations between us and I hope that such would be the relations in future. It is my view that these relations can be so adjusted that the Chogyal would have no cause for complaint in future.

The Chogyal has married an American lady. She has identified herself completely with the women of Sikkim. Women in Sikkim speak in a very low voice and the Maharani has imitated that style so effectively that I found it difficult sometimes to carry on conversation with her.

I went to see the place where the schemes made for the development of small industries in Sikkim were exhibited. The arrangements there impressed me greatly. We had useful talks about the industrial development of Sikkim. I told the Chogyal that India could help Sikkim in her industrial development. I told him also that India had been already helping in the development of Sikkim. The Indian representative who was there, had been instructed to render all possible help to the State. I believe that the relations between Sikkim and India have now been improved considerably and the former bitterness has disappeared.

Many Nepalis have settled down in Sikkim as citizens and form a large proportion of its population. This has made a considerable impact on the politics of Sikkim. There had been some demonstrations against India in Gangtok sometime before my visit. I explained to the Maharaja that such demonstrations would harm the relations between the two countries and it was desirable that they did not take place. When he told me that Sikkim was not allowed her national anthem, I told him that there could not be any objection to their having one. The military forces which were guarding the borders could not become effective without the full cooperation of the Sikkim Government. The relations between the two countries must be close and full of trust. Distrust on either side was harmful to both the countries, I pointed out to him.

The Chogyal told me that he was very satisfied with our discussions. I invited him to stay with me as my guest when he next visited Delhi. I showed my readiness to be helpful in solving outstanding questions and after my return to India some of them were solved satisfactorily.

I went to see the Nathula Pass during my visit to Sikkim. It is on the Tibetan boundary and the Indian forces guard it. China's forces are creating tension on the other side of the pass and some actions are occasionally taken by the Chinese troops to harass our men. The Chinese forces were asking our jawans for some days through loudspeakers to leave that region and threatened to destroy them if they did not do so. But our jawans replied firmly that if they took any such step, they themselves would be destroyed. China denied soon after that any such threats were given. As a matter of fact, they had attacked our posts. But they were repulsed with great losses. After this incident there is now peace in that area. It was after this incident that I went to see the place. I went there by helicopter and met many army officers there. It is a very difficult place to operate in—covered as it is with snow for a large part of the year and without any human habitation or trees. The men of our army are guarding the pass with great courage in spite of the harsh climate and are carrying on their duties with cheerfulness and enthusiasm. I was very happy to see this. I congratulated them on their devotion and courage and thanked them. My visit to Nathula and the observation of the splendid work of our army increased my respect for, and pride in, our forces and I am confident that there is no risk in this area so long as we get the cooperation of Sikkim in this matter.

During this period there was an intense agitation going on in some of the areas of Assam. There was a strong demand for the separation of some of the hill areas from Assam. Prof. Swell was the representative in Parliament from those areas. Discussions on this matter were going on for some time before I joined the Cabinet and a declaration was made by the Home Minister which created an impression that a separate State of the hill region would be created. A Committee was appointed in this connection under the chairmanship of Shri Asoka Mehta who was a member of the Cabinet at the time. He proposed that while Assam State should include the hill region, the latter, would get autonomy within the State. When this proposal was discussed, I pointed out that the declaration made by the Home Minister could not mean that this area was promised a separate State. The Home Minister confirmed my contention. The declaration only promised a consideration of the proposal.

I tried to impress on the Prime Minister in my discussion with her that if this area was separated from Assam, it would be very risky for India's security and there was a danger that the boundary on that side would not remain secure. I, therefore, held the view that this area should not be separated from Assam. The ultimate proposal that was made was that the area should remain with the Assam Government but should be, on the whole, autonomous. The scheme contemplated the transfer of the police department to the autonomous authority. I was against such autonomy as it would immediately pose the question of a separate State. The Chief Minister of Assam, the late Shri Chaliha, had consented to giving autonomy to the area, but not to the transfer of the Home Department.

When this question was discussed in the Cabinet, the Prime Minister and several other colleagues wanted to hand over the Home Department, i.e. the police, to the autonomous authority of the hill area within the State. I opposed this proposal and said that I could not agree to this on any condition, as it created a danger for the integrity of Assam. The Prime Minister was firm in her view and was ready even to cancel her visit to Australia for which she was due to leave the next day. I advised her not to cancel the visit but to take whatever decision she wanted to take after her return from Australia. She did not accept my advice at first but after some time she accepted it and postponed her decision.

After her return from Australia she had discussions in the Executive Committee of the Congress Parliamentary Party and the Working Committee. There was strong opposition to the proposed autonomy in both these bodies. After some discussions the Prime Minister gave up her insistence on full autonomy and took a decision to give autonomy to the hill area, reserving the Home Department, including the Police, with the Government of Assam for the whole State. The Bill was then presented in the Parliament and it became law.

This is how this question was solved at the time. I felt that this again left some prejudice in the Prime Minister's mind against me. After I left the Cabinet in 1969, the separate State of Meghalaya was constituted.

I went to Iran in the month of July 1968, as I had received an invitation from the Government there to visit that country. They had till then close relations with Pakistan but not with India. It appeared to me that there was a change in the attitude of the Iranian Government and they wanted to forge better and closer relations with India. I met their Prime Minister, Foreign Minister and Minister of Industries. I had long talks with those who were in charge of Iran's economic planning. These talks were very friendly and helpful. They were very eager to see that the Tata fertiliser scheme was sanctioned by the Government of India. They talked to me about it. As this scheme was not sanctioned until then and was delayed, they expressed some dissatisfaction about it.

The Shah of Iran was at that time resting at a summer resort. A meeting with him was arranged at that place and I went there to see him. It was a pleasant region. I had long talks with the Shah who showed a friendly attitude. He treated me with much courtesy and impressed me as an able administrator. He had visited Bombay some thirteen or fourteen years ago when I was the Chief Minister of Bombay where we first met. This visit, therefore, revived our old acquaintance and strengthened it. I learnt that the Shah of Iran very often flies with his whole family in a helicopter and is not afraid of any accident. Such risks are not ordinarily undertaken by emperors, kings and VIPS. But he was deterred by no such risks as he had full faith in God.

I went to Isfahan where I saw 2,000-year old monuments discovered by their archaeological department. I saw a very ancient, large and beautiful mosque there as well as two swaying minarets. These minarets were a product of the unique skill of the engineers and architects of that time. We do not find such engineers and architects at the present time.

I also paid a visit to Shiraz which is a large city and after seeing several important places there, I returned to Tehran. The Indo-Iranian Association in Tehran gave me a reception in Iranian style. In thanking them I said, 'The Aryans migrated from central Asia to India and some of those who broke their journey on the way in Iran settled in Iran permanently. Others went to India and settled there and became Indians. Iran is, therefore, a second home for Indians.' This reference to history made the people who were present very happy.

I saw the museum containing very valuable jewels of the Shah of Iran. I had never seen this kind of museum elsewhere. It contains a fabulous collection of diamonds and other jewels worth crores of rupees and it was impossible to make a proper valuation of this treasure. This treasure of Iran is unique and beyond comparison. One can infer from this treasure how prosperous Iran was in the past. I got a strong impression from the talks I had with the Shah and others in Iran that they wanted to come closer to India and had a strong desire to strengthen mutual cultural relations.

I had an opportunity to meet, in Tehran, an old Iranian friend, Mr. Saif Azad, who was with me in Yeravada prison in Bombay State in 1942. He was a detenu in this jail as a suspected Nazi supporter at the time of the Second World War. He had stayed for a few years in Germany and was considered to be a supporter of Hitler and was, therefore, detained in the jail in which I was also housed as a detenu. We were together in jail for more than two years and came to know each other very well and became friends. I had discussions with him about the common words in Sanskrit and Persian languages. I learnt from him that there were about twenty-five per cent common words in these two languages.

I inquired about him when I went to Tehran and he had also learnt about my visit. He inquired about me and sent me a letter that he was unable to move out as he was suffering from rheumatism and that he was very anxious to meet me. I went to see him at his place which was very near the place I visited for some discussions. He is a journalist and had a deep interest in journalism. We met at his place with great affection. Both of us were very happy to have met after many years.

He was always very cheerful while in jail and I found him to be equally cheerful when we met in Tehran. We talked about the past and also about our present activities. He once met me in Bombay during the interval when the Shah of Iran visited Bombay. Our meeting in Tehran was after a lapse of thirteen to fourteen years and we were very happy to have met after such a long period. Even though he could not walk without assistance, he came out of the house to see me off with the help of a friend despite my begging him not to take the trouble. He came to the end of the lane to see me off. He must have been 86 to 87 years of age at that time.

40

Discussion with Kosygin

MR. KOSYGIN, Prime Minister of the USSR, visited India in the month of November 1967. The discussions that our Prime Minister had with him were not conveyed to me or to any other member of the Cabinet. Only Russian interpreters were present in their private discussions. Mr. Kosygin expressed a desire to see me. I could not accept the time at first fixed for this appointment as it did not suit me. When I informed him about this, another time was fixed which was convenient to both of us. The ambassadors and interpreters of both the countries were present during the talks.

Mr. Kosygin told me that he felt that progress in the industries which had been established here with their collaboration had been satisfactory. He then suggested that some other industries should also be taken up in the public sector. I told him that we could not take such a decision without considering the question from all sides and it would not be helpful to have industries in the public sector which did not produce goods at proper prices. I also said that we must, therefore, be cautious and should take decisions in such matters after careful consideration. He then told me that he had heard that I was not in favour of the public sector. I replied, 'Your impression is very incorrect and whosoever conveyed this information to you has misled you.' He added that he had not read any statement of mine on this subject and that this was his impression. I replied:

'I have made several statements in Parliament in this connection and if you read some of them, you would have known the facts. But it is clear that you have not done so.

'I have not only not been against the public sector, but have, on the contrary, advocated its growth. But that sector has not worked efficiently so far and has involved large investments of public capital. It is, therefore, essential that decisions in this field should be taken after a careful consideration of the relevant factors.'

Mr. Kosygin left this discussion at this point and gave me the impression that he believed in what I said. This is a very significant example of the skill with which my opponents spread false stories against me.

Mr. Kosygin then started discussing politics and told me that the Jan Sangh was a very disruptive force in India and that it was getting stronger as its strength in the Parliament had also increased. I told him:

'Until recently the largest group in the opposition in Parliament was that of the Communists. The Communists are divided into two groups, one favouring Russia and the other China. The two groups have, therefore, become smaller than the Swantantra Party group which became the largest group in the opposition. The Communist parties have, therefore, lower positions.'

'The Communist Party which favours Russia is a nationalist party and is serving the people of India very well,' he said.

I replied that I did not agree with him in that statement. The Communist Party was not fully nationalist as it had more affection for Russia than for India. He asked me whether I opposed international cooperation and collaboration. I said:

'Your question is based on a wrong assumption. There cannot be international cooperation without strong nationalism. Nationalism must be conducive to international cooperation, and internationalism must support nationalism and strengthen it. Would you safeguard the interests of Russia first or would you consider our interest first?'

When he accepted this contention of mine, I told him that India must first bear in mind her own interests and should then look to international interests. This discussion ended at this point.

After discussing some other common problems, we parted.

The Russian representative who had accompanied the Russian Prime Minister saw me and invited me to visit Russia again as some years had passed since my last visit. They suggested that I should break my journey at Moscow on my way back from a tour abroad in 1968. I told him that I could not break my journey at Moscow at that time but that I would visit Russia some other time. When I returned from my foreign tour via Moscow in 1968, two Ministers of the Russian Cabinet and some other representatives met me at Moscow Airport, where they entertained me to dinner and I had some discussions with them. When they suggested that I should inform them in advance about my next flight via Moscow, I told them that I could not go via Moscow without their knowledge, even if I did not give them the information, as they had efficient ways of keeping informed. I added that I would like very much to visit Russia. I also told them that they were very efficient in their administration and added with a smile that if anybody opposed them, they would make him feel their displeasure, which would be strong and effective. I returned to India after halting at Moscow Airport for about 75 minutes.

I decided to go to Russia in July-August 1969 but I could not do so as I resigned from the Cabinet in July 1969.

In 1968, after returning from my visit to Sikkim, I went to Manila, the capital of Philippines, to attend the 2nd Annual Meeting of the Asian Bank. This bank had been established two years earlier. It started very well, but as it was a new bank its operation could not expand quickly. The contribution of India to the bank ranks third, next to that of USA and Japan. There was a good deal of useful discussion at this meeting concerning the development of Asian countries. When I spoke I said that it was India's intention to avoid drawing loans from the Asian Bank as far as possible and that we had decided to help as much as possible in the development of other Asian countries.

Shri Krishnamurthy was the Vice-President of the Asian Bank at the time. He had had experience of such work in the World Bank and the International Monetary Fund and is a very capable person. I stayed with him in Manila. I met the President of the Philippines and discussed with him how best relations between Philippines and India could be made stronger. The law and order situation in Manila at the time was such that it was difficult for women to be out of doors after dark.

From Manila I went to Bangkok, the capital of Thailand. I believe that India should have very close relations with these South East Asian countries. We have not been able to establish such relations with them so far and have paid more attention to our relations with the developed and stronger countries of the West and Russia. The people of these countries also want closer relations with India. I met the Prime Minister and Foreign Minister of Thailand and discussed with them how we could make our relations stronger and closer. Thailand is a fairly prosperous country on the whole. Several Indians have settled down there. I met some of them. I was glad to note that these Indians maintained good relations with Thai nationals.

I went to see the temple in Bangkok which has a very large gold idol of the Buddha. This impressive idol was brought to Thailand from Burma years ago and was lying buried underground. It is said that a sadhu learnt about this in a dream which led to its discovery. It is a very fine and large idol. I also went to see another temple in Bangkok where I saw a 28-foot long idol of the Buddha in a reclining position. It is a very beautiful and majestic idol.

The Buddhist religion has great hold in Thailand and I could see that Indian culture was also in much evidence.

After staying in Thailand for a day I returned to India.

41

Refutation of Allegations against My Son, Kantilal

SHRI MADHU LIMAYE, MP, made several allegations in the Lok Sabha against my son Kantilal during the discussion on the budget in 1968. He first took objection to his being my private secretary and then made an allegation that there had been a leakage of the budget through him. I replied that the allegation about the budget leakage was totally false. It had not been substantiated. Kantilal did not help me on the Government side and did not draw any salary from Government. He was only helping me in my non-official and political activities. I made this fact clear and said, 'My son joined me as private secretary after I resigned from the Cabinet in pursuance of the Kamaraj Plan. I was not in power then and my son has not been running any business since he joined me.'

I put the facts about my son's joining me as my private secretary in 1965 before the Parliament. Kantilal wrote to me at the end of 1963 or in the beginning of 1964 that he did not want to continue in business or industry henceforth and wanted to serve the country. He told me that he had resolved when he started doing business in 1951–52 that he would remain in business only until he could earn and save enough for his future livelihood. When he had saved enough to get an income of Rs. 2,500 per month he would give up business and engage himself only in public activities to serve the country. He wrote in his letter that he wanted to begin his public activities by serving me first, as I was not a minister then and was not occupying any Government office. Nobody could, under these circumstances, find any fault with the step he took. Both of us felt that this was a convenient time to take it.

I was not in a position at that time to engage any personal staff and would, therefore, get welcome help in my public life if my son was my private secretary. It was with this in mind that I agreed to Kantilal's proposal and told him that he should give up his business before coming to me. He assured me that he would do so and that he was taking this step only after taking such a decision. He gradually sold his interests in Permanent Magnet Company which he was running. He took the minimum time for freeing himself from all his business occupations and joined me in the beginning of 1964.

After some time Shri Madhu Limaye again returned to the charge in Parliament and wrote to me that my son had not until then got out of business and was still engaged in it. He also wrote to the Prime Minister about this. I sent the Prime Minister a copy of my reply to Shri Limaye. He had alleged that Kantilal was still receiving remuneration from Dodsal and Company and that he was still working for them and that, therefore, I had given false information to the Lok Sabha. He also moved a privilege motion in this connection in the Lok Sabha.

Kantilal had closed all his business connections with Dodsals in 1964 and this had been done by mutual agreement. At that time Dodsals decided to give him Rs. 2,000 per month for a period of three years as retirement benefits. This was a kind of pension for three years.

I did not hold any Government office when my son joined me in 1964. I was then only a member of Parliament and it would not have been improper if Kantilal had continued his business activities. But both of us decided that he should not remain in business. This was to preserve proper values in public life which both of us believed in. He continued as a director in one or two companies but was not doing any active work for them. It could not, therefore, be said that he was actually doing business. But one who is out to find fault could make such allegations. This was the temperament of Shri Madhu Limaye. He considered himself the only honest person in the country and did not miss an opportunity of making allegations, right or wrong, against people to whom he was opposed. My strong reply in Parliament to his earlier allegations had offended him as I could see from his conduct. He used regularly to make allegations against people who were not in his party. I gave all the facts in Parliament and showed conclusively that the allegations made against Kantilal were all false. The records of Parliament will bear me out in this matter.

When Shri Madhu Limaye demanded my resignation in Parliament, I said that if the Prime Minister had any doubts in any of these matters and if she felt that there was some substance in the allegations, I would immediately resign from the Cabinet. This was the only way in which the correct values of public life could be maintained. But if Shri Madhu Limaye thought he could force my resignation at any time he liked, I would not oblige him, as it would not be proper to do so.

The Prime Minister said publicly and also in Parliament that she did not have any doubts whatsoever about my integrity and accepted my contentions fully. She had discussed this matter with me before speaking in Parliament. I had told her that she could make enquiries with the Finance Secretary in this matter if she wished and satisfy herself about the facts. She told me that she was already completely satisfied. I also wrote to the Prime Minister about the allegation concerning the leakage of the budget. I told her that it was quite false and baseless and that she could make an independent inquiry through any source she deemed proper. The Prime Minister, however, did not consider this necessary. I, however, felt that her statements in these matters in Parliament were not as strong and effective as the occasion demanded.

Attacks against Kantilal continued and Shri Bhupesh Gupta, a Communist member, made several allegations in the Rajya Sabha about the Permanent Magnet Company. One of the allegations was that Shri Tonpe, who had worked with me as Private Secretary when I was Finance Minister, had written some letters to the Ministry of Industry requesting help for Kantilal. Some questions were asked in the Rajya Sabha in this connection. I had no knowledge about these letters till then and so I made a full enquiry and found no substance in the allegations. I also learnt at the time that Shri Gulzarilal Nanda who was Home Minister in 1965 had already made an enquiry into this matter through the CBI. I had heard about it in 1965 and had also heard at that time that a search had been ordered of Kantilal's 'Oceana' flat in Bombay. No such search was ultimately carried out.

The Prime Minister called me one day in connection with the file of the 1965 CBI inquiry. She had obtained the file direct from the Home Ministry. I heard at that time that it had gone to her through Shri Dinesh Singh about fifteen days earlier, without the knowledge of the Home Minister. The Prime Minister herself told me that the Home Minister had protested against this. She showed me only one letter from the file which was a photostat copy. I saw that there was nothing objectionable in the letter and the Prime Minister said that this was the only letter which required any clarification. The photostat copy which was shown to me was of a letter written by Shri Tonpe to an officer in the Industry Ministry. Shri Tonpe had only requested expeditious action in connection with the issuing of a licence that had already been granted to Kantilal. This was done to remove delays in implementation. There was no suggestion in the letter that any new licence or any other advantage be granted. I told the Prime Minister that many letters were issued from my office requesting prompt action on various matters and that this must be one of them. There was no question of showing any favour. The Prime Minister showed no other letter to me. She only said that there was nothing else in the file about which anybody could say anything adverse.

The Home Minister, Shri Chavan, met me soon after this. He talked to me about the CBI inquiry and showed me the file containing the original of Shri Tonpe's letter. I saw that several endorsements had been made by concerned officers of the Industry Department on the original letter. But the photostat copy which the Prime Minister had shown me had no such remarks on it. This gave me the impression that some game had been played in this matter. The question in the Rajya Sabha related to this very letter. An attempt was made to show that some favour was shown to Kantilal. I explained the whole matter clearly and said that this was a routine matter and the letter had contained no request or suggestion of any improper or irregular recommendation about the issue of the licence. The letter was intended only for expediting action. It was obvious, therefore, that an attempt had been made to raise a scandal in a very wrong manner. The Home Minister and other members of the Rajya Sabha were convinced that there was no substance in the allegation and that the only object was to defame me. When four months earlier several allegations were made against the Prime Minister and repeated questions were asked in relation to a diamond necklace and a mink coat supposed to have been given to the Prime Minister, I refuted the allegations and the reply was so clear-cut that the chapter was closed immediately.

The Prime Minister should have made an enquiry if she had any doubts and if not she should have defended me strongly. Her attitude was not quite clear to me. I, therefore, began to feel that the Prime Minister had included me in the Cabinet as a result of pressure and that she was not happy about it. I had said definitely in both the houses very clearly while refuting the allegations that I could not remain in the Cabinet even for a minute if she had any adverse information against me or even a suspicion against me in these matters. The Prime Minister did not say that she had any reservations in the matter. I received reports later about a meeting of some advisers of the Prime Minister at her house in connection with this episode and that there was a proposal at this meeting that I should be relieved from the Cabinet. I received this information from one of those who attended. But the Prime Minister was told by one of her friends that she would be harmed if she took any wrong action in this matter and that no harm could come to me as the story was false. It was only after this that the Prime Minister talked to me about the CBI file and supported me in the Parliament.

Just when this episode was closed, there was a demand from Shri Chandra Shekhar, MP, for an enquiry against the Birlas. He wrote to me asking for some information in this connection. I supplied all the information I could and, for the rest, I informed him that I could not supply it. He had made some thirty to forty allegations against the Birlas and demanded the appointment of a commission of enquiry to investigate these. This matter was raised by Shri Fakhruddin Ali Ahmed in the Cabinet twice or thrice. Some of the associates of the Prime Minister had created a climate to show that I was coming in the way of the appointment of a commission of enquiry. This was not correct. My attitude in the matter was clear. I told the Prime Minister in the Cabinet that I had made enquiries into all the allegations relating to my department and that the rest would soon be enquired into and that whatever punishment was called for would be meted out. Decisions on matters depended on the reports of the CBI which had been asked to make an enquiry. There was, therefore, no meaning or purpose in appointing a roving commission of enquiry. No advantages had been gained from such commissions in the past which had only landed Government into huge expenditures. The reports of the commission had not hurt the persons against whom they were made and were in fact helpful to them in their defence. I then said that it would be better to appoint a high ranking police officer to make an enquiry into the allegations where criminal action could be taken. If the official was of the grade of an IGP it would not be possible for anybody to influence him. Such an officer should make an enquiry and if he found evidence of crimes he should prosecute the persons concerned. This was the only useful action that could be taken. In other matters, the departments concerned should enquire departmentally and take the necessary action.

The Prime Minister had some talks with the Birlas in this matter, but I did not talk with any one of them about it. This was clarified also in the Rajya Sabha and yet Shri Chandra Shekhar continued making his attacks. He even raised questions about the budget which was presented four months earlier and in which some tax concessions were given. I refuted all these allegations in the Rajya Sabha. The Executive Committee of the Congress Parliamentary Party asked Shri Chandra Shekhar to explain his conduct and also gave him a hearing. It disapproved of his conduct and decided to convey its displeasure to him. It was also decided that Smt. Gandhi would convey this censure to Shri Chandra Shekhar.

The Prime Minister told me that she had orally conveyed the decision of the Executive Committee to Shri Chandra Shekhar. The letter which she wrote later on did not mention it and Shri

Chandra Shekhar made a public statement that the Prime Minister had not conveyed to him any censure or disapproval of his action. The attitude of the Prime Minister in this matter was, therefore, criticised by many. She did not say publicly that she had conveyed the censure to Shri Chandra Shekhar. As she had told me twice that she had done it, I did not pursue the matter. This episode is a further indication that the Prime Minister's attitude towards me was not very clear and that, in actual practice, it was ambivalent in nature. On the whole, the Prime Minister's attitude towards me did not appear very friendly. She used to discuss some matters with other colleagues of the Cabinet but not with me. The discussions with me were mostly in the Cabinet.

The Prime Minister did not pull up her supporters who were criticising me publicly in a very loose manner. If there was any criticism against the Prime Minister, she did not tolerate it and got very angry about it. I made it very clear in the Executive Committee of the Parliamentary Party that if any member publicly criticised any other member of the party and necessary action was not taken against him, the party would not be able to maintain discipline and would be weakened. But I did not get any response from the Prime Minister. Her outward behaviour with me was always correct and courteous. I did not at that time have any reason for resignation from the Cabinet. If any such occasion had arisen I would immediately have done so.

42

Another Foreign Tour

I WENT ABROAD again in September 1968. I went to London and Washington for the annual meeting of the Commonwealth Finance Ministers in London and meetings of the World Bank and International Monetary Fund in Washington.

Mr. McNamara had taken charge as President of the World Bank before I went to Washington. He had visited India soon after when I had had discussions with him. He made an assessment of the progress made by India when he came here and showed his readiness to help in making further progress. He was very impressed by what he saw as I learnt from him when I met him in Washington.

Mr. Nixon was elected as President of the USA in November 1968. He had visited India before his election as a private American citizen. I had invited him to lunch and had had discussions with him on several matters for about an hour and a half. I had heard and seen the television discussion between him and Kennedy when they had contested for the Presidentship of the USA as I was in Washington at the time. I saw a great change in him from that time. He impressed me as a person who wanted to understand things without prejudice and was very frank in his discussions. I could not meet him in September 1968, when I went to Washington, as he was engaged in his election work. I met President Johnson who did not contest the election. Vietnam events had exposed him to very serious criticism which had a worrying effect on him.

After returning to India, I toured some parts of India as usual. I particularly visited Jammu. The people of Jammu had a grievance that the people of India went to Srinagar but did not visit Jammu. I met representatives of several associations there and also addressed a large public meeting. I explained to the people that we did not attach less importance to Jammu than to Srinagar and were always keen to visit Jammu as well as Srinagar. I also replied to Sheikh Abdullah's criticism of India. I said, "The merger of Jammu and Kashmir with India is final and unalterable. I have no doubt that nobody can change it. Sheikh Saheb was asking for a plebiscite but this has been held three times already as there had been three elections on the basis of adult franchise.' I also delivered a convocation address to the students in Jammu.

I went again to Washington at the end of March 1969 to attend ex-President Eisenhower's funeral. The Prime Minister was to go but she was in Rangoon at the time. She sent me a message that I should go in her place. As I had to leave for Washington within twelve hours, I got ready and took a direct flight via London to Washington. As there was not enough time to go from the airport to the place of funeral by car, I went there by a helicopter.

I went straight from the helipad to the place where the body of President Eisenhower was lying in state. After paying my tribute there, I joined the funeral procession which started soon after. The funeral procession took two to three hours to reach its destination. I then met two of the new Secretaries to Government who had been appointed by the President. As President Nixon was very busy at the time, arrangements were made for me to see him only for a few minutes, soon after the reception in the evening. It was not possible for him to see me during the day. I attended the memorial service for President Eisenhower. A number of heads of States had come to attend the funeral which was very efficiently organised.

I had to leave straight for New York from the President's reception at the White House to catch the plane at New York for returning to India. It was, therefore, doubtful whether I would get any time to see the President. But the President had made arrangements to see me for a few minutes and I was taken to see him in another room before I left. When I met the President at the reception, he introduced me to his wife with great cordiality. He was sorry that he could meet me only for a few minutes and said that we should meet for a longer time next time either in Delhi or Washington. He told me that he wanted to make the relations between our two countries better and more cordial and added that if any message was to be conveyed to him, it would reach him soon if it was sent through the newly appointed American Ambassador to India who was a very close colleague of his. He referred to our meeting in Delhi and thanked me again for the lunch I had given him.

I was out of India for three nights, two of which I spent in planes and one at the residence of Nawab Ali Yavar Jung, our then Ambassador in Washington.

I knew that a straight flight from India to America and back was very tiresome and that the person travelling straight from America to India got so tired that he had to have complete rest for two to three days after arrival in India. This is a general experience. I, therefore, rested completely during my air journey from India to Washington and back and did not do any reading. I also ate very sparingly during the journey, with the result that I did not feel tired when I returned to India. I had had to go to Sydney to attend the Annual Meeting of the Asian Bank soon after my return and I could do so easily.

This was my second visit to Sydney. I had first gone there in 1965. Sir Robert Menzies was Prime Minister of Australia then but he retired of his own accord a short time after my visit. He was succeeded by Mr. Holt who had earlier been Treasurer in the Australian Cabinet for several years and whom I had known for about five years. He was drowned early in 1968 when sea-bathing. As the sea was very stormy, he could not be rescued. Mr. Holt was extremely fond of swimming and a man of great courage. He went to swim at Port Baron even though it was not considered a very safe place. It was not necessary for him to go there and one can only say that death dragged him there. Destiny cannot be avoided, and it was the hand of destiny that led him to his death.

Mr. Gorton succeeded Mr. Holt. I had not met him before in Australia or elsewhere. I met him first for two or three minutes at President Nixon's reception at the White House when I told him that I was going to Sydney in a few days. In Sydney I met the Governor-General Lord Casey as well as the Prime Minister and some other ministers. I had met the new Treasurer, Mr. MacMahon, who had invited me to visit Australia when he had come to India the previous November. I called on him and his wife.

On my return journey from Sydney I went to Singapore where I met the Prime Minister. I was put up at the state guest house. It was my usual practice to stay with our ambassadors whenever I went abroad. But our Ambassador at Singapore told me that he had made the special arrangement as there were no air-conditioning arrangements in his house. The Prime Minister of Singapore, Mr. Lee, is a very able politician and statesman of very progressive and strong views. I had long talks with him on many subjects. He has a reputation of talking for a major portion of time in his conversations with others, but during our discussions he encouraged me to take more time than him as perhaps he got much interested in what I was telling him.

I met some Indians living in Singapore and saw the Singapore port. I also went to see the housing arrangements which the Government had made on a very large scale. Singapore is a City State and is very prosperous. It has well-developed industries and the people are very industrious and disciplined. More than 30 per cent of the population lives in houses built by the Government. This shows the extent of the housing activities of the Singapore Government. The housing is very well worked out. The houses and the surrounding areas have a very pleasant appearance and the arrangements in the houses are worth imitating.

I also met the Foreign Minister and the Finance Minister of Singapore. They showed a desire for closer relations between Singapore and India. India must cultivate close and friendly relations with the countries of South East Asia especially as close relations amongst these countries can be very helpful for defence against a common danger. There is no question of making any alliance but, where there are mutual common interests, close relations are essential. I am confident that any danger from China can be averted if these countries have close relations and informal links with one another. I am fully convinced of the necessity of also having very close relations between Japan, Australia, India and other South East Asian countries.

43

Dr. Zakir Hussain's Death and the Choice of a New President

I RETURNED TO Delhi from my visit to Australia and Singapore at about 11 a.m. on 3 May 1969 and went to office later than I usually did. Soon after reaching the office, I received a message on the telephone from the ADC of the President from Rashtrapati Bhavan informing me that Dr. Zakir Hussain had had a severe heart attack and there was a very little hope for his recovery. I immediately rushed to Rashtrapati Bhavan. The Prime Mnister was away on a tour of Rajasthan. When I reached Rashtrapati Bhavan, I found that the doctors were doing all they could but there was no effect and it was certain that he could not be saved. I went to his room to pay my respects to him. I got the impression that he had already passed away. I suggested to his Secretary and the ADC that Dr. Wig and other eminent doctors should be called in to examine the President. After examination they declared that the President was dead.

Dr. Zakir Hussain had gone to the bathroom. When he did not come out after fifteen or twenty minutes, one of the members of his personal staff opened the door and found that the President was lying unconscious on the commode. The doctors who happened to be at Rashtrapati Bhavan to give the President a check up that morning were called in immediately. Dr. Hussain had told the doctors that they could examine him after he returned from the bathroom. They tried to revive his heart, but did not succeed. Over the telephone, in my office, I was not informed that he was dead. Only when the experts who were called to examine him confirmed this, was it officially announced that the President had passed away.

The Prime Minister could not return to Delhi before 5.30 that evening. It was, therefore, decided to have the funeral the next day and the body of the President was kept lying in state in the hall so that people might pay their last respects to him. This arrangement was made after discussing it with the Prime Minister on the telephone. I then returned to my office and all public offices were closed soon after the announcement. Dr. Hussain was laid to rest in Jamia Milia which he had founded.

Dr. Zakir Hussain was a great personality. He had a very

simple and fine nature. He was a noble-hearted person. He must have been seldom angry with anybody as he had an unruffled temperament. He was a great lover of humanity. He was very fond of flowers as well and many flowers of various types were grown by him in the Rashtrapati Bhavan gardens. Gandhiji had appointed him Chairman of the Basic Education Committee which drew up a scheme for basic education for the whole country. He was deeply interested in this subject and was very unhappy that his scheme was not being implemented in many states. He was a very religious person. He was a true Indian and considered himself an Indian first and then a Muslim. He believed in Gandhiji and had very great and equal respect for all religions. He had made a very fine impression by his personality and work and was considered one of the great men of the country. He had never desired any office but accepted whatever work was entrusted to him with pleasure. He did not express any desire for any office after he became Governor of Bihar, but when he was pressed to become the Vice-President of India, he accepted the office and performed his duties with great efficiency and dignity. When Dr. Radhakrishnan was elected as President of India in 1962, Dr. Zakir Hussain was elected as Vice-President.

He felt very unhappy at the turbulent behaviour of certain members of the Rajya Sabha of which he was the presiding officer, but he tolerated it all with patience and magnanimity. He said in 1967 that he did not want to continue in that office. He was suffering from heart-trouble and felt he would not be able to cope with the strain of handling the turbulent Rajya Sabha members. He was chosen to succeed Dr. S. Radhakrishnan as President in 1967.

Two or three members of the Congress Parliamentary Board wanted Dr. Radhakrishnan to continue as President for another term as he had earned a very great reputation and credit both in the country as well as internationally. But the majority of the members were in favour of Dr. Zakir Hussain being elected as President. All agreed to this proposal and he was elected unanimously by the party. Some members in the opposition were saying that his election reflected communalism as, according to them, he was selected as President on that consideration. But the opposition was ineffective and Dr. Zakir Hussain was elected with a thumping majority.

Dr. Hussain was very unhappy on account of the incidents which were taking place in the country, particularly in West Bengal and Kerala, and also on account of the differences amongst Congressmen. When I called on him after he was sworn in as

President, he received me with great affection. He told me that I was like his elder brother. I told him that as he was the President, he was an elder for all of us. Whenever I met him, I found him worried about conditions prevailing in the country. He discussed these conditions with the Prime Minister some days before his demise and when I met him I found that he was feeling very much worried. He told me that whenever he asked the Prime Minister about the condition in the country, she told him that there was nothing to worry about. The President told me that while the country was in a condition which caused him concern, the Prime Minister did not seem to be worried. The fine gentleman that he was, he would not speak disparagingly about anybody. It was clear that he was feeling very uneasy about the dangers facing the country.

He made a very fine impression by his personality in whatever foreign countries he visited and the whole country was terribly shocked by his sudden passing away. It is no exaggeration to say that he gave distinction and honour to the high office of the President by his personality and work.

The Prime Minister called me for a discussion in the evening after the funeral or the next day—I do not remember exactly. She expressed her shock at the sudden passing away of the President and discussed with me about the new President to be elected as she was not quite sure what she should do in the matter. It was a problem for her to decide who should be elected. I told her:

'We have been lucky in having found persons of great dignity and capacity as the last three Presidents. All the three Presidents brought great credit to the office which they occupied. We should, therefore, select a person of the same calibre. I have no person in my mind in this connection. But we should see that the tradition of selecting the President is maintained and that he should be elected unanimously. This is how we can solve the problem.'

She then asked me whether I had any objection to having Shri V. V. Giri elected to the post. I replied:

'There is no question of my having objections in the matter. But you were unhappy, and have often told me that you were unhappy even about his Vice-Presidentship. When he was proposed for this office, you did not like it and said that he would not do as President if such an occasion arose. You had even then told me that there should be no convention or rule that the Vice-President should be the next President.'

I then added that, in my view, Shri V. V. Giri could not be the President and asked her how his name could be proposed in view of these facts. I further said, 'I do not know how I can suggest the name of Shri V. V. Giri as President. You believe and I also believe that there should be no convention that the Vice-President should be promoted as President. On this count also we cannot select Shri Giri.' I further told her that Shri Giri had attracted a great deal of criticism on account of his fondness for touring with his family. This is also one of the objections. 'As this is the Gandhi Birth Centenary year,' I went on, 'some colleagues might propose that a Harijan should be selected for the President's office. We have only two persons who can be thought of in this connection, Shri Jagjivan Ram and Shri Sanjivayya. Shri Jagjivan Ram has not filed his income-tax return for his additional income for the last ten years and has also not sent in his return for wealth tax. This would debar him from being a candidate. Shri Sanjivayya is very young. If he is selected as President he would be in a difficult situation after retirement. There is nothing lacking in his personality. We are friends, but he has not yet attained the necessary status in the country and hence it would be difficult to select him for this office. I do not make any suggestion myself.'

As several colleagues felt that someone from the south should be chosen, Shri Sanjeeva Reddy's name was suggested by some of them. Shri Reddy was at that time Speaker of the Lok Sabha. The Prime Minister was not quite satisfied with his work and had occasionally expressed her dissatisfaction about it.

After a few days, when I went to see her again in connection with some other matter, she told me that Shri Jagjivan Ram had told her that he did not want to be a candidate for the Presidentship and it was so reported in the newspapers. I told her that it was possible that he might really want to be selected as President, but might be expecting to be pressed to stand for the post. But the affair about the income-tax return went against him and was a bar to his candidature. There was a propaganda in the newspapers that the Prime Minister supported Shri Giri's candidature and that she wanted that the candidate should be of her choice. Shri Kamaraj had met her earlier, as I learnt from him, and he had then reminded her about Shri Sanjeeva Reddy's candidature. The Prime Minister had told him that she had not proposed the name of Shri Sanjeeva Reddy but had no objection to his being proposed. But she told me when I saw her that she apprehended that, if Shri Sanjeeva Reddy became President, he might create difficulties for Government. I told her that he would be a constitutional President and could not embarrass the Prime Minister. The President was bound to act according to the advice of the Prime Minister and her apprehension was not justified. I again brought to her notice that it was necessary to discuss this matter with all her colleagues. It would be better to have an informal discussion and, if there was no unanimity about it on some person, we should unanimously adopt the person whom the majority favoured. It would be, therefore, proper and necessary, in my view, that she should have an informal discussion with all the colleagues. She said nothing about this and our discussion ended.

When we met for a third time she told me that Shri Jagjivan Ram had expressed his willingness to stand. I told her that I could not support him and that I considered that Shri Sanjeeva Reddy had the support of the majority of our colleagues. Personally, I had no names to suggest. I again requested her to discuss the matter informally with all her colleagues. She did not then reject the suggestion, but she did not also show any interest in it. She asked me which body would select the person for the President's office. While she asked me this question, she knew of course that the Congress Parliamentary Board had to make the selection. This was how the selection was made in 1957, in 1962 and in 1967. It was the right and duty of the Parliamentary Board. She did not talk any further about this.

A propaganda was going on in the newspapers about Shri Giri and Shri Jagjivan Ram to the effect that the President must be chosen by the Prime Minister as she had to work with him. This was not a proper attitude or argument as the Prime Minister could be changed but the President could not be changed and whoever was the President had to work according to the advice of the Prime Minister in office, according to the Constitution.

Gandhi Centenary Committees were appointed in India and in foreign countries, one of which was West Germany. Mr. Kissinger was the Chancellor of West Germany at that time. He had invited me to attend the first meeting of the Committee formed there and to inaugurate it. He also wanted to have discussions about our mutual relations. I, therefore, went to West Germany in the beginning of July. I went to Frankfurt and then to Bonn where I met the Chancellor, Vice-Chancellor, Mr. Brandt, Mr. Walter Scheel and others. I had very friendly and useful discussions with them about the industrial development of West Germany, politics and our mutual relations. Mr. Kissinger was the Chairman of the Gandhi Centenary Committee. He could not go to the city where I had to deliver the inaugural speech as he had to attend another meeting in another city in connection with the impending elections in West Germany. The Vice-Chancellor, Mr. Brandt, was very hopeful of succeeding in the elections and becoming the Chancellor if he won a majority.

From Bonn I went to Hamburg and one or two other places to see the latest development of industries. I also went to see the well-known factory for the manufacture of cars known as Volkswagons. I was impressed by the efficient management of that factory. The West German Government expressed their willingness to give all possible help for manufacturing small cars in India. After returning to Bonn, I went to Frankfurt, where we have our trade centre and the Indian Investment Centre Office, on the last day of my tour. There I gave my inaugural speech in the presence of many well-known people of that place. They seemed to be very well impressed by what I said. As the speech was considered important it was given wide publicity in the country's newspapers.

I then returned to Bombay from where I flew straight to Bangalore on 9 July where meetings of the AICC and the Working Committee were to be held. It was decided, at the suggestion of the Prime Minister in a meeting of the Parliamentary Board which was held in Delhi in the previous month, that the selection of the candidate for the Presidentship should be made at Bangalore and that we should meet and discuss the matter on the evening of 9 July. A message was received from the Prime Minister that she would not be able to attend the meeting of the Working Committee on the 9th due to ill health. We could not, therefore, discuss the matter there on 9 July. The Prime Minister came to Bangalore the next day. But before coming she had sent a note on economic problems. She had put in a remark at the end of the note that she had jotted down her thoughts in the note in a hurry. The next day we discussed it in the Working Committee.

There was nothing new in the note, but she had mentioned some matters which were under discussion in accordance with the guidelines the Congress had laid down and also the nationalisation of banks, mentioning that some people were not satisfied with mere social control of banks. She suggested in the note that either five or six big banks should be nationalised or that, in the alternative, more funds should be released by the banks for industries in pursuance of the social control in force. This note had been sent with Shri Fakhruddin Ali Ahmed and was not addressed to the Congress President. As there was no consensus on the question, Shri Chavan suggested that the whole note should be placed before the AICC for consideration and proposed a compromise resolution. All members agreed with it. Several members suggested that I should move that resolution in the AICC and I accepted the suggestion as almost all the members had agreed to it. I moved the resolution in the AICC accordingly and explained all the points in the note and the steps taken about several of them. I suggested that the remark at the end of the note made by the Prime Minister that some stray thoughts were jotted down in a hurry should be removed and that change was made. Shri Chavan supported the resolution. I told the AICC that the principle of nationalisation had been accepted but the Working Committee had to decide when to do it after taking all factors into consideration. The most important point to bear in mind was that we had all to work together and in cooperation.

There was much discussion on this resolution and several amendments were moved. One amendment was for the nationalisation of some banks. At the end of the debate I replied to it and explained my stand on these matters very clearly. I requested the movers of the amendments to withdraw their motions in view of what I had explained. All the amendments were withdrawn within half a minute. This was evidence of the fact that the members were satisfied with my reply. But some of the supporters of the Prime Minister talked even then behind my back that I had not moved the resolution as I should have done. Such propaganda was being made by these people for some time. I was neither surprised nor worried by it. The resolution was passed unanimously. Anybody will be convinced from the fact that the manner in which I explained the situation satisfied most of the members of the AICC. There was hardly any precedent of amendments having been withdrawn so quickly on very important resolutions.

The meeting of the Congress Parliamentary Board was fixed for 12 July at Bangalore for selecting the candidate for the Presidentship of India. But even on that day the Prime Minister did not show any inclination or desire to discuss the matter informally and for two or three days before the meeting she used to call members individually and talk to them. She had told Shri Kamaraj that I had proposed the name of Shri Jagjivan Ram. I reminded her of what I had told her on the very first day of our discussion on this matter and she admitted that what I had said was correct. I reminded her that I had said, 'If a Harijan was to be selected for the office, two names can be considered. I shall not be able to support Shri Jagjivan Ram's name on account of his default in the matters of income-tax and wealth tax.' I was clearly of the opinion that he should not continue even in the Ministry and I had given an indication of this view in the discussion with the Prime Minister at the time of my talk with her. But this matter was ultimately for the Prime Minister to decide and I could not, therefore, assert my view in the matter. I had also told her that while Shri Jagjivan Ram could not be supported as President, there was a majority support for Shri Sanjeeva Reddy. Some members were suggesting that the consideration of this matter should be postponed again for consideration in Delhi and that I should discuss the proposal with the Prime Minister. The Prime Minister agreed with me that there was no advantage in postponing this decision, but I saw that she was then in favour of Shri Jagjivan Ram and had dropped the idea of proposing Shri Giri.

During her talks with me, she mentioned Shri Rajaji's letter to her in this connection. Shri Rajaji had suggested to the Prime Minister that she should be the President. It was clear that she did not want to accept this suggestion. There was also a suggestion that I should become the President, but I did not accept it.

When we went to the meeting of the Parliamentary Board the atmosphere was not at all happy as neither of the two sides was prepared to make a compromise. The Prime Minister started the discussion saying that though she had first thought of Shri Giri for the office, she found in her discussion with others that there was no consensus in his favour. She also said that she felt that the majority was in favour of Shri Jagjivan Ram and that, therefore, she proposed his name for the office of the President. Shri Fakhruddin Ali Ahmed supported her. Shri S. K. Patil then said that in his view the consensus was in favour of Shri Sanjeeva Reddy. The Congress President Shri Nijalingappa also said the same thing. Shri Fakhruddin Ali Ahmed argued that it should be left to the Prime Minister to take the decision in the matter. I told him that when Shri Jawaharlal Nehru was the Prime Minister, on two similar occasions decisions were taken against his view and he had accepted the majority decision as he had full faith in democracy. It would be better if this time also the majority decision was accepted. But the Prime Minister and Shri Fakhruddin Ali Ahmed were not prepared to agree. I then said that we should not discuss the merits or demerits of the persons concerned but should find out on whose side the majority of the members was and the decision should be taken accordingly. Merely prolonging the meeting would not bring any solution.

Shri Nijalingappa then asked every member to give his opinion as it was not possible to determine where the majority was without such a procedure and nobody objected. The Prime Minister was sitting next to Shri Nijalingappa. She supported Shri Jagjivan Ram's nomination. I was sitting next to her and when asked about my view I supported Shri Sanjeeva Reddy. Shri Jagjivan Ram was the next member who naturally supported his own candidature and it was not necessary for him to speak about it. Shri Fakhruddin supported him. All the rest, i.e. Shri S. K. Patil, Shri Kamaraj and Shri Yashwantrao Chavan, supported Shri Sanjeeva Reddy. Shri Nijalingappa was also in favour of Shri Reddy. Thus there were three votes in favour of one and five in favour of the other. Shri Nijalingappa then said that we must accept the fact that the majority was in favour of Shri Sanjeeva Reddy.

The Prime Minister refused to accept this and said that it would have serious repercussions. When she said this, a suggestion was made by some members that Shri Sanjeeva Reddy's candidature should not be declared immediately and that the Prime Minister and Shri Nijalingappa should discuss the matter. We all said that if they agreed on a name, we would all support it. It was, therefore, decided that the name should not be declared until a discussion between the two took place. The resolution of the Parliamentary Board meeting was recorded in the minute-book as one passed by a majority. There was a general convention in the Working committee that a majority decision should be considered as unanimously accepted.

The Prime Minister did not meet Shri Nijalingappa that day at all. The next day she saw him but the meeting did not end in an agreement. She called a Press Conference after the discussion and sent a message to Shri Nijalingappa that he could declare the name as decided by the Parliamentary Board. The Congress President accordingly told the Press after about 11.00 a.m. on the 13th that Shri Sanjeeva Reddy had been selected. I returned to Delhi by plane that evening.

44

I Quit the Cabinet

In the Press Conference she held at Bangalore, after the meeting of the Parliamentary Board, the Prime Minister gave expression to her dissatisfaction with the decision taken and also said that she was insulted thereby. I learnt about this when I reached Delhi. A Government officer informed me on the night of 14 July that he had learnt during his talk with an officer close to Shri F. A. Ahmed that it had been decided to drop me from the Cabinet. When I was told about this, I told the person concerned that I had absolutely no objection to it. It was not in any way pleasant or advantageous to continue in the Cabinet in these unhealthy circumstances. There was, therefore, no cause for unhappiness for me if the Prime Minister relieved me.

When I was in my office in the Finance Ministry on 16 July 1969, a special letter from the Prime Minister was handed over to me at about 12.30 p.m. Soon after, at about 1.30 p.m. an announcement was officially made that the Prime Minister had taken over the charge of the Finance Ministry. This made it clear that the Prime Minister did not want to discuss the matter with me at all and that her decision had already been implemented. I could only read in this action that the Prime Minister desired that I should not continue in the Cabinet. She had stated in her letter that I should continue as Deputy Prime Minister and that she would discuss with me later on what work should be entrusted to me. This was an amazing proposal and a very clever move. I replied to her immediately that in view of the manner in which she had written to me and the Finance Ministry had been taken over by her, I could not continue in the Cabinet and that, therefore, I was resigning.

Shri Hitendra Desai came to Delhi soon after this incident and had a meeting with the Prime Minister. He told me that she was worried as to how she could meet me. He had told her that he was sure that I would see her immediately she asked me to do so. I received a telephone call from the Prime Minister at about 8 p.m. that night expressing a desire to see me. I informed her that it was not possible for me to meet her that night as it was late and that, if she had no objection, I would see her the next day. I went to see her next morning. She told me she wanted me to continue in the Cabinet. I told her, 'The way you have hurt my self-respect and the fact that you have not even had the courtesy to discuss the matter with me, makes it very clear that you do not want me to continue in the Cabinet. I have, therefore, no alternative to resigning. If you wanted a change in the Finance Ministry, you should have discussed it with me. You know very well that I have never discussed any matter with you in an improper manner. Even when I have differed from you in some matter, I have never been guilty of impropriety or discourtesy. What I have felt is that you have behaved towards me in a manner in which no one would behave even with a clerk.' She accepted that the method was wrong. I then said, 'If you now feel you acted wrongly, you can retrace your steps.' This, she said, was difficult to do.

'If you feel that a mistake has been committed,' I told her, 'you have to rectify it; if you do not want to do so, I will not press you to do so. You should do it only if your are convinced that you have to do it.'

The Chief Minister of UP, Shri Chandra Bhan Gupta, had told me that the Prime Minister had told him that I was opposing her. I had mentioned this talk in my letter to the Prime Minister, saying that it was not proper that she should make such a false allegation against me. She denied having done so. I checked with Guptaji and he confirmed what he had told me earlier and that the Prime Minister was trying to get out of an awkward situation by denying the truth. I, therefore, again wrote to the Prime Minister to say that Guptaji had confirmed the talk that had taken place between her and Shri Guptaji. To this there was no reply.

After this incident, when the meeting of the Congress Parliamentary Party took place on the 19th, she presented the matter in a different manner. She said in the meeting that she had taken over the Finance Ministry as she wanted to gain experience of that Ministry. She also asserted that all must accept the decision of the Prime Minister in every matter. I replied with her permission:

'If the Prime Minister had told me that she wanted to gain experience of the Finance Ministry, I would have willingly handed over the Ministry to her because it is the right of the Prime Minister to retain whatever Ministry she wants for herself. But she gave me a different reason in the letter she wrote to me. It is against democratic tradition for the Prime Minister to say that everybody should accept her every decision. No single individual can have such a blanket power of decision in a democracy. The right of making decisions lies with the Cabinet. The Congress

President also cannot be vested with such powers. The policy is laid down by the Working Committee and its implementation is done by the President. There is nothing wrong if the Cabinet accepted the view of the Prime Minister voluntarily. But if many members held a different view and gave expression to it, the Prime Minister must accept the majority decision. I have always acted in accordance with these principles as the Chief Minister of Bombay. I have always executed every decision of the Congress as if it was my own view, even where I have disagreed with it, if it were passed by a majority. Nobody has been able to point out any departure on my part from such behaviour.'

The Prime Minister accepted my resignation after this meeting at 3 or 4 p.m. by a letter she wrote to me. I sent my reply to her immediately. She took the decision to nationalise fourteen banks and made a public declaration about it the same night.

Shri Jagannathan who was Economic Secretary in the Finance Ministry, was appointed as a Director of the World Bank in 1968 and was sent to the USA with the rank of an ambassador. This created a vacancy in my Ministry. Shri I. G. Patel was the Chief Economic Adviser at the time with the rank of Additional Secretary. He had also worked in the USA. A member of the ICS cadre had always been appointed to this post in the past and no economist had previously been appointed to this post of Economic Secretary. Shri I. G. Patel is an economist and was taken in the Ministry of Finance as Economic Adviser when the late Dr. J. J. Anjaria, with whom he worked for a few years, was Chief Economic Adviser. He decided in 1962 not to continue in Government service and to go back to his job as Professor of Economics. He talked to me accordingly. But soon after my leaving the Ministry Shri T. T. Krishnamachari succeeded in persuading him to come back to the Finance Ministry. Shri Patel is a very capable officer with very balanced views. He is very progressive in his outlook and has impressed everybody as an able administrator. I came to the conclusion, after considering the matter, that it would be advantageous if an economist was appointed as Economic Secretary and that it was not necessary to appoint a member of the ICS or of a similar service to this post. My decision created some discontent in ICS circles at the time.

When I discussed this matter with the Prime Minister she agreed with my proposal. But later on she showed her unwillingness to appoint Shri I. G. Patel as Secretary and ultimately decided that he should be appointed as a Special Secretary in that post. As the status of a Special Secretary was similar to that of a

Secretary, I did not ask the Prime Minister to reconsider her decision. I could not understand what led the Prime Minister to change her mind in this matter. I felt that she did so fearing that perhaps Shri I. G. Patel owed personal loyalty to me. He continued as Special Secretary when I resigned from the Cabinet and there was no reason for anybody to believe that Shri I. G. Patel had any special loyalty to me.

Shri Patel is a man of great independence and his loyalty is more to principles and Government than to any individual. This is why Shri Krishnamachari and Shri Sachin Chaudhari as Finance Ministers both trusted him fully. He expressed no desire to be appointed as Economic Secretary. He did not speak to me about it at all. He did not ask me why he was made Special Secretary and not Secretary. He is a very quiet and self-respecting person, completely engrossed in the performance of his duties. He constantly thinks of how the country's interest can be promoted and he worked extremely hard for days together at the cost of his health. This was a special trait of his character. Very few officers could be compared to him in calibre. He accompanied me on my foreign tours for meetings of the World Bank and gave me very valuable help on many occasions. He is very shy by nature and all knew him as a very capable officer who had no desire to put himself forward.

Before closing this chapter I would like to mention an incident. After I had joined the Cabinet in 1967, I had some discussion with the Prime Minister about her residence. The house that she was occupying at that time was not quite convenient and therefore there was a proposal for constructing a new house for her. She was at first considering selecting one of two houses which were available; either 5, Dr. Rajendra Prasad Road, or the house which had been occupied by the late Shri Lal Bahadur Shastri. When I went to see 5, Dr. Rajendra Prasad Road, I was told that she was going to see the house for herself. I then told her that she should first make her selection and that I would occupy what was left. She ultimately did not select either of these houses. She next thought of occupying Hyderabad House. This is a very large house and I felt she would be criticised if she occupied it. There was then a proposal for purchasing Darbhanga House for the Prime Minister, but it was dropped as the cost was very high. I understood from my talk with the Prime Minister that she had no objection to occupying the house on Teen Murti Marg which had been occupied by Shri Jawaharlal Nehru and which had been assigned to the Jawaharlal Nehru Memorial Trust after his death. She told me that she had felt that Shastriji should have occupied that house. I told her that that house was very appropriate for the Prime Minister. If she went there, it would be a proper decision in my view. If such a decision was taken, the Government could sanction funds for constructing a proper museum for the Jawaharlal Nehru Memorial Trust. But I said that it was she who must take the decision and that I would agree with it.

After some time Shri Dinesh Singh told me one day that the Prime Minister desired that the Cabinet meeting which was to be held that day should take a decision about her house. She would not attend that meeting and had suggested that I should preside over it. I made it clear to Shri Dinesh Singh that I would agree to preside over that meeting if the Prime Minister agreed to accept the decision of the Cabinet pertaining to the house. He should, therefore, consult the Prime Minister about it.

He did this and told me that the Prime Minister would accept the decision of the Cabinet without any hesitation that the Teen Murti Marg house should be occupied by the Prime Minister. I myself asked her for confirmation as I was eager to see that there was no room for any misunderstanding. The Prime Minister confirmed her talk with Shri Dinesh Singh. A decision was then taken in the Cabinet with only one member dissenting. I had said in the meeting that as the President of India was the President of the Jawaharlal Nehru Memorial Trust, he would have to be consulted and his approval obtained. I accordingly went to Dr. Zakir Hussain and consulted him. He told me that the decision was most appropriate and that he agreed with it fully. I conveyed all this to the Prime Minister.

She told me that the decision of the Cabinet would be implemented. But after a few days, as there was some opposition from some members of the Jawaharlal Nehru Memorial Committee, the Prime Minister took a decision, without consulting the Cabinet, that she would not go to that house and the Cabinet decision would not be implemented. This decision of the Prime Minister was absolutely arbitrary and one-sided and was against the assurances she gave me. I did not protest as it would have created misunderstanding.

A decision was then taken to constructing a new house for the Prime Minister. I did not consider this decision very proper as such construction would be very costly. But I did not oppose the proposal especially as I had told the Prime Minister in the very beginning that the decision concerning the Prime Minister's house must be taken by herself and she would be responsible for it. I had provided in the budget for funds for the construction of the

Jawaharlal Nehru Memorial Museum and Library when it was decided that the Prime Minister should go to Teen Murti House, but when it was decided ultimately not to implement the Cabinet decision and to continue the Teen Murti Marg House as the Jawaharlal Nehru Memorial and to construct a new house for the Prime Minister, I refused the grant for constructing a new building for a museum.

45

The Split in the Congress Party

THE PRIME MINISTER launched a powerful propaganda campaign about the nationalisation of banks soon after the announcement of the decision about it. She had taken the step in order to impress upon the people that she was progressive and dynamic, to win popularity and to strengthen her political image. Shri Yashwantrao Chavan praised her in very flattering terms for nationalising the banks and his opposition to her weakened.

There was an intense feeling of displeasure amongst many members of the Congress Working Committee with the manner in which the Prime Minister had behaved with me. It was decided to consider the matter in the meeting of the Working Committee which was called by the President of the Congress for the evening of 21 July.

I explained fully why I had resigned from the Cabinet on the first day of the meeting of the Lok Sabha, clarifying the whole situation. The Prime Minister spoke after me and tried to defend her action after speaking some words of praise for me. But she could not give any adequate explanation for her action or reply to the reasons that I had given for my resignation. When the party secretary went to her before the meeting of the Working Committee to request her to propose the candidature of Shri Sanjeeva Reddy, she refused to do so. As she considered it very probable that the Working Committee would show displeasure at her behaviour, she talked to Shri Yashwantrao Chavan about it, suggesting that some compromise could be made if the Working Committee did not pass any resolution. She talked also to Shri Kamaraj and some other members. But she did not talk to me. I did not even know about these talks at the time.

Shri Yashwantrao Chavan said in the meeting of the Working Committee in the evening that it was not advisable to pass any resolution at that stage, and that it would be better if some arrangement could be made for a happy compromise after a cooler consideration of the matter. Shri Kamaraj said that the step taken by the Prime Minister was unfair and unjust and that she should not have behaved with me as she had done. The Prime Minister said that she was sorry if anything wrong had been done and suggested that the Congress President and she might discuss and find out a mutually acceptable solution. No resolution was, however, passed to that effect in this meeting.

The Prime Minister signed the nomination paper of Shri Sanjeeva Reddy the next day and proposed him for the Presidentship of the country. I warned my colleagues at that time that if they did not take suitable steps to meet the hostile attitude taken by the Prime Minister in respect of the Congress candidate for Presidentship and deferred consideration of the matter until the election was over, I had no doubt that the Prime Minister would change her mind in the end and would defeat Shri Sanjeeva Reddy. It would be no use repenting after inaction and the Prime Minister would have weakened everybody. It was the opinion of Shri Sanjeeva Reddy, Shri Yashwantrao Chavan and some others that it was probable that Shri Sanjeeva Reddy would be more easily elected if no step was taken before the election was over. I again tried to persuade them to see the danger lurking in this attitude and warned them that they were making a serious blunder in deciding that way and that they were being caught by the Prime Minister's deceiving move. But they had no courage to take appropriate steps at that time.

The Prime Minister refused to issue a written appeal to the Congress MPs and MLAs to support the Congress candidate. On the pretext that the members of the opposition would raise legal objections against this, she said that she could not make such an appeal. This was a lame excuse as the Supreme Court had clearly ruled in a suit which was lodged after the election of the late Dr. Zakir Hussain as President that there was nothing improper or illegal if the Prime Minister appealed to the members of her party to vote for the Congress candidate. It was obvious to me that while the Prime Minister wanted to make a show of supporting the candidature of Shri Sanjeeva Reddy, she in reality wanted to defeat him. This was why she did not issue any written or oral appeal. It was then decided to solve this issue by calling a meeting of the Parliamentary Party. I did not attend the meeting, but I learnt after the meeting that Shri Nitiraj Singh, MP, raised a point of order about what had happened, saying that it was an unjustifiable criticism of the Prime Minister. I learnt that he was put up to raise this protest. Soon after, he became a Minister of State. Shri Nijalingappa appealed to the members of the Party to help Shri Sanjeeva Reddy in getting elected. The Prime Minister only said that she agreed with it but she did not make any appeal to the members directly. She did not also issue any written appeal.

Her supporters started propaganda against Shri Sanjeeva Reddy within four or five days of that meeting.

Shri Jagjivan Ram and Shri Fakhruddin Ali Ahmed sent a letter to the Congress President on the 11th or 12th of August in which they made allegations that there were rumours that the Congress President was having some negotiations with the Jan Sangh Party and the Swatantra Party and that this had created great excitement among the members of the Congress Party. Giving this as a justification, they asked for permission of the Congress President to vote according to their conscience for Shri V. V. Giri instead of for Shri Sanjeeva Reddy. The Prime Minister, who was supporting Shri Giri from behind the scenes, wrote a letter to the Congress President supporting the allegations and the demand of the two Ministers. She thus openly started propaganda against Shri Sanjeeva Reddy. I advised the Congress President even at that time that disciplinary action should be taken against those two Ministers and other members of the Working Committee and the Parliamentary Party who were responsible for such behaviour. Such disciplinary action would have cleared the atmosphere which had been vitiated by their actions. Shri Nijalingappa and Shri Kamaraj agreed with my view but the step was not ultimately taken as a result of persuasion to the contrary by Shri Yashwantrao Chavan, Shri C. Subramaniam and others. This strengthened the propaganda against Shri Sanjeeva Reddy who, as a result, was defeated. The result of the election was known on 20 August, but I saw it very clearly much earlier. This was why I had warned the Congress President and my other colleagues about it a month earlier. However, whatever is to happen happens, and this is why even wise people make mistakes. I did not therefore think it proper to blame anybody in this matter.

The Congress President called for explanations from the Prime Minister, Shri Jagjivan Ram and Shri Fakhruddin Ali Ahmed on the 21st and called a meeting of the Working Committee on the 25th to consider the matter. Shri V. V. Giri had been elected as President. Shri Yashwantrao Chavan had supported Shri Reddy. He had told me earlier very clearly and firmly that if the Prime Minister got Sanjeeva Reddy defeated disciplinary steps should be taken against her. But he had now weakened completely. He might perhaps have felt that as the Prime Minister had strengthened her political position, it was not expedient to oppose her. He said in the Working Committee that they had drafted a compromise resolution in which there was an appeal for forgetting the past and for not taking any disciplinary action.

The Working Committee met in a very tense atmosphere. It was first demanded by some members that Shri Jagjivan Ram and Shri Fakhruddin Ali Ahmed and also the Prime Minister give explanattions for the allegations they had made against the Congress President and that they should either prove them or withdraw them. The allegations were false and therefore could not be proved. Both Shri Jagjivan Ram and Shri Fakhruddin Ali Ahmed therefore immediately explained that as their information was wrong their allegations were wrong. The Prime Minister also accepted this position in silence and a resolution was passed to that effect.

Shri Yashwantrao Chavan then moved the resolution for unity. Shri Kamaraj and some other members said that the Prime Minister and her colleagues must express regret for defeating the Congress candidate, Shri Sanjeeva Reddy, and if that was not done organisational discipline would disappear. When this was said, the Prime Minister said very clearly that whatever had happened was proper, that no regret would be expressed and that if any pressure was applied for such action, the Congress would be destroyed. She also said that those who were proposing such a step must understand that they would be responsible for it. Many members then got tempted by the desire to maintain unity. They had been weakened by the threat of the Prime Minister and gave up their demand for an expression of regret by her and her two colleagues. I refused to accept this position and wanted to leave the meeting. But Shri Kamaraj and other colleagues requested me not to do so. I could not disregard the request. I said that as I did not agree with Shri Chavan's resolution I did not accept it. But I did not insist on recording my opposition as, if all the other members agreed to the resolution and I insisted on recording my dissent, I would have been held responsible by them for destroying the unity of the Congress. I was quite clear in my mind that this 'unity' move was a very clever one by the Prime Minister and others were deceived by it. She was continuously strengthening her position and was waiting for an opportunity to show her strength. But my colleagues did not see this clearly and their sentimental attachment to unity made them weak. This is how the meeting of the Working Committee concluded.

A few days after this meeting of the Working Committee, the Prime Minister's supporters started propaganda against the Congress President. At the end of September or beginning of October 1969, a strong opposition had arisen in the Tamil Nadu Pradesh Congress Committee against the behaviour of its President, Shri C. Subramaniam, and the differences between Shri

Kamaraj and him had reached the maximum level of bitterness. Shri Subramaniam felt convinced that he would be removed from the Presidentship of the Pradesh Congress Committee and so resigned from that post voluntarily. Thereby he automatically ceased to be a member of the AICC as he was an ex-officio member as President of the TNCC. As he was elected to the Working Committee as a member of the AICC, his membership of the Working Committee also automatically ended. On 7 or 8 October the AICC Secretary, Dr. S. D. Sharma, put before the Congress President a draft of a letter to be sent to Shri Subramaniam informing him about this position. The Congress President made a remark on that draft that before sending the letter it was necessary to obtain the full facts and that it was also necessary to find out whether Shri Subramaniam had been elected a member of the AICC. Such a letter could be sent to him only after verification of these facts. A copy of this draft, however, must have reached the Prime Minister soon after it had been put before the Congress President. She, along with four other colleagues—Shri Yashwantrao Chavan, Shri Fakhruddin Ali Ahmed, Shri Jagjivan Ram and Shri Umashanker Dixit—wrote a letter to the Congress President on the 8th informing him that the action taken by him against Shri Subramaniam was unconstitutional and that he was thus going against the spirit of the 25 August resolution. They also objected to the efforts he was making to remove the Presidents of the Andhra Pradesh and UP Congress Committees and to get new Presidents elected in their places. This illustrated the saying that 'the thief punishes the sub-inspector'. In fact, the Congress President had sent no letter to Shri Subramaniam up to that time. But he would not have been wrong even if he had sent it as Shri Subramaniam, according to the Congress Constitution, had ceased to be a member of the Working Committee by his own action. This move was clearly in conformity with the tactics adopted by the Prime Minister so far as I could see from the facts before me.

The Congress President replied to them in strong terms. When some people asked two or three signatories of the letter as to why they had made these false allegations even though no steps had been taken against Shri Subramaniam until that time, they replied that they did so as they did not want any steps to be taken against him. As this purpose had been served by the letter, it did not matter to them even if the step was considered wrong. This was their code of conduct. Shri Yashwantrao Chavan had also joined the company of the Prime Minister and her colleagues. A demand was then made by the Prime Minister's supporters for summoning the Congress Working Committee and the AICC soon. They suggested 1 and 2 November as being suitable to the Congress President and the Prime Minister. A meeting of the Working Committee was called to consider the situation on those dates.

The propaganda against the Congress President by the supporters of the Prime Minister meanwhile continued and some ministers and their colleagues were openly collecting signatures to requisition a meeting of the AICC.

Shri Fakhruddin Ali Ahmed held a press conference on 29 October. He strongly criticised the Congress President in that conference. He also said that, as many changes had been made in the Congress constitution at the Faridabad session and as the work of holding organisational elections had become difficult and had been delayed, the election of the Congress President had been postponed for a year. A requisitioned meeting of the AICC was therefore proposed to be called only in order to elect a new Congress President. This requisition was handed over to Shri Sadiq Ali, the General Secretary of the AICC, at 2 a.m. on the night of 31 October. Shri Fakhruddin Ali Ahmed was guilty of very wrong conduct as a member of the Congress Working Committee in making propaganda against the Congress President in a press conference. He thus forfeited the confidence of the Congress President. The Congress President, therefore, removed him from the Working Committee. He also wrote to Shri Subramaniam that he would not be invited to the Working Committee as he had ceased to be its member.

The meeting of the Working Committee was held on 1 and 2 November. When we met on the morning of the 1st, ten members were present and Shri Abraham of Kerala had sent word that he would be arriving half an hour late. He arrived before 11 a.m. Eleven members out of the total membership of 21 in the Working Committee were thus present at the Working Committee meeting. Of the remaining ten, Shri Subramaniam had constitutionally ceased to be a member and Shri Fakhruddin Ali Ahmed had been removed from membership. The Prime Minister had already taken a decision that she would not attend the meeting and had called her supporters to her residence for a parallel meeting. Shri Abraham came to the Working Committee and told us that he had been called by the Prime Minister to see her at her residence in the morning. As Shri Subramaniam went personally to take him there and pressed him very hard, he went to the Prime Minister's house. Shri Abraham had met the Prime Minister the previous night when he learnt that she had decided not to attend the Working Committee meeting the next morning. He did not, therefore, want to go to her house as it would serve no purpose. He ultimately went only under pressure from Shri Subramaniam. When he met the Prime Minister in the morning, she explained to him her stand. Shri Abraham told her clearly that he was not with her and came away straight to the Working Committee meeting at 7 Jantar Mantar Road. The Prime Minister alleged that the Congress President had removed Shri Subramaniam and Shri Fakhruddin Ali Ahmed as he did not have a majority in the Working Committee and wanted a majority. This allegation was totally false as is clear from the facts I have given above. The Prime Minister had gone very far in making propaganda against the Congress President. Even if the two members Shri Subramaniam and Shri Fakhruddin Ali Ahmed had not ceased to be Working Committee members, the Prime Minister's supporters in the Working Committee could not muster the support of more than ten as eleven members of the Working Committee were present in the meeting at 7 Jantar Mantar Road on 1 November.

Dr. Shankar Dayal Sharma who was assuring the Congress President until the night of 31st that he was loyal to him, went over to the Prime Minister's side the next morning, before the meeting of the Working Committee. He then started making propaganda against the Congress President. I had warned the Congress President six months earlier that Dr. Sharma's loyalty to him was doubtful and that he was the Prime Minister's informant. It was my inference that it was only on his information to the Prime Minister that she and four of her colleagues had written a letter to the Congress President on 8 October. Dr. Shankar Dayal Sharma, who had placed before the Congress President the draft of the letter to Shri Subramaniam, must have sent copies to the Prime Minister and her colleagues. This led them to write to the Congress President as they did. Dr. Sharma could not have then realised or learnt that the Congress President had not sent that letter to Shri Subramaniam and had postponed taking action on it.

The conduct and actions of the Prime Minister were considered in the Working Committee meeting of 1 and 2 November. In the meeting with her collaborators at her place she had decided to requisition a meeting of the AICC. The Congress President had asked for an explanation from her in this connection also. The next meeting of the Working Cmmittee was called on 13 November but as the Prime Minister, who had called the meeting of the Congress Parliamentary Board on the 16th, changed that date to the 13th, the Working Committee meeting was called on the 11th. When I went to the meeting of the Working Committee at Jantar Mantar Road on the 11th I saw that Smt. Subhadra Joshi, Shri Bhagat,

Shri Shashi Bhushan and some others had organised demonstrations against the members of the Working Committee that morning and were trying to prevent them from entering the compound. I had learnt from the morning newspapers about the arrangements made by these people for demonstrations. In spite of the news in the newspapers, the Prime Minister did not prevent them from going to 7 Jantar Mantar Road but she sent many policemen there.

The police neither removed the demonstrators nor took appropriate steps or legal action against them. When I reached the place the demonstrators surrounded me outside the gate and made it impossible for my car to enter the compound. I therefore got down from the car. They then surrounded me but in spite of the cordon I entered the compound and reached the office. At the meeting I learnt that they had attacked the Congress President also. Fortunately he did not suffer any physical injuries.

After about an hour and a half the Congress Secretary received a telephone message from Shri Kapoor, Private Secretary of the Prime Minister, to the effect that the Prime Minister was very much pained by the demonstrations. She, however, did not have the courtesy to talk to the Congress President herself. She perhaps made this show only to show her innocence in the matter.

After a very full discussion, we decided to take disciplinary action against the Prime Minister. It was clear that the Congress would not survive if these steps were not taken. During the day, Shri Vasantrao Naik, Shri Mohanlal Sukhadia and others were talking to Shri Chandra Bhan Gupta with a view to arriving at a compromise. We discussed the conditions which were offered for this compromise. As these were acceptable, we postponed the resolution on disciplinary action. But in the evening we received a message from the Prime Minister that the compromise was possible only if the Congress President withdrew all the charges made against her. This was very improper and unreasonable for if the charges were withdrawn and no compromise was ultimately made, the Congress President and the Working Committee would not have any basis left for taking any steps. We suggested that the representatives of both the sides should meet and discuss the matter and the representatives whose conduct was considered wrong would admit their mistake. It was not possible for the Congress President to withdraw the facts of the charges which he had sent to the Prime Minister without a discussion. The efforts at compromise failed because the Prime Minister stipulated that she would agree to compromise only if her condition was accepted.

The eleven members of the Working Committee who were

present in the meeting decided unanimously to remove the Prime Minister from Congress membership and the Congress Parliamentary Party was informed and asked to elect a new leader as the Prime Minister had ceased to be a member of the Congress.

We did not attend the meeting of the Congress Parliamentary Party which had been called by the Prime Minister on the 13th. All those who attended it disapproved of the Working Committee resolution and declaraed their confidence in the Prime Minister. Those members of the Congress Parliamentary Party who were present there thus revolted against the Congress and opted out of the Congress by their conduct. As the Prime Minister had ceased to be a member of the Congress she should have resigned her office. If she had a majority of members of Parliament with her and got elected leader of a new party, she could then have become Prime Minister again. But she did not do this and continued as the Congress Party Prime Minister and claimed that those who had revolted against the Congress were the only proper members of the Congress Parliamentary Party. This conduct was against the constitution of the Congress and immoral too. But as she had the power of Government to back her, she acted on the maxim 'might is right'. When her meeting was going on in the Central Hall, a large crowd of her supporters gathered outside Parliament House. This crowd could not really have collected there because, for some years, Section 144 of the Criminal Procedure Code prohibiting the assembly of five or more persons used to be enforced near Parliament House, but that year they deliberately did not issue any such order and allowed their supporters to collect there so that they could get the necessary support. The Prime Minister thus preserved her position by a complete misuse of Government power.

Several members of this crowd surrounded Smt. Tarakeshwari Sinha, a Member of Parliament, who went there at the time, and behaved with her in a very rough and violent manner. Some leaders of the crowd asked her to leave the place, but Smt. Sinha refused to do so and said that she had a right to be there as a member of Parliament. The police also advised her to leave the place. Soon after this somebody from the crowd slapped her from behind in the presence of the police. Smt. Sinha did not leave the place and the police arrested her and took her to the police station. This again was illegal as, instead of arresting those who had assaulted her, the police arrested Smt. Sinha, the person who was assaulted. This was totally improper and illegal. The dictum of Tulsidasji, 'The powerful do no wrong', was aptly illustrated by this incident. Later on, the Prime Minister went to the crowd, but she did not condemn the assault on Smt. Tarakeshwari Sinha. On the contrary, she congratulated the crowd for the enthusiasm shown by them. Anyone will see from this conduct of the Prime Minister that she did not disapprove of the rough and rude deal given to Smt. Sinha and that she did not even regret it.

When many members of the Congress Parliamentary Party revolted in this manner, against the Congress, the remaining sixty-five members who were loyal and disciplined met at Shri Nijalingappa's residence on the 16th and elected me as the Chairman of the Legislature Party and Dr. Ram Subhag Singh and Shri Shyam Nandan Mishra as the leader of the Congress Party in the Lok Sabha and the Rajya Sabha, respectively. Dr. Raju was elected the Deputy Leader of the Congress Parliamentary Party in the Lok Sabha. The Constitution of the Congress Parliamentary Party had not envisaged the creation of these offices when it was drawn up twenty-two years earlier as there was no idea then that the party might have to sit on opposition benches some day. It had been drawn up on the assumption that the Congress Party would always be the ruling party. A meeting of the Parliamentary Party was held after this incident and necessary amendments to the Constitution were adopted providing for the election of a chairman and two leaders of the party in the two houses. The chairman and the two leaders were elected on the 16th in anticipation of these amendments.

This is how the opposition Congress Party was formed in Parliament. There was no recognised opposition party in the two houses until then as none of the opposition parties till then possessed the necessary membership of not less than 10 per cent of the total strength of each house to be recognised officially as an opposition party. They were considered as only opposition groups. It was for the first time that Dr. Ram Subhag Singh and Shri S. N. Mishra became leaders of the opposition in the Lok Sabha and Rajya Sabha respectively. Their recognition was delayed in both houses for a long time as the Chairman and the Speaker could not disregard the wishes of the ruling party. Ultimately, the opposition party was properly recognised but our party was called 'Congress Party (O).' Some considered 'O' as standing for opposition, while we consider that 'O' stands for organisation.

Smt. Indira Gandhi called a meeting of the so-called AICC on the basis of the signatures of the members who had sent the requisition. There is no provision in the Congress Constitution for such a meeting and it was a completely unconstitutional action. The requisition was received with 407 signatures on 31 October at about 2 a.m. as I have mentioned earlier. This requisition was considered by the Working Committee. The signatures were not on one paper but were spread over several sheets, none of which contained more than twenty signatures. Some sheets contained only one signature. One can, therefore, clearly understand how these signatures were obtained. Among these signatures, three or four from Gujarat were false as I could immediately see when they were shown to me. There were other false signatures also. There were the signatures of two former members of the AICC from the Punjab who had left the Congress several months earlier. The Working Committee rejected the requisition as being unconstitutional, but it decided to call an ordinary general meeting of the AICC in the third week of December in Gujarat and the press was accordingly notified. The Prime Minister, Smt. Indira Gandhi and her colleagues claimed that the majority of the AICC members were with them. If their claim was correct, they should have attended the meeting of the AICC which was called by the Working Committee and should have opposed the resolution of the Working Committee. They could have thus expressed their 'no confidence' in the Working Committee. But they were sure that they had no working majority at the time. This is why they took the improper and unconstitutional action they did.

The meeting called in the name of the AICC by the Prime Minister was held at Delhi and was presided over by herself. She had ceased to be a member of the Congress as she was legally and constitutionally removed from membership by the Working Committee. A meeting presided over by her could not therefore be a legal and constitutional meeting of the AICC. Anybody who possesses even a little knowledge of constitutional law can understand this. They also decided to call the open sessions of their 'Congress' in Bombay, which was also wrong.

The meeting of the AICC and the open session of the Congress which were fixed by the Working Committee were held at Gandhinagar which was the new capital of Gujarat State, situated about twelve miles from Ahmedabad and where the Government had not yet shifted. It was generally estimated that about 5,00,000 people assembled at this meeting at Gandhinagar. Such a large presence was not seen in any of the Congress sessions during the past several years. The meetings were very well attended for both the days. The arrangements and discipline were also of a high order. It was a matter to be specially noted that there was neither any accident nor any pick-pocketing incident in spite of such a large crowd having collected there. This kind of enthusiasm was not displayed at the meeting called by the Prime Minister in a very large city like Bombay. It was not possible for the place where the Bombay meeting was held to accommodate such a large crowd as was seen in Gandhinagar. Considering the area of the place where the Bombay meeting had taken place it could not have accommodated more than 1,50,000 people, whereas they claimed that more than 5,00,000 people had attended. Nobody could prevent them from making such wild propaganda as the radio and the newspapers were under their control. Nobody could earlier have imagined that such misuse of the radio, as is being made by the ruling party, could have been made by a democratic government in this country or in any other part of the world.

This and the later conduct of the Prime Minister will be properly assessed by history. I have no doubt that the like of this attitude has not been seen either in this country or in any other democratic country so far. It must be admitted that she has succeeded in her tactics so far and that she has great intelligence and courage, which serve her well in such moves and manoeuvres. However, it cannot be said, considering the manner and purpose for which these natural gifts are being used, that they are being properly utilised.

46

My Family

I HAVE ALREADY referred piecemeal to my family in earlier chapters but I would nevertheless like to deal with some family matters at one place even at the risk of occasionally repeating myself. As I have said in an early chapter, my father was a teacher in the former Bhavnagar State and I was brought up in my early childhood at my maternal grandfather's place at Bhadeli. The family there consisted of my maternal grandfather, maternal grandmother, two maternal uncles and their families. I received much affection from them all and was also fortunate in profiting from their very good influence.

My father died when I was in the matriculation class and soon after that tragic incident, I was married. After passing my matriculation examination from the Bai Avabai High School, Bulsar, I attended Wilson College, Bombay from 1913 to 1917. After graduation, I joined Government service in May 1918. I gave up Government service in May 1930, from which time I have been serving the people of this country to the best of my capacity.

Even though married in 1911, I could live with my wife only from 1917 as I was studying until then and both of us were very young. I, therefore, started my married life after passing my BA examination. When I joined service in 1918, my mother, my wife, my brothers and a sister lived with me in Ahmedabad. One of my two sisters died in 1912 from burns suffered as her clothes caught fire when she was firing crackers during Diwali. From that time I resolved not to allow the use of crackers in my family and have so far stuck to this resolution.

I had become the father of five children by 1928, but only four of them, two sons and two daughters, were living when I gave up service in 1930. One son died in his childhood. My children were with me until I gave up service. My eldest daughter Viru was born in 1921. My first son was born after her and died when he was 18 months old. My second daughter Indu was born in 1925 and my son Kantilal was born in 1926. The third son who was born in 1928 died within a month of my leaving service in 1930. Thus two daughters and one son were surviving after 1930.

I went to jail within a few months after I had left service in

1930 and the education of my children was completely disorganised as my wife had also gone to jail as a satyagrahi and I had to make some arrangement for my children's education. I got my eldest daughter admitted in the Girls' Gurukul at Itola near Baroda. My second daughter was staying with my younger brother Ambubhai and my son Kantilal was sent with my brother Chhotubhai who had gone to Sind as an assistant engineer in Government service in 1931. Thus I could not give any attention to the education of my children. From 1930 to 1934, I was either in jail or was touring Gujarat for Congress work. After I returned from jail in 1934, I lived with my younger brother Ambelal in Ahmedabad. My two daughters were studying in a municipal school there and my son was attending another school. He then joined the Gujarat Vidyapith for some years. In the last year of high school, he lived and studied with my friend the late Shri Mangaldas Pakvasa in Bombay.

Till 1929 I used to scold my children and even punish them physically if they lied or did some mischief causing destruction of something. I had been considering the necessity of controlling my anger from 1921, but as I considered it also necessary to use it for getting work done, I did not succeed in my efforts to control it. I realised in 1929 that I should not try to improve my children or others by physical punishment. They were born with the influences of their past lives and I could not make any improvement in them by punishing them harshly and it was also not proper for me to do so. Moreover, they were not able to retaliate when I punished them. It was, therefore, not proper for me to punish them physically. I, therefore, gave up giving physical punishment to my children from 1929.

When I joined the Bombay Government as a Minister in 1937, my children were in Bombay with me and my son Kantilal was then studying in Kabibai High School in Bombay. When I resigned as Minister in Bombay in 1939, I went to Ahmedabad and stayed with my brother Ambubhai. It so happened that all of us four brothers were staying together in Ahmedabad at that time. The brother next to me, Ambubhai, was manager of a mill. The one younger than him, Nanubhai, returned to India about that time from London after passing the FRCS examination and the youngest, Chhotubhai, was serving as engineer in the Ahmedabad Municipality. He was transferred from Sind to Ahmedabad a short time before I went to Ahmedabad.

When I went again to jail in 1940—41 and 1942 the education of my children again got interrupted. Just before I resigned Ministership in 1939, the marriage of my eldest daughter was fixed with the brother of my brother-in-law on my wife's side. This betrothal was arranged only after ascertaining the willingness of both of them. They were married at the end of 1941 at Navsari after I had returned from jail. I issued no invitations for that marriage but almost all my relatives came uninvited. Their number was more than a hundred. They came even though I did not want them to do so as they had much love for me and this was the first marriage in my family.

My son joined college after passing his matriculation examination, but as he failed in the inter-science examination, he did not want to study further to carry on his studies. One of the reasons for his failure was that he took science at my instance so that he could go in for engineering. But science subjects did not interest him and he failed in his examination and decided to give up his studies. I suggested to him to take training as an aircraft ground engineer. The Tata Airways Company was at that time taking apprentices for training as ground engineers. The required fee of Rs. 1,000 was paid and he joined there as an apprentice, receiving a stipend of Rs. 50 per month.

After taking this training for about one and a half years, one of his friends told him that the future was not very bright in that line financially and that he could not go very far in it. The friend suggested that he should join the insurance business. Kanti asked for my advice. He was then over 24. I told him that he could go to the insurance business if he wanted to, but that I would not be able to recommend him to anybody. He told me that he would join that line if I would approve of it and that he would get service in the New India Insurance Company. I then told him, 'If you have already found service you can certainly join it, but you must join it on the distinct understanding that you cannot canvass for insurance through or with the help of any Government official.' He accepted this condition and joined the New India Insurance Company.

Shri R. D. Birla had come to see me one afternoon three or four months before this change of his occupation. As I was engaged with some other person, he was waiting in the drawing room. When he saw Kantilal, he enquired from him what he was doing. He told Shri Birla that he was taking training as a ground engineer. Shri Birla suggested to him that it would be better if he went to America for training instead of taking it here. Kantilal told him that he had no resources for going to the USA. Shri Birla then told him that he was prepared to send him to America for training if he desired as he was sending some other students for study abroad. Kantilal did not give any reply to him.

When I learnt about this conversation from my son, I told him that he should have replied to Shri Birla in the negative immediately and that he should have also told him that he did not want to go abroad with help from anybody. He told me that he had not shown any desire for or agreement with the suggestion. I then talked to Shri Birla and told him that he should not have spoken in that manner to Kantilal as it was improper to tempt him in this manner. Shri Birla told me that he had made the suggestion innocently and had no motive in doing so.

Shri B. K. Shah was the General Manager of New India at the time. I had little acquaintance with him. Shri A.D. Shroff who was Chairman of the company at the time was against me in those days on account of the prohibition policy. One day I invited Shri B. K. Shah to see me and asked him to let me know his reasons for engaging my son for insurance work. 'I want to understand the reasons for engaging him for insurance work,' I said, 'I do not know whether you have examined him to find out whether he had the necessary capacity for doing such work. If you have taken him without his being fit for it only because he is my son, it will not only unnecessarily bring me disrepute but harm Kantilal also. When I am not in power, it is possible that he will lose his job if he was not fit for it. I, therefore, want to understand from you on what basis you have engaged him in your service and whether he is fit for the work.' He replied, 'We engage, from time to time, young persons whom we consider suitable for this work as probationers and we have engaged Kantilal in pursuance of this policy. We have not taken your position into consideration at all and we have not taken him because he is your son. He, too, has not given me any reference to you. I found after talking to him that he would be able to do insurance work very well. This is why he was engaged by us and I am sure he will work very well.' I then asked him to let me know whether the salary given to him was larger than that given to others. He told me that they had not given him a rupee more and that they were giving him a salary according to the scale fixed for the purpose.

When the ordinary general meeting of the New India Insurance Company was held after a few days, Shri A. D. Shroff was asked by a shareholder a question about the engagement of Kantilal in the service of the company. Shri Shroff replied, 'There is no question of influence or recommendation in this matter. All know that relations between Shri Morarjibhai and myself are not quite good. There is, therefore, no possibility of any concession being made in this case as can be easily understood. We pay him according to his capacity and fitness as we pay all other people in similar services.'

If I remember correctly, the insurance work put in by Kantilal in the very next year was larger than that put in by his colleagues and he was awarded a prize for his good work. He thus proved his efficiency and ability for the work. He observed the rule of not insuring persons in Government offices and of not canvassing business with their help.

Shri Manubhai Shah said one day during a talk with some friends that Kamanis had given a very large insurance to Kantilal and that this must have been done only because of Morarjibhai. When I learnt about this I inquired immediately from Shri Poonamchand Kamani on the telephone about the facts of this matter. I had very little contact with Shri Kamani till that time. We knew each other, but not closely. He immediately informed me that he himself knew Kantilal and had therefore given him insurance and that I had nothing to do with it. I told him, 'You must have given this insurance business to Kantilal instead of giving it to your usual agent. This must have given cause for this complaint in my view. If you have given this work to Kantilal, depriving somebody else of it, is it not natural that the other man will feel aggrieved? You ought to take this point of view into consideration.' If my memory is right, that insurance work was held back that year from Kantilal. I understood later on that Shri Manubhai Shah had also learnt about it. Kantu was doing his insurance business very well and had made great progress in it. As he was living with me with very little expenditure from his own income, he could save almost all his earnings. It is with the help of those savings that he started dealing in general stores and selling goods on a commission basis.

A Gujarati young man wrote me a letter from which I learnt about the expansion of Kantilal's business. He wrote to me : 'Your son deals in mill stores. He takes away the business that we are doing and comes in our way. This is because of your position and power. You should, therefore, send him away from Bombay and let him do his work in any other state.' I wrote to him asking him if he could give me any evidence that Kantilal had deprived him of his business so that I could inquire into the matter. I called the mill-owner whose name he had quoted in his reply and asked him whether he had given Kantilal an agency to purchase all his stores. He told me: 'This is a completely false allegation. The only truth in this matter is that the offer that Kantilal gave me for two items of stores which I wanted to buy was at lower rates than those given by others and the quality of the goods was superior. This is why I gave him the order for these two items. I have purchased all other items from other dealers.' I informed the young man who had complained to me that what he had written to me was not correct according to the facts given by the gentleman whom he had quoted and who had given the order to Kantilal for two items only and that he should not make such false allegations. The young man wrote to me again: 'Even if he did his business in a proper manner it is natural that we would get less business as he shares in our business. You had better engage him in Government service and I would not consider it improper if he is given a salary of Rs. 2,000, but he should not carry on this business in Bombay as it puts people like me to a loss. If you do not take action as I have suggested to you, I shall have to write to the Prime Minister Shri Jawaharlal Nehru.'

I replied immediately: 'I am sending your letter myself to Shri Jawaharlalji so that you may not be put to the trouble of writing to him. I am also sending him a copy of the reply that I have sent you. If you want to write anything more to him you can do so.' I sent the letter to Shri Jawaharlal Nehru requesting him to make an enquiry in the matter as he deemed fit. It would have been a grave injustice to Kantilal to ask him not to do business because he was my son. I could not deprive him of his right to do business independently. I would not keep him with me and would take suitable steps against him if he did anything wrong or improper in his business. I had warned him about this from the very beginning. But as long as he did business honestly, no honest man could say that he was doing anything wrong. Nobody, however, can prevent those who want to malign others through prejudice or jealousy from doing so. But if I came in the way of my son's doing business through fear of being maligned, I had no doubt that I would be doing injustice to him. I enquired fully whenever somebody made a complaint against him while I was in Bombay. I even enquired through police officers. I was assured by every such officer, after making his enquiry, that the complaint was totally false and that it was a result of jealousy or made with the motive of maligning him and me.

When I am writing about this matter I should also mention here one or two other matters concerning Kantilal. A few days before I relinquished the Chief Ministership of Bombay State in October 1956, Kantilal rented his own flat on Netaji Subhash Road, Bombay. I learnt about it after he had taken it. He was not helped in this matter by any Government official directly or indirectly. I went to live with him in the flat after I vacated the

Government bungalow. He has been living independently in that flat since that time and whenever I go to Bombay I live there with him. It is a peculiar feature of the joint Hindu family of India that parents live with their children. When my detractors cannot raise any objection against my conduct, they try to make allegations against Kantilal in order to defame me. One or two newspapers, whose business it has been for several years to malign people whom they do not like, have been indulging in such writing. I made enquiries even about what was written therein and no doubt was left in my mind that the allegations made were totally wrong.

In 1962–63, Shri Jawaharlal Nehru sent to me for information a letter which he had received from somebody making allegations against Kantilal. It was obviously pseudonymous. I wrote to him immediately saying, 'The allegations made in the letter are completely false but I do not expect you to take my word for it. I wish that you make full enquiries into these allegations through any agencies that you may consider proper so that you may be satisfied about the facts and can reply to the people who write to you from your own information. I would also get reassured in these matters.' Shri Jawaharlalji immediately replied to me : 'I do not intend to make any enquiry as it is not called for at all. I sent the letter to you only for your information. The contents of the letter are obviously such that they cannot be believed. I had no idea that you would have any doubt about my attitude in this matter.'

It is a common experience in India that many people indulge in character assassination, right or wrong, against people whom they dislike or whom they consider hostile or whom they want to harm. One sees a deep-rooted tendency in many people to believe in false stories spread against others. This is a result of the want of freedom in this country for centuries. This also makes the work of the people who desire to malign others easy. But I am sure that as people become fearless in the country and get tired of false accusations, this tendency will disappear. Anybody who is constantly making honest efforts to act in accordance with truth and who, in spite of such behaviour, has to suffer such defamation by others, should consider it a test for himself and bear such malicious slander fearlessly and cheerfully without being ruffled. It is my faith that truth ultimately prevails and many incidents in my life have confirmed me in this faith.

As I have mentioned earlier, three of my children were living in 1951, i.e. two daughters and one son. The elder daughter was married in 1941 and the younger, Indu, who was one year older than Kantilal was studying in a medical college. She had to appear at the final MBBS Examination in April 1952 and I wanted to send her to the hostel to prepare for it. But as I was out of Bombay a great deal on account of the elections and as my wife had no other company at home, she did not agree to send Indu to the hostel. Indu was very much devoted to me and she always said that she did not want to marry and that she wanted to serve me. She used to quote often the example of Maniben, the daughter of the late Sardar Vallabhbhai Patel, in this connection. I did not press her to marry. She carried on with her studies and was preparing herself for the examination as well as she could. My defeat in the elections in the beginning of 1952 gave her a terrible shock and her mind was affected, resulting in a very serious nervous breakdown. As her nerves had weakened very much, she tried once in 1952 to commit suicide by burning herself. After making the attempt she withdrew from it. She could not appear at the final examination in April on account of the nervous breakdown and decided to appear in October or November. When she appeared for the examination in October, she had taken my pen to write her answer-papers. When she came back, I could see from the small amount of ink that she had used that she must have written very little in her papers. But she was under the impression that she had done well and was shocked when she found that she had failed in the examination when the result was declared. I was told that she was given an impression by some doctors that she was deliberately failed because she was the daughter of the Chief Minister. This had a very serious and adverse effect on her unsteady mind and she pressed me to get her marks recounted by the university. In my view, she had been given a very wrong impression by some doctors and I could not pursue her request. My refusal also had an adverse effect on her.

She was still refusing to consider marriage, but some months before she passed away she expressed a desire to marry a co-student of her college who belonged to another community and was three years younger than her. I asked her to reconsider mainly on account of the difference in ages, but as she persisted in her desire I gave my consent to their betrothal. We had thought of performing the marriage in May 1953. I learnt later on that there was some quarrel between them in the interval and that this had given her a great shock. I went to rest for a few days to Juhu at the end of June 1952 and took her with me. Early one morning at Juhu she went into the sea outside our compund and went on until the waters reached her shoulders. But she returned from that point, perhaps, because her courage failed her then. When I learnt about it, I sent her back to my residence at Malabar Hill. Before I returned from Juhu to Bombay, she made a successful attempt to commit suicide by setting fire to her clothes. She was very badly burnt but she did not utter even a single word about pain and all the while said that she should be allowed to die and she should not be medically treated. She died as a result of severe burns on 3 April 1953. I learnt later on that the person whom she was to marry had spurned her a few days earlier. She took this step as a result of the consequent frustration, because her nerves had gone very weak and her mind had also become unsteady. This incident gave me at the moment a very deep shock, but I immediately regained my peace of mind as a result of my faith that everything happens in accordance with God's will.

At present I have two surviving children, both of whom are living independently. My wife has been sharing my good and bad days as my life partner and has been giving me all possible cooperation. We have been able to lead our lives with contentment and cheer by the grace of God.

47

Experiences of Illness

As I HAVE already mentioned earlier, I have been fortunate in having a healthy and trained physique from my childhood. I have, however, had experiences of illness three or four times so far and had to undergo operations three times. It would perhaps be appropriate to describe briefly some of these experiences here.

I had a black mole the size of an old pie coin on the right side of my forehead just under my hair from my birth and another which was a smaller one on the left side. A surgeon friend of mine, Dr. Dhaka, who is now no more, happened to notice these moles in 1952 and told me immediately that they should be removed as otherwise they might develop into a more difficult, i.e. a malignant, condition. Doctors are generally very careful in such matters, especially as they fear that this might lead to cancer in the long run. One or two other surgeons also confirmed this opinion and my daughter Indu who was at that time studying for the MBBS and was in the last year of her course was also pressing me to have the moles removed by an operation. When six or seven persons pressed me to have the operation, I wanted to be free from the pursuit of the doctors and asked Dr. Dhaka to carry out the operation if he considered it necessary. I went to his private surgical rooms for this purpose. The operation was made under local anaesthesia which was administered by an injection. The operation lasted for about an hour and a half since the doctor was keen to see that the incision left no scars. It so happened that the anaesthesia was not fully effective. When the doctor applied his knife, I felt some pain, but I did not give any indication of it to the surgeon as I was in the midst of the operation and bore all the pain with fortitude. As my face was covered by a napkin during the operation, the doctor could not see it and could not therefore notice that I was suffering from pain. When I informed the doctor about it after the operation was over, he was extremely unhappy, but I assured him that there was no reason for being unhappy as I had not suffered any damage.

Dr. Dhaka considered me his elder brother and I had no doubt that he operated on me with great care. He stitched the surgical wound with great care and in such a manner that no marks would remain. But in spite of all his care, the skin broke up, with the result that the operation left a scar on my forehead. The doctor felt very sorry about this but I have no doubt in my mind that he was not to blame. After the wound was properly bandaged, I left the hospital for home within fifteen minutes and began to attend to my routine work after a few hours.

Within a few days after this, I went to attend the AICC meeting which was held at Indore. The bandage was taken off before I left for Indore. This was my first experience of a surgical operation. I was operated upon twice after this; once for removal of a kidney stone and the other time for hernia.

When the Bombay Government was in Poona in the monsoon of 1949, suddenly one morning I got an attack of pilitis. As I believed in nature cure, I refused to take allopathic medicines and fasted to cure myself. I was getting high fever and was bedridden. My colleagues, doctors and friends were pressing me for taking allopathic medicines. Dr. Dinshaw Mehta who was conducting a nature cure centre in Poona at the time and used to treat Bapu also and was a firm believer in nature cure used to look after me. Doctors and colleagues, including Shri Balasaheb Kher, tried hard to persuade me to take allopathic medicines. At Balasaheb's instance, Dr. Dinshaw Mehta asked me to take *auriomycin* and was willing to give me the drug, saying that there was no bar to taking *auriomycin* while under nature cure treatment. I did not agree with him at all in this view, but it became difficult for me to argue with Balasaheb Kher when the nature-cure expert expressed this view. I took *auriomycin* under these circumstances. This drug was newly discovered at the time and I was given a heavy dose of it. I suffered from much weakness after taking it. I am sure my weakness was a result of taking that medicine and that I had erred in doing so. I then resolved not to repeat this error in future.

About two years later, in 1951, while I was at Dahanu, I suddenly got severe pain in the right side of my stomach. I was touring in that area for two days. On the day in question I had fasted in accordance with my habit of fasting once a week. I was given coconut water three to four times by my host. I stayed that night at Dahanu at the house of the President of the District Congress Committee. At about 1.45 a.m. I had very severe pain on the right side of my stomach and my sleep was broken. The pain increased steadily.

Others were sleeping in the adjoining room and I decided not to disturb any of them as they could not have helped me at all and would have been worried if I had informed them. As Bombay was more than seventy miles away, it would have taken many hours for a doctor to come there from Bombay. Moreover, I was to return to Bombay in the morning. I therefore decided not to say anything to my friends. I was uneasy with the severe pain for a few minutes. But I soon remembered my prayer. It has been my practice to pray on rising in the morning and going to bed at night. I pray to God to send me all the pains that I have to undergo on account of my past actions immediately and also to afflict me with all the diseases from which I have to suffer on the same count so that I may suffer them in this life and be free from the bondage of past actions. I found the four Sanskrit verses of my prayer in *Anugita* in 1926, from which time I have invariably used them in prayer. I told myself that after having offered this prayer before sleeping I must not worry if I got pain which I had asked for and that I should bear it with cheerfulness and fortitude. I offered a prayer to God with an apology for being uneasy and immediately felt relief and went to sleep. When I got up in the morning I had no pain and there was no necessity of getting any treatment.

I got another attack of pilitis in the beginning of December 1955. This was a more serious attack than the earlier one and my fever went up to 104°F. At the time of the first attack I had taken antibiotic tablets under pressure, but this time I stuck to my determination not to have any medicine and took only nature cure treatment.

When Dr. Jal Patel and some other doctor friends learnt about my illness, they immediately came to see me. They told me after examining me that I was suffering from some infection and that I must take antibiotic drugs. They also warned me that the infection would not be removed without that treatment. I told them that I did not believe in that treatment and that I had no doubt that I would be cured by fasting. They tried for an hour to persuade me but failed. Ultimately I told them : 'It is not good that you should carry on this long discussion with me when I am suffering from 104° temperature. This will aggravate my illness and you should therefore close this discussion. I am determined not to take medicine. However, if you find it necessary you can give it to me yourself when my condition becomes so serious that I may not survive. You can use whatever medicine you want to use at that time.' The doctor friends were displeased at my attitude and gave up their attempts.

I was free from illness after fasting for ten days. Dr. Jal Patel examined me then and told me that the infection had disappeared and that I had been cured on account of my will power. I then told him that if he accepted that position he should bear it in mind and that in future he should not press me to take any medicine. I then went to rest at Juhu for a few days and recovered completely in a short time.

I realised as late as 1958 that the pain which I suffered from in 1949, 1951 and 1955 was due to a kidney stone. As a result of taking a good deal of coconut water during the day at Dahanu the stone must have descended to the ureter from the right kidney, which had caused the pain which I then suffered. I did not suffer from any pain after that till 1958. I had four or five painful attacks after June 1958. I used to endure the pain silently without allowing anybody to know about it and did my work as usual.

I went to Nainital in June or July 1958 to attend the annual function of a school there as the chief guest. Pantji had also repeatedly asked me to go to Nainital. I stayed there at Government House. I reached there at about noon and when I was resting, just after lunch, I got very severe pain, more severe than what I had got at Dahanu in 1951. I had to attend a meeting which Pantji was addressing at 5 p.m. but the pain did not subside. I did not mention the pain to anybody and went to Pantji's meeting in spite of it. The pain continued during the meeting and I sat there without showing it. The pain abated only when I returned to Government House at about 7 p.m.

I had to climb 1,500 ft. to the top of the hill where the Birla School was located in the afternoon the next day and I was advised to go up on a pony or in a palanquin. I refused to do either and climbed the whole distance on foot. I descended from the place after the function was over and did not suffer any more pain. I returned to Delhi the next day. But soon after I began again to get repeated attacks of pain and realised that it was due to the kidney stone. I came to the conclusion that the best remedy was to remove the stone by an operation and felt that it was possible that other complications might arise if I allowed the stone to remain any longer in the kidney.

I got operated upon in the Bombay Hospital by Dr. Shantilal Mehta in December 1958. I had believed for a long time that Dr. Shantilal Mehta was the best surgeon in Bombay. He was a co-student of my younger brother Nanubhai who is also a surgeon. They were studying together and were good friends. It is possible that it was due to my soft corner for him that I considered him such a good surgeon. From the experience that I had of the operations he carried out on me, I am convinced that he is a surgeon of great skill and that a patient can trust him completely. He is very conscientious in the performance of his duties and treats all patients equally. He is known for his plain speaking and giving correct advice to every patient which, in my view, is a great virtue.

As he was not attached to the Bombay Hospital then, some difficulty was encountered in getting him to operate upon me in that hospital. I requested the persons in charge of the hospital for the necessary permission.

I was taken to the hospital the previous night. I was not informed about it earlier, but after going there, the surgeon came to me at about 9.30 p.m. and told me that he wanted to give me an injection. When I asked the reason he said that the injection was to be given to me in order that I might not worry and that the operation could be done with ease. I told him, 'I do not believe in such injections and am not worried about the operation. It is only the fear of death that makes a person worry about an operation. But I have no fear of death as I believe firmly that death is inevitable and its moment is also fixed. Nobody can avoid or postpone it. There is no reason to feel unhappy about death as it is futile to worry about what is unavoidable.' Then I said in a lighter vein, 'Why should I worry ? If I die during the operation I will be unconscious at the time as a result of anaesthesia. I will not know anything about it and, therefore, there is nothing for me to worry about. It is you who would have to worry because you would have to explain the circumstances of my death. You have, therefore, to take the injection and not I.' The doctor enjoyed the joke and after having a good laugh agreed that there was no need for any injection in my case.

Dr. Mehta performed the operation in a beautiful manner in about an hour. I was then taken to my room. When he told me that night that he would like to give me an injection to help me sleep, I again declined it and said that the pain would not be removed by it and that the only thing the injection would do was to remove the severity of pain. I did not believe in this method and did not, therefore, require the injection. He accepted my view. I had made a condition with him before undergoing the operation that he should not give me any medicine which had any animal substance in it, under any circumstances. I would undergo the operation only if he assured me about this. He assured me accordingly and did not give me any such medicine. I had no objection to blood transfusion as such blood is donated voluntarily. But it was not necessary to give me any blood transfusion at the time. As the stone had stuck to the wall of the ureter, it had to be removed with great care. The surgeon did this with immense skill and attached a very small tube for the outlet of urine from the ureter as it could not be stitched. It took a few days for the ureter to heal up completely. The doctor told me that it would soon heal if I did some walking. I carried out his advice and the wound healed within two or three days. I was discharged from the hospital after twelve or thirteen days.

My niece Dr. Usha and Dr. Sarla Mistri, who is also like a daughter to me, nursed me in the hospital. There was also a professional nurse looking after me. I took care to see that I gave them the least trouble. I got pain for the first two or three days, but I did not allow anybody to know this. The day after the operation I did not find it possible to pass motion while lying in bed. I, therefore, requested the surgeon to give me permission to sit on a commode. He told me that he would give such permission if I was prepared to bear the resulting pain and I said that I was willing to do so. I then used a commode and my bowels moved and I was completely relieved.

The doctor had advised me not to lift any weight for three months after the operation and I carried out his instructions fully. I took a daily walk of five or six miles for three months after the operation, which helped me to recover my former health. As the operation was very neatly done, there was no necessity for any aftercare. I recovered from the resultant weakness in two to three months.

I was staying at 7 Thyagaraja Marg at the end of 1963 and the beginning of 1964 when I was not in office. One day I brought down a heavy bag from the top of the cupboard. It was very heavy and I lost sight of the fact that I had advanced in age and my body, however healthy, would not be able to bear such strain at that age. My action in bringing down the bag from the cupboard gave me hernia. Dr. Bhonsle who used to massage me with great affection once or twice a year, had come to massage me a couple of days after the incident. When he massaged me on the joint of the right thigh I said that I had some pain. He asked me whether I had lifted any weight. I told him that I had done so. He then told me that I had got hernia as a result. It was thus that I learnt about it. Hernia, as I was assured, could be cured by an operation completely. So I was operated upon for it in July 1964.

This time the operation was performed in the Harkishandas Hospital where Dr. Shantilal Mehta was attached as a surgeon. When I got myself operated upon in Bombay Hospital by Dr. Shantilal Mehta in 1958, somebody spread a rumour after the operation that it had failed. This rumour reached the ears of the surgeon's father-in-law who was in his office at the time and he made enquiries about it. It was from him that we learnt that somebody had spread this rumour in order to discredit Dr. Shantilal Mehta. I, therefore, decided to go to the Harkishandas Hospital for operation to avoid repetition of such an incident. As a result of Dr. Shantilal's experience of the first operation he did not get me to the hospital the previous evening and called me only an hour before the scheduled operating time. He operated on me soon after some preliminary preparation. He had told me before the operation that it was necessary to do a vasectomy on me to ensure that hernia would not recur. I agreed to this and he carried out the operation very well. I returned home after a few days. I have been taking the necessary care since then in this matter and am sure that there is now no necessity for worrying about it any further.

48

My Faith

As MY deep faith in God and the principles flowing from there have been influencing me in all my activities, it is necessary to define them as clearly as I can.

My parents and my maternal grandfather had very deep faith in God. I observed from my childhood that they were unselfish in their actions and tried to stick to the truth throughout their lives. I feel that I have been born with a similar faith from my past life as this faith has been governing me from my childhood.

I see that the universe is quite unlimited in its extent. There are innumerable orbs like our earth in the universe and they all have regular movements. Such a universe cannot go on indefinitely unless it is governed by specific and unalterable rules. I have, therefore, no doubt that it is governed by specific rules. Pondering over the nature of this law, I believe that the principle of *karma,* i.e. action and result of action must be the basis of this rule. The law of action and reaction which scientists have discovered has its counter part in the principle of *karma* which lays down that action and reaction are equal and opposite. The law of *karma* or action which I believe in is similar to this law of the physical sciences. Just as action must have its reaction, every action has its result. This law which applies to the universe applies equally to man.

If our world was not governed on the basis of unfailing and uniform justice, it could not survive as in its absence there will be complete confusion and chaos. Scientists have now no ground to doubt that the universe is eternal. The changes which are constantly taking place in the universe must be governed by a law and the increase and decrease involved in the changes are quite equal which means that there is no loss or gain of the substance on account of change. I have arrived at the belief that every person has freedom of action and that action may be good, bad or neutral. The life of every person is governed by his actions.

Happiness or unhappiness, pleasure or pain, which man experiences is the result of his own action and he has to undergo it fully. No person can be made happy or unhappy by another person. It would not be justice if one person could make another person unhappy or miserable and if that happens man cannot be considered free to act in his life. If a person is thus dependent on another for what he does he cannot be considered good or bad. Whatever a man enjoys is as a result of his own past actions. Somebody can become an instrument of giving him that happiness or unhappiness, but the instrument cannot be held responsible for it. The responsibility is that of the person's action itself. The belief in birth and rebirth flows from the law of *karma,* i.e. action. This is the basic principle of Indian culture. There is no belief in rebirth in Western culture.

Man is responsible for very many actions in his life and is unable to enjoy or suffer the results of all of them in one life. It is in consequence of this that he is reborn to enjoy that which remains to be enjoyed, and his actions go on accumulating. The chain of birth and rebirth thus goes on. I have no doubt that there must be a definite rule which governs the time and the method of enjoyment of the results of different actions. It would not be right to say that there is no such rule because we do not know it. The scientific advance and researches, which great men of science are constantly making are also in accordance with the law of the universe which alone makes them possible. The scientific knowledge of today which is limited, even though rightly considered as amazing by us, is insignificant when compared with the deep secrets of the universe. What I mean is that it is little when it is compared to the secrets of the universe which are still undiscovered or are hidden from us. We are able to predict the time and quantum of rain, earthquakes and their time of occurrence, windstorms and several such phenomena by knowing more and more of the rules of the universe. All these visions and knowledge about them prove, in my view, the fact that the universe is governed by a definite law or a set of rules. It is inherent in the belief in birth and rebirth that there would be no rebirth if a man has enjoyed the results of all his past actions and has ceased to do new actions which give him results to enjoy.

Actions in this belief are of three kinds, viz. 1. good action (*punya karma),* 2. evil action (*papa karma*), and 3. action which is neutral, i.e. neither good nor evil (*papa-punya rahita*). The action by which we serve or benefit somebody and which is performed with the motive of earning some dividend or merit is a good action. The result of such an action gives enjoyment of some material happiness to the person who does it. The action which is done with the purpose of harming somebody or to benefit oneself at the cost of another is an evil action. It gives us as its result what we consider to be material unhappiness. As long as a man works with affection or ill-will, i.e. with some self-interest, he cannot be free from the cycle of birth and rebirth and his actions belong to the category of good or evil. But the person who goes beyond feelings of affection and ill-will, i.e. is unattached to anything, does not do any action with a view to getting anything for himself and does his actions without any desire to enjoy their fruits. His actions do not involve the enjoyment of any results of either happiness or unhappiness. Such actions are not, therefore, binding and only when he does such actions is he free from the cycle of birth and rebirth. These actions are known as actions with detachment. When a man, therefore, becomes detached and free from affection or ill-will and performs all his actions with detachment (*anaskti*), there is no rebirth for him after he finishes the enjoyment of the result of his past actions done with good or bad motives.

Most people are ordinarily governed by feelings of affection or ill-will and yet all these people also do not do all their actions with such motives. Such people also do a few actions with a sense of duty only and without any motive. Such actions do not involve them in the enjoyment of any results.

The result of every good or bad action is two-fold : 1. the resultant happiness or unhappiness which one has to undergo and cannot be evaded or avoided; 2. the desire (*vasana*) to do the same kind of actions again. The second result gives every man both good and bad tendencies. If he goes on doing good actions, his good tendency gets increased or strengthened and if he does bad or evil actions, his good tendency gets lessened and his evil tendency increases. Everybody knows within himself what is right or wrong, good or evil, but when he does not prefer the good and the right action and acts wrongly, he gets into the habit of doing wrong or evil actions and the evil tendency goes on increasing. A man gets the desire to do right or wrong actions according to the right or wrong desire or tendency which he gets from his past actions. But if he gets determined to stick to what is right, in spite of wrong desires or impulses, he prevents himself from getting involved in wrong actions. He has this freedom to check or prevent himself from doing new wrong actions.

Man cannot avoid undergoing happiness or unhappiness according to his past accumulated actions. But he can save himself from his wrong desires or tendencies which form his nature and which make him act wrongly, if he makes a correct use of his freedom. Ordinarily men do not search for truth or have such a philosophy of life. They would like to live as men generally live in the world. They behave, therefore, in a routine manner and travel on the beaten track. But those few who are in search of the fundamental truth of life and pursue it thoughtfully and diligently and with intense application, do realise the truth. Then they get freed from the cycle of birth and rebirth. Thus they get merged in the fundamental principle of the universe. As this is my faith in life I have always believed that it is the duty of man to search for truth in life and that all activities in life must be carried on only to find out truth.

Three paths have been prescribed by Indian philosophy for the pursuit of truth : 1. the path of knowledge (*gyana*), 2. the path of devotion (*bhakti*), and 3. the path of action (*karma*). The path of devotion and the path of action are two different aspects of *karmayoga* or can be considered as two forms of the same path. When a person takes to the path of knowledge, he turns away from the world, engages in constant meditation, renounces worldly life and accepts a life of solitude. There he pursues truth through meditation and contemplation. He thus obtains freedom from attachment, i.e. likes and dislikes, and when he gets that knowledge he returns to society to serve the people by giving them advice about true religion, to help them free themselves from the cycle of birth and rebirth. While he is engaged in the service of the people, he is also tested on whether he has really imbibed the true knowledge. One cannot realise God or truth without serving creation. It is, therefore, considered that service of the people is service unto God and that it is the real instrument for reaching the truth. In this process a person cultivates detachment.

Man learns to act with detachment also by engaging himself fully in devotion to God. It is because of this belief that I consider that the path of *karma* and the path of devotion are nearly the same. A man can serve people truly only if he serves without any desire of enjoyment of its fruit. It is only thus and by doing his actions with the spirit of detachment that he can be free from likes and dislikes. All the three paths ultimately lead to total detachment and I believe that complete detachment is the same as the vision of God or truth. Belief in destiny flows from the belief I have mentioned. It is alleged by some people that belief in destiny makes people idle and inactive. But correct belief in destiny does not make man idle or inactive.

No man can blame somebody else for the happiness and unhappiness which he undergoes from birth to death as it is all in consequence of his own actions. When a man stumbles against a rock and suffers pain, he does not blame the rock, but considers it his own fault. In the same manner, if a person suffers harm or injustice through another person, the former should not consider the latter responsible for it. He should realise that it was a result of his past actions. It is not possible to avoid the enjoyment of happiness or unhappiness which one may have to enjoy. He can, however, save himself from the feeling of pleasure or pain if he looks at both happiness and unhappiness with equanimity. What I mean is that if he keeps his peace of mind in both circumstances he enjoys both equally. He can then remain peaceful, contented and unruffled under all conditions. He cannot avoid pain, but he can save himself from feeling unhappy or miserable.

The belief that whatever man enjoys is due to his own actions does not make him inactive or indifferent in his actions, but makes him more alive to the necessity of doing good actions. It gives him knowledge that, howsoever wrong his past action may have been, he can start doing new actions with a good motive and can make his future better. This is the hope that it always gives. If one does not believe in rebirth, one would not desist from doing bad actions as nothing is to be carried over after death, there being no rebirth. But when one believes that one will have to enjoy the results of his actions if not in this life then in another life, he will hesitate and avoid doing wrong actions and will be encouraged to do good actions.

This belief, however, does not mean that it is futile to help somebody in grief or pain on the ground that whatever pain he is undergoing is a result of his own previous actions. The person who believes in birth and rebirth and the law of *karma* has, on the contrary, to strive constantly to have sympathy with others in their misery and to share it by serving them selflessly. Because man can know truth and God only through the service of men, he has to serve others by striving constantly to give relief to those who are in pain. One cannot actually remove the pain of another or lessen it by sharing in his unhappiness, but one can help him undergo the pain with greater ease and cheerfulness and this is one form of disinterested service. Man can attain detachment only if he has a deep and true faith in God and can serve others with detachment and without self-interest only if he is humble. He can be humble only when he surrenders himself, i.e. his ego, to God.

There is no selflessness where there is expectation of a return for the service done to another. There is also scope for suffering from frustration on account of hopes not being fulfilled or expectations not being realised. One indulges in many undesirable actions as a result of such frustration. This is what I have believed from my childhood. I must have inherited this faith from my past birth. Experiences of life have given me a correct understanding of this faith and have made it firm and complete. It is due to this that it becomes easy for me to attain peace of mind quickly under all circumstances. It is also because of this faith that there is no desire in me to blame somebody else for whatever I may have to suffer and thus my efforts to obtain freedom from attachment are made easier.

My faith has been confirmed by my study of the Gita and its application to my life has become easy. My belief in having equal respect for all religions has been strengthened by what is taught by the Gita. Every living being has the same right to freedom of developing himself as I have. I have, therefore, learnt not to be intolerant when there is a difference of opinion between me and others. It is most advisable that I should act according to my own view where I am not convinced about the truth of the differing view and I am sure of the truth of my view. I, therefore, understand that it is equally desirable or advisable for the other person holding his view to act according to his own view in a similar manner.

From this I have also arrived at the belief that every person aims at going up and not going down, spiritually. One can, however, develop only according to the extent of one's own effort. One can help another in this process if he asks for help and it cannot be given otherwise. But one should always be ready and anxious to give help to others whenever it is asked for. God's law is always benevolent and whatever happens according to that law leads to one's welfare or good. Whatever condition one finds oneself in, is in accordance with the law of God. It is, therefore, one's duty to be cheerful in every condition and see His grace in it. We do not know what is to happen. Men should, therefore, go on acting according to what they consider is right and must accept the result as being in conformity with God's law. At the same time, one should constantly try to go on doing good actions selflessly. Gandhiji's life has also confirmed me in this faith.

Mahatma Gandhi was born an ordinary child. He rid himself of likes and dislikes and attachment by following the path of truth and non-violence in his life and became a mahatma or a great soul. Any man who makes similar efforts can without doubt become equally great. Nobody can improve or spoil another person but if one leads a good life one can create a desire to be good in others. The other man will decide to go on the same path if he sees that going on that path leads to happiness. If he asks for help after getting that desire for proceeding on that path, one can and should help him. Nobody can spoil me if I do not want to be spoiled. I can make my life better and richer by constantly learning lessons from wherever I can learn them. I believe that this rule has universal application, and I have been constantly trying to live accordingly.

This is how my faith in religion has been confirmed and my

unshakable faith in the law of *karma* has affected my method of action in my life. It is this faith which has given me the principle which I follow of not being a party to group formation wherever I work. It is because of this that I believe in the non-alignment policy of my country. I have adopted this non-alignment policy in my life and have therefore not considered it proper to indulge in any intrigue. I have considered every experience of my life as the grace of God.

As I have said above, whatever happiness or unhappiness I enjoy is a result of my past actions and I do not consider the person through whose agency I may enjoy it, responsible for it. I have, therefore, never considered anybody as my enemy in my life. There might be many who consider me as their enemy, but I have not considered anybody as my enemy and have never hesitated to help others whenever I was in a position to do so and persons were in need of my help.

Several persons, including my colleagues, have spread a belief about me that I am rigidly obstinate and that I do not listen to anybody. When I meet such persons, I ask them to quote some instance of my rigidity that they may have observed. None of them is able to quote any such instance. When I ask them why they consider me rigid, some tell me that I do not pay any heed to others' views and do not accept them. When I ask them whether I discussed matters with them for an hour or two, they admit that I did so but say that I did not accept their viewpoint. I have never refused to see anybody in my life so far because I firmly believe that it is my duty to meet everybody who wants to see me. I can understand his viewpoint only if I can see him. In any case I can give him the satisfaction of hearing him and knowing his viewpoint.

Again, as I said earlier, it is my firm belief that it is possible to realise God only through rendering service to humanity. It is due to this belief that I have adopted this way of life. I do not consider anybody inferior to me or myself superior to anybody, as I am subject to the law according to which every human being has both good and evil tendencies in him and it has been my constant effort to behave with others in that manner. When somebody tells me that I have not heard him I remind him about my long discussions with him. He then admits that I heard him out but complains that I did not accept what he said. It often happens that I have not been able to accept the viewpoint of another because I was not convinced about its correctness or truth. I then tell such persons that while I did not accept their viewpoint, they did not equally accept my point of view and that I have not complained about it. I ask them, 'If I do not accept your viewpoint, I am considered obstinate and rigid. Would you also not consider yourself rigid when you do not accept my view ?' Then these persons admit that their charge is wrong.

What I understand by rigidity is a person sticking to his view even when he realises that he is wrong. Such an attitude is full of untruth and I consider it a vice. But I stick to my viewpoint only as long as I am convinced that I am correct. I consider that everyone who seeks truth must act according to what he thinks is right. When others act according to their beliefs, I do not consider them rigid or obstinate and respect their views. I try to explain my view to the other person when I have a discussion with him, at the same time making a full effort to understand his viewpoint. If I find that his viewpoint is correct I invariably accept it. I try to follow the path of my own duty and have never tried to come in the way of others doing their duty or to deflect another person from acting according to his conception of his duty.

Ever since I became an adult, I have been convinced that one should form no habits except the one of telling the truth. All other habits enslave one and make one dependent and weak. It has, therefore, been my constant and persistent effort to be free from all other habits. This has given me control of my mind and a capacity for taking decisions. Some have charged me with being rigid in order to make me give up my firm views and to accept their views out of fear of being defamed. I was convinced soon after completing my college education that one should not do anything out of fear. It has also been my firm belief that one should not have the desire or expectation to get something from anybody if one wants to be free from fear. Man cannot free himself totally from desire. His desires can, however, be merged in the overwhelming desire for realising truth or God and for doing selfless service to man. Then alone can he be free from fear. I have also realised that one should not have greed even in the matter of doing service to others. I also believe that one should not have attachment to one's family also. It is due to this belief that I have considered it my duty not to leave any property to my family and to serve my family as I serve others. Therefore, I have made arrangements for leaving nothing to my children from whatever I have saved and have willed it for public use.

Appendix 1

Chagla-Morarji Correspondence

Letter from Shri M. C. Chagla

10th October, 1950

My dear Morarji,

I was very much touched by your letter and I hasten to reply to it in the spirit in which you wrote to me.

I have told you in private and I have stated it in public that one of the most cheering aspects of my work as Chief Justice has been my association with you. We may have sometimes differed but I have always appreciated your point of view—the more so as I have always felt that your decision has never been coloured by the slightest suggestion of communalism or nepotism.

But I have been noticing recently a growing feeling in Government circles—you may not be sharing it—that the High Court is a sort of third chamber and is out to throw out Government and so its powers should be curbed. This uneasy feeling receives some justification by some incidents that have recently taken place.

In my letter to the Chief Minister, I have referred to the manner in which the High Court was completely ignored when it was deprived of its jurisdiction in Charity Suits by a legislative fiat. Why do you blame me if I feel a little sore ? As I have always said the power is yours, you have the right to take the final decision—but at least consult us, hear what we have to say and then come to your own conclusion.

We are all pledged to a democratic secular state—and I agree with you that to be truly democratic and secular is the most difficult thing in the context of present times. I have often felt that you have not availed yourself of my services not as Chief Justice but as a friend and as a lover of our country in the course that you and I both have at heart. After all, why are we working day and night suffering heartaches and headaches, were it not for the fact that we hold the belief that our work will not be wholly wasted and that, when we defend our country, will be a little better and stronger than when we started our labours.

I violently differ from you in your outlook on life and with some of your views. You will concede to me the right to do so. But I have the greatest admiration for your fundamental integrity and honesty of purpose. We both have the same goal in view. We may try to appreciate it by different ways. But so long as we love our country passionately and desire her well being, there ought to be an unseverable bond between us.

Yours ever,
M. C. Chagla

Letter from Shri M. C. Chagla

25th November, 1950

My dear Morarji,

Your letter came to me as a painful surprise. But I am glad you have written this letter becuase it clearly shows how much you dislike my being in the position that I am in, and how much you would have preferred a more docile and tractable Chief Justice. I am sorry you have got to put up with me but perhaps you will be able to do so better if we understand each other, and so I proposed to write to you with the utmost frankness—even at the risk of making you more angry than you obviously were when you wrote the letter.

I should have thought that the Director of Publicity has more important things to do than to scrutinise every utterance of the Chief Justice in order to find out whether he has said anything against Government which should be brought to the notice of his employers. May I humbly suggest that he should spend a little more time in elucidating the law to the citizens, so that they should know what their duties and obligations are—a subject about which many are woefully ignorant.

After reading your letter I have definitely come to the conclusion to which I was being driven more and more every day that the Government of Bombay do not relish any criticism—so much so that they cannot tolerate even a humorous remark. Government possess the monopoly of wisdom, statesmanship and patriotism and anyone who differs from them is either a fool or a knave. You do not realise how independent thinking is fast disappearing from Government officials. Several of them have told me that they dare not express their honest opinion because if they did so they would immediately lose their jobs. If you resent the humorous remarks of the Chief Justice what would you do, I wonder, if they had been uttered by someone who was subordinate to you. We have the recent example of Dr. Phadker of Poona who had to resign because he had the temerity to criticise your prohibition policy. If you really believe in democracy you should welcome men like Dr. Phadker. As it is you get furiously angry if someone even makes a joke about Government—so angry that you do not even realise that it is a joke.

I have never been in the habit of considering, when I speak on a subject, whether my remarks are going to please or displease anyone. I did not acquire that habit under the British Government. I do not propose to acquire it under our own Government.

I do not think you even know how Governments are criticised in England. A Chief Justice of England in recent times wrote a book called 'The New Despotism.' I strongly recommend it to you. I do not think the Home Secretary wrote a rude letter about it to the Chief Justice. The British Government have been governing democratically for centuries. They respect criticism and welcome it. Because they know that they are not infallible and they want to know and understand public opinion so that they should correct their mistakes and make their rule acceptable to all sections of the people.

I wonder whether you found only the two sentences you have quoted from my speech of any substance. I suppose the rest of it was not worthy of the consideration of the Director of Publicity and of yourself. I am sure anyone who is not violently biased would see the humour of these two sentences. I was merely pointing out that laws are being passed sometimes too quickly and on too many subjects and the public have no time to digest them. In several addresses presented to me by the Bar Association pointed attention has been drawn to this aspect of legislation. I would also like you to study the recent rules published in the Gazette under the Prohibition Act. Do you seriously think that any citizen can or does understand what the law is ?

In season and out of season I have been preaching respect for the law. You have never shown any appreciation of what I have been trying to do for the establishment of the rule of law. I do not expect it nor do I want it. But it comes with an ill grace from you when you sarcastically insinuate that I break the law or keep company with those who do so. I admit I do not mix with saints or supermen. My friends are fallible and full of human frailty and weakness. But they are a thousand times better than those who don the garb of unblemished virtue and have neither understanding nor tolerance.

You have asked me how I would like propaganda against myself. Well, I have never descended to a personal level in any public utterance. Unbeknown to you I have stood up for you against your detractors—and they are many—in private. I have always expressed my admiration for your integrity and sincerity of purpose. I hope I shall have the strength and charity to tolerate any propaganda that Government may start against me. If I don't then I shall be unworthy of being considered as possessing a democratic spirit.

You say you are apprehensive about the future. So am I. I love my country with the same intensity and fervour as anyone else. And I am seeing tendencies which, if not checked, will lead us to unbridled dictatorship. You and I don't count. Our vanity, our amour-propre, our sensitiveness are nothing compared to the future destiny of our people. In Heaven's name let us not do anything which may deflect that destiny into channels unworthy of a great nation.

Yours sincerely,
M.C. Chagla

P.S.: I have typed this letter myself so that no one should see it. You did not show me even that courtesy.

Letter from Shri Morarji Desai

Bombay
26th November, 1950

My dear Chagla,

I thank you for your reply of the 25th. When you have seen anger and dislike of your independence in my letter instead of pain on account of misrepresentation from a friend, I can imagine how angry you are with me and what prejudices you have regarding our policies.

I wish you had not been so unnecessarily hard on the poor Director of Publicity who only did his duty. He was present at the meeting and he saw the effect of your remarks which you say you made in humour. I readily believe that your intention was to be humorous but was it not prompted by prejudice and a dislike of our policies?

When you say that this Government does not like any criticism, are you quite fair to us? This Government has never considered itself to have possessed a monopoly of all wisdom, statesmanship and patriotism and we have never considered anyone who differs from us either a fool or a knave. The freedom and impunity with which criticism and allegations are made against us in press and on platform would be a standing and clear testimony to our regard for liberty of expression and criticism in the eyes of any impartial or unprejudiced observer. You have made several assumptions one of which is that independent thinking is fast disappearing from Government officials. If you had seen the files in the secretariat and reports from officials you could never have made this unwarranted assertion. If you were present at the discussions we have with our officers you would never have carried this prejudice. This only shows how much credence you give to the stories you hear from the people who see you and talk to you against us.

You have quoted the example of Dr. Phadke. It was Dr. Phadke and not Dr. Phadker. Have you cared to inquire about the incident as it took place. As far as I know the facts, this gentleman stood up to propose a vote of thanks and gave a *homily* on birth-control and the failure of Government in this direction. It was a wrong advantage that he took of the occasion. This was not a subject for the occasion at all and a vote of thanks cannot be made an occasion for such a lengthy criticism to which the Government has no chance to reply. Dr. Gilder who was the guest of the institute pointed out the unfairness to the persons who had invited him and they asked Dr. Phadke to express his regret for the discourtesy shown by him in spite of a warning to him by his colleagues. The most painful part of your criticism in this respect is that you have coupled Dr. Phadke's criticism with prohibition. This shows how readily you believe what the press writes against Governmnent and how the prohibition policy of Government has irritated you against us.

Please don't think that I am not able even to see a joke because it makes me terribly angry. A joke would be appropriate in its proper place. It would be disastrous if made at a wrong place and with respect to an unsuitable incident. It should not have been necessary for me to point out this difference. I do not know what you did under the British Government but I do know that you did not criticise their actions in public meetings half as frequently and sharply as you do now.

I am surprised that you consider my letter rude. Will you please point out the rudeness so that I can make amends for it ? If you consider what I have written to you as a friend as rude, it will be difficult for me to point out to you frankly even in a personal letter what I considered harmful for the future of this state. It is possible you consider me wrong in my understanding but was that a justification for the attack that you have made on my supposed intolerance and want of appreciation of humour and civil liberties ? Would you not allow me to convey to you my apprehensions without making you angry ? Is this your idea of toleration, broad-mindedness and friendship ? You wrote to me yourself last time that I have not availed myself of your service not as a C. J. but as a friend and as a lover of our country in the same cause which both of us have at heart too, and yet when I try to draw your attention to the effect your remarks would have on the public mind, you fly into a rage and attribute to me an intolerant mind and a desire to have a very docile Chief Justice. This only shows how prejudiced you have been against me and my colleagues ever since the prohibition policy was finalised and brought into effect. I know you have differed from us violently in this matter but I had no conception that your annoyance would go to this length.

You have cited to me the English parallel. May I also request you to consider the English conventions which the judges there observe ? Even though they are members of clubs, they seldom go there and never take part in meetings which would by any means land them into a controversy. I do not think either in England or America or in any democratic country they have been able to make their rule acceptable to all sections of the people. This would be a fact impossible of accomplishment by any party consisting of human beings.

Is it fair for you to assume that I did not find the rest of your speech of any substance because I mentioned only the two objectionable sentences ? Would it have made a difference if I had mentioned that the rest of the speech was not only without objection but was also instructive ?

I know you have emphasised respect for law but have you ever publicly stated that this Government is trying to do everything that it can according to its capacity to establish a rule of law as it should be in a democracy. On the contrary, has not your criticism in public given support to the criticism of some sections of the public and the press that we are not mindful of civil liberties and the principles of democracy ?

I am very grateful for your defending me against my critics and for your admiration for my integrity and sincerity of purpose. How does this fit in with your contempt for those who don the garb of unblemished virtue and have neither understanding nor tolerance—by which I suppose you refer to me and to people like me ? I make this inference from the context of the reference.

There was no sarcastic insinuation in my reference to the breaking of law. The reference to the unavoidability of breaking some rule of law under the existing Government in your speech could have either come from personal experience or experience of people whom you know well. How was I otherwise to explain your sweeping statement ? You explain it by saying that it was a joke. Was it not a sarcasm ? Would it not expose the Government to ridicule coming as it did from the C.J.? Would you not allow me even the friendly privilege of letting you know how I was hurt by your sarcasm ? May I request you to consider whether you have not become intolerant of my views and have taken consequently a very uncharitable view of my reactions to your public criticism ? Would I be unreasonable if I expect the Chief Justice to be very tolerant and balanced towards frailties of people like myself who, though lacking understanding and tolerance, still possess sincerity of purpose and integrity in your view ? Is not more expected of the Chief Justice in such matters ?

You hope that you will have the strength and charity to tolerate any propaganda that Government may start against you. But have you shown this towards the criticism that I have made in my letter to you as a friend ? When I asked you in my letter how you would feel if those whom you chide publicly did the same to you, you seem to conclude that it is going to be done. I have not done anything of that nature so far and have tried to prevent others from doing it wherever possible. If you ask any member of the press who comes to my conferences, you will be easily convinced about the truth of what I have said. I posed the above question only in order that you may make a comparison and realise my feelings. I always pray to the Almighty that He in His kindness and forgiveness may save me from any attempt of retaliation in any matter, whatsoever may be the provocation.

If dictatorship overtakes this country in my lifetime, I shall not be in the seat of Government but am sure to suffer terribly and even lose my head in an attempt to fight the dictatorship with whatever little strength of purpose God may have given me.

I am very sorry I had to get the letter typed because I do not know typing. I shall not commit the mistake again and apologise to you for the discourtesy that has been felt by you as a result. I hope you will forgive me for this.

Your letter has made me so unhappy and apprehensive that I do not know whether in future, I should let you know my feelings if such occasions arise in future. I consider it very essential that I shall give no offence to or irritate the head of the Judiciary as cordial relations between the Executive and Judiciary are vital in the interest of a democratic State which both you and I want to build up. I shall be very grateful if I receive a frank guidance from you in this respect.

Yours sincerely,
Morarji Desai

Letter from Shri M. C. Chagla

27the November, 1950

My dear Morarji,

I thank you for your letter of 26th November.

I can assure you that I will never resent any criticism of my action offered by you as a friend. My resentment proceeded from the tone of your letter and from the fact that it seemed to be written officially as a Minister of the Government of Bombay and not as a friend. May I suggest that in future we should talk over our differences ? You know how welcome you are to come over to my place. Things look very different in black and white than when they take the form of the spoken word. One has the line, the love and the gesture to go by. In cold print there is no guidance except the words themselves.

I am as anxious as you are that cordial relations should be maintained between the Judiciary and the Executive and also that our personal relations should not be impaired by our differences in outlook or policy.

I do not write to recover the ground which I have already done in my last letter but there are two or three points raised in your letter which require a reply.

(1) In writing about Dr. Phadker I went by newspaper reports. I had no other sources to go by.

(2) It is very unfair to me to suggest that I have been prejudiced against you and your colleagues since prohibition was launched. You are attributing to me petty-mindedness of which I hope I am not guilty. I have made no secret of the fact that I differ from you with regard to that policy. I think it is a mistake, that it will do harm to public interest and that ultimately it will fail but only after causing a great deal of irreparable damage. But I do possess a sense of *proportion.* I realise and I try to make others realise that after all prohibition is one item in the programme of Government and Government cannot be judged only by that item. I have always given expression to my view that our Government is the best of all Governments in India and we should consider ourselves proud and happy to be living in the State of Bombay.

(3) With regard to the convention observed by the English

judges you are not justified in having a fling at me about going to clubs. The private life of a judge is his own and everyone in England respects it. It is entirely incorrect to say that judges do not visit clubs. Some like to go to clubs and do so. Others do not and accordingly are not clubmen. I agree that they do not take part in meetings which raise controversies. Have I ever attended a political meeting or spoken on a controversial subject ? Have you ever known me say anything about prohibition ? If you only know how many invitations I declined to speak at meetings because I feel that the subject might be even remotely controversial. Of course I do speak on questions affecting the administration of justice and I will continue doing so. That is not only my right but my duty and in doing so I am following the highest traditions. I also cannot forget that besides being a judge I am also a citizen interested in the welfare of my country—and so I am deeply interested in educational, social and cultural matters.

(4) It is not correct that I have never publicly praised Government for anything it has done for the establishment of the rule of law. Wherever I have replied to Bar addresses I have told them what you have been doing for the separation of the Executive from the Judiciary. It is true I have also criticised you. But it has not been all criticism.

(5) You say that I criticise our Government more again and more strongly than I ever had the British Government. Surely you know that that is not correct nor is it taking a fair and impartial view of my past record. My public life before I came to the bench is an open book and I think I can proudly say that I always was a consistent and continuous critic of the policy of the British Government.

One happy result of this unfortunate and rather acrimonious correspondence has been that it has emphasised the fact that both of us—however much we may differ as to the means—are agreed in our belief in democracy and our hatred for dictatorship. So long as that basis remains we will always be friends, and I shall continue to have for you the same regard which I have always had ever since we came into contact with each other.

Yours sincerely,
M. C. Chagla

P.S. Please forgive the handwriting. I had no time to type this letter.

Appendix 2

A Note on Discussions held at Shri Ram Nivas Ruia's Residence on 11th December, 1952

Among those present on the occasion were :

Myself, Chief Justice, M.C.S., Secy., H.D., Pranlal D. Nanji, Dharamsey Khatau, Navin Chandra, Motilal Tapuria, Chimanlal Parikh, Collector of Customs and Commissioner of Income-tax.

I reached the place at about 8.05 p.m. Others were there from about 7.30 p.m.

We sat down to dinner at about 8.30 p.m. and finished it at about 9.15 p.m. I was sitting all the while with the Chief Justice. Until about 9.30 p.m. C.J. and I had a very friendly chat on general topics.

At about 9.30 p.m. Pranlal started a discussion as regards the condemnation of businessmen as dishonest generally by Ministers. I told him that we in Bombay had never done any general condemnation and that he need not be worried as the criticism applied only to those businessmen who were dishonest. But he would not give up his complaint and blamed Government for not putting down corruption in administration. I told him that Government's task became very difficult as people readily gave bribes and were not prepared to give information to Government and help them in punishing corrupt officials. Pranlal said that people had to suffer losses if they did not get work done by paying bribes.

The C. J. joined in this criticism and added that controls created corruption. I then told him that controls became necessary as there was general corruption in society. It can only be said that existence of controls did not help in removing corruption. The C. J. did not quarrel with this but persisted in his general argument against administration regarding corruption. He gave us an instance that it was not possible to get a flat without giving a *pugree.* I told him that the statement was not quite correct as I know of many instances when people got flats, without giving a *pugree*, directly or through Government. He would not accept this and said that he knew better because people talked to him more frankly and not to me. I then told him that the C. J. could never be in touch with public opinion as he could not meet people as freely as we could but he persisted in his argument. I then told him that the *pugree* evil was fairly successfully tackled but the decision of the High Court that first informers should not be given flats about which they give information, made Government work difficult and the present position had arisen. He got angry and began to discuss the decision. I said that that was not the place for such a discussion and that it could best be done when we were alone. He would not however take the hint and became more vehement in his criticism. I then told him that if he felt that we were working wrongly or inefficiently, he should give up his safe position and get into politics and try to get in charge of Government so that he could show how Government could be run better. He said that he knew that and that he might one day take that step. Then he attacked those in Government by saying that power corrupts and makes people intolerant and that there should not be intolerance. As he harped more on power corrupting, I told him that it is not only those who are on the executive side who have power. The Judiciary also has power and whereas the executive power has checks and is responsible to several quarters, the judiciary has no check and holds irresponsible power. This enraged him and he said I called the High Court irresponsible. I told him that that was a wrong interpretation as we were discussing the kind of power and its effects. He was therefore unfair in his inference. He then got excited and told the businessmen that it is because of this that he has been advising friends to get power as that was the only remedy in a democracy and agreed that power was in the hands of voters. I agreed immediately that that is the only democratic method. But if the voters had given power to one party, it cannot hand it over to others because they want it. All who are dissatisfied with Government should contest elections on definite issues and try to change the Government according to their rights for the elections were very free in this country as demonstrated in the last elections. The C. J. said it was good that the High Court had powers and I told him that it was the Congress Party who framed the constitution and gave these powers to the High Court.

During the course of the discussion the C. J. defended people who had to give bribes because they were helpless against corrupt officials and even stated that if a man in dire need committed a crime, he would consider it justifiable and would publicly say so. I said that this was a very strange attitude for the C. J. to adopt.

Pranlal D. Nanji and Chimanlal Parikh very cleverly tried to encourage the C.J. in this discussion and the C.J. went all out in his severe criticism of those in authority.

20.12.52 M. R. DESAI

Appendix 3

Discussion with Vinobaji

Shri Narayan Desai had given me a note of the discussion which I had with Acharya Vinobaji in May 1955. *Shri Narayan Desai is the only son of the late Shri Mahadev Desai. He passed his whole life in Bapu's contact as long as the latter was alive. He received his education also under his guidance, and has imbibed the spirit of Mahadev Desai and Gandhiji very well. He has devoted his whole life to the service of the people and works with Vinobaji in the field of sarvodaya. As his note has been very well drawn up, I am giving it as recorded by him, so that the readers can have a correct idea about our discussion and also about my views on some of the problems. Our discussion went on the* 7, 8 *and* 10 *May* 1955. *The whole discussion was in Hindi except once when Khandubhai Desai also joined in our discussion, when we spoke in Gujarati for about* 4 *or* 5 *minutes.*

7.5.1955

VINOBA : Are we not meeting after a long time ?

MORARJI : It is so. We have not been able to meet until today after I met you in Bombay.

VINOBA : I could meet Pantji also after I had toured UP for seven months. It happens like the stars in the sky, that is, it happens when it has to happen.

MORARJI : If you had come to Bombay I would have met you often. You are, however, touring far away. I have discussions sometimes with Ravi Shanker Maharaj, Narayan Desai and others. I saw Maharaj after he returned from Puri. He will also now move on foot and it will be difficult therefore to meet him.

VINOBA : I believe he is now 60 years old.

MORARJI : Yes, that is so, and he will move on foot for two and a half years.

VINOBA : The life of hikers gets lengthened.

MORARJI : I do not believe any life can be lengthened.

VINOBA : I sometimes say humorously that one who walks cannot be caught up by the God of death from behind.

MORARJI : I believe firmly that nobody can live for a moment more than the span fixed for him.

VINOBA: My mother had given me a stratagem for life. It helps man certainly to keep control over himself. She told me that it is decided for every person how many times he has to take food. If therefore one eats only once a day he can live twice the span fixed for him.

MORARJI : The control or self-restraint which is exercised without understanding its true meaning, does not last.

VINOBA : But the helpless world requires some support.

MORARJI : Man should never despair and should have confidence in himself. One may take help when one is shaken up, but it is not useful to take help from the very beginning. Vows are also in the same category. Every man can derive strength from vows but it will be better if one can do without them.

VINOBA : A vow is not always the resort of the weak. Bapu was a great believer in vows and there can be no question of weakness in his case. Vows decide and fix our path.

MORARJI : Vows are certainly useful, but a great difficulty is encountered when one has to be broken. When a man deceives himself in order to break a vow, he suffers a great deal of harm.

VINOBA : Bhagwan Manu has suggested a very fine way. He said that vows should be taken for the most important matters, but for smaller things one should only have rules.

MORARJI : There is a danger of self-deceit in taking such vows. One has to find one's own way. If a vow is taken at the instance of others, it becomes harmful. If one proclaims one's determination, one is saved from breaking it. It is therefore good to declare one's determination, but one should not declare it in order to be praised by some people. A man can save himself if he is careful. Where he is not able to decide himself, he may act according to the advice of the person in whom he has faith. But one should not get anything done by anybody out of regard or respect. This also comes in the way of one's development, for if he cannot abide by what you tell him, you will feel that he does not have faith in you.

VINOBA : This is quite true. It is not a sign of freedom or independence to make somebody do something as one desires.

MORARJI : Such an atmosphere cannot be created without democracy. Some people are arguing that democracy is not helpful in eradicating poverty quickly and one should therefore resort to dictatorship. But if democracy disappears in this country we shall all be destroyed. There is fear in this country but the people will be far more fearful under a dictatorship. Fear is the most degrading thing for man. It is very important to save man from fear. As long as somebody is afraid of me, I am bound to be afraid of somebody else.

VINOBA : Bapu made the fullest effort to see that nobody was afraid of him.

MORARJI : The country would not have come up to this position if Bapu had not been there. It is also due to the effort of Bapu that democracy functions in this country. He always maintained democratic functioning in the Congress. Our strength will be increased only if we continue to tread on that path. If we do something else merely in order to get quicker or better results, we shall be greatly harmed. While we are on this subject, I should like to mention some things about myself in the very beginning. One of my delusions was removed as a result of the 1952 elections. My defeat subjected me to one punishment, not the punishment of defeat but the delusion, that I would be able to be free from ministership and go my own way to serve people, was removed. I have never started any activity to get anything and I have never tried to avoid any responsibility that has come my way. I had thought that after the elections I would be able to take up work of my choice if I was defeated. This was a delusion. The events that followed the election removed that delusion. I realised that I had to do the work which was in store for me.

Balasaheb said that he would not contest the elections of 1952. Shri Shanker Rao Deo had charged him with being untrue to the people. Balasaheb took it ill and took it to heart. He therefore decided not to stand for elections and pressed me to take his place. There was a question of how to solve the difficulties inherent in the composite state of 4 divisions—Bombay, Maharashtra, Gujarat and Karnatak. It is a difficult task to run a government, especially for one who wants to realise his soul or realise truth. There has always been a belief that one can resort to lies in running a government. This is how all governments have been conducted so far. This was also the view in the times of Mahabharata. Bapu showed the new way. Bapu demonstrated that truth must be practised in every field and every moment of life. This can be realised only when those, who believe that truth must be practised in running governments, undertake the responsibility of running governments. It will not do to run away from the responsibility of government, but one must constantly be careful to see whether truth is observed in everything that one does. One has to rely to a smaller or larger extent on colleagues and members of the administration in running a government. If those people resort to untruth, I have to be guilty of untruth when I rely on them. I had therefore thought twice or thrice within myself that I should be saved from such a contingency if I was defeated in the elections. I have made a rule in life for years that I must not run away from a task which comes to me from God. I, however, thought of running away from it by wishing to be defeated. As I thought of being wiser than God I was defeated. If the counting of the votes had been done once again I was sure I would have won, but I gave up that idea deliberately. I could not save myself from joining the government even after being defeated.

Balasaheb sent me word that I must not make any statement when I got the news of defeat. When I discussed the matter with him, he told me that I could not give up getting into the government. I told him that the people did not want me. When he said that it would not be possible to do without me, I answered that the government would have gone on if I was dead. He then said that as long as I was alive I had to do the work. Then he asked me to suggest some other person who would do the work as well in my place. I could not honestly suggest an alternative. There was a greater pressure for me to continue in the government from Maharashtra. I consulted Shri Nathji and Kishorelalbhai. Both of them gave me the same advice. Balasaheb then promised me that I should undertake the responsibility only if the Congress Working Committee asked me to do so and not merely at his instance. I then asked him not to suggest it to the Working Committee. If they themselves suggested it I shall certainly act on it. I, however, received a letter immediately from Jawaharlalji that I must get into government without any other consideration. The Working Committee took the same decision and I had to take the responsibility. This removed also my pride or vanity, gave me humility and increased my capacity to some extent. I had to hear taunts every day that I was a defeated Chief Minister, which gave me some humility. I had made a condition that I would not undertake the responsibility if there was opposition even from one member of the Congress Party of the newly-elected legislature, but all of them unanimously elected me. I even said that if my view differed from the view of all the other members of the party they would have to abide by my decision. If they did not do so, I will give up the leadership. They gladly accepted the condition.

Let usconsider your suggestion that everything should be

decided unanimously. This is how we conduct party affairs, but it is not possible always to get the consent of the opposition. We should certainly have such an attitude towards the opposition that they would not consider us as their enemy and we do not consider them as enemies. This certainly gives good results because we gain everybody's goodwill. It is therefore that the work of the Bombay Legislative Party goes on smoothly.

VINOBA : In spite of Bombay being a mixed State ?

MORARJI : That is so. This question arose when I formed the Ministry. I had insisted that the Ministry must be so formed that it worked with cohesion. We decided after a great deal of thought and consultation that there should be 4 Maharashtrians, 3 Gujaratis, 1 from Karnatak and 1 from Bombay. If I fixed a larger number the question would arise of taking Muslims and other persons also and similar other questions would have arisen. I had taken the consent of all concerned for this number. I had also discussed the names with others and with the Presidents of the Pradesh Congress Committees. As Kanjibhai and myself were of the same view in most matters, his agreement was there. Shri S. K. Patil wanted me to take some other person from Bombay, but when I said no, he himself agreed that the name suggested by me was better than that suggested by him.

Shri Hiray agreed with me as regards two names out of the 4 which I suggested from Maharashtra. He did not agree to the names of Nimbalkar and Tapase. He wanted two persons who would support him. I then told him that that was not possible. Nimbalkar was a fine man. We had to take somebody from the State area when it merged and Shri Nimbalkar had transferred to the Bombay Government, when the State was merged, 40 lakhs of rupees. He used to conduct the government in his State very well. When I asked him to join the government, he said no. As he had spent Rs. 8 lakhs on agriculture after the merger of the State he could not suffer that loss. I then told him that his sons would look after the agriculture. Ultimately, he gave up all these interests and joined the government. How could I give him up now ? He would not do whatever Hiray would ask him to do and he did not believe in distinctions between Brahmins and non-Brahmins. The same consideration was there about Tapase. We had to take somebody from the Harijans, Muslims and Christians, and there was no better man than Tapase for this purpose. Hiray then told me that he would not join, and this is how he created difficulties in the formation of the Ministry.

He approached Jawaharlalji. I told him that he could tell Jawaharlalji in my presence whatever he had to tell him. I would not be able to work with a person who would have great dissatisfaction about me. Hiray did not agree to the names that I had given him.

This happened on a Sunday. I had to give the names to the Governor on Monday. I had asked Shri Yashwantrao Chavan as to what would be his attitude if Shri Hiray did not join. He expressed his readiness to join the Cabinet, but he asked me to advise him. I told him that if he agreed with Hiray he should follow him, but if he did not agree with him he should certainly join the Cabinet. I would have no objection if even after agreeing with me he did not join. I would not be unhappy if I failed. But the question of his whole life was before him. He should therefore decide for himself. He took no time and decided immediately and said he would join me. I then asked Hiray to join the Cabinet and see by experience whether he could work well. If he felt any injustice being done, he could resign. I satisfied him about the portfolio to be given to him and told him that I would give him the work according to his capacity.

Shri M. P. Patil wanted that I must take three men from Karnatak in the Ministry. I could not take more than one. I told him that if he wanted to join he may do so, otherwise he may not. But he agreed in the evening. After we started working together there was no trouble. There was only a dispute about the question of Dangs but we had no discussion about it. The States Reorganisation Commission was to decide it.

I know that you are in favour of the formation of linguistic states. But Bombay State is better as it is at present. It avoids weaknesses. If it is divided into linguistic portions it would create regionalism. The good reputation which Bombay has today will be destroyed. It will have adverse effect on the whole country. Bombay has a very high standard of public life and it has a good effect on the other states. We have to undertake large responsibilities. If Bombay State is united, it would have a better credibility and one can get more resources. This is what we experience today. We have more resources even than UP. Some people think that more work will be done if there is a separation in the different parts of Bombay, but that is not correct. I did not like even the appointment of the States Reorganisation Commission, and did not also appreciate the formation of a separate Andhra

State. Everything, however, happens according to God's law. When Bapu could not stop partition and the formation of Pakistan, even though he opposed it till the last moment, who are we in such matters ? If Bombay State is divided, it will not make me unhappy. We have fared well so far by God's Grace.

I wanted to talk with you on many subjects besides bhoodan. It is therefore that I have explained to you my viewpoint, so that you can understand me correctly.

VINOBA : I did not know until now all that you have told me now.

MORARJI : If I had met you before, I would have told you all this earlier. The attitude that I adopted had a good result. I told Panditji that he had made an exception in my case in respect of nominating the defeated persons for ministerships and people would charge him with partiality. But he told me that if I did not continue in the government everything would be damaged, and I must do my level best in the task that I had taken up. I then told myself that I must go on doing what God wanted me to do. That is the only way I could gather more strength. But when you say that I must work by taking the assent of all parties, it appears to me an impossible proposition.

A society without government may appear theoretically correct, but is impossible in actual life. Only God can be perfect. I do believe that government should govern less and less. We cannot acquire strength by remaining in the government and we have to increase our capacity. Where there is no capacity, it requires a government to remove the weaknesses. In a welfare state, the government functions not for exercising power but for rendering service. One should therefore be a public servant and not an officer or a master. This too is not very easy. It is impossible to do without government altogether. There should be more and more decentralisation of power. The states should have less functions and power, by delegating more and more powers to gram panchayats, local bodies, municipalities, etc. No village will remain without a gram panchayat after two or three years. Our elections are very expensive and result in corruption and dishonesty. It is a very important question as to how to save ourselves from this evil. One of the methods is to take votes by collecting the people in a meeting and asking them to vote by raising their hands. There is a danger lurking in this method too. The unsocial elements can influence such direct elections very adversely. As long as the people do not develop capacity to save themselves from such unsocial elements, government cannot accomplish it. It can happen only when everybody becomes so strong that society can become free from wrong action. As we could not establish panchayats in small villages, we have arranged for a common panchayat for a few villages. We are at present giving a grant of 15 per cent of the land revenue to village panchayats. We shall increase it to 30 per cent and will give more as it becomes necessary to do so. We will get more and more work done through them. There are other methods also of transferring power to the lower levels, such as development projects, labour institutions, forest societies, etc. There will be difficulties also in this arrangement, but we will have to face them and solve them.

We cannot take the cooperation of those who come in the way of achieving cooperation with all and want to destroy that system. I have decided myself not to resort to untruth in running the administration. We have to censor the posts of some people. Somebody asked me a question whether we are censoring some post, and I immediately admitted it. I can reduce this censoring to a minimum and if I am asked about it I shall not deny it. I am also asking my officers and the police not to speak an untruth, and warn them that I shall not excuse them if they practise untruth. But I will excuse honest errors or weakness. The method adopted by the police of using violence or beating people cannot be defended and I have told them so. I am happy and feel proud that nobody was beaten by the police in the investigation of Bapu's murder case. There cannot be as much strength in untruth as there is in truth. All do not agree with this, but have sympathy for my insistence. The police do not play hide and seek with me, that is, they do not conceal anything from me. If they do so, I would feel that they were afraid of me. I consider it my fault if anybody was afraid of telling me the truth. I cannot say that I have succeeded fully in this effort, nor can I claim it about my colleagues. My colleagues also try to save themselves from wrong actions and it has its good results. The results may come in slowly, but they do come in. I do not think many think on these lines. The Gita also says that most of the people do not think about truth. Very few think about it and out of those who think about it and practise it, very few succeed. It is our task to persuade all people to think on these lines. There is a good standard of public life in Bombay, but the credit does not go to me. It is because the people cooperate. The police cannot achieve everything. The people at the top must improve themselves. The Gita has said that the ordinary people follow or imitate the actions of those at the top. The main work therefore is that of making improvements at the top. If ministers, lawyers and doctors behave better, it will have an effect on everybody. It is in this direction that I am making my efforts. But how is one to cooperate with those who do not believe in truth ? I cannot say that all in the Congress believe in truth. I cannot therefore work in cooperation with those who do not believe in truth.

Mridulaben had once asked me why I did not cooperate with members of the socialist group. I told her that they believed in untruth and some of them believed that the Marxist way would serve the country better. Jayaprakashji at that time was a Marxist and believed that Gandhism was inimical to socialism. Everybody in the socialist group is a leader and there is hardly any discipline. The Congress has believed in discipline. How can I therefore work with those who do not believe in discipline and truth ? A complaint was made to Bapu in this connection. I had then told Bapu that I could not work with those who did not believe in these ideals. Bapu also approved of my attitude, and this is how I work even today.

Our discussions remained unfinished on account of prayer time. They were continued after the prayers.

VINOBA : There is hardly any difference of opinion in what you have said about the absence of government. I am agreeable that there should be no impediment in the welfare work of the people, that the states should function less and less and the people govern themselves more and more. The extreme statement of total absence of government resembles the proposition in geometry by some that two parallel lines never meet, or by others that they do meet at infinity, making an angle at $0°$. It is only a difference in expression when you say that there cannot be a society without government and when I say that it can be done. When some people said that there should be a society without government, I corrected them and told them that it will not be a society without government, but a society free from government. But this is an ideal position and one need not go into a controversy about it. There is very little difference of opinion in the other things that you have said. You tell me that it is difficult to work with those who do not believe in non-violence and that one can hope to change those who believe in non-violence. But as I said in today's prayers, a change can be made in anybody if we have faith in humanity. It so happens that sometimes those who claim to be truthful have no faith in it, while those who deny it are more truthful. One should therefore settle these things by experience. It is my experience that everybody tells me whatever he really feels. Jayaprakash tells me everything. The Congress leaders also talk to me frankly. It is therefore that I feel that some programmes can be worked together. By doing so we will get used to work together and distrust will lessen. If people can work without a party view and keep only the moral view before them, many things can be accomplished by mutual adjustment. I, however, agree on the whole with whatever you have told me.

MORARJI : It will not be proper if we trust somebody about whom we are sure that he is a liar. One can believe such people once, but not again and again.

VINOBA : This is a matter relating to the limitation of experience. A person who has remained a villain until today can improve tomorrow.

MORARJI : I agree. One who is an atheist can believe in God and the person who says that he believes in God may not have full faith. But it is not possible to have confidence in a person who does not want to believe in God.

VINOBA : Who can make him have a desire to believe ? But we should keep a possibility before our minds that he can be changed.

MORARJI : I agree. One should not have any dislike about such a person. I cannot claim that I am free from all prejudices or dislikes, but I am making an effort to get free from them. If I get a wrong idea, it is my own weakness. My conduct should be such that people should trust me. If people do not trust me, it only means that there is untruth in me. But it is very necessary to work with great care in such matters.

VINOBA : It is our duty to be careful. One should be careful both in his inside and outside behaviour. He only can pursue truth who is constantly careful, but to be suspicious is not a sign of carefulness.

MORARJI : Carefulness and suspicion are two quite separate matters.

VINOBA : I have derived knowledge from the same Guru from whom you have got it. How much difference can there therefore be between us ?

MORARJI : It can be only in some details. One can cultivate a truly humane attitude in all matters only by adopting Bapu's methods. It is one's duty to make an effort in that direction. If this effort is made by all adopting your way only, I do not think success can be achieved. It is only when administrators and men of religion work in cooperation that this can be achieved. Both are complementary to each other. People will worship you but they will imitate the rulers as they want to be like them. People approach a man of religion only for their conscience. If therefore both work together, it will have a healthy effect. The people will acquire truth only when the government functions truthfully. The reverse also is true as ultimately the representatives of the government come from the people and are chosen by them.

VINOBA : I too agree with these propositions. I would express it in another way. Governmental power may be represented by 0 and the people's power by the digit 1. But when both these come together it makes 10.

MORARJI : Such an expression or example might create a misunderstanding that government is of no use, and by such different expressions, a delusion is created that the governement does not belong to the people. I do not believe in dictatorship under any conditions. If somebody asked me to be a dictator, I would consider it a degradation for me. Even God has not kept all the power with Himself. The government also has to behave in the same manner, and this is our effort. One should go in the direction of perfection from imperfection, but everybody has not got this desire or aim in him. It is our duty to create this desire in everybody. If I do not behave accordingly, I would be devoid of religion. But if you preach every day freedom from the government, there will be contempt created against the government. One has therefore to be very careful in speaking about it.

VINOBA : Some people said there should be no government. I said there should be freedom from the government. The words used also therefore should be used carefully. There is a great difference between freedom from action and inaction.

MORARJI : Ordinary people do not understand these differences.

VINOBA : I think they understand. The people of India understand this more than the rest of the people in the world.

There is a greater understanding in our people. If your advice is that one should not talk of freedom from government, it would be against religion. I do believe that one should be very careful in this matter. If I err anywhere people tell me about it. People like me will go on talking about freedom from government.

MORARJI : You can certainly do so.

VINOBA : I am willing to persuade other people about this. If I did not believe in government today I would not have talked of the law of prohibition. I have not had any particular difference of opinion with you in this. But I must constantly keep before me the ideal, otherwise there will be great harm.

MORARJI : I do accept that position. Today you had asked for closing umbrellas during the prayer. I did close my umbrella at that time, but if there had been rain at that time I would have had to go away as I had no spare clothes with me then. I do not believe that God cannot be seen below the umbrella.

VINOBA : This only relates to a sense of humour.

MORARJI : Everybody is not endowed with it.

NARAYAN DESAI : Would you wish that others should not speak about freedom from the government ?

MORARJI : How can I prohibit others ?

NARAYAN DESAI : You should give a warning if there is want of care in somebody's referring to it.

MORARJI : I can give that warning if there is no danger of its being misunderstood. I am only careful to see for myself whether I have acted rightly or wrongly.

VINOBA : I have accepted the government even in prayers. Did I not refer to the story of the Marathas ?

MORARJI : You have also governed and that too in the name of government. (*Laughter.*)

VINOBA : I can ditto everything that you have said so far.

MORARJI : You have asked all people to do only bhoodan. This does not appear to me to be appropriate and it is not even possible. There can be no dispute about those who have faith in this work to be busy with this work or to do only that work, but who will do the other things that are to be done ?

VINOBA : As you apply all your energy to elections during election time, bhoodan also should be attended to for four months with all the energy that everybody can command.

MORARJI : I do not give up attending to other things even while attending to elections, and I was applying my capacity to other things also at the same time.

VINOBA : If that much capacity is applied to this work also there is no objection.

MORARJI : But in the Bombay State some people are asking members to resign from the Legislative Assembly. Deshpande resigns, Bhonsle resigns as MLA. This would necessitate bye-elections that would again involve expenditure. Bhonsle's constituency is such that there would be a dispute about

Karnatak and Maharashtra in that election. I would say that he can remain present for a day only in the Assembly and attend to bhoodan for the rest of the days.

VINOBA : These are two separate cases. One has donated his whole life and the other has not. But if he joins bhoodan, he has to observe the rules obtaining there.

VAJUBHAI SHAH : Can one claim that he has fulfilled his moral responsibility by attending the Assembly for a day and doing other work for the rest of the period.

MORARJI : Yes.

VINOBA : I do not agree. This may be a practice.

MORARJI : Jayaprakashji has donated his life to you. Why has he gone to Rangoon ?

VINOBA : Did he not go before he donated his life to me ?

MORARJI : I am referring to his going now.

VINOBA : I do not know about it. But if he has gone there I believe that he must be talking about bhoodan and sarvodaya there too.

MORARJI : Who can say anything about it ? But how can one accept the donation of life from the person whom I have referred to earlier. He is governed entirely be emotions. He married only three years ago and has children. How will he look after them ? I do not know. I had asked him what he would do if his wife did not agree with this donation. Then he began to evade the issue. There is a dispute between Maharashtra and Karnatak with reference to the Belgaum District. He (Shri Bhonsle) did not ask me But he must have given you some word when he came to you. This is therefore a dispute between religion and irreligion. You can please give your opinion. (This is about Bhonsle).

VINOBA : When he came, he came of his own accord. It is only a question of a year and a half. He can then leave it. There is no objection. If he leaves now it will create difficulty. I therefore asked him to help me.

MORARJI : I have told them clearly that I will not accept the resignations. If somebody wants to come to the Congress Party from another party, I would ask him to resign from that party and then join the Congress. I do not consider it proper that in Travancore-Cochin the Congressmen from Tamil Nadu were taken by them. One should not make any one a sanyasi without his being fully ready for it.

VINOBA : I have not appealed to anybody individually.

MORARJI : (I related the story of a sadhu in Parnera Hill near

Bulsar.) This is how one should test a person who wants to be a sanyasi.

VINOBA : You will also be tested.

MORARJI : Bapu had asked people to take vows. But hardly four or five out of the eighty persons who accompanied him to Dandi must have continued to observe those vows. Such cases lessen the ordinary man's faith in religion.

VINOBA : Whatever it may be, Bapu has made gold out of earth only with the help of such faith.

MORARJI : I agree with it entirely. How would I have the capacity that I have today without him. I have heard that you have a dissatisfaction about firing by the police in Bombay State. I shall therefore refer to it in some detail. There were riots once when I was Home Minister. Bapu then asked me to remove the military and the police from duty and asked me to sacrifice myself. He had also told me before ending his advice that ultimately I should act only according to my capacity. In his evening prayer also he said the same thing. I examined myself. I did not feel any joy in making a sacrifice in this manner. I did not feel that such a sacrifice would bring some solid good result. If I removed the police and the military, I would be killed. But after I was dead, the military would have acted in the same manner as they acted before. I therefore tried to go to the extent to which I could go according to my capacity. I suspended the operation of Section 144 CPC from the morning and toured the turbulent areas. Thousands of people met me. A stone was thrown at one place, but I disregarded it. This gave very great results. The tension in the atmosphere disappeared. I informed Bapu about all this afterwards. He told me that I had acted properly. Mavalankar went to the extent of asking Bapu why he had given such an advice to me. Bapu then asked me about it whether he had advised me wrongly. I asked Bapu why he was putting such a question to me. He explained why he was asking me. I replied: You had advised me correctly and you had trusted me also. If I did not act accordingly it was due to my weakness. I did not come to seek advice from you as I wanted it to be given for I could act only according to my capacity of non-violence. It is not my claim that I have acquired truth completely. If that had been so, all would have believed in me. The fact that some do not believe in me means that there must be some untruth in me.

VINOBA : Demonstrators have some limitations. They can act only within those limitations.

MORARJI : I should like to give you my view as regards your call for preventing cow-slaughter by legislation. There is a law in Bombay prohibiting the slaughter of useful and young animals. There is no prohibition against slaughter of old and useless animals. There are two difficulties in passing such a legislation. It is only the peasants who sell such animals. They know to whom they are selling them. If we can persuade them not to sell them, the task would be easier, otherwise it would be difficult. They would not look after old animals and would not keep them. If government undertakes to maintain such useless animals, it will have to incur a lot of expenditure which is not so very possible at present. When government cannot provide for old human beings today, how can it provide for old animals ? Peasants will let loose such animals if they are not allowed to sell them, and then these animals will do a lot of damage to crops which will lead to serious disputes. Will this lead to an implementation of religion ? If such animals are taken care of by government, such people will be encouraged and a very large area of land will have to be set apart for maintaining such asylums for cows. 60 to 70 per cent of the opposition members in the Assembly were against making such a legislation. I had explained this in a meeting at Jalgaon and they also accepted the position. I can give many arguments in this connection, but today I am referring only to some specific points. Just as a cow gives milk, a buffalo also gives milk. Other animals also would be included in the same category for being kind to animals. I had a peculiar experience at Godhra in Panchmahals. There the farmers used to let loose some of their animals which became so wild that they could not be controlled, and used to damage the crops a great deal.

VINOBA : The UP people must have perhaps thought of a remedy.

MORARJI : I do not think that they have any remedy, and how many people belonging to the RSS take only cow's milk ?

VINOBA : I am not referring to them. The committee which has been appointed by the government for legislation for cow protection has taken a unanimous decision in this matter.

MORARJI : This must have been done through popular fear.

VINOBA : That is not so. It is more important to consider that the recommendation is unanimous in Madhya Pradesh and in Kashmir.

MORARJI : There are a few cows in Kashmir. There is a law in Saurashtra against cow slaughter, but they migrate to Bombay and are even exported to Pakistan.

VINOBA : This is a very complicated subject and it relates to Indian culture. We need not discuss it today. We cannot put up with what happens in Calcutta even for a minute.

MORARJI : I know nothing about it.

VINOBA : I learnt about this from Miraben. There good cows are slaughtered. They are kept hungry for three days before they are slaughtered. All this is cruelty.

MORARJI : What can be said about such people and their decisions ? They keep even fish hungry for the whole day until they are eaten up.

VINOBA : These are matters to be tackled by all together, and we shall have to take both positive and negative actions. I am taking all the positive steps that I can.

8–5–1955

MORARJI : How can there be a government of all parties ?

VINOBA : It is a very wide subject. All the work at the lower levels must be done without party considerations and more and more powers should be vested with villages so that they are made very strong. The government would have only the power of planning, and the elections can be indirect.

MORARJI : I agree with this suggestion, but it is not practical today. This can be brought into effect only when panchayats are properly run.

VINOBA : Whatever can be implemented out of these propositions should be implemented today. The rest can be done later on. This idea does not belong to a mere bhoodan movement. I do not believe in the principle of working for the good of the greatest number which is based on a majority decision of 51 : 49.

MORARJI : Theoretically I would agree, but it will be difficult to put it into practice. Those who run the government must keep this in mind. People will go on saying that I am acting on the strength of the majority, but that should not in any way irritate or excite me, although those who are in power get easily excited or angry. I am in favour of basic education. At present it is run in such a manner that basic education costs more than ordinary education. I agree with you that education should not be with government. But how is government to give up its responsibility as long as society is not prepared to undertake the responsibility. We have left the running of colleges and secondary schools education to the people. For primary education we have set up school boards. There was, however, party spirit created even in this in Maharashtra. When Dinkerbhai became the Education Minister, he believed that we must give up education and leave it to people, but now he has changed his view. There is nothing but intrigue in universities. It will not be beneficial to think of democratic procedures in everything that we do.

KHANDUBHAI DESAI : There must be some direction by somebody. Whose will it be ?

MORARJI : Government will give directions and also finances.

KHANDUBHAI DESAI : There should be no regimentation or rigid control.

MORARJI : I agree.

KHANDUBHAI DESAI : That is a correct attitude.

MORARJI : I am requesting my friends in Saurashtra to launch this experiment. There is a saying in Gujarati that 'the successful are wise'. As long as no experiments are made for freeing education of government control, the problem will not be solved. When I am not able to make my colleagues agree what can I do with others ? I cannot force my opinion on others.

KHANDUBHAI DESAI : What should one do when there is a difference of opinion with a minister colleague ?

MORARJI : One has to make a compromise in such matters. But there can be no compromise in matters of principle.

VINOBA : One should not bring in principles in small matters.

KHANDUBHAI DESAI : I agree.

MORARJI : I have some experience about prohibition. A committee was formed for it. I then insisted that only those who believed in prohibition should be on that committee. Jawaharlalji did not like it. But I remained firm, and Jawaharlalji yielded. One has to remain firm about matters of principle.

VINOBA : It is believed that there can be a government of all parties under two conditions. This can happen in times of war and where no party gets a majority.

MORARJI : I do not like the other contingency, because in that arrangement unscrupulous people demand their price. I do not therefore like coalitions much. A government which is formed under duress cannot run well. One has to make compromises in Congress work. I had opposed one name publicly for an anti-corruption committee, as I considered the inclusion of that name a weakness. When I asked Panditji, he said, 'Set a thief to catch a thief.' But how can this be effective ? One cannot clean a room with a dirty broom.

DHEBARBHAI : There is something else which we have to discuss with Morarjibhai. There is much difference of opinion amongst the followers of Mahatma Gandhi as regards the setting up of a society without a government vis-a-vis democracy. It would be better therefore to discuss subjects relating to the programme for a society free from a government.

VINOBA : We have discussed it. This is a subject which, even if we discuss it by staying together for a few days, will not be complete. He has accepted one position that, considering the present conditions, the government should be reduced to a minimum, keeping in mind the welfare of the society. I asked what would be the end result. Will government remain or disappear? This is an academic discussion. We did not go deeper into that distinction. I had not praised either side of the question. You have now broached it. More power should be given to villages thus enabling them to look after their affairs themselves. Whatever may be your system, it can be properly executed only if the village people are ready to undertake the responsibility.

We have got some villages where we have got all the land in donation, as for example, Mangaroth. They are going to decide next year that they will not get any cloth from outside. As the government is agreeable, they can be helped in that matter. Otherwise, if the people are self-sufficient in the matter, there would be no obstacle in carrying out the project. We should on one side reduce the government's responsibility and, on the other, go on strengthening the villages.

MORARJI : I have no objection to this. Ultimately the government will remain in the villages. But we need not discuss this matter now. I, however, accept the proposition that sarvodaya is different from democracy. I do not believe merely in the majority of 51 : 49.

VINOBAJI : I shall recapitulate in short all that we have talked so far :

(1) Power to the lowest level.
(2) The people above should have only planning power.
(3) The people at the top should have moral strength, so that their advice would be accepted as an order.
(4) There would be no party working at the base. All discussions in gram panchayats should be unanimous.
(5) Elections should be indirect, so that the evils inherent in them are minimised.

We also considered one other matter besides this about coalition ministries. These take place during war or when there is no majority.

We are in a very difficult position today. It is not desirable to have more difficulties, and if, at this time, the people of different parties work together, would it not be right ? If there is no common programme intellectual dissensions will be created.

MORARJI : If all can talk with one voice, it will be good, but that will not happen. If all parties work together it will be good, but at present many of them do not believe in the purity of means. Also they do not have a proper picture for the future. We did consider the question of working together in villages, and we have also considered the same procedure for municipalities, but that did not seem to be possible. We even considered that Congress may not go to the municipalities. But what will be its result ?

VINOBA : The only question is whether the suggestion is practical or not. I believe it is. It requires only proper intelligence. One should have also proper trust and no suspicions.

MORARJI : One has to be very careful. One who has faith in God. . .

VINOBA : God is so elastic that everybody can do whatever he likes under his name.

MORARJI : Nobody would otherwise believe in Him.

VINOBA : As the negotiations between Jayaprakash and Jawaharlalji have broken down, the strength of the former's party has lessened.

MORARJI : I must give my view as I am somewhat responsible for it. Jawaharlalji mentioned this matter, all of a sudden, in the Working Committee. It was not appropriate for me to say much in the full meeting. But Jawaharlalji called some of us after that meeting. He told us that those people (Jayaprakash and others) are prepared to come to us subject to some conditions. I requested him to do whatever he wanted to do after a full consideration. These people might be ready to come with us today. But they will leave us when there are elections. They will work with us now and will criticise us outside. On the contrary, you will not be able to criticise your opponents. I have no dispute with the fact that there are good people in every party, but one cannot work with them only because of that consideration.

VINOBA : Good people do not mean only those with spiritual qualities. We ought to believe that we can work with people who agree to work after clarifying the ideology and thoughts and if there is similarity in them.

MORARJI : I had once a discussion with Shri Asoka Mehta and

Meherali, who asked me to prepare a programme for working together. I asked them whether they believed in Marxism, and when they replied in the affirmative about some of them, I told them: 'If you believe in violence, we cannot work together.'

VINOBA: It would be a good thing if such discussions take place at higher levels.

DHEBARBHAI: There are three groups amongst the Socialists today: those who follow J.P., others who follow Ram Manohar Lohia, and the third consists of hidden Communists.

VINOBA: As the talks with Jayaprakash and Jawahar broke down, the former's capacity got lessened.

DHEBARBHAI: You desire that all those who believe in non-violence should get together in a useful programme.

VINOBA: Yes, that is so.

MORARJI: But there must be some political thinking in all these matters, and if one runs a government, he has to think politically to a large extent.

VINOBA: I do not understand from this how Gandhiji then influenced us. The arguments that I have heard so far are not new. Veteran democrats have thought of these things.

MORARJI: We are influenced by Gandhiji in that one should work with good will with the opponents, and howsoever much they may criticise us, one should not get angry. But one cannot work in cooperation with them.

VINOBA: We should make attempts to take those who believe in non-violence with us.

VAJUBHAI: You have something to say about the salaries of ministers. It is my thesis that as long as the leadership does not behave with equality, there cannot be equality in society. There are two kinds of leadership, one at the lower levels which is in the hands of teachers; the other at the higher level which is in the hands of ministers. There should be no difference in the salaries of teachers and those of ministers, governors and the president. If they take the same salary, it will have a great effect on society.

MORARJI: It would be quite correct to say that there should be no difference in the salary between ministers and the chief minister as well as between central ministers and the prime minister. But there must be some difference between the salaries of the ministers and the president, and the ministers and the governor.

10-5-1955

MORARJI : I was very happy with your speech yesterday. Not only I but all of us have been happy. But do you think that all will work on land ?

VINOBA : Not in the present conditions, but that would happen in ideal conditions.

MORARJI : Then it is correct.

VINOBA : Agriculture is an activity where man comes constantly in contact with nature. We should not deprive anybody of this advantage.

MORARJI : Those who live by agriculture today, do not have sufficient knowledge about it.

VINOBA : We should educate them, and if any other means of maintenance can be given, that should also be done.

MORARJI : I am in agreement with you about your stand regarding basic education. But from where are we to bring such teachers ? It is a very difficult task to change the minds of teachers. I had offered to Aryanayakam to hand over all powers to him, so that he could make whatever experiments he liked; but he found some difficulty in putting it into practice. It is hoped that much will be achieved in three or four years. I wanted to take charge of the Education Ministry, but I had to take the Home Ministry in which the work is in a direction different from that of education. I am ultimately responsible for all the firing that takes place under my Government. I sometimes feel helpless. The people adopted wrong methods as a result of the 'Quit India' movement.

VINOBA : These people say that they have contributed to the winning of freedom.

MORARJI : I wanted to attend the Sarvodaya Sammelan. But I did not do so as I find that the ministers are humiliated there.

VINOBA : You are entitled to come there. But if you give up your field, others will take possession of it.

MORARJI : I did not want to enter into a dispute by coming here.

VINOBA : I have said in one place that the ideal for those who run the government should be that of Janaka and those who work outside government should have the ideal of Shukdev.

MORARJI : This is quite correct. But it is difficult to reach that ideal. I am constantly trying to see that a wrong thing is not done, but Janaka did not even think wrongly. This is difficult. I am, however, in a fairly good position. My party trusts me. This, however, enlarges my field of activity and my responsibility and the work also sometimes becomes difficult.

VINOBA : The rulers have to protect both truth and non-violence, and it is the sum and substance of your arguments that if an occasion comes for giving preference to one of them, one should prefer truth.

MORARJI : There you are right. One can compromise about non-violence, but a compromise with truth is indefensible. It is futile to be angry. Even though I know this, sometimes I get angry. I do not know what I should do. I have not been able to persuade even members of my family to accept my ideals.

VINOBA : Mahadevbhai was praising Shri Purshottam Maharaj who was living in Godhra. Bapu asked what kind of a person he was and whether he was married. Mahadevbhai said he was married. Then Bapu asked what kind of a wife he had. Bapu was told that she was a very saintly woman and he said then that Purshottam Maharaj was a real saint.

MORARJI :Knowing all these things I lose my pride and vanity and my feet get steady.

(*Somebody asked, 'Has the discussion on bhoodan taken place ?'*)

MORARJI : Yes. If anybody takes the help of officers to get bhoodan, it will be injurious. People will then give bhoodan through fear or with the hope that their influence will increase. What happened in the collection of war-funds should not be repeated in this movement. It is the aim of bhoodan to transform man. If I give up my present duties, I would certainly engage myself in bhoodan. Then I would go from village to village, but I cannot give up the work that has been entrusted to me by Jawaharlalji.

Jawaharlalji has great regard for truth, though sometimes his process of thinking becomes very dangerous on account of Western influence. It may be also because he has not experienced poverty,but he does not consider himself superior to anybody else, and that is why I respect him very greatly. No dictator will have more powers than what he has today and yet he considers himself equal to everybody. It is good that you remain in close contact with him.

VINOBA : I am temperamentally incapable of taking the initiative in these matters.

VAJUBHAI : This is correct. But aggression of love is beneficial.

MORARJI : No aggression is ever beneficial.

VINOBA : That is quite correct.

MORARJI : One finds difficulty in one's work as long as the ego is there.

VINOBA : Even when we believe firmly that there should be no ego, something still remains with us.

MORARJI : I have been making an effort for the last thirty-five years to be free from anger. In the beginning I used to believe that it was necessary to show anger sometimes in running the administration. I realised after eight or ten years that anger is bad under all conditions. I used to get angry when somebody lied to me. Then I realised that that was no reason for me to be angry. One gets angry when one finds oneself helpless or incompetent to argue.

VINOBA : If the person who believes that anger is not good gets angry, he should keep some sugar-lumps with him and take the same when he gets angry. (*laughter*)

MANIBEN : Those who had gone from Gujarat to Puri for the Sammelan, told us that they were unhappy as a result of going there, as the atmosphere was full of adverse criticism of the Congress.

VINOBA : This impression is not correct. If anybody had said anything about the Congress there, it was only I.

MORARJI : They did not refer to speeches. They got this impression from talking to several people.

VINOBA : You have done well in drawing my attention to this. If there was such an atmosphere it only meant that there was no non-violence. I shall try to correct it.

MORARJI : Satire has a very bad result. It would be better to make a direct attack.

VINOBA : In any direct talk, truth is preserved. I believe you must attend this Sarvodaya Sammelan.

MORARJI : Those who did not fully believe in truth and non-violence when Bapu was in Congress are now talking of non-violence.

VINOBA : One should get conscious about the futility of violence in this atomic age.

MORARJI : That is so. Jawaharlalji also has begun to have faith in the purity of means. He does not now make fun of people who have faith in God.

NARAYAN : J.P. believes in both God and the purity of means.

MORARJI : Yes, that is so. I do believe that he has made progress in this direction, but he has not yet grasped it fully.

NARAYAN : He has full faith in non-violence.

MORARJI : Does he believe in a class war ?

NARAYAN : No. He believes in removing classes.

MORARJI : That is not possible. There cannot be only one class and there should be class cooperation.

NARAYAN : Can there be classes of poor and the rich ?

VINOBA : No. But there would be different professions.

NARAYAN : That means there will be difference of professions and not of classes.

MORARJI : You may say so. I cannot understand why people cannot have faith in God.

(*These talks ended after some talk about Vinobaji's health. The whole discussion occupied seven to eight hours.*)

Index